Public Debt
Sustainability

Public Debt Sustainability

International Perspectives

Edited by
Barry W. Poulson, John Merrifield,
and Steve H. Hanke

LEXINGTON BOOKS
Lanham • Boulder • New York • London

Published by Lexington Books
An imprint of The Rowman & Littlefield Publishing Group, Inc.
4501 Forbes Boulevard, Suite 200, Lanham, Maryland 20706
www.rowman.com

86-90 Paul Street, London EC2A 4NE

British Library Cataloguing in Publication Information Available

Library of Congress Cataloging-in-Publication Data

Names: Poulson, Barry Warren, 1937- editor. | Merrifield, John, 1955- editor. |
    Hanke, Steve H., editor.
Title: Public debt sustainability : international perspectives / edited by Barry W. Poulson,
    John Merrifield, and Steve Hanke.
Description: Lanham : Lexington Books, 2022. | Includes bibliographical references and
    index.
Identifiers: LCCN 2021041044 (print) | LCCN 2021041045 (ebook) |
    ISBN 9781666902563 (cloth) | ISBN 9781666902587 (paperback) |
    ISBN 9781666902570 (epub)
Subjects: LCSH: Debts, Public—Case studies. | Public administration—Case studies. |
    Fiscal policy—Case studies.
Classification: LCC HJ8015 .P824 2022 (print) | LCC HJ8015 (ebook) |
    DDC 336.3/4—dc23
LC record available at https://lccn.loc.gov/2021041044
LC ebook record available at https://lccn.loc.gov/2021041045

Contents

Foreword   vii
Xavier Debrun

Acknowledgments   xi

Introduction   1

**PART I: RULES-BASED FISCAL POLICY IN
THE UNITED STATES**   **11**

1   Organizing Congress for Budget Reforms   13
     Kurt Couchman

2   Debt Fatigue and the Climacteric in U.S. Economic Growth   37
     John Merrifield and Barry Poulson

PART II: RULES-BASED FISCAL POLICY IN EUROPE   **67**

3   Preparing for the Next Crisis: Lessons from the Successful
     Swedish Fiscal Framework   69
     Fredrik N. G. Andersson and Lars Jonung

4   The Swiss Federal Debt Brake and Its Unbudgeted Surpluses   101
     Vera Z. Eichenauer and Jan-Egbert Sturm

5   The German "Debt Brake": Success Factors and Challenges   117
     Lars P. Feld and Wolf H. Reuter

**PART III: RULES-BASED FISCAL AND MONETARY
POLICY IN EMERGING NATIONS**   **137**

6   A Money Doctor's Reflections on Currency Reforms
    and Hard Budget Constraints   139
    Steve H. Hanke

7   Fiscal Rules and Public Debt: An Emerging Market Perspective   171
    Pablo E. Guidotti

8   Populist Economic Thought: The Legacy of Juan
    Domingo Perón   201
    Carlos Newland and Emilio Ocampo

**PART IV: IS NON-CONVENTIONAL MONETARY
POLICY SUPPORTING OR UNDERMINING FISCAL
STABILIZATION POLICY?**   **217**

9   Monetary Policy and the Worsening U.S. Debt Crisis   219
    Norbert J. Michel

10 The Federal Reserve and the Debt Crises   241
    Thomas R. Saving

11 The High Costs of Fiscal and Monetary Anomie:
    Argentina since 1945   259
    Emilio Ocampo

**PART V: THE ULTIMATE CHALLENGE FOR FISCAL
SUSTAINABILITY: ENTITLEMENT REFORM**   **285**

12 The Failure to Establish Effective Rules for Financing
    U.S. Federal Entitlement Programs   287
    Charles Paul Blahous

13 Fiscal Rules for Social Security and Medicare: Would Accrual
    Accounting Help?   337
    James C. Capretta

Appendix A   353

Appendix B   357

Index   363

About the Editors   369

About the Contributors   371

Foreword

Xavier Debrun

The government is special. It is not expected to die, it provides goods and services that no one else can effectively produce and deliver, it can insure against otherwise uninsurable risks, it can be a lender and rescuer of last resort, and it can legitimately redistribute income from the rich to the poor. To be able to do all that, the government is sovereign: it funds operations through taxation, and on occasions by reneging on its financial obligations without facing dire legal consequences or by printing fiat money. Because it can do all that and get the means to do it, the government has ended up being rather big, representing between a third and a half of the economy in most emerging and advanced countries.

Government debt is special too. It allows policymakers to smooth taxes over time, to shelter the economy against macroeconomic shocks, and to provide a safe asset to the financial system. Having a liquid market for securities expected to generate the promised income stream in virtually all states of the economy is essential for adequate risk pricing, for financial stability, and in the end, for an efficient allocation of resources.

To be that safe asset, public debt must be backed by a credible commitment to service it in all circumstances. As economies governed by serial defaulters are unlikely to thrive, government solvency is key to prosperity. However, assessing solvency is one area of economics where conceptual clarity meets practical fuzziness. Conceptually, public debt cannot exceed the present value of all future budget surpluses (net of interest payments). That is simple. In practice though, this means that solvency is a mere prediction about an unknowable and indefinite future. And if uncertainty about the future was not hard enough to tackle, servicing public debt is a sovereign decision, a strategic choice resulting from a cost-benefit analysis mixing economic and political calculations. All this explains why statistically, the debt level is not a good predictor of sovereign default.

Economists nevertheless know a couple of things suggesting that the debt level nevertheless matters a great deal. First, there is a limit to indebtedness because future surpluses are bounded upward for economic (the Laffer curve, incompressible spending) as well as political reasons (nobody likes austerity and large surpluses are hard to sell). Second, high public debt dents into potential growth by draining resources from the private sector (crowding out and high taxes dampen private investment), constraining investment in desirable infrastructures, and limiting governments' ability to shelter the economy against bad shocks, let alone tail events like the COVID-19 pandemic.

Since the early 1970s, public debt has ratcheted up in most advanced economies. Just before the COVID-19 shock, debt was often at or close to a peacetime high. What could be worse than a war for public debt? Politics. Yared (2019) summarizes the argument as follows: "[. . .] [N]ormative theories cannot deliver a complete justification for the increase in government debt across advanced economies. This suggests that the widespread increase in debt partly reflects a political failure."[1] A considerable literature has explored the various reasons why well-intended governments might have a penchant for excessive fiscal deficits and debts. Among those reasons, the relative neglect for what happens after the next election is a prime culprit: it makes immediate spending with instant effects more valuable in the eyes of politicians. This comes at the expense of future expenditure and of present outlays whose benefits are only visible in the future (e.g., investment and education).

The traditional response to this "fiscal commitment problem" cannot be the institutional fix used to solve the "monetary commitment problem" (i.e., a penchant for excessive inflation). Although depoliticizing the money supply was not easy, it happened, and it is generally thought to have delivered the goods: low and stable inflation. The same institutional arrangement cannot apply to the government budget, which is by essence the financial translation of a political platform. That makes fiscal policy "messy," "darn hard," and a form of "alchemy" to quote just a few expressions recently used to describe it.

Thus, constraining fiscal policy relied on rules, which can be numerical—typically in the form of legal caps on aggregate budget indicators—or procedural—a prime example is the PAYGO rule preventing new programs to increase the deficit. Perhaps the most comprehensive system of rules-based fiscal governance is found in the European Union where two layers—at the national and supranational levels—coexist to constrain policymakers' discretion.

The empirical evidence on fiscal rules' effectiveness is generally mixed. On the one hand, fiscal deficits seem to be lower where rules are in place.

On the other, the likelihood of formal compliance rarely exceeds that of winning a toss. In Europe, efforts to improve compliance loaded the system with contingencies and new rules to the point of making things unmanageable. Independent fiscal institutions have also been created to raise the profile of rule compliance in the public debate, the hope being that vocal watchdogs could increase the reputational costs of fiscal indiscipline and rules' infringement. The evidence in that respect remains inconclusive. Elsewhere, rules have either been abandoned or diluted.

Perhaps the bigger threat to rules-based fiscal policy is the recent increase in the demands on fiscal policy. The budget is now expected to plug public infrastructure gaps that grew large in some countries, to smooth the transition toward a carbon neutral economy, and to play a much more prominent role in actively stabilizing the economy. In a world where excess savings chase too little investment, the fall in equilibrium interest rates has indeed constrained monetary policy space, effectively shifting the burden of stabilizing the economy to fiscal policy.

The implications for fiscal discipline and rules-based fiscal policy are potentially daunting. First, zero or negative interest rates create the impression of a giant fiscal free lunch, where debt accumulation is essentially free or even rewarded. Second, traditional boundaries between monetary and fiscal policies are blurred. For instance, one may wonder about the remaining difference between cash and public debt at zero interest rate. Calls for central banks to organize "helicopter drops"—a fundamentally fiscal measure—are not even taboo anymore. Third, tail events like the COVID-19 pandemic have required an unprecedented coordination between monetary and fiscal policies to provide enough macroeconomic policy support to the economy. Numerical fiscal rules were suspended and large purchases of government bonds by central banks have created welcome fiscal space at the cost of artificially compressing risk premium.

Such monetary-fiscal coordination is certainly welcome to face crises of the COVID-19 magnitude: monetary or fiscal policy alone could not provide enough support. However, one should keep in mind that such coordination works only if the credibility of the two basic commitments to stable price and debt levels is not questioned. Losing that credibility would have disastrous consequences seen many times in developing economies: default would materialize through runaway inflation.

As all crises end, the burning question will be when and how to normalize monetary and fiscal policies in a way that does not scar the economy further and preserve the credibility of the two basic commitments. To be sure, constraining policymakers' discretion through rules and independent institutions will remain as desirable in the post-pandemic economy than in the pre-2008 "great moderation." But deep crises are always learning experiences and the

rules-based macroeconomic frameworks of tomorrow may significantly differ from those of today.

While independent central banks have been working hard to revisit their
policy strategies, that process has been slower and trickier on the fiscal side.
Beyond the timing for de-activating escape clauses or re-introducing fiscal
rules, fiscal frameworks will have to be revisited with the fresh pair of eyes
stemming from new experiences. The same old questions may find new or
different answers: How can we better navigate the trade-offs involved in the
design of fiscal rules (credibility, flexibility, and simplicity)? How can we
effectively enforce fiscal rules? What can we expect from independent fiscal
institutions and can we expand their role without impinging on democratic
controls? As argued above, today's challenges go well beyond addressing
some penchant for deficit spending. Answers to these questions will have to
take into account the new demands on fiscal policy: from addressing infra-
structural gaps to absorbing some of the transitory costs of decarbonization,
and from maintaining intergenerational fairness during a dramatic demographic transition to occasionally coordinating closely with monetary policy.

This book offers an excellent starting point to think productively about
macroeconomic frameworks that preserve policy credibility and show resilience to the new challenges of our time.

NOTE

1. P. Yared, "Rising Government Debt: Causes and Solutions for a Decades-old
Trend," *Journal of Economic Perspectives* 33, no. 2 (2019): 115–140.

Acknowledgments

The editors wish to thank the Koch Foundation for their support of the Friedman Research Project and sponsorship of the symposium of scholars which was the basis for this book. We also wish to thank the team at Lexington for their work in editing and publishing the book.

Introduction

Over the past half century virtually every country has at some point experienced debt fatigue, allowing debt to increase more rapidly than gross domestic product (GDP). Debt fatigue has been accompanied by increasing vulnerability to economic shocks, retardation in economic growth, and in extreme cases, debt default. Only a small group of countries have been successful in stabilizing and reducing debt burdens to sustainable levels in the long term.

There is controversy regarding the point at which a country is likely to experience the constraints imposed by debt fatigue. A broad consensus within the European Economic Community and other international institutions suggests a benchmark ratio of debt to GDP of 60%. When debt burdens approach or exceed this benchmark, a country is likely to encounter greater risk of default and other constraints on its ability to borrow.

Arguably, the most successful country in stabilizing and reducing debt to sustainable levels in the long term is Switzerland. The turning point in Switzerland can be traced back to the economic recession experienced in the early 1990s. At that point Switzerland experienced a recession accompanied by a sharp increase in debt. As Feld and Kirchgassner (2006) relate, the response to this debt burden was conditioned by the perception of Switzerland as a small country with limited financial resources. Switzerland did not have a central bank with the capacity to finance large government deficits, and as an independent country it did not have access to the reserves of the European Central Bank. With these constraints in mind, Switzerland enacted new fiscal rules to effectively constrain the growth of debt at all levels of government.

The Swiss debt brake enacted at the national level became the model for fiscal rules enacted in Germany. Similar fiscal rules were later enacted in other European countries and by the European Economic Community. The

1990s launched a new era as fiscal rules to constrain debt were enacted in countries around the world (Debrun et al. 2018). During that decade of rapid economic growth many countries were successful in stabilizing and reducing their debt burden. In the United States, that decade is referred to as the "Great Moderation" in fiscal and monetary policy. With new fiscal rules in place, the United States was able to balance the budget and generate a modest surplus in the primary balance.

Over the past two decades, however, most countries have not been successful in achieving debt sustainability (Boccia 2020; Merrifield and Poulson 2016a, b, c; 2017a, b, 2020). Economic shocks have been accompanied by sharp discontinuous increases in debt. One group of countries responded to rising debt burdens with more vigorous policies of fiscal consolidation. Other countries have failed to do so; economic shocks pushed their debt burdens well above levels considered sustainable, and their debt burdens continued to increase even in periods of economic recovery and growth.

During the financial crisis in 2008 many European countries circumvented the fiscal rules designed to constrain the growth of debt, and exceeded the guidelines set in EEC fiscal rules. During the economic recovery from the financial crisis Germany and other EEC countries enacted refinements in their fiscal rules designed to make them more effective constraints on the growth of debt. These countries pressured other members to follow EEC fiscal guidelines.

Following the financial crisis in 2008 deficit hawks in the United States also supported a return to rules-based fiscal policy and fiscal discipline. Research by Debrun and Jonung (2019) suggested that the United States had returned to the indicative fiscal and monetary rules of the "Great Moderation." Xavier Debrun and his colleagues at the IMF referred to a "second-generation" of fiscal rules designed to correct flaws in the original rules. Based on a growing consensus within the financial community, the IMF published guidelines for the design of effective fiscal rules (Debrun et al. 2018).

This optimism regarding rules-based fiscal policy was short lived. Even before the coronavirus pandemic many countries, including the United States, abandoned their fiscal rules in a rebellion against the fiscal austerity imposed by the rules. There is no longer a consensus regarding the role that fiscal rules should play, or how countries should respond to rising debt burdens. We are left with a relatively small group of countries in Northern Europe that are more vigorously enforcing their fiscal rules (Merrifield and Poulson 2016a, b, c; 2017a, b; 2020).

The divergence in responding to increasing debt burdens has been especially true during the coronavirus pandemic (*Wall Street Journal*, 2020). The economic impact of the pandemic has been comparable to that experienced during the Great Depression. Most countries have fallen off a fiscal cliff in which the fiscal stress of declining revenues and increased expenditures has required unprecedented increases in debt.[1] A great divide emerged in how different countries responded to the increasing debt burdens resulting from the pandemic. A good analogy is how countries responded to rising infection rates during the pandemic. A country's response to the pandemic is considered successful when they are able to bend this infection rate downward in the long term. Similarly, a country's fiscal policy is considered successful to the extent that they bend the debt/GDP curve down in the long term.

The countries enacting effective fiscal rules have had fiscal room to pursue countercyclical fiscal policies in response to the economic shock of the coronavirus, and are projected to bend their debt/GDP curve down in the long term. Unfortunately, most countries, including the United States, did not have much fiscal room to pursue countercyclical fiscal policies. Policies pursued in response to the coronavirus pandemic have again resulted in a sharp discontinuous increase in debt burdens, leaving them even more vulnerable to economic shocks. The cost of responding to economic shocks, and especially the coronavirus pandemic, has left many countries with debt fatigue. It is not that they are unable to enact and enforce effective fiscal rules to constrain debt; these countries are unwilling to enact and enforce effective fiscal rules.

Unsustainable debt levels incurred in response to economic shocks over the past two decades is a challenge for many countries. Restoring debt sustainability will require even greater fiscal consolidation. More countries will encounter debt fatigue as they attempt to stabilize and reduce debt/GDP ratios to sustainable levels. Some countries will find that the cost of fiscal consolidation will outweigh the benefits of achieving sustainable debt levels. The outcome of this debt fatigue is not clear. This book explores the challenge of debt fatigue from the perspective of three groups of countries: low debtor countries, high debtor emerging nations, and high debtor developed nations.

LOW DEBTOR COUNTRIES

Low debtor countries are able to avoid debt fatigue. Because they have maintained low debt/GDP ratios they have the fiscal space to pursue countercyclical fiscal policies without incurring unsustainable growth in debt. If they do incur deficits and increase debt in response to the economic shock they are able to pursue fiscal consolidation policies that stabilize and reduce debt. In general the Northern European countries that are members of the European Union have been most successful in maintaining low debt/GDP ratios in recent decades. The most successful of these low debtor nations are those enacting and enforcing new fiscal rules, following the precedent set by

Switzerland. Germany has emerged as a strong proponent of rules-based fiscal policies within the European Union in recent decades.

HIGH DEBTOR EMERGING NATIONS

High debtor emerging nations have little fiscal space to pursue countercyclical fiscal policy in response to economic shocks, and are more likely to experience debt fatigue. Many of these countries have increased their debt/GDP ratio to levels that expose them to the risk of default. An economic shock results in a deterioration in their primary balance that shifts them toward the debt limit. The *debt limit* is defined as the level of debt at which interest rates are infinite, that is, the country can't borrow at any interest rate. Even before they encounter this debt limit the country is likely to encounter higher interest rates on sovereign debt that increases the risk of default.

Most emerging nations have significantly increased debt in response to the economic impact of the coronavirus pandemic. They have issued this debt at sharply higher interest rates. The spread in interest rates between emerging market debt and U.S. Treasury debt increased about 4%. HSBC analysts estimate that about a quarter of emerging market sovereign debt is at risk of falling into distressed territory. The one exception to this fiscal stress in emerging nations is China. China has large reserves of foreign currency, and maintains strict control over international capital flows.

Some emerging nations, such as Argentina, have increased their debt/GDP ratios to levels that expose them to default. Economic shocks result in a deterioration in their primary balance that shifts them above the debt limit. Argentina is in fact a serial defaulter, having defaulted on debt in response to several economic shocks in recent decades. The International Monetary Fund has extended loans to these nations, providing them with access to international capital markets. But Argentina demonstrates that there are limits to these IMF bailouts when they fail to respond to rising debt/GDP ratios with fiscal consolidation policies.

HIGH DEBTOR DEVELOPED NATIONS

The economic impact of the coronavirus has again exposed high debtor European countries to risk of default and created major divisions within the European community (Badia et al. 2019). Greece defaulted on its debt following the 2008 financial crisis. All of the Southern European countries have been exposed to risk of default during the pandemic. The European Central Bank is purchasing bonds and extending funds to shore up the banking system in these high debtor countries. Now there is pressure for the European Central Bank to issue common debt which would ease the fiscal burden in these high debtor counties. However, Germany and the Netherlands have opposed the creation of common bonds, arguing that it would allow the European Central Bank to finance governments in member nations. Germany has also challenged the legal authority of the European Central Bank to purchase bonds.

Debt fatigue is perhaps most evident in Japan. Until the late twentieth century, the debt burden in Japan was similar to the United States and other advanced economies. When debt burdens increased, the Japanese government responded with prudent fiscal policies, balancing its budget and reducing debt. In recent decades, however, the Japanese government has allowed its debt burden to increase continuously, leaving Japan with the highest ratio of debt to national income in the world, at 250% (Debrun et al. 2018). Because of decades of deficit spending and debt accumulation, Japan continues to experience economic retardation and stagnation. Japan has not experienced insolvency because the Bank of Japan holds large reserves, and the Japanese yen is a reserve currency. Also, the Japanese debt is largely held by domestic lenders such as Japanese households and banks.

The debt crisis in Japan is especially relevant to the United States. In America, debt is on a similar trajectory as the one experienced in Japan. Like Japan, the United States will probably not experience insolvency in the near term. The U.S. dollar is unique as the dominant reserve currency in international financial markets. A significantly larger share of U.S. debt is held by foreign lenders compared to Japan. To date, foreign lenders have been willing to hold larger dollar reserves, although there is some evidence that this is changing as debt burdens in the United States increase. As the United States accumulates more debt, the greatest risk for the nation is economic stagnation. Like Japan, in recent decades the United States has experienced a slowdown in economic growth. The Congressional Budget Office projects that retardation in economic growth will continue over the next three decades, with annual growth rates falling below 2% (Congressional Budget Office 2020).

Over the next 30 years, the United States will look more like Japan in other ways as well. As the population ages, a smaller share of the labor force in the population means that tax burdens used to support expanding entitlement programs fall on a smaller share of the population. The magnitude of these transfer payments is just as incredible as the size of the national debt. After three decades the CBO estimates the government will pay out each year $4 trillion in Social Security payments and $4.5 trillion in Medicare benefits (Congressional Budget Office 2019). A slowdown in economic growth would make it difficult, if not impossible, to generate the tax revenues needed to meet these obligations. As the trust funds used to finance Social Security and Medicare are exhausted, it is less likely that these entitlement programs will be viable when our grandchildren retire.

As the debt crisis in the United States worsens, we should expect intergenerational transfers of wealth to be accompanied by generational conflicts and political instability. Slower economic growth means fewer opportunities for young people to find good jobs or pursue entrepreneurial ventures. Younger generations are losing faith in the ability of elected officials to pursue prudent fiscal policies. We should not be surprised that younger people are attracted to a progressive agenda that promises even more ambitious entitlement transfers paid for by taxing the wealthy.

When high debtor countries, such as Japan and the United States, experience debt fatigue, the outcome is less certain. Because these countries have reserve currencies and maintain large reserves they are less likely to experience currency devaluation when they incur debt. In recent years these countries have pursued non-orthodox monetary policies designed to drive interest rates toward and below zero, reducing the interest cost in issuing sovereign debt. The economic impact of the coronavirus has not exposed these countries to risk of default on their debt, at least in the near term. Thus far the expansion of their monetary base has not resulted in inflation rates in excess of the target rates set by their central banks.

There is growing evidence, however, that higher debt levels in Japan and the United States have resulted in retardation and stagnation in economic growth. In the long term, slower economic growth will make it even more difficult for these countries to pursue fiscal consolidation policies necessary to reduce their debt to sustainable levels. It is possible that debt fatigue in the long term could expose these high debtor countries to default on their debt as well. There is ample precedent for debt default by developed countries in the first half of the twentieth century, especially during the Great Depression.

QUESTIONS EXPLORED IN THIS BOOK

As countries recover from the coronavirus pandemic, they are confronted with an even more challenging debt crisis. Xavier Debrun argues that in deciding where we go from here there is no longer a consensus regarding the optimum design and enforcement of fiscal rules.[2] Rather we must address a series of questions and challenges to the conventional wisdom. This book provides an opportunity for scholars to explore these questions from an international perspective, with reference to European countries and emerging nations, as well as the United States.

Who Needs Fiscal Rules and Why?

Over the past half century there has been an explosion of debt at all levels of government. This rapid growth in debt cannot be explained by neoclassical theories of public finance. The public choice literature provides an alternative explanation for the debt crisis focused on deficit bias in democratic societies. This book provides new perspectives on rules-based fiscal policy designed to constrain fiscal policy and maintain sustainable levels of debt. The book provides a critical appraisal of the new fiscal rules enacted to address the debt crisis, and the divergence between countries that have enacted effective fiscal rules and countries that have failed to do so.

How Do We Design and Enforce Effective Fiscal Rules?

New fiscal rules have often proved to be ineffective in reducing debt to sustainable levels. "Second-Generation" fiscal rules refer to the more recent refinements in fiscal rule design and enforcement that have proven to be more effective. The International Monetary Fund, as well as other organizations, has drafted guidelines for fiscal rule design and enforcement.

The book critically evaluates new expenditure limits, deficit and debt brakes, and the way in which these rules are incorporated into the budget process through compensation and amortization accounts. Emergency funds and capital funds give legislators flexibility in implementing the rules. An important issue is the role for automatic stabilizers and discretionary fiscal policies to provide flexibility in responding to business cycles. New budget institutions, such as fiscal responsibility councils, have been introduced to provide transparency and accountability.

What Institutional Setups Favor/Hinder Effective Fiscal Rules?

Some scholars argue that effective fiscal rules require fundamental institutional reforms in the polity and economy, and question the effectiveness of "Second-Generation" fiscal rules in the absence of these institutional reforms.

The book explores the political institutions within which fiscal rules have proven to be both successful and unsuccessful. One prerequisite for effective fiscal rules is fiscal autonomy for subnational governments. If state and local governments depend upon the central government for bailouts this can undermine fiscal discipline. Fiscal federalism is linked to decentralization and a strong federalist system. Some scholars argue that checks and balances have eroded, and must be restored for effective fiscal rules. Scholars point to the important role for direct democracy, initiative, and referendum, in countries with effective fiscal rules.

The book also focuses on reforms in private markets to complement effective fiscal rules. Capital markets can play an important role in signaling the credit worthiness of government borrowers. No bailout rules and bankruptcy laws can create the right incentives for both private lenders and public borrowers.

What Is the Role for Monetary Policy in Supporting/ Undermining Fiscal Responsibility?

Milton Friedman argued that fiscal responsibility could be undermined by discretionary monetary policy. More recently, scholars such as John Taylor have proposed fiscal rules to complement rules-based monetary policies. Some scholars maintain that in the United States in recent decades fiscal and monetary policies approximated a Fiscal Taylor Rule, and argue that these indicative rules can achieve sustainable debt levels even in the absence of formal "Second-Generation" fiscal rules. New monetary theories even question whether we should be concerned about deficits and debt. But, the return of trillion dollar deficits, and projections of even higher debt/GDP ratios in the United States call into question sanguine views of fiscal policy. The book explores the role for monetary policy in supporting or undermining fiscal responsibility.

The Challenging Future for Rules-Based Fiscal Policy in Developed Countries

Long-term projections by the Congressional Budget Office reveal a challenging future for fiscal policy in the United States. Similar studies in other developed countries suggest that long-term trends will put upward pressure on debt, making it difficult to achieve sustainable debt levels.

Demographic trends project an aging population with increased demands for public pension and health benefits for retirees. These entitlement expenditures are driving higher debt/GDP ratios in the long run. A major challenge for rules-based fiscal policy will be reforms to constrain the cost of these entitlement programs. Prudence suggests that countries should impose stringent fiscal rules in the near term in order to create the fiscal space needed to respond to these trends in the long term. Responding to this challenge will be especially difficult for countries that are experiencing retardation in economic growth.

Some countries have responded to this challenge by enacting reforms in their entitlement programs. Permanent commissions have been created to study long-term trends and to recommend policy responses. However, most countries are far behind this learning curve, and are doing little to understand the impact of these long-term trends or enact reforms.

NOTES

1. For forecasts of debt/GDP ratios in the wake of the coronavirus pandemic, see International Monetary Fund 2020.
2. The editors wish to thank Xavier Debrun for his advice and support in helping to launch this book project. Xavier encouraged us to challenge the conventional wisdom, and to provide an international perspective in exploring debt issues.

REFERENCES

Badia, M., P. Medass, P. Gupta, and Y. Xiang, 2019, "Debt is Not Free", *IMF Working Paper WP/20/1*, International Monetary Fund.

Boccia, R. 2020, "The United States vs. Switzerland and Sweden: Three Approaches to Fiscal Restraint", in *The Fiscal Cliff: New Perspectives on the Federal Debt Crisis*, edited by J. Merrifield and B. Poulson. Cato Institute, forthcoming.

Congressional Budget Office, 2019, *Long Term Budget Outlook*.

Congressional Budget Office, 2020, *Long Term Budget Outlook*.

Debrun, X., and L. Jonung, 2019, "Under Threat-Rules Based Fiscal Policy and How to Preserve It", *European Journal of Political Economy*, 57, March: 142–157.

Debrun, X., J. Ostry, T. Williams, and C. Wyplosz, 2018, "Public Debt Sustainability", in *Sovereign Debt: A Guide for Economists and Practitioners,* IMF Conference, edited by S. Abbas, A. Pienkowski, and K. Rogoff, International Monetary Fund, Oxford University Press, forthcoming.

Feld, L., and G. Kirchgassner, 2006, "On the Effectiveness of Debt Brakes: The Swiss Experience", Center for Research in Economics Management and the Arts, Working Paper No. 2006-21.

Merrifield, J., and B. Poulson, 2016a, *Can the Debt Growth be Stopped? Rules Based Policy Options for Addressing the Federal Fiscal Crisis*, New York, NY: Lexington Books.

Merrifield, J., and B. Poulson, 2016b, "The Swedish and Swiss Fiscal Rule Outcomes Contain Key Lessons for the U.S.", *Independent Review*, Vol. 21, No. 2, pp. 251–275.

Merrifield, J., and B. Poulson, 2016c, "Stopping the National Debt Spiral: A Better Rule for Solving the Federal Fiscal Crisis", *Policy Brief*, The Heartland Institute.

Merrifield, J., and B. Poulson, 2017a, "New Constitutional Debt Brakes for Euroland Revisited", *Journal of Applied Business and Economics*, Vol. 19, No. 8, pp. 110–132.

Merrifield, J., and B. Poulson, 2017b, *Restoring America's Fiscal Constitution*, New York, NY: Lexington Books, 2017b.

Merrifield, J., and B. Poulson, 2020, *The Fiscal Cliff*: New *Perspectives on the Federal Debt Crisis*, Cato Institute, forthcoming.

Office of Management and Budget, 2020, "President's Fiscal Year (FY) 2021 Budget"

Wall Street Journal, 2020, "Pandemic's Economic Fallout Puts Euro to the Test", Saturday/Sunday, May 9–10: B13.

Part I

RULES-BASED FISCAL POLICY IN THE UNITED STATES

Chapter 1

Organizing Congress for Budget Reforms

Kurt Couchman

INTRODUCTION: MISSED OPPORTUNITIES

In 2010, the Tea Party shook the country. The incoming House majority had the most Republican members since the late 1940s, and the massive class of Tea Party freshman was ready to shake up DC.

Democrats would still hold the Senate majority and the White House in the 112th Congress, but a brutal election helped raise the status of Democratic proponents of fiscal prudence. That combination of energy and a spirit of compromise was a promising opportunity to establish new rules and to improve old rules for controlling the debt.

Yet they failed. Advocates lacked mature and realistic proposals. Members and groups were not organized to build bipartisan—and therefore enduring—support.

The greatest accomplishment of the 112th Congress, the Budget Control Act (BCA) of 2011 (U.S. Statutes at Large 2011), primarily inflamed the squabbling over the annually appropriated discretionary spending, a relatively small and declining share of spending (CBO 2021). It had bipartisan support, but it was largely a punt: the Joint Select Committee on Deficit Reduction that the BCA established failed to agree on deficit reduction, and eventually Congress increased the discretionary caps for every fiscal year from 2013 through 2021 with progressively less discipline.

A presidential election consumed most of 2012. As the years passed, Congress' attention shifted. Work to improve the budget system continued, but for most policymakers, it became a secondary priority at best.

New windows may open soon. Mirroring the Republican revolt against the Democrat-dominated American Recovery and Reinvestment Act in 2009 and the Democrat-only Affordable Care Act in 2010, among other legislation,

13

Democrats reacted intensely to the Republican-only, deficit-boosting Tax Cuts and Jobs Act of 2017. After Democrats captured the House, however, members of both parties have backed major spending increases and tax cuts in the 116th Congress (2019–2020), usually without even a pretense of off-sets (CRFB 2020b). After gaining unified control in the 117th Congress by winning the White House and a razor-thin majority in the Senate, Democrats pushed through the $1.9 trillion American Rescue Plan (CBO 2021b) on a purely partisan vote in March 2021.

The fiscal and monetary policies from pandemic response on top of an already unsustainable debt trajectory seem likely to generate even more public anxiety about the debt. As of this writing, a waning emergency, a strengthening economy, and inflation concerns are strong headwinds for a big spending agenda. Yet, looking back beyond the immediate situation makes clear that members of both parties share the blame.

Fortunately, champions of fiscal responsibility exist in both parties as well. Public demands for deficit reduction could empower prudent members of both parties to check other demands under narrow majority or closely divided government, rather than polarizing one party against the other. President Biden has been involved with budget negotiations over his decades of public service. His administration may be amenable to and perhaps even an advo-cate for restoring fiscal sustainability. Early signs are mixed, suggesting that context matters.

Important questions include the following: (1) How can responsible mem-bers gain influence within their party and political systems? (2) When might windows of opportunity open and how long could action be feasible? (3) What options could attract broad support? (4) How can the groundwork for reform be laid?

These questions cannot be neatly separated, at least not without losing sight of the connections. Politics, policy, and process are inextricably inter-twined. Policymakers need both means and motivation to act, and reformers can improve both substantially.

Increasing issue salience; empowering champions and allies; developing specific policy, process, and structural changes; and generating support for both personnel and policy are all necessary.

"NO ONE'S TALKING ABOUT IT". . . SO TALK ABOUT IT

As individuals, our priorities shift with time and circumstance and along with social cues from those around us. Policymakers are the same. On any issue at a specific time, some may be enthusiastic, others tepid, and still others dismissive, if not opposed. Those sentiments are driven by personal preferences, electoral and fundraising calculations, the esteem of colleagues, and the ability to gain and retain influence and to advance policy outcomes, among other factors.

If policymakers sense that an issue has become more salient with peers and the public, they tend to give it more attention. They become more willing to talk about it.

In recent years, some policymakers concluded that sound budgeting wasn't politically salient. Why? After intense focus in 2010–2013, it went "out of cycle." Legislators don't hear from their constituents, from advocacy and interest groups, or from colleagues about it as much as other priorities.

Yet pre-pandemic polling (Peterson 2020) showed that supermajorities of the American people—by age, ideology, political affiliation, race, gender, and other factors—want policymakers to reduce deficits and to budget carefully. More recent polling confirms this (CRFB 2021). Elevating awareness of such polling and other indicators with policymakers can help change the narrative.

Another tactic is to organize existing champions, whether currently energized or more latent, in a public way that elevates those issues on the policy agenda. Several examples from the 116th Congress follow. Representatives Jodey Arrington (R-TX) teamed up with Representative Scott Peters (D-CA) to build an informal working group and lead a letter (Arrington 2020) with 30 Republican and 30 Democratic signers to House leaders in June 2020 asking for budget reforms to be included in upcoming pandemic legislation.

Senators Mitt Romney (R-UT) and Joe Manchin (D-WV) worked with Representatives Mike Gallagher (R-WI) and Ed Case (D-HI) on a bill to create bipartisan commissions meant to restore solvency to endangered trust fund programs such as Social Security, Disability Insurance, Medicare, and highway programs (CRFB 2019).

Senate Budget Chair Mike Enzi (R-WY) and Senator Sheldon Whitehouse (D-RI) put together a package (Enzi 2019) to reinvigorate the congressional budget process with the budget resolution playing the central role. A bipartisan supermajority of the committee approved it. These are among the most prominent examples, but they are only a handful of the budget initiatives from the 116th Congress.

Each initiative has spillovers. They individually and collectively bring attention to and engagement from members of Congress on fiscal issues. They show that bipartisan support exists for meaningful improvements. Efforts like these can help sustain and increase the momentum for reform. Policy innovation also creates more "on-the-shelf" options for the fleeting moments when windows of opportunity open.

Kurt Couchman

RULES: THE LANDSCAPE FOR DELIBERATION

Budget reformers are often attracted to big changes, like a constitutional balanced budget amendment (BBA) or new statutory targets. I am too. I've written two innovative BBAs and have developed ideas for statutory budget goals and their enforcement (Amash 2011; Brat 2015; Couchman 2017, 2020).

Broad goals and big initiatives are necessary. They are not sufficient. They are not sustainable if they are not compatible with the micro-incentives and processes facing decision makers. Even in Congress, macro outcomes emerge from micro-decisions and choices, all shaped by a constantly shifting kaleidoscope of influences (Schelling 2006). Among the sources of its evident dysfunction are the chamber and party rules.

Chamber Rules

The rules and voluminous precedents governing the House of Representatives (U.S. House Rules) and the Senate (U.S. Senate Rules, Riddick and Frumin 1992) are the operating systems of each body. They—and the customs guiding their use—are the terrain of the procedural landscape. Process has substantial effects on policy outcomes. Process sets boundaries on how, when, and which members can inject ideas and proposals into congressional proceedings.

Committee jurisdiction is a potent example. Highway programs are generally reauthorized for five years at a time. The House Committee on Transportation and Infrastructure and the Senate Committee on Environment and Public Works have authority over most of the spending, while the House Committee on Ways and Means and the Senate Committee on Finance are responsible for the revenue. The spenders get the political gain from handing out goodies, while the taxers bear the pain of paying for it. The unsurprising result is undisciplined spending growth with revenue shortfalls and a trust fund that would have run out of money long ago except for bailouts from the general fund of the Treasury (Kirk and Mallet 2020). In 2020, however, the revenue committees showed no appetite to even pretend to pay for the transportation-committee-approved wish lists (Snyder 2020).

The scope of potential amendments to chamber rules is broad. Focusing only on a few budget-related aspects, committees are supposed to remain within budget constraints, but the rules lack binding penalties—or even transparency—for those that do not. The rules require a cost estimate from the Congressional Budget Office before a vote on a measure can occur, and legislation is not supposed to increase the debt. Yet both rules can be waived, and they are when it is politically expedient. Establishing self-discipline for a body that writes and enforces its own rules is the central challenge.

For overall fiscal policy, the rules grant the Budget Committees plenary oversight and control over all significant fiscal matters. In recent years, that power is more nominal than real. Strengthening the Budget Committees has been a common theme in recent budget process efforts such as the Joint Select Committee on Budget and Appropriations Process Reform in 2018, the Enzi-Whitehouse Bipartisan Congressional Budget Reform Act of 2019 (Enzi 2019), and the Convergence Project (Convergence 2018).

Yet power, unlike prosperity, tends to be zero-sum. Vesting more power in the Budget Committees could reduce the power of leaders, of the Committees on Appropriations, or of various authorizing committees.

The rules could reflect state experience to merge the Budget and Appropriations Committees while pushing almost all substantive policies other than spending amounts to the authorizing committees (discussed below) and putting more of the boilerplate appropriations law into permanent statute. Such an overhaul would require revising nearly all budget statutes.

A third approach could involve stronger Budget Committees and putting appropriations within the authorizing committees (Perdue 2016). Though these structural overhauls seem ambitious—and they are—an ineffective process creates appetite for fresh thinking.

Rules reforms are usually considered at the start of a new Congress. In the House, the majority party re-establishes the rules on the first day of session, usually with a substantial package of changes developed almost solely by the majority party (Hoyer 2019). Ultimately the House package requires only a simple majority for adoption. Organizing is challenging in the months immediately before and after a general election. After the elections, outgoing members can't participate much (and are often job-hunting anyway), new members don't know what they're doing and have few relationships, leadership elections and committee jockeying happens, end-of-year lawmaking is under way, holiday parties are ubiquitous, and nearly everyone is making holiday plans.

Unlike the House, the Senate is a "continuing body" and need not re-adopt rules each Congress. Moreover, formally amending Senate rules requires two-thirds of members to approve a change. That high bar for amendment, the lack of a pressure point to establish rules, and the evolution of Senate precedents mean that the formal Senate rules undergo less change.

Another sore spot is dissatisfaction with Congress' increasingly top-down orientation. Deliberation has become more and more suppressed over the last three decades. Under leaders of both parties—Senate majority leaders Harry Reid (D-NV) and Mitch McConnell (R-KY) and House Speakers Nancy Pelosi (D-CA), John Boehner (R-OH), Paul Ryan (R-WI), and Pelosi again—the floor has become more tightly managed (Wallner 2018, U.S. Senate). Leaders control the agenda, and neither committees nor rank-and-file members have much influence. Discontent is widespread, but that energy must be shaped and directed with specific changes advanced through organized efforts to be useful. Otherwise, idle hands are the Devil's playthings, as the saying goes.

Members have succeeded in reclaiming power from leaders before. A revolt against the top-down rule of Speaker Joseph Cannon (R-IL) came to a head on March 17, 1910. Then, a coalition of Democrats and progressive Republicans forced rules changes through the chamber over the strenuous objections of and obstacles from the Speaker and his allies (U.S. House History). Though it was far from an ideal system, committees had much more influence on the agenda until Speaker Gingrich began to re-centralize power starting in 1995.

Despite today's centralization, the vestiges of a committee-driven system remain. House Rule XIV(4) indicates that each committee chair will have a turn to bring legislation to the floor. In practice, this process is short-circuited by what the Rules call a "special rule." These special rules are, in fact, the only way that measures without overwhelming support are considered in the House. In addition, House Rule XI(2)(c)(2) and Senate Rule XXVI(3) enable a majority of committee members to force a special meeting—a hearing or even a markup of legislation—over the chair's objections.

In both cases, members still possess the latent power under the formal rules to reject special rules on the floor and to demand special meetings in committees. In both cases, the power of party leaders to enforce partisan discipline prevents these outcomes except in the most extreme circumstances. Indeed, the House Freedom Caucus was created as an organizational obstacle—a voting bloc and a pre-commitment device—to check the power of Republican leaders to push through special rules that those members opposed (DeSilver 2015). Further, the majoritarian nature of the House does not necessarily mean that it must operate under total control of the majority party's leadership. House majorities on any given measure could instead be bipartisan, committee-driven, or otherwise ad-hoc coalitions.

Despite the filibuster and other constraints, the Senate majority leader controls the agenda largely through his "right of first recognition" (Wallner 2018). Power is never unlimited, and leaders must accommodate pressures from their respective conferences, as Speaker Cannon learned the hard way (Huder 2018). But the power to choose how and when to accommodate gives leaders tremendous ability to guide the flow of their respective houses and conferences.

Finally, concentrated power in congressional leaders empowers the president compared to Congress. Under current practice, the president can negotiate for a pre-baked package with not more than the four conference leaders. Usually just the Senate majority leader and the Speaker of the House, one of whom is often of the president's party, are the main players. If legislation in each house were open to deliberation, floor amendment, and Congress-wide negotiations instead, the president's ability to dictate terms to Congress would recede (Amash 2020).

Conference and Caucus Rules

The rules of each house can be improved, but parliamentary practice under the rules and norms may be more important. The incentives guiding member behavior—including strong norms of deference to leaders—are shaped substantially by the power structure within each conference or caucus.[1]

In some ways, the power structures are organic and subjective. Their contours come from the perceptions that members have of each other, their ideas, and their influence as much as explicit powers. Relationships with key personnel in the administration, the other chamber and the other party, subject matter expertise, compelling communications, prolific fundraising, effective organizers of other members, and institutional knowledge all affect the "political capital" of a member.

Even so, written conference rules play a big role, as they help structure and are in turn, at least potentially, shaped by the forces above. House Republicans, Senate Republicans, and, since July 2020, House Democrats have published their rules online.[2] Senate Democratic Caucus Rules are still secret.

Conference rules establish the formal relations of each party: how conferences select leaders, including steering, policy, and campaign officials; committee and subcommittee chairs (or ranking members); and committee membership (Swift 2020). Positions of authority bring responsibilities. Some are explicit, like representing the position of the conference. Some are made explicit to members outside of the rules, like party fundraising goals tied to official positions.

A majority of each party conference can revise the rules. This usually occurs at an organizational meeting shortly after a general election, but it can occur otherwise during a Congress. Revisions matters most before a new Congress—before decisions about who will serve in which capacity are set for the next two years.

In one sense, changing conference rules seems easy: only a bare majority of that party needs to support a rule change, and a relative handful of members can demand a secret ballot. In other ways, it's quite challenging. The organizing conference takes place at the end of the preceding Congress, but it excludes outgoing members and their institutional knowledge. It includes incoming members, who are overwhelmed by their recent victory and by absorbing information as they prepare to take office. Members-elect have thought little—if at all—about the conference rules (or the chamber rules), and most feel obligated to the leaders who helped campaign and fundraise for them. Moreover, nearly all members have been focused on regaining or retaining power in Congress and perhaps the White House until the week before.

In addition, would-be reformers must act at the apex of leaders' relative influence. Members select or reaffirm leaders as the most popular members of the conference shortly before they consider rules amendments. Furthermore, leaders have disproportionate influence in choosing committee chairs and committee members, decisions which they make in the months after organizing conferences. Even many members deeply dissatisfied with current arrangements are hesitant to rock the boat when facing uncertain payoffs.

The status quo delegates extraordinary power to congressional leaders. The House Democratic Steering and Policy Committee and the House Republican Steering Committee are the arms of each conference that generally determine who serves on or leads each committee. Members are selected in several ways, yet the direct or indirect influence of the Speaker or Minority Leader is vast (Swift 2020).

Chipping away at that concentration of power is key to making Congress more of an effective, deliberative body again. For any individual member or small group of them, taking on entrenched power is perilous. The individually prudent course is often to avoid the deeper pursuit of the public interest and to seek individual advancement in an unhealthy system.

Reformers must therefore choose their battles strategically, build coalitions well in advance, and develop compelling policy and political narratives to explain why their proposals are necessary and helpful to the interests of most members. The rules that rule the rulers must be agreeable to enough of them. And they must navigate the process to get their amendments on the agenda and to a vote.

It can be done and has been recently. At the end of the 114th Congress in November 2016, House Republicans adopted several conference rules changes to democratize the selection of members of the steering committee, the leadership-dominated body that generally selects committee members and leaders. Due to these changes, regional representatives on steering are apparently more responsive to members of each region.

At the end of the 116th Congress in November 2020, House Republicans clarified the process for considering resolutions before the conference, which could include rules changes. They also eliminated a minor perk of leadership, the ability to designate issues as "leadership issues."

In January 2021, Senate Democrats limited members' ability to chair both a full committee and an appropriations subcommittee (Shutt 2020). The public still doesn't know the rest of their rules, but distributing responsibility more broadly is a healthy step for the Senate Democratic Caucus.

Further moves along those lines may be feasible. Something like proportional representation for the steering, policy, and campaign committees or re-establishing one-person-one-vote (the top Republican gets four and the second Republican gets two) may have potential, as may otherwise shifting away from leaders' discretion and toward the conference's choice.

Another approach could be ensuring that membership on each committee is close to a representative sample of each conference. This would likely improve conference dynamics and policy outcomes in the near term. It may be imperative in a committee-driven Congress, and it would likely expand the possibilities for bottom-up policy initiatives. Each committee as a microcosm of the conference would facilitate bargaining within each committee from all relevant factions of each conference.

In addition, conference rules could include more budget-related provisions. Conferences could set expectations for leaders and members that would guide subsequent assignments and responsibilities. Committee leaders could be responsible for introducing legislation to cultivate the laws—that is, reauthorize, update, streamline, consolidate, and so on—within their committee or subcommittee jurisdiction. Leaders and chairs could be expected to produce a budget resolution and to uphold their budget allocations for both direct and discretionary spending. Committee leaders could be obliged to ensure deficit neutrality or reduction in any legislation they report. Similar reforms to both chamber and conference rules can reinforce each other.

Better rules make little difference if they are ignored or evaded. A critical mass of members must have incentives to resist rule breaking. For some, personal ideological conviction is sufficient. For others, upholding the rules may provide electoral, fundraising, grassroots, or institutional influence. Politicians, including leaders (the most popular among them), generally follow the path of least resistance. Rules changes may be able to redirect that path toward healthier outcomes.

ORGANIZING FOR REFORM

The institutions established by the rules largely establish the landscape on which public policy deliberation takes place. Using that terrain effectively requires bringing members together to advance objectives.

Members organize when they foresee comparatively large net benefits. They are busy, and they have many choices for spending their time and energy. Successful advocates consistently provide value. This includes not only re-election-focused political activities, like organizing fundraisers or campaign volunteers, but it can also mean helping them rise in influence in Congress by supporting issues they care about.

Assistance with policy can serve multiple goals for members, including winning the good graces of the political base (primary voters), the district generally (swing voters), monied interests (campaign contributors), fellow partisans, as well as the public interest as they see it. These can overlap. Advocates' comparative advantage is often expertise and sustained attention.

Getting re-elected and gaining influence take many forms. One path includes becoming a leader through expertise on issues that are salient to other members and other constituencies. An issue's prominence ebbs and flows, but many issues retain a dedicated core of champions nonetheless. They can continue to learn about the issues and to develop policy innovations, ready to seize the moment when opportunity arises.

Preparation for successful engagement requires advocates to provide continued support and encouragement to members, staff, and other policy professionals. This includes connecting academics to policy analysts to advocates to policymakers. The insights in the academic journals must be mediated by those who engage with the politics, policy, and procedures of governance and can present them in forms that are useful and beneficial to policymakers.

Congress is usually not self-organizing. It is mostly a reactive institution. For both members and staff, simply responding to and keeping up with the floor, committees, fundraisers, campaigns, party conferences, member organizations, lobbyists, grassroots, constituents, and so on consume almost all their time. The highest priorities usually advance the members' interests across several domains, including by building relationships with other members.

Engaging with Existing Entities

Advocates can find insertion points at existing organizations such as committees and member organizations. After finding potential champions—someone with interest but needing direction—advocates can help convert that energy into concrete actions and initiatives. Building many relationships expands the chances of matching ideas with proponents.

Budget reformers have a natural home in the budget committees and a few others. In the 116th Congress, Senate Budget Committee Chair Mike Enzi (R-WY) and Senator and Budget Committee member Sheldon Whitehouse (D-RI) negotiated the Bipartisan Congressional Budget Reform Act (Enzi 2019). This sweeping package of provisions focused on reinvigorating the budget resolution, and it was approved by the committee on a bipartisan 15–6 vote in November 2019 (U.S. Senate Budget 2019).

In the House, Budget Chair John Yarmuth (D-KY) and other leading House Democrats proposed the Congressional Power of the Purse Act (U.S. House Budget 2020) to shift power and accountability toward Congress when implementing appropriations. It incorporated Senator Mike Lee's (R-UT) ARTICLE ONE Act (Lee 2019) to reclaim congressional power over emergency declarations, which the Senate Homeland Security and Governmental Affairs Committee approved on a voice vote in July 2019 (Senate HSGAC 2019). Last Congress, House Budget Ranking Member and appropriator Steve Womack (R-AR) and his staff seemed to have been working with members to propose targeted budget changes as well (Burchett 2019; Case 2019; Meuser 2019).

Congressional membership organizations provide resources and create opportunities. The House Republican Study Committee has produced an annual budget proposal for many years with numerous savings options and reform options (Hern 2021). The Congressional Progressive Caucus used to produce a "People's Budget," (CPC 2019) though fiscal responsibility has not been a primary focus. The Blue Dog Coalition of moderate Democrats proposed a Blueprint for Fiscal Reform (Blue Dog 2019) and otherwise engages frequently on budget-related matters. Fiscal Responsibility is listed as a core issue for the New Democrat Coalition as well (New Democrats).

Committees and these membership organizations generate important positions, principles, and proposals. Even so, each has constraints based on party leadership, official jurisdiction, or a limited range of ideological scope. Other groups, like the bipartisan Problem Solvers Caucus, provide some possibilities (Problem Solvers 2020) but generally have other priorities (Problem Solvers).

Organizing Additional Efforts

When existing organizations leave gaps, it can be useful to form new venues. The BCA of 2011 established the Joint Select Committee on Deficit Reduction (U.S. House Budget 2011). The Bipartisan Budget Act of 2018 established the Joint Select Committee on Budget and Appropriations Process Reform (Lynch and Saturno 2019). Both failed to produce recommendations with enough support for floor consideration, but they elevated budget reform on the congressional agenda, created new champions, and indicated opportunities for bipartisan progress. Though only touching on budget process, the Select Committee on the Modernization of Congress was created through the House Rules package for the 116th Congress (Hoyer 2019) and included budget reforms in its final recommendations (U.S. SCMC 2020).

Less formally, Reps. Jodey Arrington (R-TX) and Scott Peters (D-CA) have led bipartisan meetings with House members to seek consensus on and to build relationships around bipartisan budget improvements. Their first public product was a letter to House leaders with 30 Republican and 30 Democratic signers asking for budget reforms in the next pandemic response legislation (Arrington 2020). Though the members support continued public health and economic support funding, they stated that Congress must lay the groundwork for future deficit reduction through improvements in budget transparency, accountability, and responsibility (details below).

Like support to individual members, creating and sustaining groups require providing members and staff with benefits across multiple domains. Demonstrating that fiscal responsibility is popular (Peterson 2020) and good politics (Fall, Bloch, Fournier, and Hoeller 2015, 48-49), while strengthening relationships with other members, can raise the priority level enough to justify putting their limited time and resources into those efforts. Smart members can reap additional benefits through the observation that a lower debt burden increases the prospects for emerging priorities to be addressed in a timely way.

Ad-hoc efforts can also form around specific legislation or at least a concept. Following the long government shutdown that spanned the end of the 115th and the beginning of the 116th Congress, proposals for automatic continuing resolutions to prevent shutdowns proliferated. Some were partisan, while others were bipartisan. One version was considered and approved by the Senate Homeland Security and Governmental Affairs Committee (U.S. Senate HSGAC 2019), and attempts to enact it continue.

PROPOSALS WITH POTENTIAL

Whether a focal point of current member discussions or not, crafting legislation is crucial. Times change. Senator Rob Portman (R-OH) advocated for automatic continuing resolutions for many years before a long shutdown brought it nearly within reach in 2019 (Portman 2019). A BBA languished for 15 years between votes in 1996 and 2011, and a better-crafted version might have succeeded then (Couchman 2017).

Productive reforms take time to develop and circulate within the policy community, even when advanced by well-respected legislators with sound proposals. Here are some of those stories.

The TRUST Act

Four major trust fund programs are projected to exhaust their reserves in the next 15 years: highway programs in 2022, Medicare Hospital Insurance in 2026, Social Security Old Age and Survivors Insurance (OASI) in 2032, and

Social Security Disability Insurance (SSDI) in 2035 (CBO 2021). When that happens, spending will be limited to each trust fund's incoming revenue, a substantial spending cut.

This grim reality has created momentum for the bipartisan, bicameral Romney-Manchin-Gallagher-Case legislation to establish bipartisan, bicameral commissions to seek agreement on protecting these programs, including by extending their cash-flow solvency. The updated version of the bill, the Time to Rescue United States Trusts (TRUST) Act, would have the commissions (termed "rescue committees") work for six months after enactment (Romney 2021). The pressure from looming depletion dates combined with each commission's sole focus on one program provides four separate chances to strike a deal. This approach could succeed where prior all-or-nothing-and-everything-is-on-the-table fiscal commissions (without a crisis point) have not.

The TRUST Act illustrates the benefits of outside support. Sen. Romney and his team have been in close contact with advocacy groups from soon after the concept was born in July 2019 through the initial bipartisan, bicameral introduction in October 2019. Those advocates have continued to generate interest within the policy community, promoted it with congressional offices, and published numerous resources (CRFB 2019a, 2020a, c, d, f, g; MacGuineas 2019).

Less than a year after its conceptual origin, the TRUST Act became part of the HEALS Act, the Senate Republican pandemic response package (McConnell 2020). Budget reforms rarely move onto congressional leaders' agenda so quickly. It does, however, show how a prominent, engaged, and energetic member with good staff, a thoughtful proposal, and outside support can successfully navigate the politics, policy, and process.

Combining Budget Targets with Debt Limit Reform

Beyond affecting trust fund exhaustion, the pandemic's vast increase in the national debt seems likely to bolster efforts to control the debt and related processes during the 117th Congress and beyond. The current debt limit suspension expires on July 31, 2021 (U.S. Statutes at Large 2019), so combining debt limit reforms with enforceable budget targets could be feasible. It already has bipartisan support, as indicated by the Peters-Arrington letter, which also backed the TRUST Act (Arrington 2020).

Many options are available for reforming the debt limit, setting budget targets, and enforcing them (CRFB 2020h). Some ideas—usually the simpler approaches—have already been drafted or proposed. Others have not yet been proposed in legislative form, but developing them now, well ahead of anticipated opportunities, is important work.

Structural Primary Balance

For instance, debt-to-GDP targets are seen by experts as the gold standard for fiscal sustainability. Such goals are abstract to the public, however. The public wants balanced (cash flow) budgets. Full balance is likely out of reach for the foreseeable future, but a path to primary balance—excluding net interest on the debt—may be achievable within a decade or so. Turning that concept into a plausible legislative proposal requires working through a range of policy, political, and process issues, and then putting it in the form of a bill.

A discussion draft of such legislation was developed but not introduced during the 116th Congress. The conceptual work goes back at least a decade. This version targets primary balance over the medium term (roughly, over the business cycle) including emergency spending. Mechanically, it would set an annual, fiscal year, primary spending cap, adjusted for timing shifts and automatic stabilizers. That cap would grow with a trend of GDP growth—the average of the prior five years of GDP growth—which would stabilize primary spending as a percentage of GDP. The growth rate for spending would decrease, cumulatively, following primary deficits (and increase following primary surpluses, not to exceed trend GDP growth). Emergency spending would be offset subsequently, not immediately (Couchman 2019). Increasing the revenue baseline would allow greater spending.

Those mechanics make for a realistic rule. It would be easy to implement. Each year, the Congressional Budget Office would produce a top-line primary spending level as a starting point for the budget resolution. If members want more non-emergency spending, they could raise revenue.

This rule design would produce a smooth structural spending path despite an inherently volatile revenue base. It would promote policy stability—and reduce regime uncertainty for public and private actors—compared to many other budget target possibilities, especially annual balance. It would also allow emergency spending, subject to reasonable oversight and discipline through later offsets.

Budget Target Enforcement

Budget targets are not self-enforcing. The Bipartisan Congressional Budget Reform Act from Senators Enzi and Whitehouse anticipates a special reconciliation process to achieve deficit targets set in the budget resolution (CRFB 2020e). The Reforming America's Fiscal Toolkit (RAFT) Act from Representatives Tim Burchett (R-TN) and Ed Case (D-HI) would have the budget resolution choose a reconciliation-like process or a bipartisan, bicameral joint select committee on fiscal responsibility (Burchett 2019). Another possibility could be that whenever (primary) deficits are projected in every year of the next decade, the most popular (by cosponsors) major deficit-reducing bills would get expedited consideration in Congress.

Alternatively, automatic adjustments to spending and revenue programs could occur. In the current law, across-the-board sequestration enforcement is required under the BCA of 2011 and the Statutory Pay-As-You-Go Act of 2010. Yet it is a blunt instrument, and Congress always waives it. Another approach could incrementally tweak existing parameters in current law and add new parameters to tweak until desired savings are obtained. This incremental approach is more difficult to draft, but it could be more reasonable in its application and thus more likely to be politically sustainable.

Debt Limit

The debt limit could be automatically waived as long as the fiscal targets are on track, within a reasonable margin of error. Then it becomes a carrot for fiscal responsibility and a stick against shirking. It could be set as a percentage of GDP instead of as a nominal amount. Many other possible improvements exist (CRFB 2015). If the debt limit were again raised in dollar terms instead of suspended, Congress could have to include a debt limit increase when passing deficit-increasing legislation—a stick—or when passing deficit-reducing legislation—a carrot.

Balanced Budget Amendment to the Constitution

Fully balancing the budget is politically out of reach for now. Even so, BBAs are worth keeping warm. Politics can change quickly in a crisis.

Some versions are better than others (Couchman 2017). One model provides broad scope for implementing legislation. The Principles-Based BBA would require balance, which may occur over more than one year like a structural concept, and it could be full balance or primary balance, depending on implementing legislation (Brat 2015). The Business Cycle BBA specifies the mechanics, but it also permits full or primary balance (Amash 2011).

Primary balance is more politically achievable than full balance because it excludes interest costs. It would require only about half as much fiscal consolidation. Perhaps after reaching primary balance, the public would insist that Congress revise the implementing legislation and go the rest of the way to full structural balance.

A constitutional rule would buttress a statutory rule in three main ways: (1) create an enforceable supermajority for emergency spending, (2) identify a timeline to reach balance (however defined), and (3) generate a national conversation during ratification to help re-establish fiscal responsibility norms for Congress.

Resilience Agenda

Following the pandemic, interest in improving public and private capacity to handle emergencies may emerge. Some federal borrowing has been driven by the so-called automatic stabilizers of revenue reductions from less economic activity and increased demand for spending programs such as unemployment and nutrition assistance. Some federal borrowing supports the states and businesses. Less such aid may be needed if the federal government reduced its encouragement of indebtedness throughout the public and private sectors.

Congress could encourage states to consider structural balance instead of annual balance. Then states could borrow more during recessions while giving lenders the confidence that they'll be paid back during boom years. States wouldn't need to sacrifice their sovereignty to pursue congressional bailouts, and their spending and revenue policies could be more stable.

Business tax and regulatory policy—especially in financial services—strongly favors debt over equity finance like stocks. This artificially suppresses the financial cushion they would otherwise have to help them get through tough times. Federal loan programs such as direct loans, loan guarantees, and related programs subsidize borrowing, so we get more debt. Meanwhile, our tax code constrains our ability to avoid the double taxation of savings compared to a consumption tax base, and these burdens on saving naturally reduce national savings. Reversing these disincentives to save and incentives to borrow could help the private sector be more financially robust (Couchman 2018).

Strengthening the Budget Committee

Patches to the budget process could get it running again, but an overhaul may be in order. Making the Budget Committees into leadership committees is one way, as the 2018 Joint Select Committee on Budget and Appropriations Process nearly recommended (Lynch and Saturno 2019) and as the Enzi-Whitehouse proposal did (Enzi 2019). This model envisions putting chairs and ranking members of the major committees with fiscal jurisdiction onto the Budget Committee. It is thought that their collective weight would facilitate policy bargaining as input to the budget resolution and stronger incentives to carry it out as output.

This could counteract the unfortunate reality that most members don't get excited about the budget resolution, budget process improvements, budget enforcement, or, except under unified control for partisan priorities, budget reconciliation. Until and unless the Budget Committee has greater institutional heft, it could continue to struggle to overcome the forces that push the budget resolution toward being a messaging document rather than a blueprint for governance.

Toward Unified Budgets

In the states, however, the budget and appropriations functions are combined (White 2015), and the state budget processes generally work well. One reason may be that nearly all members have requests for appropriations allocations and report language, leading to greater deference to the committees with those responsibilities. Another could be that state budgets include everything, so the deal isn't final until everything is agreed to. A single package also has the virtue of integrating the detailed policies for spending and revenue line items with budget targets and other aggregate measures. In addition, state budgets focus mostly on allocations and leave most other policy decisions to the authorizing committees.

Congress' process has largely already collapsed into a single, end-of-year omnibus appropriations package. Sometimes it is preceded by a budget resolution, but increasingly a budget resolution is only a vehicle for partisan reconciliation. The appropriations package, however, lacks a connection to broader budget targets and excludes direct spending—70% of the pre-pandemic spending and growing—and all revenue.

Shifting toward state budget practices would substantially change the congressional budget process. It would require modifying the budget statutes, House and Senate Rules, all four sets of conference rules, committee assignments, relationships with other committees and other entities, and more. Even so, the process isn't working, so reviewing what works—the states—for best practices and inspiration is appealing. Perhaps strengthening the Budget Committees will work well, but if it doesn't, we may need a backup plan.

The Budget Committees could still exist in a reimagined process. Authorizing committees could send "Views and Estimates" outlining their fiscal agendas to both the Budget and Appropriations committees. After a budget resolution with reconciliation instructions—or just as a normal practice—authorizing committees could transmit direct spending and revenue proposals to the Appropriations Committee to be integrated into the appropriations package. The 12 appropriations bills could continue being reported from each appropriations subcommittee, and then the full committee could combine the 12 bills into a single omnibus package with changes to direct spending and revenue included, ultimately similar in form to the conclusion of the states' budget processes. That way, the pudding (discretionary spending like defense, transportation, and education) helps Congress eat their peas (overall fiscal management, including needed consolidation).

WHEN OPPORTUNITY KNOCKS

Virtually all process changes affect power dynamics. Turf and ego are part of Congress. Yet they need not be insurmountable. It is almost impossible to innovate thoughtfully and quickly in a crisis, or when opportunity knocks otherwise. Forget about innovating and persuading when other demands overwhelm most members.

Reformers must lay the groundwork well in advance and when few seem to care about their issues. They must carefully study the policies and institutions, both those they seek to amend or replace and those that may inspire productive alternatives. They must accurately diagnose the root causes of dysfunction and studiously develop ideas for addressing them as concrete proposals. Then they must adapt proposals into legislative form, keeping the process and political constraints and prospects always in mind. They must build coalitions with other members and with external expert organizations to reach a critical mass to inspire credibility, if not outright deference, often with little advance warning.

Some changes have the most impact prior to or just at the start of a Congress. Revising committee jurisdictions and membership would be messy within a Congress. Revamping conference rules after the organizational meetings would postpone many benefits until the next Congress, though that is preferable to never addressing them.

The debt limit is a perilous opportunity. Many members resist using it as a bargaining chip because they believe the stakes—immediate default on the debt—would be catastrophic. Even so, a fully developed and bipartisan-backed combination of enforceable budget targets combined with debt limit reform could succeed in advancing both aspects of fiscal responsibility: controlling the debt growth and protecting the full faith and credit. Other options could be ripe for negotiation then too, especially a bipartisan commission approach.

The end of the fiscal year, the end of the calendar year, and trust fund depletions are long-anticipated opportunities. It may be as important to prepare for those that are not scheduled, however. International incidents, executive actions, rating agency reports, financial crises, and much more can provoke intense pressure on Congress to "do something." If reforms are ready and appropriate for those moments, the prospects for their enactment rise dramatically. Chances usually come and go quickly as deadlines and other crisis points pass. Reformers may only have weeks—or even days—to act.

CONCLUSION: BE PREPARED

The United States has not been successful in using rules-based fiscal and monetary policy to head off a potential debt crisis. Not yet at least.

Federal policymakers have many promising options for restoring fiscal sustainability and otherwise improving the way Congress develops budgets and chooses priorities. Much can be learned from other countries and from the states, but Congress' unique features require tailoring ideas to work with its unique political, policy, and procedural context.

Advancing plausible reforms requires understanding the influences on players within the U.S. political system. This includes a detailed grip on the policy landscape established by the explicit rules and informal norms from both chambers and all four conferences as they interact with each other, the administration, and others.

Within that framework, being organized within Congress and among outside groups is a crucial determinant of effectiveness. Champions don't just happen—they need ongoing support to stay active and to break new ground. The community of reform can provide technical, organizational, public relations, political, grassroots, and other assistance so congressional champions experience tangible benefits across multiple domains for doing public interest work.

Continued expansion of well-developed policy ideas with established support maximizes opportunities. Even if some details need to change to fit emerging situations, initially working them out makes legislation far easier to get into a form that can be enacted.

The budget process can be altered, but not by waiting for the last minute. Understanding the political, procedural, and policy landscape and investing the time to develop thoughtful ways to improve the system and to build relationships is the necessary groundwork. With preparation, patience, and vigilance, much is possible.

NOTES

1. House Republicans and Senate Republicans each form a "conference," while House Democrats and Senate Democrats each form a "caucus."

2. House Republican Conference, "Conference Rules of the 117th Congress," https://www.gop.gov/conference-rules-of-the-117th-congress/. Senate Republican Conference, "History, Rules & Precedents of the Senate Republican Conference," https://www.republican.senate.gov/public/index.cfm?a=Files.Serve&File_id=11 2F6AFB-A1F0-4C3F-8E78-788AC85C344E. House Democratic Conference, "Rules of the Democratic Caucus," https://www.dems.gov/imo/media/doc/DEM_CAUCUS _RULES_117TH_April_2021.pdf.

REFERENCES

Amash, Justin. 2011. "H.J.Res. 81. Business Cycle Balanced Budget Amendment." Introduced, October 14, 2011. https://www.congress.gov/bill/112th-congress/ house-joint-resolution/81.

Amash, Justin. 2020. "Who Broke Congress?" *Free Thoughts Podcast*, June 12, 2020. https://www.libertarianism.org/podcasts/free-thoughts/who-broke-congress-rep-justin-amash.

Arrington. 2020. "Arrington, Peters Pen Bipartisan Letter on Need For Budget Reform, Debt Reduction." June 1, 2020. https://arrington.house.gov/news/do cumentsingle.aspx?DocumentID=326.

Blue Dog Coalition. 2019. "Blue Dogs Release Blueprint for Fiscal Reform." July 18, 2019. https://bluedogcaucus-costa.house.gov/media-center/press-releases/blue -dogs-release-blueprint-for-fiscal-reform-0.

Brat, Dave. 2015. "H.J.Res. 55. Principles-based Balanced Budget Amendment." Introduced, May 20, 2015. https://www.congress.gov/bill/114th-congress/house -joint-resolution/55.

Burchett, Tim. 2019. "Bipartisan Legislation Limiting Public Debt Introduced by Reps. Burchett, Case." November 20, 2019. https://burchett.house.gov/media/ press-releases/bipartisan-legislation-limiting-public-debt-introduced-reps-burchet t-case.

Case, Ed. 2019. "Case Introduces Bill to Tackle Exploding National Debt." November 21, 2019. https://case.house.gov/news/documentsingle.aspx?DocumentID=99.

Committee for a Responsible Federal Budget. 2015. "The Better Budget Process Initiative: Improving the Debt Limit." March 12, 2015. http://www.crfb.org/paper s/better-budget-process-initiative-improving-debt-limit.

Committee for a Responsible Federal Budget. 2019. "Bipartisan Group Introduces TRUST Act." November 1, 2019. http://www.crfb.org/blogs/bipartisan-group-in troduces-trust-act.

Committee for a Responsible Federal Budget. 2020a. "Support for TRUST Act Grows." January 7, 2020. https://www.crfb.org/blogs/support-trust-act-grows.

Committee for a Responsible Federal Budget. 2020b. "President Trump has Signed $4.7 Trillion of Debt into Law." January 8, 2020. https://www.crfb.org/blogs/pre sident-trump-has-signed-4-7-trillion-debt-law.

Committee for a Responsible Federal Budget. 2020c. "GAO: Fiscal Sustainability Is a Growing Concern for Some Key Federal Trust Funds." January 31, 2020. https:/ /www.crfb.org/blogs/gao-fiscal-sustainability-growing-concern-some-key-federal -trust-funds.

Committee for a Responsible Federal Budget. 2020d. "Major Trust Funds Headed for Insolvency Within 11 Years." July 22, 2020. https://www.crfb.org/blogs/major-tr ust-funds-headed-insolvency-within-11-years.

Committee for a Responsible Federal Budget. 2020e. "Correcting the Record on the Enzi-Whitehouse Budget Reform." June 10, 2020. http://www.crfb.org/blogs/corr ecting-record-enzi-whitehouse-budget-reforms.

Committee for a Responsible Federal Budget. 2020f. "Correcting the Record on the TRUST Act." July 24, 2020. https://www.crfb.org/blogs/correcting-record-trust -act.

Committee for a Responsible Federal Budget. 2020g. "Explaining the TRUST Act: Just the FAQs." July 28, 2020. https://www.crfb.org/blogs/explaining-trust-act-ju st-faqs.

Committee for a Responsible Federal Budget. 2020g. "Pairing Debt Limit Reform with Budget Goals." August 27, 2020. http://www.crfb.org/blogs/pairing-debt-l imit-reform-budget-goals.

Committee for a Responsible Federal Budget. 2021. "New Poll Finds Americans Worry About the Debt and Want the Budget More Balanced Between Generations." May 13, 2021. https://www.crfb.org/blogs/new-poll-finds-americans-worry-about -debt-and-want-budget-more-balanced-between-generations.

Congressional Budget Office. 2020. "Summary of Estimated Budgetary Effects of Rules Committee Print 116-54, H.R. 2, the Moving Forward Act, Including Manager's Amendment (DeFazio 228)." June 30, 2020. https://www.cbo.gov/syste m/files/2020-06/HR2.pdf.

Congressional Budget Office. 2021a. "The Budget and Economic Outlook: 2021 to 2031." February 11, 2021. https://www.cbo.gov/publication/56970.

Congressional Budget Office. 2021b. "Estimated Budgetary Effects of H.R. 1319, American Rescue Plan Act of 2021." March 10, 2021. https://www.cbo.gov/pub-lication/57056.

Congressional Progressive Caucus. 2019. "The People's Budget FY 2020." August 30, 2020. https://cpc-grijalva.house.gov/the-peoples-budget-fy-2020/.

Convergence Project. 2018. "Final Report: Building a Better Budget Process." March 2018. https://www.convergencepolicy.org/wp-content/uploads/2018/04/ B3P-Report-Final_4.18.18.pdf.

Couchman, Kurt. 2017. "A Well-Crafted Budget Amendment Can Succeed." *The Hill*, January 20, 2017. https://thehill.com/blogs/pundits-blog/the-administration /315423-a-well-crafted-budget-amendment-can-succeed.

Couchman, Kurt. 2018. "Huge Trade Deficits Reflect and Create Bigger Problems." *The Hill*, June 27, 2018. https://thehill.com/opinion/international/394319-huge-t rade-deficits-reflect-and-create-bigger-problems.

Couchman, Kurt. 2019. "We Should Offset Emergencies—Just Not Right Away." *The Hill*, January 15, 2019. https://thehill.com/opinion/white-house/425384-we-should-offset-emergencies-just-not-right-away.

Couchman, Kurt. 2020. "Effective Fiscal Rules Build on Consensus." In *A Fiscal Cliff: New Perspectives on the U.S. Federal Debt Crisis*, edited by John D. Merrifield and Barry W. Poulson, 147–184. Washington: Cato Institute.

Desilver, Drew. 2015. "What is the House Freedom Caucus, and Who's In It?" *Pew Research Center*, October 20, 2015. https://www.pewresearch.org/fact-tank/2015 /10/20/house-freedom-caucus-what-is-it-and-whos-in-it/.

Enzi, Michael. 2019. "S. 2765, the Bipartisan Congressional Budget Control Act." Introduced, October 31, 2019. https://www.congress.gov/bill/116th-congress/senat e-bill/2765/text/rs.

Fall, Falilou, Debbie Bloch, Jean-Marc Fournier, and Peter Hoeller. 2015. "Prudent Debt Targets and Fiscal Frameworks." Organisation for Economic Co-operation and Development, 48–49. July 1, 2015. https://doi.org/10.1787/5jrxtjmmt9f7-en.

Hern, Kevin. 2021. "Hern, RSC introduce FY22 Budget – 'Reclaiming our Fiscal Future.'" May 19, 2021. https://hern.house.gov/news/documentsingle.aspx?Do cumentID=349.

Hoyer, Steny. 2019. "H.Res. 6, Adopting the Rules of the House of Representatives for the 116th Congress." January 9, 2019. https://www.congress.gov/bill/116th -congress/house-resolution/6.

Huder, Joshua. 2018. "The House and Senate Go Rogue?" May 22, 2018. https://ww
    w.legbranch.org/2018-5-22-the-house-and-senate-go-rogue/.
Kirk, Robert S., and William J. Mallett. 2020. "Funding and Financing Highways and
    Public Transportation." Congressional Research Service. Updated May 11, 2020.
    https://fas.org/sgp/crs/misc/R45350.pdf.
Lee, Mike. 2019. "Sen. Lee Introduces ARTICLE ONE Act to Reclaim Congressional
    Power." March 12, 2019. https://www.lee.senate.gov/public/index.cfm/2019/3/
    sen-lee-introduces-article-one-act-to-reclaim-congressional-power.
Lynch, Megan S., and James V. Saturno. 2019. "The Joint Select Committee on
    Budget and Appropriations Process Reform." Congressional Research Service.
    Updated March 26, 2019. https://fas.org/sgp/crs/misc/R45111.pdf.
MacGuineas, Maya. 2019. "Utah Statesmen Seek to Fix Our Most Pressing
    Problems." *Salt Lake Tribune*, December 13, 2019. https://www.sltrib.com/opinion
    /commentary/2019/12/13/maya-macguineas-utah/.
McConnell, Mitch. 2020. "McConnell Outlines Historic Relief Proposal
    for 'An Important Crossroads in this Battle.'" July 27, 2020. https
    ://www.republicanleader.senate.gov/newsroom/remarks/mcconnell
    -outlines-historic-relief-proposal-for-an-important-crossroads-in-this
    -battle-.
Meuser, Dan. 2019. "Meuser Introduces Legislation to Increase Accountability and
    Transparency for Federal Budget Process." July 25, 2019. https://meuser.house
    .gov/media/press-releases/meuser-introduces-legislation-increase-accountability-
    and-transparency-federal.
New Democrat Coalition. 2020. "Fiscal Responsibility." Accessed August 30, 2020.
    https://newdemocratcoalition.house.gov/policy/issues/fiscal-responsibility.
Perdue, David. 2016. "Perdue Proposes Dramatic Reshaping of Budget Process."
    September 29, 2016. https://www.perdue.senate.gov/news/press-releases/perdue
    -proposes-dramatic-reshaping-of-budget-process.
Peter G. Peterson Foundation. 2020. "Do Voters Care about the National Debt? The
    Polls Say They Do." February 20, 2020. https://www.pgpf.org/blog/2019/12/do
    -voters-care-about-the-national-debt-the-polls-say-they-do.
Portman, Rob. 2019. "As Shutdown Continues, Portman, Senate Colleagues Introduce
    Bill to Permanently End Government Shutdowns." January 11, 2019. https://ww
    w.portman.senate.gov/newsroom/press-releases/shutdown-continues-portman-sen
    ate-colleagues-introduce-bill-permanently-end.
Problem Solvers Caucus. 2020. "Problem Solvers Address Need to Confront Budget
    Crisis with Principles." October 19, 2020. https://problemsolverscaucus-gotthe
    imer.house.gov/media/press-releases/problem-solvers-address-need-confront-bu
    dget-crisis-principles.
Problem Solvers Caucus. 2021. "About the Caucus." May 23, 2021. https://problem
    solverscaucus.house.gov/about.
Riddick, Floyd M., and Alan S. Frumin. 1992. *Riddick's Senate Procedure:
    Precedents and Practices*. Revised and edited by Alan S. Frumin. January 1, 1992.
    https://www.govinfo.gov/app/details/GPO-RIDDICK-1992/GPO-RIDDICK-
    1992-1/context,.

Romney, Mitt. 2021. "Romney Leads Bipartisan Coalition in Introducing the TRUST Act." April 15, 2021. https://www.romney.senate.gov/romney-bipartisan-coalition-introduce-trust-act-inclusion-next-relief-package.

Schelling, Thomas. 2006. *Micromotives and Macrobehavior*. New York: Norton.

Shutt, Jennifer. 2020. "Democrats' Rule Change Could Spark Senate Appropriations Shakeup." *Roll Call*, December 10, 2020. https://www.rollcall.com/2020/12/10/democrats-rule-change-could-spark-senate-appropriations-shakeup/.

Snyder, Tanya. 2020. "House Sends Massive Infrastructure Bill to the Senate, Where It Has No Path Forward." *Politico*, July 1, 2020. https://www.politico.com/news/2020/07/01/house-infrastructure-bill-347355.

Swift, Taylor J. 2020. "Who Steers the Ship? An Examination of House Steering and Policy Committee Membership." July 20, 2020. https://firstbranchforecast.com/2020/07/20/who-steers-the-ship-an-examination-of-house-steering-and-policy-committee-membership-in-the-116th-congress/.

U.S. House Committee on the Budget. 2020. "Congressional Power of the Purse Act." Accessed August 30, 2020. https://budget.house.gov/CPPAct.

U.S. House Committee on the Budget. 2011. "The Joint Select Committee on Deficit Reduction." August 30, 2020. https://budget.house.gov/issues-initiatives/joint-select-committee-deficit-recution.

U.S. House Committee on Rules. "Rules and Resources." https://rules.house.gov/rules-and-resources.

U.S. House History, Art & Archives. 2020. "The House's All Night Session to Break Speaker Joe Cannon's Power." August 30, 2020. https://history.house.gov/Historical-Highlights/1901-1950/The-House-s-all-night-session-to-break-Speaker-Joe-Cannon-s-power/.

U.S. House Select Committee on the Modernization of Congress. 2020. "Recommendations." November 28, 2020. See recommendations 85–92. https://modernizecongress.house.gov/recommendations.

U.S. Senate. 2020. "Majority and Minority Leaders." September 6, 2020. https://www.senate.gov/artandhistory/history/common/briefing/Majority_Minority_Leaders.htm.

U.S. Senate Committee on the Budget. 2019. "Bipartisan Reforms Get Budget Committee OK." November 11, 2019. https://www.budget.senate.gov/bipartisan-reforms-get-budget-committee-ok.

U.S. Senate Committee on Homeland Security and Governmental Affairs. 2019a. "Committee Passes Bipartisan Bill Introduced by Senators Hassan, Lankford to Prevent Government Shutdowns." June 19, 2019. https://www.hsgac.senate.gov/subcommittees/fso/media/committee-passes-bipartisan-bill-introduced-by-senators-hassan-lankford-to-prevent-government-shutdowns.

U.S. Senate Committee on Homeland Security and Governmental Affairs. 2019b. "Assuring that Robust, Thorough, and Informed Congressional Leadership is Exercised Over National Emergencies Act, Report of the Committee on Homeland Security and Governmental Affairs." Senate Report 116-159. November 18, 2019.

U.S. Senate Committee on Rules and Administration. 2020. "Rules of the Senate." Accessed August 30, 2020. https://www.rules.senate.gov/rules-of-the-senate.

U.S. Statutes at Large. 2011. "The Budget Control Act of 2011." Public Law 112–25. Enacted August 2, 2011.

U.S. Statutes at Large. 2019. "The Bipartisan Budget Act of 2019." Public Law 116-37. Enacted August 2, 2019. See sec. 301.

Wallner, James. 2018. "What Makes Senate Leaders So Powerful?" August 1, 2018. https://www.legbranch.org/2018-8-1-what-makes-senate-leaders-so-powerful/.

White, Kathryn Vesey, Lauren Cummings, Bruckie Gashaw, Stacey Mazer, Brian Sigritz, and Leah Wavrunek. 2015. *Budget Processes in the States*. National Association of State Budget Officers. Spring 2015. https://higherlogicdownload .s3.amazonaws.com/NASBO/9d2d2db1-c943-4f1b-b750-0fca152d64c2/Uploade dImages/Budget%20Processess/2015_Budget_Processes_-_S.pdf.

Chapter 2

Debt Fatigue and the Climacteric in U.S. Economic Growth

John Merrifield and Barry Poulson

THE CLIMACTERIC IN U.S. ECONOMIC GROWTH

Economists in the United States are debating whether the economic recovery from the coronavirus pandemic will be V-shaped, U-shaped, or W-shaped. Whatever the pace of recovery from this recession, the assumption was that in the long term the United States will recover to rates of economic growth experienced prior to the pandemic. An alternative view is that the United States is experiencing a "climacteric" in economic growth.

A *climacteric* in economic growth refers to long-term retardation and stagnation in economic growth beyond the short-term economic shock of the pandemic. The term "climacteric" was first introduced to describe the slowdown in economic growth experienced by Great Britain at the end of the nineteenth century, and by the United States in the early twentieth century (Poulson and Dowling 1973). This secular retardation in economic growth reflected slower growth in factor inputs and factor productivity.

The United States is experiencing a climacteric in economic growth in the twenty-first century, comparable to that in the early twentieth century. The Congressional Budget Office (2019a, 2020f) documents this secular retardation in economic growth. Over the past three decades real GDP growth averaged 2.5% per year. The CBO projects that over the next three decades the annual rate of economic growth will average 1.6%. The CBO finds that the economic outlook for 2020–2050 has deteriorated significantly compared to previous forecasts.

The CBO finds that over the past two decades economic shocks have been a source of retardation in economic growth (see table 2.1). Total output has been about half a percent below potential output, and this is projected to continue in the long term. This reflects the fact that during and after economic

Table 2.1   Real GDP Growth (Percent Annual Rate of Growth)

1990–2019	2020–2030	2031–2040	2041–2050	2020–2050
2.5	1.6	1.6	1.5	1.6

Source: Congressional Budget Office 2020f.

downturns actual output has fallen short of potential output to a greater extent and for longer periods of time than actual output has exceeded potential output during economic booms (Congressional Budget Office 2015). Each of the recent economic shocks has been more severe and has left actual output even further below potential output.

The CBO finds that retardation in economic growth in coming decades reflects slower growth in factor productivity as well as factor inputs.

Over the next 30 years the average annual rate of growth in productivity is projected to be just under 1.3%, nearly 0.3 percentage points slower than the average annual rate of growth over the past 30 years (CBO 2020f, p. 20).

Slower growth also reflects the impact of fiscal policies, most importantly, the influence of increases in public debt. The CBO notes that there is considerable uncertainty regarding the impact of these variables.

> Another source of uncertainty is the global economy's longer term response to the substantial increase in public deficits and debt that is occurring as governments spend significant amounts to attempt to mitigate the impact of the pandemic and the economic downturn. (CBO 2020d, p. 5)

DEBT FATIGUE IN THE UNITED STATES

The climacteric in U.S. economic growth is directly linked to debt fatigue and unsustainable growth in debt. The figure 2.1 traces the primary balance and debt as a share of GDP in the post–World War II era.

The debt/GDP ratio fell during the post–World War II era until the mid-1970s.While the government ran deficits in most years, the deficits were modest and more than offset by the growth in GDP. From the mid-1970s until the early 1990s the government consistently incurred deficits exceeding the growth in GDP, marking the beginning of unsustainable growth in debt.

During the "Great Moderation" of the 1990s the government incurred lower deficits, and generated surplus revenue from 1998 to 2001. The debt/GDP ratio was reduced to levels comparable to the 1970s.

Debt fatigue is most evident during the last two decades, and is linked to the economic shocks experienced during these years. The first economic shock was the relatively mild recession in 2001.

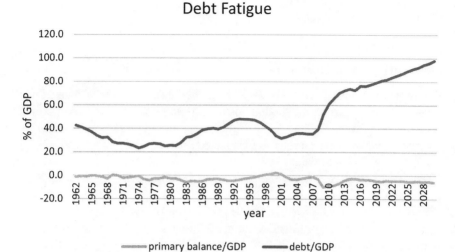

Figure 2.1 **Debt Fatigue.** Calculated by authors using the simulation model described in Appendix A.

Countercyclical fiscal policy in these years again boosted deficits and the debt/GDP ratio. During the economic recovery from that recession, deficits were reduced and the debt/GDP stabilized.

The financial crisis in 2008 resulted in the sharpest recession of the post–World War II era. The deficits incurred during that recession were greater than that incurred in any other post–World War II recession, and resulted in a sharp discontinuous increase in the debt/GDP ratio. In the years following that recession deficits were reduced, but the debt/GDP ratio continued to increase. It is at this point that debt fatigue becomes most evident. Even before the coronavirus pandemic the government again incurred trillion-dollar deficits increasing the debt/GDP ratio at an unsustainable rate.

The CBOs most recent forecast captures the devastating impact of the coronavirus pandemic on the budget and the economy (CBO 2020b). Deficits are projected to grow to unprecedented levels, 17.9% of GDP in 2020 and 9.8% of GDP in 2021. Debt held by the public is projected to increase to 101% of GDP in 2020 and 108% of GDP in 2021. The CBO projects continued growth of debt to more than 195% of GDP over the next three decades (CBO 2020f).

Over the past two decades each major economic shock has been accompanied by a sharp discontinuous increase in debt. In years of economic recovery the United States exhibits debt fatigue in which debt continues to increase relative to GDP. Slower economic growth makes it more difficult to pursue the fiscal consolidation required to stabilize and reduce debt. The fiscal rules and fiscal policies now in place are flawed in that they have failed to prevent an unsustainable growth in debt.

Debt Fatigue and Risk of Default

Future generations of Americans will bear the burden of debt fatigue in the form of direct taxation, the hidden cost of inflation, higher borrowing costs, or some combination of the three. Higher taxation and inflation have yet to emerge; however, interest rates are projected to increase, and to diverge even further from that in low debt countries.

The CBO forecasts that while the federal funds rate will remain at 0.1% over the next decade, the interest rate on 10-year Treasury notes will increase from 0.9% in 2020 to 4.8% by 2050 (CBO 2020f, p. 13).

The higher interest rates reflect increased uncertainty and risk associated with U.S. debt. The CBO (2019b) estimates the average long-run effect of interest rates ranges from about 2 to 3 basis points for each 1 percentage point in debt as a percentage of GDP.

An important proposition in this literature is a non-linear relationship between yields and debt levels. Yields may not rise smoothly with increases in the debt levels. Yields may rise gradually at first, but eventually yields increase in a steep non-linear way, and at some point credit markets respond by denying borrowers credit.

A study by Turner and Spinelli (2012) estimates that each percentage increase in government debt as a share of GDP raises the interest rate differential about 5 basis points.[1] The impact of debt on interest rates depends on whether it is financed domestically or externally. In the United States, the share of debt financed externally has increased; as a result, the impact of higher debt on interest rates has also increased. This relationship holds even when taking into account the effects of quantitative easing on interest rates. Like the heavily indebted countries in Europe that are dependent on external finance, the United States has become more vulnerable to a financial crisis.

The CBO notes that as debt levels continue to rise a major uncertainty is the willingness of lenders to purchase U.S. debt (Congressional Budget Office 2019, 2020c). This has not really been tested in recent recessions because the non-orthodox monetary policies pursued by the Fed expanded the share of U.S. debt in the Fed portfolio. However, there is growing evidence that debt levels in the United States have increased to levels that risk default.

Some credit agencies have downgraded U.S. debt. S&P Global Ratings downgraded U.S. debt to AA+ in 2011 (www.spglobal.com/ratings/en/).

In July 2020 Fitch Ratings downgraded U.S. debt from stable to negative, citing —deterioration in the U.S. public finances and the absence of a credible fiscal consolidation plan.

—Treasury flexibility, assisted by Federal Reserve intervention to restore liquidity to financial markets, does not entirely dispel risks to medium—term debt sustainability, and there is growing risk that U.S. policy makes will not consolidate public finances sufficiently to stabilize public debt after the pandemic shock has passed. (www.fitchratings.com/).

Fitch further noted that the United States has the highest debt of any AAA-rated sovereign. Fitch has become pessimistic regarding U.S. debt even though the country has a higher debt tolerance level than other AAA sovereigns.

High deficits have often led to debt crises, but there is considerable uncertainty regarding the debt levels where a country risks default (Reinhart and Rogoff 2009; Reinhart et al. 2003). IMF guidelines (2013) set public debt benchmarks at 85% of GDP for advanced countries, suggesting that debt in the United States has now increased to levels that risk default.

Causes for Debt Fatigue in the United States

Debrun et al. (2018) explore the causes for the growth of debt in high debtor developed countries, contrasting the experience of a high debtor country, Japan, with that of Germany, which has had more success in limiting the growth in debt. There are many parallels between the growth of debt in Japan and the United States; therefore, it is worth exploring the causes for debt growth examined in Debrun et al. (2018) to determine their relevance for the United States.

Debrun et al. (2018) suggest four possible explanations for why high debtor countries allow debt to grow at unsustainable rates:

1. Implicit or explicit strategy of eventually defaulting
2. Confusion between trend and cycle: the authorities observe lower growth and adopt expansionary policies that fail to deliver the expected boost
3. Conflict with the central bank that responds by raising interest rates
4. Lack of domestic support for fiscal discipline, which leads to destabilizing budgetary cycles when fiscal fatigue sets in (Debrun et al. 2018, p. 16).

The first explanation can be ruled out for both Japan and the United States. For strategic reasons, it would be too costly for either country to default on debt. The best evidence for this in the United States are the extraordinary measures taken by the Treasury to meet debt obligations in periods when actual debt approaches statutory debt limits.

The other explanations for the growth in debt involve failures in monetary and/or fiscal policy. For Debrun et al. (2018) an important question is whether monetary and fiscal rules in place have proven to be effective constraints on debt in the long run. There is an extensive literature on this question for the United States, extending back to the seminal work of John Taylor (Taylor 1993).[2]

MONETARY RULES AND MONETARY POLICY

The role of the central bank and monetary policy has emerged as crucial in determining the success or failure of fiscal policies designed to achieve sustainable debt. In his seminal article Taylor (1993) proposed a monetary rule, since referred to as the "Taylor Rule." That rule would adjust the nominal interest rate in response to changes in inflation and output. He recommended a relatively high interest rate when inflation is above its target, or when output is above its full employment level, to reduce inflationary pressure. He recommended a relatively low interest rate in recessions to stimulate output and suggested that as a rule of thumb, when inflation rises by 1%, the nominal interest rate should increase by about 1.5%; if output falls by 1%, the interest rate should be decreased by about 0.5%.[3] Since his original paper, Taylor and others have suggested numerous refinements to the Taylor Rule (Orphanides 2007; Davig and Leeper 2007).

Taylor (2010) follows in the positivist tradition of his mentor Milton Friedman by exploring the role of monetary policies during fluctuations in economic activity in the United States. He traces shifts in rules-based and discretionary monetary policy over several decades. Taylor (2010) finds a discontinuous shift in monetary policy beginning in the late 1970s and early 1980s when the Fed pursued an aggressive policy to reduce inflation. Taylor and others find evidence that during the late 1980s and 1990s, the Fed pursued monetary rules designed to stabilize inflation at a full employment level of output (Taylor 2010; Clarida et al. 2000). While the Fed has never committed to an explicit monetary rule, Taylor maintains that monetary policy in the late 1980s and early 1990s followed a de facto Taylor Rule:

> It certainly appears that the changes in inflation and real GDP influenced the path of the federal funds rate. This evidence is especially important because monetary policy pursued during the period by the administrations of Ronald Reagan and George H. W. Bush are generally regarded as contributing to economic stability. (Taylor 1993, p. 203)

Taylor and other economists maintain that during this Great Moderation, growing confidence in Fed monetary policy led to expectations of low inflation (Taylor 2000, 2010; Eichenbaum 1997; Feldstein 2002).

Taylor (2010) maintained that a shift back toward discretionary monetary policy occurred with the Fed's decision to hold the target rate of interest below the level implied by monetary rules during 2003–2005, and the interventions by the Fed during and after the Great Recession that began in 2008.

When the economy fell off a cliff in 2020 the Fed responded by reducing interest rates to close to zero and purchasing more than $2 trillion in Treasury and mortgage-backed securities. The Fed has since expanded its bond purchases to include corporate bonds, and has committed to maintaining the current pace of purchasing Treasury and mortgage-backed securities. Chairman Jerome Powell announced that the Fed plans to keep interest rates close to zero for years. He stated that "We are strongly committed to using our tools to do whatever we can and for as long as we can to provide some relief and stability" (*Wall Street Journal* 2020c, A1). Chairman Powell's commitment to use the tools of monetary policy is a clear signal that the economic recovery from the coronavirus pandemic will be a long and difficult task. Until the recovery is complete, the Fed will in effect be monetizing government debt.

Powell's aggressive policy has been described as the "Powell Put," a reference to the monetary policies pursued by Fed Chairmen dating back to Alan Greenspan. After the 1987 stock market crash Greenspan lowered interest rates and injected liquidity to prevent further deterioration in the market. This policy has been criticized as a support for asset pricing that shifts the risk of investing from the private sector to the public sector.

There is a fundamental difference between the "Powell Put" and the "Greenspan Put." The aggressive monetary policy pursued by Greenspan in 1987 was followed by more than a decade of moderate monetary policy, approximating the benchmarks set by the Taylor rule. In his recent statements regarding monetary policy Chairman Powell paid lip service to the Taylor rule, stating that "Officials continued discussions about whether to tie their rate plans to certain economic outcomes, such as inflation returning to 2% and unemployment returning to its recent lows" (*Wall Street Journal* 2020c, A1).

But the Fed is also considering imposing a cap on government bond yields (*Wall Street Journal* 2020b, B11). They would commit to purchase Treasuries in whatever amounts are required to keep borrowing costs from exceeding a specific range. This policy was pursued by the Fed during World War II, and in the postwar years to help the government finance war expenditures. The Fed commitment to this policy now would aid the government in financing increased expenditures in the wake of the coronavirus pandemic.

Policymakers anticipate that interest rates will be near zero at least through the end of 2022. Given the commitments made by Chairman Powell there is little likelihood that the Fed will again be guided by the benchmarks set in the Taylor rule, and restore moderation in monetary policy, at least in the near future.

In his analysis of the "Great Moderation," John Taylor poses a counterfactual hypothesis (Taylor 2009, 2010, 2014; Cogan et al. 2013a, b). What if the rules-based approach to monetary policy that emerged in the late 1980s and 1990s had continued over the past two decades? He and his coauthors simulate the impact of a "Taylor Rule" on monetary policy. They conclude that a Taylor Rule-based monetary policy could have avoided the destabilizing effects of the discretionary monetary policies pursued in this period. Taylor and others argue that we can no longer rely on the Federal Reserve to pursue discretionary monetary policies to approximate a rules-based policy, and that formal monetary rules, such as the Taylor rule, should guide monetary policy (Poulson and Baghestani 2012).

Subsequent research has explored different versions of the Taylor rule as the basis for explaining monetary policy over business cycles in the United States (Orphanides 2008; Poulson and Baghestani 2012; Davig and Leeper 2007).

In Search of a Fiscal Taylor Rule (FTR)

Taylor recognized that commitment to a monetary policy rule such as the Taylor Rule was not a sufficient condition for price stability. If fiscal expectations are inconsistent with a stable price level, this could preclude price stability, even with a Taylor Rule in place.[4] He advocated a rules-based approach to fiscal policy (Taylor 1993, 2000). The FTR is a rule providing benchmarks to guide discretionary fiscal policy. The objective of the FTR is to promote economic stability over the business cycle, while maintaining debt sustainability in the long run.[5]

The FTR requires that a structural surplus is maintained over the business cycle. Application of the FTR means that fiscal policy is anchored in the sense that debt converges to a sustainable level in the long run. The nominal budget balance allows automatic stabilizers to support aggregate demand when actual output is below potential output and for reductions in expenditures when actual output exceeds potential output. Taylor maintains that this FTR provides a good fit for the fiscal balance in the United States in the long run. He fits the FTR to U.S. fiscal data for 1960 to 1999.

A number of studies have built upon the original Taylor design for a FTR (Carnot 2014; Debrun and Jonung (2018); Kleim and Kriwolusky 2013; Kumhof and Laxton 2013; Lukkezen and Teulings 2013). Debrun and Jonung (2018) recently generalized the Taylor FTR in a model that they also fit to U.S. data. Their model provides benchmarks for the nominal budget balance to provide for economic stabilization over the business cycle, and convergence of the debt/GDP ratio to a given target. They assume the 60% target for the debt/GDP ratio adopted by the European Union and the OECD. They fit the model to U.S. fiscal data for the period 1990 to 2017.

Debrun and Jonung (2018) find that in the United States the actual budget balance in the 1990s exceeded the benchmark budget balance. In other words, the fiscal policies pursued during the "Great Moderation" were actually more prudent than that consistent with their FTR benchmarks. However, over the past two decades the actual budget balance was significantly below that consistent with the benchmarks. This suggests that over the past two decades fiscal policy no longer approximates the rules-based fiscal policy pursued during the "Great Moderation."

Debrun and Jonung (2018) are somewhat sanguine regarding the prospects for a rules-based approach to fiscal policy in the United States. They argue that while the actual budget balance has been below the benchmark budget balance over the past two decades, there is evidence of convergence toward the benchmark after the financial crisis. They conclude that as the output gap closes deficits will move back to levels consistent with long-term debt objectives. They seem to suggest that we should expect a return to a rules-based fiscal policy similar to that pursued during the "Great Moderation."

Debrun and Jonung (2018) are also supportive of discretionary fiscal policy to stabilize the economy over the business cycle. The benchmarks in their FTR model provide for discretionary fiscal policy as well as automatic stabilizers. Taylor and other monetary economists are more skeptical of the effectiveness of discretionary fiscal policy in stabilizing the economy over the business cycle.

As Debrun and Jonung (2018) note, the simulation of FTRs that they and Taylor conducted is sensitive to data vintage. They have both chosen time periods that include the fiscal policies pursued during the "Great Moderation." The Debrun and Jonung (2018) simulations ended in 2017 prior to the impact of fiscal policies pursued by the Trump administration.

We question the sanguine view that Debrun and Jonung have of the prospects for U.S fiscal policy. After the 2008 recession, the United States attempted to reduce deficits for several years but quickly abandoned these fiscal austerity measures, incurring trillion-dollar deficits, even in years of rapid economic growth. This is in contrast to Germany and other countries in Northern Europe that were successful in balancing their budgets and reducing debt burdens over the past decade (Merrifield and Poulson 2016a, b, c, 2017a, b, 2020a).

The long-term forecasts of the Congressional Budget Office (2020f) reveal that at least under current law the United States will incur greater deficits that will further deviate from benchmark budget balances required by a FTR. The debt/GDP level is projected to increase well above current levels and diverge even further from the 60% target for sustainable level in their analysis. The United States does not appear to be returning to the rules-based fiscal policies pursued during the "Great Moderation."

We conclude that over the past two decades the United States has abandoned the rules-based fiscal policies pursued during the "Great Moderation." If elected officials had continued to pursue those more prudent fiscal policies, the country could have avoided a debt crisis. But, hoping that elected officials will again be guided by a FTR to stabilize the economy over the business cycle and reduce the debt/GDP ratio to a sustainable level is wishful thinking. Because the United States has abandoned a rules-based fiscal policy it will be even more difficult to solve the debt crisis.

Debt Fatigue: The Path Not Taken

Debrun et al. (2018) conclude that we are left with the final explanation for unconstrained growth of debt in high debtor developed countries: lack of domestic support for fiscal discipline. The question is why domestic support for fiscal discipline has deteriorated in the United States in recent decades. The public choice literature identifies deficit bias of elected officials as the source of deficits and unsustainable debt.

Combined with erosion in fiscal rules constraining rent-seeking behavior, opportunities for rent-seeking have expanded greatly over the past half century. The ability to finance expenditures with debt has increased the fiscal commons, and created more incentives to engage in rent-seeking. That begs the question: Why citizens in countries such as Switzerland and Germany support fiscal discipline, while citizens in countries such as Japan and the United States have abandoned it (Merrifield and Poulson 2018)?

Feld and Kirchgassner (2001, 2006), and Blankert (2000, 2011, 2015) explore the effectiveness of Swiss debt brakes. Blankert (2000, 2011, 2015) provides a nuanced explanation for Swiss citizen's support for fiscal discipline using the concept of dynamic credence capital. The path chosen by Switzerland can be traced to a crucial court decision in 1998. In that year, the municipality of Leukerbad could not service its debt, and turned to the canton of Wallis for a bailout. The court ruled that the canton was not liable for the debt incurred by the municipality, leaving Credit Suisse First Boston and other creditors to absorb the loss.

Blankert argues that this "no-bailout" rule has been the basis for the success of fiscal rules in constraining debt at all levels of government in

Switzerland. Each level of government perceives that they are autonomous and independent in their fiscal affairs, and cannot depend on other governments to bail them out. To avoid default on their debt municipal and cantonal governments enacted "debt brakes," fiscal rules limiting the ability of elected officials to spend and incur debt. A "debt brake" was then enacted at the federal level through a referendum with overwhelming support from Swiss citizens. Blankert maintains that the fiscal discipline imposed by these "debt brakes" has resulted in growing dynamic credence capital; over time Swiss citizens have gained greater confidence in the ability of their elected officials to pursue prudent fiscal policies within the framework of these fiscal rules.

Debrun and Jonung (2019), and Merrifield and Poulson (2016b, 2017a, 2018, 2020b) explore whether the fiscal rules enacted in Switzerland and other European nations are relevant for the United States. Throughout most of U.S. history, governments operated with a "no-bailout" rule. State as well as municipal governments went bankrupt in the nineteenth and early twentieth centuries. The last state to declare bankruptcy was Arkansas during the Great Depression. In response to the fiscal stress experienced during the Great Depression Congress enact new federal laws providing for municipal bankruptcy. But no provisions were made for state bankruptcy; the federal government abandoned the unwritten "no-bailout" rule for state governments. In periods of recession, the federal government now responds to fiscal stress providing state governments with funds to offset revenue shortfalls, and states then use this bailout money to rescue municipal and other local governments.

With the collapse of financial markets in 2008 the federal government introduced a new method for bailing out state and local governments. The federal government subsidized debt issued by state governments as Build America Bonds (BABs). States issuing these bonds received a direct federal subsidy of 35% of the interest cost, and more importantly what in effect were federal guarantees of these bonds. With this federal bailout money, state and local governments continued to expand their borrowing during that recession (Merrifield and Poulson 2018).

The federal government responded to the coronavirus pandemic in 2020 with a more ambitious bailout of state and local governments (Wall Street Journal 2020d, A3). The initial coronavirus rescue package included billions in direct aid to state and local governments. The most recent rescue package includes massive aid for state and local government; a House measure proposes $3 trillion in aid, with $1 trillion earmarked for state and local governments.

For the first time, the Federal Reserve has been authorized to purchase state and local debt, with backing from the U.S. Treasury. Congress allocated $454 billion for the Treasury to offset losses in Fed lending programs, with $35 billion earmarked to backstop municipal debt. With these measures the federal government has eliminated the no-bailout rule for local as well as state government.

The federal government bailout of state and local governments has resulted in significant distortion and misallocation of capital markets. Over the past decade there has been little change in the bond ratings of the states. With the exception of Illinois, all states receive investment-grade ratings for their bonds. Despite wide variations in total debt, and especially in unfunded liabilities in pension and OPEB plans, the states are able to issue debt at low interest rates, reflecting the investment-grade rating. In recent years, with the Fed pushing the federal funds rate toward 0, state and local governments are able to issue debt at all-time low interest rates (Merrifield and Poulson 2020b).

The federal bailout of state and local governments creates all the wrong incentives. Elected officials have little incentive to enact effective fiscal rules or pursue prudent fiscal policies. Special interests have more incentive to engage in rent-seeking to capture the benefits of these bailouts. Lenders do not have the incentive to practice due diligence in assessing the creditworthiness of these governments, anticipating that in periods of fiscal stress they will be bailed out by the federal government. Bond rating agencies have no incentive to distinguish between debt issues of different state governments because it is all guaranteed by the federal government.

The United States is experiencing deterioration in dynamic credence capital (Merrifield and Poulson 2018, 2020c). In each recession the federal government incurs more debt to bail out the states, and each state issues more debt to bail out local governments. The absence of a "no-bailout" rule means that there is little incentive for elected officials to practice fiscal discipline. With the erosion of fiscal rules imposing fiscal discipline citizens have lost confidence in the ability of elected officials to pursue prudent fiscal policies.

The coronavirus pandemic has exacerbated a deep division between citizens in the states (Merrifield and Poulson 2020b, c). Support for federal bailouts comes primarily from citizens in high debtor states that have a high percentage of urban populations, and that stand to capture most of the rent from federal bailouts. Citizens in low debtor states have a low percentage of the population in urban areas, and therefore do not capture as much rent from the federal bailouts.

Citizens in states such as Utah that balance their budgets and limit debt are challenging the federal bailout of high debtor states. Citizens in Salt Lake City are asking the obvious questions about this bailout money. Why should their federal tax dollars be used to bail out elected officials in Illinois who have failed to balance their budget and where debt is growing at an unsustainable rate? Public employees in Utah, where reforms have significantly reduced unfunded liabilities in pension and OPEB plans, are asking why their federal tax dollars are used to prop up pension and OPEB plans in Illinois with unfunded liabilities that cannot be paid off within a 30-year amortization period. When the federal government addressed similar problems in Puerto Rico it enacted legislation mandating that Puerto Rico declare bankruptcy in order to restructure its debt. If bankruptcy is the solution for Puerto Rico, why is it not the solution for unsustainable debt in Illinois and other high debtor states?

The United States at a Crossroad

In 2020 the United States virtually abandoned rules-based monetary and fiscal policy. The discretionary monetary and fiscal policies pursued in response to the coronavirus pandemic are unprecedented. The question is how to restore rules-based monetary and fiscal policy when the economy has recovered from the pandemic.

There are now two competing approaches in addressing the debt crisis in the United States. Debrun and Jonung argue that the United States should return to the FTRs that proved to be effective during the "Great Moderation" of the 1980s and 1990s. These are referred to as indicative fiscal rules because they simply set benchmarks or objectives against which to measure the effectiveness of fiscal policies. This approach does not rely on formal fiscal rules or objectives that require sanctions and enforceability when the objectives are not met.

Debrun and Jonung maintain that this indicative fiscal rule approach is a more viable alternative than the formal fiscal rules enacted in many countries in recent decades. The fact that most countries have evaded or abandoned formal fiscal rules suggests that lack of enforceability is undermining the credibility and public support for rules-based fiscal policy. They conclude that indicative fiscal rules, such as FTRs, combined with institutional reforms to provide greater transparency and accountability may be the only viable way to restore rules-based fiscal policy in the long run. Further they argue that institutional innovations such as Fiscal Responsibility Councils may be required to boost reputational effects as well as provide for greater transparency and accountability.

There are several reasons why this indicative fiscal rules approach may fail in addressing the debt crisis in the United States. The FTRs that were effective in the 1980s and 1990s may prove to be ineffective in the twenty-first century. During the Great Moderation the United States experienced high rates of economic growth, with modest recessions.

Debt fatigue has put the United States on an unsustainable debt trajectory. Over the past two decades major economic shocks have left the country with a greater debt burden, and with a greatly expanded role for the federal government in the economy. The economic impact of the coronavirus pandemic has been comparable to a wartime economy; in responding to this recession the federal government has incurred unprecedented amounts of debt, and has all but abandoned rules-based fiscal and monetary policy.

The long-term forecast by the CBO is for a continuation of these trends over the next three decades. The federal government will account for a greatly expanded share of GDP, and much of this expanded role for the federal government will be financed by debt. The literature on debt tolerance suggests that debt in the United States has increased to levels that negatively impact economic growth. For example, a study by the Bank for International Settlements (BIS 2011) finds that "At moderate levels, debt improves welfare and economic growth. But high levels are damaging."

The BIS study found that when government debt exceeds 85% of GDP economic growth slows. The report also found that beyond this threshold a country is less able to respond to economic shocks.

The CBO (2020f) forecasts that higher debt levels in coming decades will be accompanied by retardation and stagnation in economic growth. Potential output is now growing at a significantly lower rate than it did during the "Great Moderation." This means that even when the gap between actual output and potential output is reduced, the economy will grow more slowly than it did two decades ago. The climacteric in economic growth is making it more difficult to bend the debt/GDP curve downward.

From an historical perspective, the CBO long-term forecast appears to be very optimistic. The CBO assumes that over the next three decades the United States will not experience a major recession. The CBO does assume that actual output will fall somewhat short of potential output over the forecast period, but that is not the same as assuming a major recession. In recent decades, after each major recession the United States has recovered more slowly, with long periods when actual output was significantly below potential output. Each major recession has left the federal government with higher debt levels and with less fiscal space to pursue countercyclical fiscal policy.

We conclude that the pursuit of indicative fiscal rules will fail in the United States for the same reason that they have failed in Japan. For three decades Japan has set benchmarks for inflation that it has failed to achieve. Inflation rates have remained stubbornly well below the 2% target rate over most of this period. Japan has also experienced retardation in the rate of growth in output and employment. Japan has failed to achieve benchmarks despite aggressive monetary and fiscal policies. The Bank of Japan has kept interest rates at or below 0%. The Japanese government has pursued a series of fiscal stimulus packages over these years, with the Bank of Japan monetizing the debt. The outcome is the highest debt/GDP ratio among advanced economies.

The combination of debt fatigue and retardation in economic growth in Japan is the most likely path for the United States under current law. The question for the United States is whether there is an alternative path to the one projected in CBO long-term forecasts, and if so how can citizens choose this alternative path. The experience in Switzerland and other European countries reveals that there is an alternative path, and that citizens in a democratic society are capable of choosing that path. In the remainder of the chapter we explore both questions. The following section explores the potential impact of Swiss-style fiscal rules on the budget and the economy over the next three decades. The dynamic simulation analysis reveals that with these fiscal rules in place it is possible for the United States to stabilize and reduce debt to sustainable levels over the forecast period. With these fiscal rules in place downsizing the federal government, the United States can restore long-term economic growth.

The empirical analysis also reveals how difficult this challenge will be (see table 2.2), and why the United States is likely to continue to experience debt fatigue. The final section explores issues of political economy in enacting Swiss-style fiscal rules in the United States.

DESIGNING NEW FISCAL RULES

There has been a dramatic increase in the number of countries enacting new fiscal rules. In 1990, only a handful of countries had enacted the new fiscal rules; by 2015, 92 countries had the new rules in place (Budina et al. 2012; Lledo et al. 2017).

The IMF and Second-Generation Fiscal Rules

There is an extensive literature on the design of fiscal rules, and no other organization has been more influential in analyzing fiscal rules than the IMF (Ayuso Casals 2012; Buduna et al. 2012; Cordes et al. 2015; Fall and Fourier 2015; Fall et al. 2015; Casselli et al. 2018; Debrun et al. 2008; Eyraud et al. 2018; Alesina and Drazen 1991; Persson and Tabelini 2000; Von Hagen 1991; Von Hagen and Harden 1995; Kopits and Syzmanski 1998; Kopits 2001; Kumar et al. 2009; International Monetary Fund (IMF) 2009, 2015, 2018a).

During the 2008 financial crisis many countries circumvented or abandoned their fiscal rules. However, following the financial crisis some of these countries enacted refinements in their rules to make them more effective in constraining fiscal policy. The IMF refers to these as *second-generation fiscal rules*. The IMF maintains that there is now a consensus based on this experience that is the basis for optimal design of fiscal rules. In addition to its extensive research, the IMF has codified this optimal design in two publications "How to Select Fiscal Rules" and "How to Calibrate Fiscal Rules: A Primer" (International Monetary Fund, 2018a, b).

IMF studies use econometric models to measure the impact of fiscal rules on budgets and aggregate economic activity. The econometric models are used to simulate the impact of economic shocks. The simulation analysis incorporates fiscal multipliers designed to capture the impact of fiscal policies in the short run. The assumption is that fiscal rules impose a tighter fiscal stance that has a negative impact on output in the short run.

There are two basic problems with the IMF methodology for analyzing the impact of fiscal rules. The assumption of Keynesian fiscal multipliers is challenged in recent studies (Taylor 2009, 2010, 2014; Cogan et al. 2013a, b). With Keynesian multipliers the IMF studies simulate a negative impact on output when fiscal rules impose a tighter fiscal stance. If the Keynesian assumptions are faulty then this assumption should not be the basis for fiscal rule design. This controversy has focused on the impact of fiscal rules and fiscal policy over the business cycle, but we must also question this assumption in designing fiscal rules for long-term fiscal sustainability.

The second problem with IMF methodology is static scoring in measuring the impact of fiscal rules and fiscal policy. As the IMF notes, their approach may miss valuable information on how the economy would behave over a forecast period. In particular, using IMF methodology "there is no feedback from fiscal policy changes to macroeconomic variables, in particular GDP." The IMF notes that their analysis assumes that growth is constant over the long run, but "in reality growth and the interest-growth differential vary with the level of debt" (IMF 2018, 2010, 2013c, 2018c, e; Schick 2010; Schaechter et al. 2012; Wyploz 2005, 2012, 2013).

The IMF surveys alternative methodologies in measuring the impact of fiscal rules and fiscal policies on aggregate economic activity (IMF 2018a, b). An alternative to Keynesian modeling are political economy models first introduced in the work of Alesina and Tabellini (1990a). That study was the first to find evidence that fiscal consolidation policies could have a positive impact on economic growth in the long term. Several features of these political economy models capture the supply-side effects of fiscal policies. The models capture the feedback from fiscal policy changes on macroeconomic variables, most importantly GDP. Fiscal consolidation policies that constrain the growth of government spending are accompanied by higher rates of economic growth, which over a long period of time result in significantly higher levels of GDP. In contrast to the Keynesian models, the political economy models utilize dynamic scoring rather than static scoring to capture these feedback effects.

A Political Economy Model for the United States

In this chapter, a political economy model is designed to measure the impact of fiscal rules and fiscal policy on budgets and aggregate economic activity in the United States. The study uses scenario analysis first introduced by Debrun et al. (2008) to simulate the impact of fiscal rules in Israel, and then expanded in other IMF studies (IMF 2009). Scenario analysis is forward looking in simulating the impact of fiscal rules over a forecasting horizon. The simulated outcome with fiscal rules is compared to a baseline, which in the IMF studies is the World Economic Outlook. In this chapter the baseline used for comparative purposes is the CBO Long-Term Budget Outlook. Debt dynamics are compared with and without new fiscal rules and fiscal policies in place.

In contrast to IMF studies this analysis uses dynamic rather than static scoring to capture feedback effects on macroeconomic variables. The dynamic simulation analysis assumes an opportunity cost when resources are shifted from the private to the public sector. Fiscal consolidation policies that constrain the growth of government spending are accompanied by higher rates of economic growth. The dynamic simulation model also captures the supply-side effects of changes in taxes in the long term. The feedback effects of changes in fiscal rules and fiscal policies that result in fiscal consolidation are captured in this dynamic simulation analysis. A combination of fiscal rules and fiscal policies that downsizes the federal government and boosts economic growth is most likely to achieve sustainable debt in the long term. As Alesina and Tabellini (1990a) argue, fiscal consolidation may or may not negatively impact output in the short run, but the primary objective of fiscal consolidation policies is achieving sustainable debt levels in the long term.

A fundamental tradeoff is that between commitment and flexibility in rule design. Rules may commit elected officials to follow a constrained fiscal policy in order to achieve a specific target, such as a spending limit or revenue limit designed to achieve a desired debt or deficit target. But the more stringent the rule, the less flexibility elected officials have in responding to economic shocks from recessions or emergencies (Azzimonti et al. 2016; Halac and Yared 2014, 2016, 2017, 2018a, b; Amador et al. 2006; Yared 2018).

The theoretical and empirical literature on second-generation fiscal rules supports a hybrid approach to rule design. In a hybrid approach, a threshold is set for target levels of debt/GDP and deficit/GDP that trigger fiscal policy responses. The optimal target thresholds must be tight enough to achieve a sustainable fiscal policy, but not so tight that policymakers cannot respond to economic shocks. This hybrid approach can resolve the tradeoff between commitment and flexibility in fiscal rule design.

The Merrifield/Poulson (MP) Fiscal Rules

We propose second-generation fiscal rules for the United States. A detailed description of the proposed MP rules is provided in appendix A; the following summarizes the main features of the rules.

Flexibility is introduced in our proposed (MP) rules in a number of ways. For example, if the policy instrument is an expenditure limit, elected officials have discretion in determining how stringently to apply the limit. In the long term, a spending limit is gradually increased to meet the increased demand for government services, such as pension and health benefits for an aging population. Elected officials can set a spending limit multiplier set at unity in the medium term, and then adjust the multiplier upward in the long term.

Flexibility is also introduced in the form of debt and deficit brakes. Debt and deficit brakes are designed to give elected officials flexibility in constraining fiscal policy in the medium term. When debt and deficits reach threshold levels this triggers debt and deficit brakes that impose a more stringent spending limit. The debt and deficit brakes provide flexibility to elected officials in the form of multipliers. A multiplier set at unity would apply a debt brake or deficit brake gradually at threshold levels. A multiplier greater than unity would apply the debt brake and deficit brakes more stringently above the threshold levels.

Our proposed deficit/debt brake is complemented by other fiscal rules. An emergency fund provides for emergencies such as natural disasters and military conflict. The MP rules allow for deficits in the emergency fund in periods of financial crisis and recession (International Monetary Fund 2017, 2018a). The MP rules address countercyclical government services demand growth with a higher spending cap equal to half the amount of revenue declines. However, like the Swiss debt brake, these deficits in the emergency fund must be offset by surpluses in the primary budget in the near term. As in the Swiss case, deficits in the emergency fund must be balanced by surpluses within a fixed time frame. The emergency fund is similar to the notional account used in Switzerland to achieve budget balance in the near term. The rules constraining the emergency fund could be suspended in the case of a war (Blanchard et al. 2010; Delong and Summers 2012; Halac and Yared 2016; Coate and Milton 2017; Lledo et al. 2017).

Some countries have enacted fiscal rules with a "golden rule" that exempts government capital expenditures from the spending limits (Bassetto and Sargent 2006). We propose a version of the golden rule that would retain the integrity of the fiscal rule. Investment spending spurs economic growth, so some countries exempt it from spending caps, and also allow debt financing. But even with a clear formal definition of *investment*, an exemption creates a loophole we want to avoid. So, the MP rule creates regular saving to fund investment beyond what the ex ante fiscal limits allow.

The capital investment fund proposed in the MP rules is patterned after the Swiss model (Geier 2011; Andersen 2013; Bodmer 2006; Beljean and Geier 2013). The capital investment fund is designed to fund infrastructure investments. In periods when economic growth is above the long-term average rate of economic growth a portion of revenue is set aside in the capital investment fund. In periods of slower economic growth money is transferred from the capital fund to help finance infrastructure investments. This method of allocating the capital funds based on the rate of economic growth assures a steady growth in infrastructure investment in the long run.

Our deficit/debt brake is designed for the unique institutions in the U.S. economy. The proposed fiscal rules are simulated for the United States over the forecast period 2019–2042, based on parameters unique to the U.S. economy over this time period.

It is important to contrast the proposed MP fiscal rules, with other fiscal rules proposed for the United States. We propose a combination of interrelated fiscal rules designed to achieve multiple targets, including a deficit/GDP ratio and a debt/GDP ratio. The long-term goal is a sustainable debt/GDP ratio. Once a sustainable debt level is reached the proposed rules approximate a cyclically balanced budget, with surpluses in periods of economic expansion offsetting deficits in periods of economic contraction.

The flaw in the current U.S. fiscal policy is the failure to set long-term goals and to incorporate those goals in the budget process. Some have argued that it is unrealistic to set long-term goals and impose fiscal rules to achieve those goals. They argue that Congress already struggles with short-term budgets, and that Congress is not able to hold on to long-term goals. But this is an argument for continuing a budget process relying on discretionary fiscal policies that created the debt crisis. Continuing to muddle along with current discretionary fiscal policies is no longer a viable option in the long run.

Critics will argue that such a complex set of rules will be difficult to enact and to implement. We simulate the proposed fiscal rules to show how they can be implemented to achieve the multiple targets. We maintain that a combination of fiscal rules is a prerequisite for fiscal stabilization in the United States over the long term.

A Dynamic Simulation of the Model

We use a dynamic simulation analysis[6] to measure the impact of the proposed rules on the budget and on the U.S. economy over the forecast period 2019–2042. The simulation results provide insight into the role that fiscal rules can play in achieving debt sustainability. A similar methodology is used in Geier

(2012), and in the Organization for Economic Cooperation and Development (OECD) (2013).

We use the national income accounting methodology adopted by the OECD. Our GDP, personal income, population, inflation, and fiscal data are from standard sources, including the Congressional Budget Office, Office of Management and Budget, Department of Commerce, and Department of Labor. The National Bureau of Economic Research produced our income elasticity of federal revenue data. Lacking an official source for "emergency spending" and inability to cobble together reliably complete annual emergency spending estimates from separate sources, we estimated emergency spending data, as the TARP revenue-adjusted difference between the planned deficit, or surplus, and the typically much larger change in the national debt.[7]

The design of fiscal rules must take into account the unique fiscal institutions of each country, and that is especially true for the U.S. budget process rules in the U.S. Congress are unlike that in any other country. The rules assume that changes in tax rates are binding over a ten-year forecast period. At the end of the ten-year period the tax rates are assumed to revert to the tax rates prior to this policy change.

Congress can propose that the new tax rates become permanent, but the assumption is that the tax rules are non-binding on a future Congress. Some provisions of the 2017 tax law (Tax Cuts and Jobs Act) are temporary while others are permanent. For a discussion of how this legislation impacts the budget see Congressional Budget Office (2017). The dynamic simulations in this chapter are based on the Congressional Budget Office forecast, and incorporate these assumptions.

The following discussion summarizes the results of the simulation analysis. The analysis includes two forecast scenarios. The first scenario is the long-term forecast by the CBO. This CBO long-term forecast is used as a baseline for comparison with the alternative scenario with the MP fiscal rules in place. That simulation assumes the CBO baseline scenario combined with the fiscal rules, and measures the impact of fiscal rules on the economy over the forecast period. The coronavirus pandemic recession has an impact on economic growth over the entire forecast period. The second scenario captures the impact of this economic shock in the long term with the fiscal rules in place.

Debt

The following graphs compare the debt forecast by the CBO (see figure 2.2), with debt simulations with the fiscal rules in place. The CBO forecasts an increase in debt from $20 trillion to $71 trillion over the next two decades. As a share of GDP the CBO forecasts an increase from 98% to 151% (see figure 2.3).

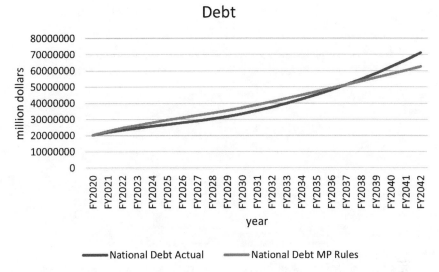

Figure 2.2 Debt. Calculated by authors using the simulation model described in Appendix A.

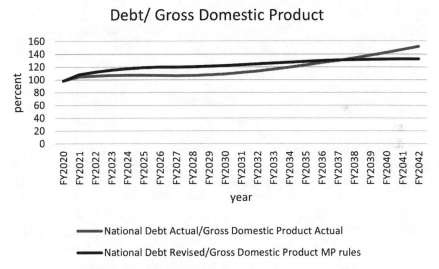

Figure 2.3 Debt/Gross Domestic Product. Calculated by authors using the simulation model described in Appendix A.

The fiscal rules significantly reduce the growth in debt compared to the CBO forecast. With the fiscal rules in place, debt increases to $57 trillion by the end of the forecast period. As a share of GDP debt increases to 132% by the end of the period.

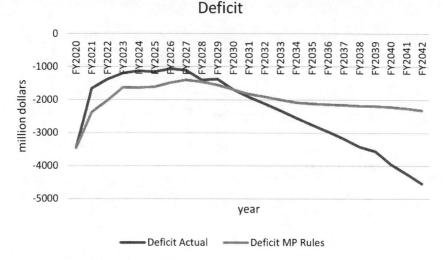

Figure 2.4 Deficit. Calculated by authors using the simulation model described in Appendix A.

It is important to note that the impact of the coronavirus pandemic recession makes it impossible to close the fiscal gap by the end of the period, even with the fiscal rules in place. While the trajectory of the debt/GDP ratio is downward by the end of the period, with debt at these levels the United States is exposed to a high risk of default over the entire period.

Deficits

In the CBO forecast deficits decrease over the next decade (see figure 2.4), and the increase significantly in the following decades. Deficits are estimated at 1.7 trillion dollars in 2021, and are projected to decrease to 1.1 trillion dollars in 2026. Deficits then increase to 4.5 trillion dollars by the end of the period. The CBO estimates deficits as a share of gross domestic product about 8% in 2021, and 10% at the end of the period.

With the fiscal rules in place, deficits are reduced, but not eliminated. By the end of the period deficits are reduced to roughly $2.3 trillion, or 5% of GDP. The fiscal rules put the country on a trajectory to reduce deficits as a share of gross domestic product.

Government Spending

The CBO forecasts that discretionary spending will grow from 3 trillion dollars in 2021 to 5 trillion dollars at the end of the period. As a share of gross domestic product, discretionary spending is projected to fall from 14% to 11% over that period.

The fiscal rules in effect freeze discretionary spending at 3 trillion dollars over the period. As a share of gross domestic product, discretionary spending falls from 14% to 6%.

Total Spending

The CBO projects that total government spending will more than double, from 5 trillion dollars in 2021 to $13 trillion dollars at the end of the period. As a share of GDP total spending will grow from 24% to 28%.

With the fiscal rules in place simulated total government spending grows from 6 trillion dollars in 2021 to 11 trillion dollars at the end of the period. As a share of GDP total spending falls from 27% to 23%.

The simulations reveal how difficult it will be to reduce government spending in coming decades, even with fiscal rules in place. Some have argued that government spending should be reduced relative to the private sector, by setting a cap of 20% or less on total government spending as a share of GDP. Simulated total government spending as a share of GDP exceeds that cap throughout out the forecast period. The impact of the coronavirus pandemic recession has been to push that target for government spending even further out of reach.

Economic Growth

The CBO forecasts that economic growth will be significantly lower over the forecast period, compared to growth over the past half century. In its most recent long-term forecast the CBO projects that real potential GDP will increase at an average annual rate of 1.6%. The average annual rate of economic growth in the second half of the twentieth century was 2.8%. The growth of GDP with the fiscal rules in place tracks closely the growth in GDP projected by the CBO.

The economic shocks that the United States has experienced in recent decades have clearly contributed to the climacteric or retardation in economic growth. As the CBO notes, actual GDP has been about half a percent below potential GDP and this is projected to continue in the long run. During and after each economic shock actual output has fallen short of potential output to a greater extent and for longer time periods than actual output has exceeded potential output during economic booms. Retardation in economic growth is especially evident in the aftermath of the coronavirus pandemic recession.

The risk of another economic shock is not incorporated in the CBO long-term forecast. If the economy experiences another economic shock comparable to the financial crisis in 2008, or the coronavirus pandemic in 2020, we should anticipate further retardation in economic growth in coming decades. The rising debt burden will make it even more difficult for the government to respond to these economic shocks.

The MP rules provide that a portion of federal revenues be earmarked for an emergency fund. With this emergency fund the government would have resources to address an economic shock, such as the financial crisis in 2008, and the coronavirus pandemic in 2020. In other words these fiscal rules would provide the federal government with more fiscal space to respond to economic shocks. Whether or not the government would have the fiscal space to avoid defaulting on the debt is an open question.

Scenario Analysis

Rules-based fiscal and monetary policy is designed to close the fiscal gap and reduce debt to sustainable levels. In this scenario analysis (see table 2.2), the simulation model is used to identify policy options required to close the fiscal gap in the United States. The following matrix reveals the impact of alternative policy options on the ratio of debt to gross domestic product in 2042. All of the scenarios assume that the MP fiscal rules are in place over the entire period. Closing the fiscal gap in the United States requires a debt/GDP ratio less than 100% by the end of the period. The scenarios with policy options that achieve this goal are identified in bold in table 2.2.

Economic Growth

The simulation analysis with the MP rules in place assumes the average annual rate of growth incorporated in the CBO long-term forecast, 1.6%. Ceteris paribus, higher rates of economic growth will of course reduce the ratio of debt to gross domestic product. In this scenario analysis we assume higher rates of economic growth as shown in the first column of the matrix. Closing the fiscal gap with policies to promote economic growth would

Table 2.2   2042 Debt/Gross Domestic Product (Scenario Analysis)

Pct Point Extra			Annual	Savings		
Economic Growth	$0	$200	$400	$600	$800	$1,000
0.0	132.4%	122.3%	114.3%	106.3%	**98.1%**	**89.3%**
0.5	121.1%	113.7%	106.5%	**99.1%**	**91.5%**	**83.4%**
1.0	112.2%	105.4%	**98.8%**	**92.0%**	**85.0%**	**77.5%**
1.5	103.8%	**97.5%**	**91.4%**	**85.1%**	**78.7%**	**71.7%**
2.0	**95.7%**	**90.0%**	**84.4%**	**78.6%**	**72.6%**	**66.1%**
2.5	**88.1%**	**82.9%**	**77.7%**	**72.3%**	**66.8%**	**60.8%**

Source: Calculated by authors using the simulation model described in appendix B.

require additional growth of 2% or more, more than double the growth rate assumed in the CBO forecast.

It is not reasonable to expect the United States to close the fiscal gap solely through policies promoting higher rates of economic growth. This would require rates of economic growth more than double that projected in the CBO long-term forecast. It would require significantly higher rates of growth than the historic average annual rates of economic growth in the United States extending back to the nineteenth and twentieth centuries.

Downsizing the Federal Government

Closing the fiscal gap in the United States will require downsizing the federal government, and earmarking the saving to reduce the federal debt. There are two potential sources of saving of sufficient magnitude to reduce the debt and close the fiscal gap, entitlement reform, and federal asset sales. Row one of the matrix estimates the impact of different levels of savings on the ratio of debt to gross domestic product. Assuming no additional economic growth, closing the fiscal gap would require average annual savings of 800–1,000 billion dollars over the forecast period.

The matrix reveals the impact of alternative scenarios combining economic growth with downsizing the federal government required to close the fiscal gap. The scenarios that close the fiscal gap are identified in bold. For example, boosting economic growth by .5% annually, and increasing annual savings by 500 billion dollars over the forecast period, would close the fiscal gap.

The CBO also explores the magnitude of savings from entitlement reform and other reforms required to close the fiscal gap. The estimates from this scenario analysis are in general consistent with the CBO estimates. The CBO also emphasizes what a formidable challenge it would be to generate savings from these reforms required to close the fiscal gap.

In the current political climate it is highly unlikely that the federal government would enact the reforms required to close the fiscal gap. The last time that the federal government generated significant savings from entitlement reform was during the Reagan administration. Neither political party now supports reform of entitlement programs sufficient to generate annual savings of 500 billion dollars.

There is a precedent for generating savings of this magnitude through federal asset sales and leasing in the eighteenth and nineteenth centuries. Massive amounts of land and other resources were transferred from the federal government to the private domain. But the closing of the frontier in the late nineteenth century ended this era of privatization. There has been some privatization of federal assets under recent administrations, but these policies generated modest savings, and the savings were not earmarked to reduce debt.

The Japan Disease

The scenario analysis reveals how challenging it will be for the United States to close the fiscal gap. Enacting the MP rules combined with policies to promote higher rates of economic growth and downsizing of the federal government could close the fiscal gap, but these policy reforms do not appear to be feasible in the current political climate.

The most likely scenario is for the United States to continue to experience debt fatigue over the next few decades. This is the scenario forecast by the CBO under current law. The explanation for debt fatigue in the United States is that suggested by Xavier Debrun, "Lack of domestic support for fiscal discipline, which leads to destabilizing budget cycles when fiscal fatigue sets in" (Debrun et al. 2018, p. 16).

We refer to this scenario as the "Japan disease." Japan has experienced debt fatigue for three decades, accruing one of the highest debt/GDP ratios ever recorded. Each economic shock in this period has been accompanied by a sharp increase in the debt/GDP ratio. The Japanese government responded to these economic shocks with a series of fiscal stimulus packages. The Bank of Japan monetized this debt, and with fiscal dominance is now required to keep interest rates at or below 0%. Over most of this period Japan has failed to achieve the benchmarks set for fiscal and monetary policy. Inflation rates have remained stubbornly below the target rate. Japan has experienced retardation and stagnation in the rate of growth in output and employment, and is projected to continue to experience debt fatigue in coming decades.

CONCLUSION

There is clearly an alternative path for the United States to pursue that would restore sustainable levels of debt. Following the precedent set in European countries, the United States could enact effective fiscal rules to constrain the growth in government spending, and reduce deficits in the long term. However, the simulation analysis reveals that after two decades of debt fatigue in response to major economic shocks, this will be a formidable task indeed.

Imposing effective fiscal rules would require a major downsizing of the federal government compared to that forecast by the CBO. Discretionary spending would have to be frozen at current levels. Total federal spending would have to be reduced far below that forecast by the CBO. This would require fundamental reforms to constrain the cost of entitlement programs, which are the major source of increased federal spending.

This simulation of fiscal rules for the United States will surely disappoint those searching for a solution to the debt crisis in the near term. Even with these stringent fiscal rules, the United States cannot achieve sustainable debt levels within the next two decades. The goal of downsizing the federal government relative to the private economy, and closing the fiscal gap, could not be achieved until the second half of the twenty-first century. Given the debt fatigue that has occurred over the past two decades, the United States is not likely to pursue this difficult alternative path.

Deterioration in dynamic credence capital in the United States means that the most likely scenario is that forecast by the CBO. The federal government will continue to expand relative to the private sector, with much of the growth in government spending financed by borrowing. By mid-twenty-first century, federal debt in the United States will increase relative to GDP to levels comparable to that in Japan.

Over the next few decades the increase in federal debt burdens in the United States will expose the country to increased risk of debt default, especially if the country experiences another major economic shock. The United States will not likely default on federal debt in the near term, the most likely outcome is that the United States will continue along the current path, with more debt fatigue and continued retardation in economic growth.

However, in the long term there is another outcome suggested by the climacteric in economic growth experienced by the United States in the early twentieth century. The major economic shocks of that era culminated in the decade-long Great Depression, in which virtually every country devalued their currency, and many countries defaulted on their debt. Such a collapse of the international economy is increasingly possible as more countries experience debt fatigue and retardation in economic growth.

NOTES

1. Turner and Spinelli (2012) measure the interest rate growth differential as the difference between the interest rate on 10-year bonds and a smoothed OECD estimate of nominal potential growth. For non-Euro area countries, an increase in the government debt-to-GDP ratio (above the 75% threshold) raises interest rates by 2.5 basis points if financed domestically, and 3.5 to 5 basis points if financed externally. This helps explain why in countries such as Japan, with debt financed domestically, the impact of debt on interest rates is moderated.

2. For a survey of this literature see Merrifield and Poulson (2016a, 2017b).

3. On his personal website, Taylor provides the following equation for the rule he proposed.

$R = 2 + \pi + 0.5 (\pi - 2) + 0.5Y$

Where R is the federal funds rate, π is the inflation rate, and Y is the GDP gap.

4. As Sargent and Wallace argued, there might be inconsistency between monetary and fiscal policy, and this outcome is most likely to exist when the government pursues a discretionary fiscal policy, Sargent and Wallace (1975).

5. For a survey of this literature see Debrun and Jonung (2018).

6. The dynamic simulation model and the simulation analysis are discussed in detail at the website objectivepolicyassessment.org/vetfiscalrules, and in Merrifield and Poulson (2017a).

7. Simulation results and sensitivity analysis of the major parameters on the model are available at the website objectivepolicyassessment.org/vetfiscalrules.

REFERENCES

Bank for International Settlements, 2011, "The Real Effects of Debt", BIS Working Papers No. 352, September.

Blankart, C. 2000. "The Process of Government Centralization: a Constitutional View", *Constitutional Political Economy*, Vol. 11, No. 1, pp. 27–39.

Blankart, C. 2011. *An Economic Theory of Switzerland*, CESifo DICE Report 3/2011.

Blankart, C., 2015. *What the Eurozone Could Learn from Switzerland*, CESfio FORUM, Vol. 16, No. 2, pp. 39–42.

Congressional Budget Office, 2015, *Why CBO Projects that Actual Output Will be Below Potential Output on Average*, February.

Congressional Budget Office, 2017, *Cost Estimate for the Conference Agreement on H.R. 1, a Bill to Provide for Reconciliation Pursuant to Titles II and V of the Concurrent Resolution on the Budget for the Fiscal Year 2018*, December 15.

Congressional Budget Office, 2019b, *The Effect of Government Debt on Interest Rates*, Working Paper 2019–01, March.

Congressional Budget Office, 2020a, *The Budget and Economic Outlook 2020–2030*, January 28.

Congressional Budget Office, 2020b, *Interim Economic Projection for 2020 and 2021*, May 19.

Congressional Budget Office, 2020c, *Federal Debt a Primer*, March.

Congressional Budget Office, 2020d, *An Update to the Economic Outlook: 2020 to 2030*, July.

Congressional Budget Office, 2020e, *CBO's Economic Forecast: Understanding the Slowdown of Productivity Growth*, NABE Foundation 17th Annual Economic Measurement Seminar.

Congressional Budget Office, 2020f, *Long Term Budget Outlook*, September.

Debrun, X., and L. Jonung, 2019, "Under Threat-Rules Based Fiscal Policy and How to Preserve It," *European Journal of Political Economy*, 57, March, pp. 142–157.

Debrun, X., J. Ostry, T. Williams, and C. Wyless, 2018, "Public Debt Sustainability," in *Sovereign Debt: A Guide for Economists and Practitioners*, IMF Conference, edited by S. Abbas, A. Pienkowski, and K. Rogoff, International Monetary Fund, forthcoming, Oxford University Press.

Feld, L., and G. Kirchgassner, 2006, "On the Effectiveness of Debt Brakes: The Swiss Experience," Center for Research in Economics Management and the Arts, Working Paper No. 2006–21.

International Monetary Fund, 2013, "Staff Guidance Note for Public Debt Sustainability Analysis in Market-Access Countries," May.

Merrifield, J., and B. Poulson, 2016a, *Can the Debt Growth be Stopped? Rules Based Policy Options for Addressing the Federal Fiscal Crisis*, New York, NY: Lexington Books.

Merrifield, J., and B. Poulson, 2016b, "The Swedish and Swiss Fiscal Rule Outcomes Contain Key Lessons for the U.S.," *Independent Review*, Vol. 21, No. 2, pp. 251–275.

Merrifield, J., and B. Poulson, 2016c, "Stopping the National Debt Spiral: A Better Rules for Solving the Federal Fiscal Crisis," *Policy Brief*, The Heartland Institute.

Merrifield, J., and B. Poulson, 2017a, "New Constitutional Debt Brakes for Euroland Revisited," *Journal of Applied Business and Economics*, Vol. 19, No. 8, pp. 110–132.

Merrifield, J., and B. Poulson, 2017b, *Restoring America's Fiscal Constitution*, New York, NY: Lexington Books, 2017b.

Merrifield, J., and B. Poulson, 2018, "Fiscal Federalism and Dynamic Credence Capital in the U.S.," ERN *Institutional and Transition Economics Policy and Paper Series*, Vol. 10, No. 16. November 28.

Merrifield, J., and B. Poulson, 2020a, *Perspectives on the Federal Debt Crisis*, Cato Institute, forthcoming.

Merrifield, J., and B. Poulson, 2020b, "How to Solve America's Debt Crisis in the Wake of the Coronavirus Pandemic," Heartland Institute, *Policy Brief*, April.

Organization for Economic Cooperation and Development, 2013, "General Government Fiscal Balance," in *Government at a Glance 2013*, OECD Publishing, Paris.

Poulson, B., and M. Dowling, 1972, "The Climacteric in U.S. Economic Growth," *Oxford Economic Papers*, Vol. 25, No. 3, Nov.

Reinhart, C., and K. Rogoff, 2009, *This Time is Different: Eight Centuries of Financial Folly*, Princeton University Press.

Reinhart, C., K. Rogoff, and M. Savastano, 2003, "Debt Intolerance," *Brookings Papers on Economic Activity*, Vol. 1, No. Spring, pp. 1–74.

Turner, D., and F. Spinelli, 2012. "Interest Rate Growth Differentials and Government Debt Dynamics," *OECD Journal: Economic Studies*, Vol. 2012/1.

Wall Street Journal. 2020a. "Federal Reserve Says It's Launching New Corporate Bond-buying Program," Tuesday June 16, 8A.

Wall Street Journal, 2020b, "Fed Looks to Put Cap on Treasury Yields," Friday June 12, B11.

Wall Street Journal, 2020c, "Fed Vows Low Rate for Years", Thursday June 11, A1–A2.

Wall Street Journal, 2020d, "More Aid Pushed for Cities and States", June 15, A3.

Part II

RULES-BASED FISCAL POLICY IN EUROPE

Chapter 3

Preparing for the Next Crisis

Lessons from the Successful Swedish Fiscal Framework

Fredrik N. G. Andersson and Lars Jonung

INTRODUCTION[1]

Prior to the outbreak of the corona pandemic in the spring of 2020, the Swedish public debt-to-GDP ratio, defined according to the Maastricht definition, had declined to 35% of GDP from a peak close to 75% in 1995 (see figure 3.1). The debt level is expected to rise to about 45% by 2021 (National Institute for Economic Research, 2020). Despite this increase, the level of public debt remains remarkably low by present international standards. The debt ratio in the euro area and the United States is expected to exceed 100% by the end of 2020. Even fiscally prudent Germany is expected to carry a debt of 75% of GDP.

Ever since the international financial crisis of 2007/08, Sweden stands out as a country with a prudent and sustainable national debt policy. Debt rises during recessions and crises only to fall back during times of growth. A low debt level before a major crisis allows Sweden to increase its public debt and support the economy during a crisis without risking a fiscal crisis. The strength of the Swedish public finances raises three questions: First, what are the determinants behind this strong performance; second, is the framework sustainable for the future; and third, are there any lessons for other countries?

The purpose of this chapter is to provide answers to these questions. The report consists of five parts. First, we give a brief account of the development of public debt in Sweden from 1750 to 2020. We show that Sweden has a long history of low and sustainable debt until the break-up of the Bretton Woods system in the early 1970s. The debt levels then rose more or less every year until the mid-1990s, when, following the economic crisis of the

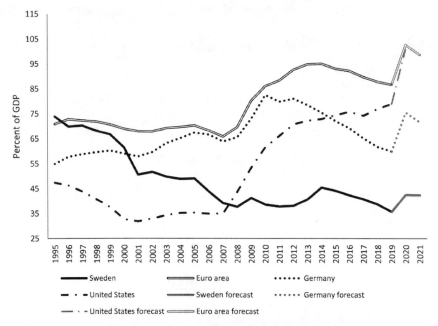

Figure 3.1   The Maastricht Debt-to-GDP Ratio for Sweden, the Euro Area, and Germany, and the Federal Debt Held by the Public in the United States. Actual data 1995–2019 and forecast data 2020–2021. Adapted from Thompson Reuters Datastream (actual data). The European Commission Spring forecast 2020, and Congressional Budget Office (forecast data).

early 1990s, the government was forced to consolidate its finances. A new fiscal framework was introduced which contributed to a quarter of a century of budget surpluses and a declining debt level.

In the second part, we describe the present Swedish framework and how it has evolved over time. Currently, it consists of four components: (i) an expenditure ceiling set in advance to keep expenditures under control, (ii) a surplus target to ensure that the budget, including those at sub-national level, is balanced over the business cycle and debt is reduced, (iii) a fiscal policy council to check whether the government follows the fiscal rules, and (iv) a debt anchor to ensure that the debt level does not grow too rapidly during major recessions when the framework allows the government to borrow.

We also discuss why the framework has been successful. In our view, there are four main reasons. First, leading politicians have had personal memory from the 1990s when public finances rapidly deteriorated, and from the subsequent period when fiscal discipline was restored through unpopular austerity measures. Second, the framework has evolved over time giving it a flexibility that has ensured that public support for the framework has remained high. Third, financial markets have responded eventually positively to the reduction in debt by reducing long-term government borrowing costs through lower interest rates. As interest rates fell, politicians were rewarded for fiscal discipline. The Swedish central bank did not bail out the government in the 1990s when debt was high and rising. Instead, interest rates were allowed to rise sharply. Fourth, the framework was designed domestically as an outcome of an internal political process, thus giving rise to public support behind the framework. It was not forced upon Sweden by outside forces. All major political parties concluded that sustainable public finances were essential for the well-being of the Swedish economy.

After this account of the past, we move, in the third part, to challenges to the framework. We identify two main weaknesses with it: the reliance on a surplus target and the strong role of the personal memory of leading politicians in maintaining the framework. We suggest potential reforms of the fiscal framework to address these shortcomings. Specifically, we argue that greater emphasis should be given to the debt anchor, that is, to debt stabilization. The surplus target is too easy to abandon, and it has no memory: bygones are bygones. A too low surplus one year is not compensated for by a higher surplus in the future. This creates an incentive to ignore the surplus target, especially when the debt level is low. There is a high risk of a return of a deficit bias in the public finances. The focus on a low and stable debt anchor removes this possibility. In addition, stressing the importance of achieving a low debt ratio prior to a crisis is one way to maintain the political support for a low debt as it allows fiscal policy to better support the economy in a crisis. Here we argue that the present debt anchor of 35% of GDP is set too high. It should be lowered to 25% to ensure that Sweden has sufficient fiscal space to meet a future crisis.

In the fourth part, we turn to the fiscal effects of the corona crisis. Here we stress the benefits of having sufficient fiscal space well in advance of a crisis like the present Covid-19 pandemic. In the fifth and final part, we discuss the relevance of the Swedish experience for the fiscal governance of other countries. We are well aware that prevailing Swedish views on debt and fiscal prudence are different from those of many other countries. Still, this should not prevent us from considering how other countries may draw lessons from the Swedish fiscal record.

SWEDISH PUBLIC DEBT FROM 1750 TO 2020

Swedish fiscal history shares many similarities with that of other European countries.[2] Before the industrialization process, and before the creation of the modern welfare state, the public debt level was relatively low and stable. It

increased during wartime and decreased during peacetime. Economic conditions had in general no effect on public debt. The Swedish debt-to-GDP
ratio during the period 1750–2017 is displayed in figure 3.2. The solid black
line represents central government debt (*Riksgäldsskulden*) and the dotted
black line shows the Maastricht debt. Data on the Maastricht debt is only
available from 1980 and onward. Most of the time, the two debt ratios are
similar, except for the latter part of the 2010s when local governments rapidly
increased their debt while the central government continued to reduce its debt
ratio.

In pre-industrial times, the Swedish government maintained a debt of
roughly 10% of GDP from 1750 until the war against Russia in 1788–1790
when the debt level increased to 30% of GDP. The debt ratio was then
reduced to almost zero in the 1820s, a level that was maintained until the start
of industrialization and public investments in railroads in the 1850s. During
a 25-year period, the debt level increased to 20% of a GDP when the government invested heavily in infrastructure. For roughly a century, from the 1880s
until 1970, the debt ratio fluctuated between 15% and 25% of GDP except
during World War II when it reached 50%. The war effect was brief. The debt
ratio was back to 20% already by 1950.

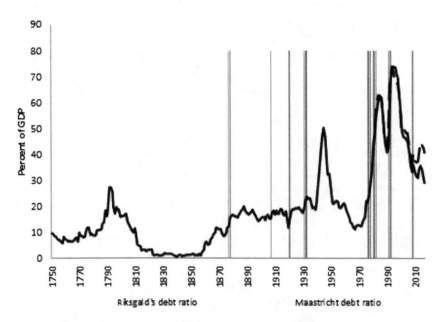

**Figure 3.2   Swedish Central Government Debt (Riksgäldsskulden) in Relation to GDP
1750–2017 (solid black line) and Swedish Maastricht Debt in Relation to GDP 1980–
2017 (dotted black line).** Adapted from Swedish National Debt Office, Statistics Sweden,
Fregert and Gustavsson (2013), and Thompson Reuters Financial Datastream.

The fact that debt never exceeded 50% of GDP from 1750 to 1970 is partly explained by the long period of peace enjoyed by Sweden. The last war Sweden fought was in 1814 against Norway. Sweden stayed out of active combat during both World War I and II. Although both world wars contributed to an increase in government borrowing, the rise was limited. During World War I, high inflation was key to hold down the debt-to-GDP level. Nominal debt increased by 155% between 1913 and 1918, but high inflation (47% in 1918) kept the increase in relation to GDP to almost zero.

The fiscal history after 1970 is a more volatile one following the demise of the Bretton Woods system and the fiscal discipline inferred by the implicit gold standard. From a low of 12.5% debt in 1970, it reached 62% in 1985 before briefly falling back to 40% by 1990, at the peak of the financial boom that followed the financial deregulation that started in 1985. The ensuing financial crisis increased debt to 74% of GDP by 1995 (figure 3.2). Three important factors contributed to the increase in debt: declining growth rates following the first oil price shock (OPEC I), the acceptance of a Keynesian view of the role of fiscal policy to ensure full employment, and expanding international financial markets.[3]

As in Western Europe, real GDP growth rates were high in Sweden following World War II, peaking in the mid-1960s before starting to decline gradually (Andersson, 2017). The post–World War II growth phase ended with OPEC I. Swedish stabilization policy was strongly influenced by the Keynesian views dominating the policy debate at the time (Jonung, 1999). Thus, the belief in the powers of discretionary fiscal policy in stabilizing the economy through economic fine-tuning was widespread among academics and politicians. The response to the decline in growth due to OPEC I was initially an expansionary fiscal program to prop up domestic demand and employment, which continued through OPEC II in 1979 and into the early 1980s. Consequently, government debt rose rapidly.

The acceptance of the Keynesian view was part of the expansion of the welfare state in Sweden in the post–World War II period. Public expenditures increased not just for health, education, and infrastructure but also for social spending and transfers. More and more of the life-cycle consumption smoothing of households over the life cycle was performed by the Swedish state through a generous social security system funded by high taxation. As wages stagnated and unemployment rose after OPEC I and OPEC II, government expenses increased to counter the decline in income. A reduction in the financial responsibilities of the state was deemed politically impossible.

Financial repression during the Bretton Woods period, including extensive controls on cross-border capital flows, restricted access to credit to largely domestic savings. Being less developed, international capital markets did not serve as a source of finance in the 1950s and 1960s. During the 1970s, following the first oil price shock (OPEC I), international capital markets began to expand, partially due to the recycling of the rapidly growing revenues of the oil-exporting countries.

Because of the negative shocks to the Swedish economy of OPEC I and OPEC II, large budget deficits emerged. The Swedish government chose to finance these deficits without draining the domestic credit market of funds by borrowing internationally. In 1974, 0.1% of the national debt consisted of external borrowing. By 1983, the share had increased to about 21% (Riksbank, 1984). The adoption of the Keynesian approach to stabilization policy making, demands through a large welfare state coupled with a reduction in economic growth, and a new source of funding outside Sweden clearly left its mark on public finances and public debt.[4]

A minor consolidation of the public finances took place in the mid-1980s. However, most of the decline in the debt ratio occurred due to an economic boom fueled by cheap credit following the deregulation of the domestic financial markets. The resulting boom, which turned to bust, and a large financial crisis in the early 1990s, partly masked the weak underlying standing of the public finances.[5] While public debt fell to 40% in 1990, it rapidly shot up to 74% in 1995 in the wake of the financial crisis.

When the Swedish economy started to recover after the financial crisis of 1991–1993, rapid fiscal consolidation took place between 1994 and 1999 when the budget was balanced. The government debt ratio continued to fall until the international financial crisis of 2008–2009. The debt ratio increased briefly during the crisis before it began to fall again. Central government debt fell, while local governments benefited from the low interest rates that followed the crisis to fund investments. By 2017, the central government debt (*Riksgäldsskulden*) was 29% of GDP compared to 74% in 1995 and 33% in 2008. The Maastricht debt was 41% compared to 74% in 1995 and 38% in 2008.

The fiscal consolidation in the late 1990s was part of a major overhaul of economic policy making in Sweden. The framework for monetary and fiscal policy making was changed in a most fundamental way. The fixed exchange rate of the krona was abolished in November 1992 in the midst of the financial crisis and replaced by a flexible exchange rate. Inflation targeting was adopted in early 1993 with a numerical target for consumer price inflation of 2% to be valid from 1995. The Riksbank was made independent in 1999. The role of fiscal policy in stabilizing the economy was reduced to that of the workings of automatic stabilizers while the main responsibility for macroeconomic fine-tuning was given to the Riksbank. Several domestic markets were liberalized and tax rates reduced, especially on capital income. Combined with a depreciation of the krona exchange rate of around 25% following the unpegging of the exchange rate, growth picked up, which contributed positively to the fiscal consolidation. The reduction in domestic demand due to the fiscal consolidation was more than fully compensated for by higher external demand for Swedish exports through the depreciation of the Swedish krona. The fiscal consolidation was also successful partly because it coincided with a break with the perceived failed policies of the past.[6] The fiscal policy framework that sets clear rules for sustainable finances was one of several components of the package of new economic policies and new institutional set-ups for policy making. Since the new consensus on economic policy was established, so far only few have argued for a return to the past system.

THE EVOLUTION OF THE PRESENT SWEDISH FISCAL FRAMEWORK

The current Swedish fiscal framework has evolved over time beginning in the mid-1990s, with the most recent adjustments agreed to by the political parties in 2016. Although the framework has changed over time, the goals have remained the same: to keep public spending under control and to ensure that the national debt ratio declines over time. Following the reforms in 2016, which came into effect in 2019, the fiscal framework consists of four major components: i) an expenditure ceiling, ii) a surplus target, iii) a fiscal policy council, and iv) a debt anchor. The surplus target is set at one-third of a percent of GDP over the business cycle for the general government (central and local government, and the public pension system). The debt anchor, the latest addition to the framework emerging from the 2016 reform, is set at 35% of GDP +/− 5 percentage points.

The Evolving Framework

When the budget deficit reached as high as 15% of GDP in 1993, the risks to the sustainability of the public finances were apparent. Because public finances had been on an unsustainable track for almost 20 years, a review of the budget process was initiated.[7] A report from the Ministry of Finance published already in 1992 was a first step, inspired by a study by Jürgen von Hagen (1992), arguing that the power of the executive was weak compared to that of the legislature in the Swedish system. The Riksdag (parliament) could easily add on expenditures beyond what was requested by the government. A string of more or less weak minority governments and a short three-year election period gave strong incentives for rising government spending without any restraining control on overall spending.[8]

To maintain control over government expenditures, the budget process was reorganized as a top-down procedure. First, the Riksdag votes on the overall spending volume for 27 expenditure areas before spending within each area is allocated. Spending beyond the amount allocated to each spending area is not possible. The Riksdag can no longer add on expenditures once the spending levels are decided upon as it could do in the past.

Second, to control the spending level for the medium term, the Riksdag votes on expenditure ceilings for total government spending less interest payments on government debt. These ceilings are set three years in advance. The Riksdag can change these ceilings. However, it has refrained from doing so with the exception for "technical adjustments," or for the election of a new government with a new economic agenda. Thus, a new government is not bound by the expenditure ceilings set by the previous government.

The expenditure ceiling has two main purposes. First, it forces the government and the Riksdag to prioritize among expenditures. An increase in one spending area is weighed against a reduction in another area. Second, it prevents the temptation to add permanent expenditures to the budget due to a temporary increase in revenues during, for example, an economic boom. The reformed budget process and the expenditure ceilings tightened the government's grip on spending. The expenditure ceiling has turned into a key policy instrument for the Ministry of Finance to control the spending of other departments.

The next step in the creation of the fiscal framework was the announcement in 1997 of a surplus target, which was subsequently phased in over four years. The target was set at 2% of GDP over the business cycle and covered general government balance, that is, central government, regional and local government, and the pension system. Part of the savings in the pensions system was later defined as private savings rather than government savings. As a consequence, the surplus target was reduced from 2% to 1% in 2007 as a technical adjustment with no overall impact on government policy.

The surplus target was introduced to reduce the government debt ratio, in preparation for the expected future strain on public finances coming from an older population. In 2016, the surplus target was reduced to one-third of a percent of GDP over the business cycle. The main reason for this step was that the debt ratio had fallen to a relatively low level and that the Swedish population was growing older.

A balanced budget requirement for local governments was enacted in 2000 to prevent local governments from undermining fiscal sustainability. Local governments are required to balance their budgets every year. They can borrow to invest as long as their yearly revenues are sufficient to cover their running expenditures and the cost of servicing and repaying their loans.

Another important part of the fiscal framework was put in place in 2007 by the establishment of a Fiscal Policy Council to monitor the government's adherence to the rules of the fiscal framework. The Council was the brainchild of Anders Borg, the minister of finance at that time in a center-right government. It was initially met with resistance from the opposition parties on the left. However, by now both sides of the political spectrum have come to accept the Council.[9]

The Swedish council is an agency under the Ministry of Finance. Its budget is proposed by the government and decided by parliament as a separate line in the annual national budget. The mandate of the Fiscal Policy Council is set out in a remit framed by the government. The present one from 2011 with minor modifications from the beginning of 2017 is short, about one page long, stating that the main task of the Council is, "to review and evaluate the extent to which the fiscal and economic policy objectives proposed by the Government and decided by the Riksdag are being achieved, and thus to contribute to more transparency and clarity about the aims and effectiveness of economic policy."

The main tool of the Council for communicating its views and analysis is the annual report published in the spring. Soon after its publication, the annual report is presented at an open hearing before the Committee on Finance of the *Riksdag* (*finansutskottet*) where the minister of finance takes part as well. The report is then taken into consideration in the Committee's evaluation of the economic policies of the government. The government responds in the Budget Bill to the report of the Council, usually in September the same year.

Although the Council has no formal powers, it is a force to be reckoned with in public debate and policy making. Sweden has a long history of open debate on economic issues and the economics profession has a relatively strong standing in public opinion. Critique from the Council has thus a likely impact on public opinion and thus it indirectly affects the government.

The fourth and latest building block of the fiscal framework is the debt anchor introduced in the 2016 review. Coming into effect in 2019, the debt anchor stipulates that the Maastricht debt ratio should be 35% of GDP +/− 5 percentage points. In principle, a debt anchor is unnecessary given the surplus target, as the debt ratio would fall as long as the government runs a surplus. However, the surplus target is set as an average over the business cycle. In addition, there is no memory in the target in the sense that the government does not have to compensate in the future for failure to meet the target in the past. It does not have to run larger surpluses in the future just because the surpluses were too small in the past. A severe recession can thus cause government debt to increase. Consequently, a government that fails to adhere to the surplus target can drive debt higher. In contrast, the debt anchor ensures that debt is kept low.

The fiscal framework contains clear rules for the level of expenditures, the budget balance, and government debt and supervision. However, the framework is also flexible. A new government can change the expenditure ceilings.

The government can ignore both the surplus target and the debt anchor if the Riksdag is willing to adopt the government's economic policy agenda. To further strengthen the framework, the revised budget law following the 2016 review stipulates that the government is forced to explain in public if its policies are in conflict with the surplus target and/or the debt anchor, and to present a plan for how the public finances are to be brought back in line with the rules of the framework. As long as public support for the fiscal framework remains high, these provisions are likely to induce governments to stick to the rules.

Lessons from the Fiscal Framework

No fiscal framework is perfect or "optimal" in its execution, not every budget since the late 1990s has been as fiscally responsible as it could have been. However, Swedish public finances have been on a sustainable path for a long time. The budget has on average been balanced with a small surplus of 0.5% of GDP since 2001. No budget deficit has been higher than 1.6% of GDP in this period. As a result, the debt ratio has fallen. Economic growth has contributed to this decline as well. Central government debt is presently the lowest since 1978.

On the negative side, we note a growing volume of local government debt. As the borrowing costs have approached zero, local government debt has increased.[10] Higher interest rate costs may put the sustainability of local finances into question. Nevertheless, the framework has successfully reduced the Swedish debt ratio to one of the lowest in Europe. Politicians have followed the rules for more than 20 years and the present framework was agreed to by seven out of the eight political parties represented in the parliament. The exception was the Sweden Democrats who objected to changing the rules and wished to maintain the old rules.

Why has the framework been such a success? There are several possible explanations, mutually enforcing each other. First, the framework has emerged through a domestic process. It was not imposed by demands or requirements from external authorities. Most likely, such reforms are more likely to succeed. They face less political resistance, are credible, and suit the country's circumstances better.[11] Politicians stick to the rules because they have designed the rules.

Second, the severity of the financial crisis in the early 1990s and the policy measures needed to stabilize the fiscal outlook have remained fresh in the memory of the public and of politicians in power. Few wish to revert to the fiscal deficits of the past. As the memory of the crisis of the 1990s fades, public support for the fiscal framework may also diminish. So far, leading members of the present government as well as of past governments have personal memories from the fiscal woes either during the crisis (1991–1994) or during the fiscal consolidation period (1995–1999). Table 3.1 shows the career position during the crisis and the consolidation period for all prime ministers and ministers of finance that have served since 2000 (i.e., after the adoption of the fiscal framework). In all governments, the prime minister, the minister of finance, or both, have private experience from the crisis and the consolidation process. Some were in government at the time as leading ministers, others served as members of parliament, while still others worked for the prime ministers serving at the time.

The government's reluctance to spend in times of low economic activity was criticized by the Fiscal Policy Council in 2009, 2010, and 2012. The Council advised the government to spend and borrow more than it did, thus proposing a more expansionary fiscal policy than the actual policy adopted by the government. In fact, the minister of finance criticized the Council for

Table 3.1 Career Positions of Prime Ministers and Ministers of Finance from 2000 to 2020 during the Financial Crisis of 1991–1994, and the Fiscal Consolidation Period 1995–1999 in Sweden

	Crisis Phase 1991–1994	*Consolidation of Public Finances 1995–1999*
Prime ministers		
Göran Persson (1996–2006)	Opposition, shadow finance minister (1993–1994).	Minister of finance, (1994–1996). Prime minister (1996–2006)
Fredrik Reinfeldt (2006–2014)	Member of parliament for ruling Moderate party.	Member of parliament for the opposition. Member of the Finance Committee.
Stefan Löfven (2014–)	Board member *Metall* (labor union).	Board member *Metall* (labor union). International secretary Metall.
Ministers of finance		
Bosse Ringholm (1999–2004)	Chairman Country Council Executive Committee (1994–1997)	Chairman National Labour Board (1997–1999) Minister of finance (1999–2004)
Per Nuder (2004–2006)	Member of parliament (1994)	State Secretary Prime Minister's office (1997–2002)
Anders Borg (2006–2014)	Political Advisor to Prime minister (1991–1994)	Private sector
Magdalena Andersson (2014–)	Part-time lecturer Stockholm School of Economics	Political advisor Prime minister's office (1996–1998). Director of Planning Prime minister's office (1998–2004)

Source: Compiled by the authors.

being too expansionary, warning that it might jeopardize fiscal sustainability in the long run.[12]

Third, the framework has so far proven flexible in the sense that there has been a broad consensus across the political spectrum concerning alterations of the rules. As the economic circumstances change, so has the fiscal framework. The surplus target has been modified and a debt anchor was introduced in 2016. A fiscal policy council to evaluate the government was established in 2007. The flexibility of the framework is likely an important reason behind its durability.

Fourth, the strong reputation of the Fiscal Policy Council forces the government in power to stick to the rules or risk public criticism from one of its own agencies. Media and the opposition parties can refer to the Council in its critique of the government, which enhances the credibility of the Council. In addition, the Fiscal Policy Council has enhanced the public's awareness of the framework, and the budget rules represent a starting point for public debate on fiscal issues. Few parties dare to promise unfunded expenditure increases or tax cuts due to the critique they may encounter in a political environment that puts a premium on fiscal prudence.

Fifth, politicians were rewarded by the financial markets for fiscal responsibility in the sense that long-term borrowing costs declined as the debt ratio was reduced. In 1995, the Swedish 10-year bond yield was 3.5 percentage points higher than the German yield despite similar rates of inflation. In 2007, the year before the international financial crisis, Swedish bond yields were 0.1 percentage point lower than German yields. This reduction in borrowing costs became a major incentive to continue to lower the debt ratio as it increased the fiscal space allowing either increased spending or reduced taxation. The Swedish central bank did not act to influence long-term bond rates when the public debt levels were high. Instead, bond yields became an important economic indicator of the state of the public finances, and politicians responded to these signals

To sum up, so far the fiscal framework has performed well during its first twenty years up to the corona crisis. It has been a source of fiscal prudence. It has received solid support from the political parties and from the public. Let us now turn to the post-corona future of the fiscal framework.

THE FUTURE OF THE SWEDISH FISCAL FRAMEWORK

The success of the fiscal framework raises the question: Why change it? Part of the success of the framework has been its adaptability. Future reforms of the framework are likely needed for it to continue to support sustainable public finances and to enjoy broad political support. In fact, the 2016 revisions of the fiscal framework included an automatic review to take place every eight years (every second parliament). The next review is thus due in 2025–2026.

Despite its success, the framework suffers from two main weaknesses that may reduce its efficiency in the future. The first weakness is the strong emphasis on the surplus target. The target has no memory. It is an ambition to be achieved over the business cycle. However, there is no mechanism to compensate for too small surpluses in the past: bygones are bygones. This creates an incentive for policymakers to miss the target deliberately. Why has the framework worked as well as it has over the last 25 years? One possible answer is the personal memory of the leading politicians of the fiscal crisis in the 1990s. This is the second main weakness of the framework: its success may be too heavily dependent on the personal memory of the leading politicians. As the memory of the 1990s fades from the collective memory, the risk of weaker public finances in the future grows.

To improve the framework, we suggest strengthening the role of the debt anchor. A debt anchor introduces a memory into the framework, as too small surpluses will cause a too high debt level. It also contributes to a political narrative of the importance of prudent fiscal policies during normal times to prepare for an inevitable future crisis. Thus, the question we should address concerns the proper size of a debt anchor for a country like Sweden.

Identifying a Proper Debt Anchor for Sweden

Finding a proper level for the debt anchor is far from trivial. The large empirical and theoretical literature on the optimal debt level and on optimal fiscal policy reaches no firm policy recommendations on the size of the public debt-to-GDP ratio.[13] One part of the literature studies the optimal size in relation to public investments and their growth-enhancing effects, arriving at no clear recommendation concerning the debt ratio. Another part of the literature focuses on finding a threshold level when the debt becomes a drag on economic growth (see for example Reinhart and Rogoff, 2010), without any firm conclusions. Research on optimal government debt suggests that there is not one optimal level fixed over time and across countries. Instead, the results appear to be time- and country-specific, as well as depending on the methodological approach adopted.

We adopt an insurance approach: in case of a major crisis, the fiscal authorities should have sufficient fiscal space, serving as a fiscal buffer, to meet the crisis at a low cost to society. We use a broad concept of "cost" here—including loss in output and employment as well as the social and political costs of crises. The Swedish fiscal consolidation processes during the 1990s, the experience of some EU member countries during the euro crisis, and the recent corona crisis illustrate the importance for society at large of having adequate fiscal space before any major crisis erupts in order to allow an expansionary fiscal response and thus to avoid unpopular consolidation measures when the economy is already depressed. In other words, having sufficient space facilitates a successful fiscal response to crises. Most likely, the size of the fiscal multipliers is larger when government debt is lower and trust in the government's ability to sustain its debt is high. Government actions to limit the real economic effects of the crisis thus become more effective and the output cost of the crisis is reduced.[14]

Having ample fiscal space implies that drastic and large austerity measures, and the political effects that come with such measures, can be avoided. This is important in any country, not least in a country like Sweden with a relatively large welfare state and public sector.[15] Swedish households rely on the government for a large share of their consumption smoothing over the life cycle and during unexpected spells of income losses (e.g., due to unemployment). Cutting back on public spending clearly hurts households financially. Households will struggle to compensate for the loss of public spending in the short to medium run. They will cut private consumption, thus making the downturn deeper during a recession or deep crisis.[16] This was the case during the financial crisis in the early 1990s when Sweden entered a debt deflation process.[17]

Sharp austerity measures are likely to have substantial political consequences as well. As Swedish voters expect the government to fulfill its welfare promises, a disappointing economic performance will fuel populism and make it more difficult to form responsible governments. Typically, erosion of trust in government, in elected politicians, and in the democratic process in general takes place during major economic crises.[18] Trust in the Riksdag and the government fell from a net of +40 in the late 1980s before the fiscal consolidation to −40 during the fiscal consolidation in the mid-1990s on a scale from plus 100 to −100, (Martinsson and Andersson, 2018). It took many years to restore trust in the government among the public.

To derive a proper level for the debt anchor, we adopt a two-step approach. First, we rely on recent economic history to decide when the cost of servicing government debt begins to increase significantly due to a rising debt level. Here, we want to identify the size of the debt limit or debt threshold where the negative effects of additional debt outweigh the positive effects. Second, we examine the fiscal cost of recent economic crises. Based on these results, we arrive at an estimate of the fiscal space required before a crisis such that the government can handle the debt after the crisis without drastic austerity measures.

When Does Swedish Public Debt Become Unsustainable?

One potential cost of high debt is that it may be a drag on economic growth. We find it difficult to establish exactly when public debt becomes too large in the

sense that it hampers economic growth. Figure 3.3 shows the contemporaneous relationship for Sweden between the public debt ratio and GDP growth in
the post-war era (1961–2019). There is no clear relationship between debt and
growth. Economic growth has been high and low irrespective of the debt level.
Average growth was slightly higher during the years when the debt ratio was
between 10 and 20%. However, these observations are from the 1960s when
growth was high in the entire developed world and thus likely not related to
the Swedish debt level. Lagging the debt ratio does not change the results. We
find no statistically significant correlation between the debt ratio and economic
growth for Sweden. Having a high debt is not directly associated with lower
economic growth, at least not at the debt levels observed historically in Sweden.

Another potential cost of high debt is the cost of servicing government
debt. This is possibly a large cost for a small open economy with its own
currency such as Sweden with limited domestic financial markets. A larger
domestic debt is likely to require external funding, where the government
needs to pay higher rates to attract investors, including taking an exchange
rate risk. The relationship between the debt ratio and the real rate of interest
is plotted in figure 3.4 for Sweden 1985–2019, starting with the liberalization
of financial markets in the mid-1980s.

Figure 3.4 displays a clear positive correlation between the debt ratio and
the real rate of interest, a relationship that we should expect. Rapidly increasing real rates during the mid-1990s was a key factor driving the government
to balance the budget from a deficit from 15% of GDP in 1993 within five

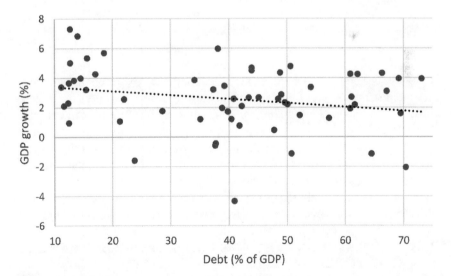

Figure 3.3 Economic Growth and the Public Debt Ratio in Sweden, 1961–2019.
Adapted from Thompson Reuters Datastream.

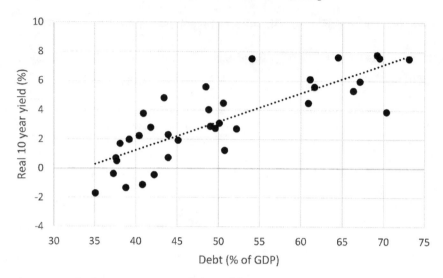

Figure 3.4   Real Interest Rates and the Public Debt Ratio in Sweden, 1985–2019.
Adapted from Thompson Reuters Datastream.

years. According to figure 3.4, an increase in the debt ratio from 40% to 70% increased the real interest rate from 1.5% to 7%.

Real interest rates have declined globally since the 1990s as part of the process of secular stagnation. The relationship in figure 3.4 is thus potentially a spurious one as a falling debt ratio and falling interest rates may coincide without being causally related. To control for globally falling interest rates, we plot the relationship between the Swedish debt ratio and the real interest rate difference between Sweden and the United States (figure 3.5) and Sweden and Germany between 1985 and 2019 (figure 3.6).

Figures 3.5 and 3.6 confirm the positive relationship between the debt ratio and interest rates. The result is especially strong when Swedish government bond rates are compared to German bond rates: an increase in the debt ratio from 40% to 70% implies 2 percentage points higher interest rates compared to German rates. In relation to the United States, the difference in interest rates between 40% and 70% debt ratio is approximately 3 percentage points.

The increases in interest rates have a relatively large effect on government finances. The rise in debt raises the cost of debt financing as well as bringing about a larger debt to service. The real interest rate in relation to Germany increases by 2 percentage points at a debt ratio of 70%. The additional cost due to the higher interest rate is 1.4% of GDP. Simply to balance the budget, the government would have to increase the primary budget surplus by 1.4% of GDP. The average Swedish primary budget balance between 2000 and 2019 was 1.1%. The increase in interest expenditure only stemming from

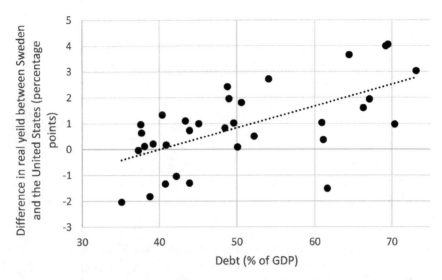

Figure 3.5 The Interest Rate Difference between Sweden and the United States, and the Swedish Public Debt Ratio, 1985–2019. Adapted from Thompson Reuters Datastream.

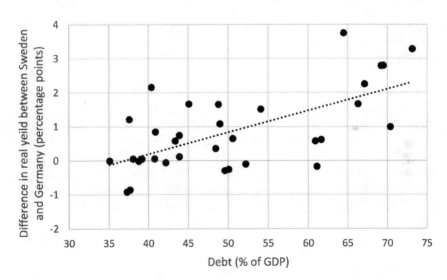

Figure 3.6 The Interest Rate Difference between Sweden and Germany, and the Swedish Public Debt Ratio, 1985–2019. Adapted from Thompson Reuters Datastream.

higher interest rates would require a twice as high primary balance to finance. The cost is not impossible to cover but sufficiently large to be avoided unless in case of a major economic crisis forcing the government to rely heavily on debt financing.

Extrapolating the results suggests that the interest rate difference compared to Germany would increase to 4 percentage points if the debt ratio surges to 90% of GDP. The additional debt service cost would be 3.6% of GDP.

We conclude from the above calculations that the central government debt to GDP should be kept at least below 40% in normal times and preferably never exceed 70–75%. We suggest, based on the historical evidence, that a 70% debt level is a reasonable debt limit or debt threshold for Sweden.[19]

Economic Crises and the Public Debt Ratio

Debt levels fluctuate with the business cycle and with economic crises. To establish an appropriate debt anchor, our second and final step is to estimate the fiscal cost of major economic crises. Sweden has experienced seven major economic crises since 1870, see the listing in Chapter 6 in Jonung et al. (2009): the crisis of 1877/78, the international financial crisis of 1907, the depression of the early 1920s, the Great Depression in the 1930s, OPEC I and II, and the financial crisis in the early 1990s. The international crisis of 2008/09, the Great Recession, should be added to this list although Sweden was only indirectly affected by the crisis and did not suffer from a domestic financial crisis as many EU member states. Still, the decline in the growth rate of GDP was sharp and sizeable.

These eight major crises were highlighted in figure 3.2, which plots the Swedish public debt-to-GDP ratio. The effect on the debt ratio of those crises occurring before World War II was modest. The welfare state had not yet been created; the public sector was limited in size. Consequently, the automatic stabilizers were small. In addition, a balanced budget was the aim of the government before the 1930s. The debt ratio shows only a modest correlation with the cyclical position of the economy. Between 1930 and 1935, during the Great Depression, the debt ratio increased by only 6.2 percentage points. Although Sweden was an early adopter of expansionary fiscal policy in the early 1930s, the actual size of the fiscal measures was limited.

Following World War II and the expansion of the welfare state and the adoption of a Keynesian approach to fiscal policy, the correlation between the business cycle and the volume of government debt is stronger, particularly during economic crises. The largest debt increase took place following OPEC I and OPEC II when the government opted for an expansionary fiscal response. The debt increased by 50 percentage points. The financial crisis 1991–1992 left its mark by an increase of 33 percentage points.

We are aware that these episodes of rising debt are time-specific. Today, the idea of a policy of "bridging over," like the policy pursued in the wake of OPEC I, would hardly find political support. Policymakers have learned from the policy mistakes of the past. The policy experiments in the 1970s and

1980s do not serve as convincing evidence for our estimates of the appropriate debt anchor today.

Instead, we are of the opinion that financial crises constitute the most severe threat facing the global economy presently. The rapid growth of the financial system following the financial deregulation of the 1980s and 1990s has increased financial imbalances. The Great Recession of 2008 has not arrested this build-up. Most of the recent crises are primarily caused by financial developments. In the case of Sweden, financial imbalances have grown significantly since the mid-1990s, raising the risk of future corrections (Andersson and Jonung, 2016).

As we deem a financial crisis the most likely future menace to the fiscal stance of Sweden, we consider the fiscal cost of financial crises internationally in the post-1990 period. Table 3.2 illustrates these costs post-1990 among EU15, Norway, Japan, and the United States according to Laeven and Valencia (2018). The first column of Table 3.2 shows the total increase of the debt level (in relation to GDP), the second column the fiscal cost of supporting the banking system, and the third column the income loss generated by the crises.

Each crisis is different as illustrated by the large variation in the estimates of the costs of crises. The least costly crisis was the Italian crisis in 2008–2009 with a fiscal cost of 8.6% of GDP. The most expensive one was the Irish 2008–2012 crisis with a fiscal cost of 76.5% of GDP. Approximately half of the cost is due to the refinancing of the banking system. The cost of the average crisis is 29.5% of GDP and of the median crisis 24.9% of GDP. The five most expensive crises have an average cost of 48.8%, the 10 costliest crises a cost of 38.7% of GDP on average; in general, the larger the cost for the support of commercial banks, the larger the total fiscal cost.

Recent changes in EU legislation have shifted the responsibility of refinancing failing banks from the taxpayers to the owners of banks. Whether this will be the case in the future remains to be seen. However, even if we exclude the refinancing costs, still we find that the fiscal cost of financial crises is high. The average refinancing costs is 9.5% of GDP and for the median crisis 6.2%. Hence, most of the increase in the debt ratio is due to lower economic growth resulting in lower tax revenues and increased costs for inter alia higher unemployment.

What conclusions should we draw from these numbers? We are of the opinion that it is reasonable that a country like Sweden should be able to meet an average crisis without running into debt problems. In other words, the government should be able to sustain an increase in the debt level of between 30 and 50% of GDP without facing rapidly increasing interest rates and/or having to seek support from the EU or the IMF. Given that Sweden should avoid debt ratios in excess of 70% to 75% of GDP, the debt ratio should be

88   *Fredrik N. G. Andersson and Lars Jonung*

Table 3.2 Fiscal Costs of Major Financial Crises in EU15, Norway, Japan, and the United States

Country	Crisis years	Increase in public debt (% GDP)	Public support to banks (% GDP)	Macroeconomic Cost GDP-loss (% GDP)
Sweden	1991–1995	36.2	3.6	32.9
Austria	2008–2012	19.8	5.2	19.2
Belgium	2008–2012	22.2	6.2	15.7
Denmark	2008–2009	32.8	5.9	35.0
Finland	1991–1995	43.6	12.8	69.6
France	2008–2009	15.9	1.3	23.3
Germany	2008–2009	16.2	2.7	12.3
Greece	2008–2012	43.9	28.7	64.9
Ireland	2008–2012	76.5	37.6	107.7
Italy	2008–2009	8.6	0.7	32.2
Japan	1997–2001	41.7	8.6	45.0
Luxembourg	2008–2012	12.7	7.2	43.3
Netherlands	2008–2009	24.9	14.3	26.1
Norway	1991–1993	19.2	2.7	5.1
Portugal	2008–2012	38.5	11.1	35.0
United Kingdom	2007–2011	27.0	8.8	25.3
United States	2007–2011	21.9	4.5	30.0
Average		29.5	9.5	36.6
Median		24.9	6.2	32.2
Top 5 most costly crises		48.8	19.8	64.4
Top 10 most costly crises		38.7	13.8	45.7

Source: Adapted from Laeven and Valencia (2018).

between 20% and 40% of GDP before the crisis. If we are to err on the side of caution, we should put the debt target in the lower part of this range.

Consequently, we view the pre-corona debt anchor in early 2020 of 35% of GDP as too high. Instead, Sweden should aim for a central point of no more than 25% with a tolerance band of +/−5 percentage points around the central point to account for normal business cycle fluctuations.

Our proposed size of the new debt anchor prepares Sweden for the consequences of a future major economic crisis. We arrive at this recommendation based on a precautionary or prudent line of reasoning. We want to have a sufficient fiscal space as an insurance against future shocks. We do not claim that we have derived the optimal debt level for Sweden. Rather, we have doubts about the concept of an optimal debt level. For this reason, we discuss the proper, prudent, or "safe" debt level from a crisis insurance perspective that would allow sufficient consumption and tax smoothing over time—ignoring any attempt of defining an optimal debt ratio for Sweden. Recent arguments by Blanchard (2019) and others suggest that the proper size of the national debt does not constitute a binding constraint for policymakers as long as the borrowing rate is below the growth rate of the economy. We find that approach risky as real yields vary substantially over time (Jorda et al., 2019). The risk of higher yields in the future is too high for the government to increase its present debt levels.

There are of course potential costs as well as benefits of a low public debt. One cost of a low debt is that the government drains the economy of economic resources, which reduces demand, or sets taxes too high. The Swedish evidence suggests these costs are non-existent or negligible. The Swedish economy out-performed most other comparable countries between 2000 and 2019 while the debt level declined. For example, GDP growth averaged 2.3% per year compared to 2.1% in the United States, 1.8% in the United Kingdom, and 1.4% in the euro area. The tax ratio fell from 49% to 42% of GDP and real public consumption grew by 29%. There is little evidence of the strong public finances having hurt society.

The New Debt Anchor

Our proposed new debt anchor has several advantages. It is a simple rule, easy to communicate with the public and the adherence to the rule can be monitored successfully by the fiscal policy council and thus by the public. Once the debt ratio has reached the 25% of GDP level, the surplus target becomes superfluous and should be abolished. A major disadvantage with the present surplus target is that it is relatively demanding to evaluate. Measuring the phase and size of the business cycle is notoriously difficult in real time. The task of estimating the structural budget deficit to quantify the surplus target involves measurement errors. Our debt anchor does not suffer from similar difficulties. It is easy to estimate in real time. Of course, they are related but it is much easier to monitor the volume of debt than the structural stance of the budget.

The other building blocks of the fiscal framework should be kept in place: the expenditure ceiling, the Fiscal Policy Council, and the debt anchor. The expenditure ceiling is an important element to keep government expenditures in line during good times under a debt anchor. In addition, once the surplus target has been abolished, the monitoring of the finances of regional and local authorities should be a prime task of the Fiscal Policy Council.

THE CORONA CRISIS AND PUBLIC DEBT

At the time of writing, the corona pandemic is causing a major economic downturn in the global economy. The fiscal situation has worsened dramatically: data from the IMF suggest an increase in the debt level for advanced countries from around 105% of GDP prior to the pandemic to more than 120% by April 2020, and it is expected to have increased by even more by the end of 2020.[20] The Swedish general government debt is expected to increase from 35% to 43%, a smaller increase compared to many other countries, yet larger than during the international financial crisis of 2008–2009.

Although still early, we can already draw some conclusions. First, the corona crisis demonstrates the importance of having a sufficient fiscal space before any crisis. The Swedish government may now substantially increase its budget deficit without worrying about the future fiscal situation or about rising interest rates. Furthermore, there is great uncertainty how the economy will develop in the coming years. The ample fiscal space allows the Swedish government to withdraw economic support from the economy gradually over time and without risking the recovery. Countries with high debt levels may have to shift from expansionary to contractionary policies while the economy still is in a recession. Such a shift is likely to cause a political reaction with growing populism and extremism as a result, which will further deteriorate the fiscal position.

Second, the Swedish central bank, the Riksbank, does not have to bail out the government by monetizing the public debt. Quickly rising debt levels increases the risk of higher interest rates, which could trigger a sovereign debt crisis, similar to the European debt crisis in 2010–2015. Such a fiscal crisis would worsen the already severe economic effects of the pandemic. Although central banks may provide temporary relief for highly indebted countries, by buying government bonds, such a policy also carries future economic risks and costs. Quantitative easing and ultralow central bank policy rates contribute to growing financial imbalances and thus raise the risk of future financial crises (Andersson and Jonung, 2020).

Third, major increases in public spending during the corona crisis may be politically difficult to withdraw after the crisis. They may also lead to further calls for public spending on other areas. The large increases in spending and the use of quantitative easing following the international financial crisis in 2008–2009 gave rise to populist calls for the people's QE and bailout for Main Street rather than for Wall Street.[21] Maintaining fiscal balance in the long run may prove difficult after the pandemic if governments spend too much during the crisis. Sustainable public finances are only achievable in a stable political environment. Crises threaten the stability of the political system. A strong fiscal framework with a low debt level prior to the crisis may help to reduce political pressures during the crisis.

CAN AND SHOULD SWEDEN SERVE AS AN EXAMPLE FOR OTHER COUNTRIES?

Sweden is in a fiscally envious position compared to many other countries. During the fall of 2019 and the early months of 2020, before the pandemic struck, the public debate on fiscal policy focused on whether the public debt was too low and whether or not to abandon the surplus target. Still, after the corona crisis, Swedish national debt remains at a low level in international comparisons. This raises two questions. First, is Sweden such a fiscal exception that other countries have not much to learn from the Swedish case? Second, should other countries follow the Swedish example?

Is Sweden an Outlier?

The Swedish fiscal framework is embedded in a unique institutional setting. However, from a historical perspective, the strength of the Swedish public finances is relatively new. The period from 1973 until 1995 was marked by growing debts and rising interest rates. It was the financial and fiscal crisis of the 1990s that forced Sweden to change course. The collective memory of the crisis in the 1990s has since helped to form a political consensus across the political spectrum concerning the importance of fiscal stability. Market signals through higher interest rates during the 1990s contributed to strengthening this consensus. Falling interest rates, once government debt began to decline, provided further incentives to continue to reduce the debt level. In the euro area, following the crisis of the late 2000s, the policy of the ECB reduced interest rates on public debt, in this way weakening political incentives to stabilize public finances. In Sweden, interest rates fell due to fiscal consolidation after the financial crisis of 1992, not due to the lack of fiscal consolidation as in the euro area after the crisis of 2008.

Countries that are struggling to get their fiscal house in order should view a fiscal framework that relies on a debt anchor as a useful instrument. The original fiscal framework for the EU as set out in the Maastricht treaty of 1992 and the Stability and Growth Pact of 1997 has proven insufficient. The Maastricht rules of a maximum debt level of 60% and a budget deficit of no more than 3% of GDP have not served as ceilings. Instead, in the best cases, they have become fiscal targets that too many governments have been aiming for. In the worst cases, the debt ceiling has become a floor rather than a ceiling—thus turning counterproductive. The Maastricht framework has clearly proven insufficient and given rise to a number of additional fiscal rules, pasted more or less ad hoc onto the initial treaty.[22]

Before the corona crisis, EU fiscal governance had turned into a very complicated affair with a wide set of rules and regulations that make the system difficult to monitor, to evaluate, and to communicate to the public. In addition, the system is a constant source of tension between "Brussels" (the Commission) and the member states. Another concern is that equal treatment across member states does not seem to be a firm principle.

As Debrun and Jonung (2019) argued, the EU system of fiscal governance before the corona crisis lacked credibility and efficiency. According to Debrun and Jonung (2019, p 155), "In practice, the focus on enforceable rules appears to have resulted in intractable complexity, to the point of putting rules-based fiscal policy at risk. The evolution of the EU fiscal framework illustrates this outcome and the related risk of de-anchoring fiscal expectations." As an alternative, they recommended in their conclusions "simple, flexible but non-enforceable rules" that work through "reputational effects." In fact, they proposed a system of fiscal governance similar to the Swedish one. Here the fiscal policy council has an important role to play due to its solid reputation. It serves as a guardian of the collective memory of the high cost of fiscal imbalances.

The corona crisis has further eroded the EU's fiscal rules by effectively removing any binding obligations. This is the appropriate response during a crisis, but raises the question: What happens next? Debt levels in the euro area have the shape of a staircase. Debt levels grow rapidly during crises. They are flat or fall just slightly during normal times, only to grow again when the next crisis hits. The result is increased fiscal vulnerabilities over time. The average debt level in the euro area is today higher than 100% of GDP. This corresponds to the Greek and Italian debt levels in 2007 prior to the international financial crisis and the European debt crisis. The debt crisis was never fully resolved. The symptoms of higher bond yields were made milder through the ECB's quantitative easing program, yet debt levels remained too high.

There is clearly a need for binding fiscal frameworks. The fiscal situation in the United States and Japan is similar. The U.S. use of debt limits and pay-as-you-go rules set by Congress have proven inadequate. The present corona-induced expansion of federal debt following the rapid rise in federal debt in recent years reveals a major weakness in the U.S. system similar to that of the EU.

One of the few frameworks that had successfully transformed the fiscal position of an advanced country during the last quarter of a century is the Swedish framework. A reformed Swedish system with a greater focus on the debt anchor is a model to be considered by other countries. Of course, we are aware that it is a far step for many EU members such as Italy, Greece, and France and countries such as Japan and the United States to move to a prudent or "safe" debt level as low as 25% of GDP. However, achieving fiscal discipline in Sweden was once regarded as an impossible task but proved possible over time. The turning point was a combination of a deep economic crisis, market forces that punished Sweden through higher interest rates, and a growing awareness of the importance of sustainable public finances. If it was possible in Sweden to turn around weakening fiscal position, it should be possible in other countries as well.[23]

Should Other Countries Follow the Swedish Example?

The Swedish fiscal framework was introduced in a different global economic environment than that reigning today. In the 1990s, Swedish long-term government yields were in excess of 5%. Interest rates have declined steadily since then. Lower rates have inspired economists such as Blanchard (2019) and Rachel and Summers (2019), among others, to argue for greater reliance on deficit financing, thus increased public borrowing and higher public debt ratios. The corona pandemic has reinforced this argument with the IMF calling for quality public investments to stimulate the economy among already heavily indebted developed countries (IMF, 2020).

The hypothesis of continuously low interest rates is a misleading one. Historically, real bond yields have varied substantially over time (Jorda et al., 2019). Figure 3.7 illustrates a trend estimate of the real 10-year government bond yield in Sweden, the United Kingdom, and the United States from 1840 to 2016. There are sustained periods of low interest rates and sustained periods of high interest rates lasting several decades. Part of the decrease in yields during the 2010s are due to central bank asset purchase programs, the so-called quantitate easing, which have expanded the balance sheet of the Federal Reserve from close to 5% in relation to GDP in 2007 to close to 35% in 2020. The corresponding numbers for the balance sheet of the European Central Bank show a rise from 15% to 60% over the same period

Although possible, it is unlikely that interest rates will remain record low forever. The historical evidence clearly shows that periods of low yields are followed, eventually, by periods of high yields. Nor is a continuous expansion of central bank balance sheets possible while maintaining economic stability. In our view, betting on low interest rates is a gamble. Only a modest increase in interest rates may cause severe harm to fiscal and real economic stability. It is easy to increase the debt ratio, but history suggests that it is difficult to reduce it. The decline in the Swedish debt ratio from 75% of GDP to 35% of GDP took 25 years. When interest rates increase again in the future, heavily indebted countries will suffer. Resisting the temptation to increase the debt during periods of low rates is part of a sustainable fiscal policy.

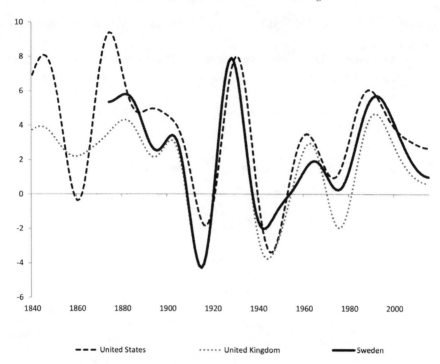

Figure 3.7   Trend Estimate of the Real 10-Year Government Bond Yield in the United States, the United Kingdom, and Sweden 1840–2015. Adapted from Andersson (2017).

CONCLUSION

The Swedish fiscal policy framework has been a success—so far. In fact, it has been too successful in the sense that it was likely to lead eventually to a too low a level of government debt. From a debt level of 75% of GDP in 1995, the debt ratio was expected to fall to 30% by 2022—before the pandemic occurred. It is now projected to peak at 45% in 2021.

Several factors have contributed to the secular decline of the debt ratio in Sweden. Widespread public support for the policy to first reduce debt and then to maintain it at a stable level has forced the political parties to compete in terms of fiscal responsibility. The experience of the crisis of the early 1990s of a rapid expansion of government debt and of ensuing large reductions in public spending is still in vivid memory. In addition, debt consolidation has rewarded governments with falling interest rates on government debt, giving the political system strong incentives to continue to reduce debt even in good times.

Although the fiscal framework has been a success until now, it does suffer from some weaknesses: one is the focus on a surplus target, another reliance on the personal memory of the crisis in the 1990s among leading policymakers. We argue that a possible reform to strengthen the framework for the future is to institutionalize the crisis memory by shifting the focus from the surplus target to the debt anchor.

As the history of government debt shows, fiscal crises are the most dangerous threat to the fiscal balance and to political stability. Thus, it is recommendable to design the fiscal framework so that it gives protection against future crises in the form sufficient fiscal space before the crisis. To derive the appropriate level of fiscal space and thus for the debt anchor for Sweden, we use a two-step approach. First, we estimate at which debt level the cost of servicing public debt begins to rise sharply. Second, starting from this debt threshold and using data from the fiscal costs of financial crises, we calculate that a debt-to-GDP ratio in the range of 20–30% would be a prudent level.

These calculations are strengthened by the recent experience during the pandemic. It demonstrates the importance of a low debt level before the crisis. Thanks to a public debt level of 35%, the Swedish response to the corona crisis allowed for a rise in public debt by around 10% of GDP without causing concerns for an unsustainable future path of public debt. This episode demonstrates the value of having a fiscal framework that creates sufficient fiscal space to meet the next crisis. This is also the major lesson from Sweden for other countries, not least in Europe and the United States.

NOTES

1. This paper builds upon and extends upon Andersson and Jonung (2019) and Jonung (2016). We have benefited from comments from Lina Aldén, Niklas Frank, Oskar Grevesmühl and Pär Österholm.

2. See Eichengreen et al. (2019) on the cross-country history of debt accumulation in a secular perspective.

3. See Persson (1996) for the development of Swedish debt from the 1970s to the first part of the 1990s.

4. See Jonung (1999) on the shifting stabilization policy models used by Swedish governments 1970–99.

5. See the analysis of boom-bust induced cycles in public finance in Sweden in chapter 6 in Jonung et al. (2009).

6. Andersson (2016) shows that major economic crises in general cause a change in policy across developed countries.

7. The rise of the Swedish fiscal framework is described in detail in Calmfors (2012) and Jonung (2015, 2018).

8. An extension of the terms of office from three to four years was introduced in 1994 as a response to the financial crisis of the early 1990s.

9. See Jonung (2018) on the establishment of the Fiscal Policy Council in 2007. Wyplosz (2002) contributed early to the arguments for a fiscal council in Sweden.

10. The average interest rate in 2017 was 0.57% (*Kommuninvest,* 2017).

11. Manasse and Katsikas (2018) argue that domestically driven reforms in Southern Europe were more successful compared to externally imposed reforms. Andersson (2016) reaches a similar conclusion. Domestic reforms are more long lasting compared to reforms imposed by external organizations.

12. It is tempting to suggest that Swedish governments have suffered from a surplus bias, not a deficit bias, a concept frequently adopted to explain fiscal profligacy.

13. See for example the survey by Alesina and Passalacqua (2015).

14. See for example Jordà et al. (2016) and Romer and Romer (2019) for the international evidence. Romer and Romer (2019, p. 12) note a "tremendous variation in the severity and persistence of output declines following financial distress." They explain this variation mainly by differences in fiscal space across countries.

15. Social spending in Sweden in relation to GDP was 26% in 2016 compared to the OECD average of 20% and 19% in the United States (OECD, 2016).

16. Swedish households have a relatively small amount of financial assets compared to households in other OECD countries. Most of Swedish household wealth is in housing (OECD, 2015).

17. See chapter 2 in Jonung et al. (2009).

18. See for example Eichengreen (2018).

19. This level is consistent with the view of Fall et al. (2015) proposing a debt threshold for high-income countries in the range of 70–90%, close to our threshold of 70%. It is also roughly consistent with the finding of Barrett (2018) of a debt limit for the UK of 90%, although calculated by a methodology different from ours.

20. See IMF (2020).

21. https://mainlymacro.blogspot.com/2015/08/peoples-qe-and-corbyns-qe.html

22. See Larch et al. (2010).

23. The Swedish experience shows that a country is not guaranteed a free fiscal lunch as suggested by Blanchard (2019). He assumes that the government can consistently borrow at low rates—a view that is clearly inconsistent with the historical evidence. This time is not different, in our view.

REFERENCES

Alesina, A., and A. Passalacqua. (2015), "The political economy of government debt", Working Paper, Department of Economics, Harvard. https://scholar.harvard .edu/files/alesina/files/political_economy_of_gov_debt_dec_2015.pdf

Andersson, F. N. G. (2016), "A blessing in disguise? Banking crises and institutional reforms", *World Development,* 83, 135–147.

Andersson, F. N. G. (2017), "Sekulär stagnation. Vad är det och hur påverkar det penningpolitiken?" *Ekonomisk Debatt,* 45(7), 13–25. https://www.nationalekonomi.se/ sites/default/files/NEFfiler/45-4-fnga.pdf

Andersson, F. N. G. and L. Jonung. (2016), "The credit and housing boom in Sweden, 1995–2015: Forewarned is forearmed", VoxEU.org. https://voxeu.org/article/cred it-and-housing-boom-sweden-1995-2015

Barrett, P. (2018), "Interest-growth differentials and debt limits in advanced economies", IMF Working Paper 18/82, IMF.

Blanchard, O. (2019), "Public debt and low interest rates", *American Economic Review*, 109(4), 1197–1229.

Calmfors, L. (2012), "Sweden: Watchdog with a broad remit", *CESifo Working Paper Series*, No. 3725, January 31.

Debrun, X. and L. Jonung. (2019), "Under threat: Rules-based fiscal policy and how to preserve it", *European Journal of Political Economy*, 57, 147–157.

Eichengreen, B. (2018), *The populist temptation. Economic grievance and political reaction in the modern era*, Oxford University Press, Oxford.

Eichengreen, B., A. El-Ganainy, R. P. Esteves and K. Mitchener. (2019), "Public debt through the ages", IMF working paper 19/6, Washington.

Fall, F., D. Bloch, J. M. Fournier and P. Hoeller. (2015), "Prudent debt targets and fiscal frameworks", OECD Economic Policy Paper Series, 15, July, OECD, Paris.

Fregert, K. and R. Gustavsson. (2013), "Financial statistics for Sweden 1670–2011", in R. Edvinsson, T. Jacobson and D. Waldenström, eds., *House prices, stock prices, national accounts and the Riksbank's balance sheet, 1620–2012*, Ekerlids förlag, Stockholm, https://www.riksbank.se/sv/om-riksbanken/riksbankens-uppdrag/fors kning/historisk-monetar-statistik-for-sverige/volume-i-exchange-rates-prices-and -wages-1277-2008/

IMF (2020), *Gross debt position*. Read 31 August 2020. https://www.imf.org/ external/datamapper/G_XWDG_G01_GDP_PT@FM/ADVEC/FM_EMG/FM _LIDC

Jonung, L. (1999), *Med backspegeln som kompass—om stabiliseringspolitiken som läroprocess*, rapport till ESO, Ds 1999:9, Finansdepartementet, Stockholm, mars, 1999. http://eso.expertgrupp.se/wp-content/uploads/1999/10/Ds-1999_9-Med-bac kspegeln.pdf

Jonung, L. (2015), "Reforming the fiscal framework: The case of Sweden 1973–2013", chapter 8 in T. Andersen, M. Bergman and S. Hougaard Jensen, eds., *Reform capacity and macroeconomic performance in the Nordic countries*, Oxford University Press, Oxford.

Jonung, L. (2018), "Homegrown: The Swedish fiscal policy framework", chapter 12 in R. Beetsma and X. Debrun, eds., *Independent fiscal councils: Watchdogs or lapdogs?*, VoxEU.org eBook. CEPR Press. https://voxeu.org/content/independent -fiscal-councils-watchdogs-or-lapdogs, January.

Jonung, L., J. Kiander and P. Vartia, eds., *The Great Financial Crisis in Finland and Sweden*, Edward Elgar, Cheltenham.

Jordà, O., M. Schularick and A. Taylor. (2016), "Sovereigns versus banks: Credit, crises, and consequences", *Journal of the European Economic Association*, 14, 45–79.

98   *Fredrik N. G. Andersson and Lars Jonung*

Jordá, O., K. Knoll, D. Kuvshinov, M. Schularick and A. M. Taylor. (2019), "The rate of return on everything 1870–2015", *The Quarterly Journal of Economics*, 134(3), 1225–1298.

Kommuninvest (2017), *Den kommunala låneskulden*, Kommuninvest, Stockholm. https://kommuninvest.se/wp-content/uploads/2017/10/Den-kommunala-l%C3%A5neskulden-2017-171016.pdf

Larch, M., P. van den Noord and L. Jonung. (2010), "The Stability and Growth Pact. Lessons from the Great Recession", *European Economy*. Economic Papers, no. 429, December, Brussels. ISBN: 9978-92-79-14915-3 ISSN: 1725-3187. http://ec.europa.eu/economy_finance/publications/economic_paper/2010/pdf/ecp429_en.pdf.

Laeven, L., and F. Valencia. (2018), "Systemic banking crises revisited", IMF Working Paper 18/206. https://www.imf.org/en/Publications/WP/Issues/2018/09/14/Systemic-Banking-Crises-Revisited-46232

Manasse, P. and D. Katsikas, eds., (2018), *Economic crisis and structural reforms in Southern Europe. Policy lessons*, Routledge.

Martinsson, J. and U. Andersson, eds., (2018), *Svenska trender 1986–2017*, SOM Institute, Gothenburg University. https://som.gu.se/aktuellt/Nyheter/Nyheter_detalj//svenska-trender-1986-2017.cid1569129

National Institute for Economic Research (2020), *Uppdatering av konjunkturbilden, augusti 2020*, NIER, Stockholm. https://www.konj.se/download/18.4171f931173cf2385f681046/1597820338698/KUaug2020.pdf

OECD (2015), *National accounts at a glance*, OECD, Paris. https://www.oecd-ilibrary.org/economics/national-accounts-at-a-glance_22200444

OECD (2016), *Society at a glance*, OECD, Paris. https://www.oecd-ilibrary.org/social-issues-migration-health/society-at-a-glance_19991290

Persson, M. (1996), "Swedish government debts and deficits, 1970–1995", *Swedish Economic Policy Review*, 3(1), 21–59.

Rachel, L. and L. Summers. (Spring 2019), "On falling neutral real rates, fiscal policy, and the risk of secular stagnation", *Brookings Papers on Economic Activity*, 1–76.

Reinhart, C. and K. Rogoff. (2009), *This time is different. Eight centuries of financially folly*, Princeton University Press, Princeton and Oxford.

Riksbank (1984), *Statistical yearbook 1983*, Riksbanken, Stockholm.

Romer, C. and D. Romer. (2019), "Fiscal space and the aftermath of financial crises: How it matters and why", BPEA Conference Drafts, March 7–8, Brookings Papers on Economic Activity. https://www.brookings.edu/bpea-articles/fiscal-space-and-the-aftermath-of-financial-crises-how-it-matters-and-why/

Roth, F., E. Baake, L. Jonung and F. Nowak-Lehmann. (2018), "Revisiting public support for the euro, 1999-2017: Accounting for the crisis and the recovery", Department of Economics, Lund University, Working Paper 2018:9. https://ideas.repec.org/p/hhs/lunewp/2018_009.html, forthcoming *Journal of Common Market Studies*.

SOU 2016:67, *En översyn av överskottsmålet*, (A review of the surplus target), Department of finance, Stockholm.

Swedish National Financial Management Authority (2018), *Prognos. Statens budget och de offentliga finanserna* (Forecast. The budget of the government and public finances), April 2018. https://www.esv.se/contentassets/903a877bc36745caa65f15044771ffb0/prognos-april-2018.pdf

Von Hagen, J. (1992), "Budgeting procedures and fiscal performance in the European Communities", *Economic Papers* 96, DGII, European Commission, Brussels.

Wyplosz, C. (2002), "Fiscal policy: Institutions vs. rules", chapter 5 in *Stabiliseringspolitik i valutaunionen*, (Stabilization policy in the monetary union), SOU 2002:16, Fritzes, Stockholm.

Chapter 4

The Swiss Federal Debt Brake and Its Unbudgeted Surpluses

Vera Z. Eichenauer and Jan-Egbert Sturm

INTRODUCTION

The Swiss federal debt brake pursues two goals: ensure medium- and long-term debt stabilization by avert (chronic) structural imbalances and grant short-term countercyclical budget leeway.[1] The federal debt brake is a constitutional rule that was introduced to correct aspects of the budget process that were perceived to be flawed. Its minimum goal is the business-cycle adjusted equalization of revenues and expenditures. The fiscal rule is asymmetric: it concerns only the expenditure side. The rule states that given expected tax revenue subject to a business cycle correction, the budget must be balanced. In principle, the Swiss Confederation can also act on the revenue side but constitutional upper limits on the main tax rates do not allow for micro-management of revenues. The debt brake was first applied in the federal budget 2003 following a steep debt accumulation in the 1990s. In 15 of the 16 years since the introduction of the debt brake, there were unbudgeted surpluses, which sometimes were large. From 2006 to 2019, the revenue growth was underestimated and the expenditure growth overestimated each year. The main contribution of this chapter is to analyze the evolution of revenue and expenditure forecasting since the introduction of the debt brake. In the decade prior the introduction of the federal debt brake, Switzerland went through a period of recession and stagnation.[2] Between 1990 and 1998, federal debt tripled starting from a debt level of 39 billion and a debt ratio of 10% (figure 4.1). In 1998, it amounted to over 110 billion Swiss francs, or more than 25% of gross domestic product (GDP). During this period of debt accumulation, the existing constitutional rule introduced in 1958 about the compensation of budget deficits proved largely toothless. The debt brake was introduced because other policy measures to curb the growth of the debt ratio were judged insufficient.

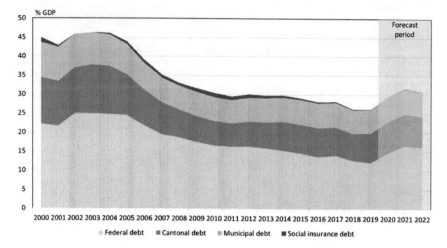

Figure 4.1   Development of the Debt-to-GDP Ratio at All Political Levels and Forecasts.
Note: 2020–2022 are projections from March 25, 2021, using recent GDP estimates that
exclude value added associated with (capital inflows following major international) sport
events. KOF Swiss Economic Institute, Sturm et al. (2020).

The debt brake is anchored in the Federal Constitution, which cannot be
changed without a popular vote. The population accepted the introduction of
the fiscal rule in 2001 with a yes vote of 84.7% and a clear majority in all
twenty-six cantons. Previously, the proposal had passed both chambers of
parliament with majorities of more than two-thirds. These strong majorities
demonstrate that in Switzerland there is widespread acceptance among citizens in the belief that federal public finances need to be tightly and conserva-
tively regulated to ensure long term fiscal sustainability.

The debt brake treats deficits and surpluses in the budget differently. While
the former need to be compensated, the latter are automatically used for debt
reduction. This modification was made by parliament to the original (symmetric) proposal by the federal government. The debt brake was an immediate
success: it stopped debt accumulation and even reduced debt. From 2004 to
2019, the federal government's gross debt fell from CHF 124 billion to CHF
88 billion.[3] The main reasons for the absolute reduction in debt were regular
budget underruns and the systematic underestimation of revenues. From 2006
to 2019, the federal revenues were larger than the expenditures almost every
year. In combination with economic growth from 2005 to 2019, the federal
government's debt ratio fell from 26% of GDP to 13%. As of 2019, the debt
brake had almost reversed the buildup of the debt ratio during the 1990s.[4]

The federal government's debt ratio has halved between the introduction
of the federal debt brake in 2003 and 2019. For international comparisons
and an overall assessment of fiscal policy, the total public debt ratio across

all layers of the public sector is relevant. Switzerland's general public debt ratio has fallen from 46% in 2003 to 26% in 2019. Since 2009, the debt ratio at the cantonal level has slightly increased while the municipal debt ratio has slightly dropped since a peak in the mid-2010s (figure 4.2). It is likely that these subsidiary federal levels have partly compensated for the decline in federal expenditures, but this is difficult to assess unambiguously. As all cantons have their own fiscal rules in place,[5] the small increase in the cantonal debt ratio is not necessarily worrisome.

Despite its obvious success, the federal debt brake has been criticized. The main criticism regards the systematic budget underruns that it appears to have created. Because many countries struggle with systematic and often large budget deficits, external observers are sometimes puzzled that a budget surplus is considered a problem in Switzerland. This is because systematic deviations from the budget in either direction undermine the budget authority of parliament and the trust in the (forecasting) abilities of the Finance Ministry.

In recognition of the intensifying debate about the debt brake caused by the repeated budget underruns, the Swiss government commissioned in 2017 a report on the topic from an expert group which was headed by Jan-Egbert Sturm, one of the authors of this chapter. The report concluded that an adjustment of the regulatory framework could undermine trust in the debt brake and thus its effectiveness. As a moral hazard, it could furthermore provoke follow-up demands. A 2012 public opinion survey demonstrated that the debt

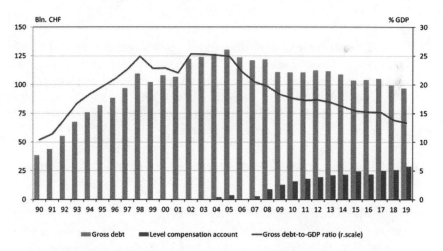

Figure 4.2 Development of the Gross Debt of the Confederation, 1990–2019, in Million CHF. Note: GDP estimates that exclude value added associated with (capital inflows following major international) sport activities. Gross debt and the level of the compensation account in billion nominal CHF. Swiss Federal Finance Administration and State Secretariat for Economic Affairs Switzerland.

brake remains very popular among the population despite the systematic budget underruns. This strengthens the political commitment to respect the debt brake and thus its effectiveness.

Besides updating parts of Sturm et al. (2017), the main contribution of this chapter is to analyze for the first time the evolution of revenue forecasts since the introduction of the debt brake. The 2017 report analyzed only the expenditure side of the budget underruns in detail. Experts considered that the measures undertaken to improve the estimation of revenues and the reform of government budgeting were likely to be sufficient to eliminate systematic revenue forecasting errors in the future. This chapter examines the claim of public officials that the positive bias in the forecasting error for revenues was indeed reduced by the introduction of an improved forecasting model implemented in 2012. We find a large overall improvement in revenue forecasts which is only partly attributable to the improved forecasting method for withholding taxes. We also find that forecasting errors for withholding tax revenues were reduced but have not become symmetrical. In the following sections of this chapter we will describe the background, design, and introduction of the Swiss debt brake. This is followed by a discussion of recent reforms, explanations for the budget overruns, and other challenges surrounding the debt brake. The final section concludes.

BACKGROUND TO THE CREATION OF THE DEBT BRAKE

Switzerland is a fiscally conservative country with a long history of fiscal rules and a strongly federalist country.[6] The competences of the Swiss federal government are delegated from the cantons and are limited compared to what we observe in other OECD countries. The maximum tax rates of main revenue components are determined by the constitution that can only be changed by popular vote. The Swiss federation accounts for 30% (2000–2019) of government expenditures in Switzerland. The largest share of government expenditures occurs at the cantonal level which is responsible for basic and higher education, police, health, and social security. On average, 40% of total government expenditures are carried out at the cantonal level while municipal-level expenditures account for 20%.[7]

After the two world wars, the federal government's debt amounted to 9 billion Swiss francs, which corresponded to about 50% of GDP at that time. In 1959, a deficit rule was introduced into the Swiss constitution to limit the debt accumulation.[8] High federal surpluses during the 1960s led to a sharp reduction in the debt ratio. Influenced by the worldwide oil crisis, this trend was interrupted in the second half of the 1970s. During the 1980s, a further decline of debt was recorded. During the recession and stagnation period of the 1990s, however, the constitutional anchoring of debt relief could not stop the increase in debt. The Swiss National Bank responded to the 1987 financial crisis with expansionary policies but reversed its approach after inflation surpassed 6% in 1990. The tight monetary policy increased interest rates, led to an appreciation of the Swiss franc, caused the burst of a real estate bubble, and led to the collapse and acquisitions of several regional banks. In a 1992 referendum, the Swiss narrowly opposed joining the European Economic Area. As a combination of these factors, the unemployment rate during several years in the mid-1990s was more than 4 percentage points higher than during the 1980s. This led to high and unprecedented federal expenditures for unemployment benefits.

More fundamentally, the expansion of federal debt was perceived to reflect flaws in the budget process. First, there was a spending bias coupled with a procyclical fiscal policy: economic upturns were not used as an opportunity for fiscal consolidation. Second, in order to raise revenues, a constitutional amendment is usually required. Spending increases, on the other hand, require only a simple majority vote in parliament.

The steep rise in the debt ratio during the 1990s was criticized early and acted upon fast. The debt accumulation was first met with several austerity packages in 1992–1994. In 1995, a brake on expenditures was introduced. Subsidy provisions, commitment credits, and payment frameworks entailing new one-time expenditures of more than CHF 20 million, or new recurrent expenditures of more than CHF 2 million required the approval of the majority in both chambers of the federal parliament. These majorities are difficult to obtain in the Swiss governmental system with a consensus rather than a majority government.

These austerity efforts and the spending brake were not sufficient to significantly reduce the budget deficit. Moreover, some economists and economic historians argued that the austerity measures at the cantonal and federal level prolonged the economic crisis.

In 1997, the Finance Ministry started planning the debt brake. As a necessary condition for its introduction, a structurally large balanced budget was required. Against this background, a budget target for 2001 was formulated in 1997: The deficit in the financial accounts was to be reduced gradually from 1999, once the economy had recovered and stabilized, and not exceed 2% of revenues until the 2001 fiscal year. In order to achieve the budget consolidation aimed for with the 2001 budget target, a new, temporary transitional provision was created in the federal constitution that obligated the Federal Council and Parliament to make savings with a binding deadline if the target was not met. The proposal for the 2001 budget target was accepted by 70.7% of the people in a 1998 referendum. Subsequently, work began on the design of the federal debt brake which was first applied in the 2003 federal budget.

The government report accompanying the original proposal makes clear that the primary goal of the regulation is to stabilize the federal debt with the secondary goal of granting short-term countercyclical budget leeway.[9] To achieve these goals, the government proposed to symmetrically compensate for surpluses or deficits. According to the proposal, the balancing of the budget would have required either an increase of the expenditure ceilings or a reduction of revenues in the following years. The reason for the planned symmetrical management was a proposed compensation account as an instrument to compensate for estimation errors in revenues. In the absence of systematic forecast errors for revenues, the balance of the compensation account would fluctuate around a stable level. The sanction in the event of a major deficit prevents a systematic overestimation of revenues and thus a constant violation of the debt brake. Conversely, the debt brake would have been overfulfilled in the event of systematic underestimation. The funds in the compensation account could then have been used to increase the expenditure ceiling or reduce taxes.

Parliament did not endorse this proposal and allowed for a more ambitious goal than debt stabilization. There should be the possibility of using surpluses to pay off the debt. In contrast to the original proposal, surpluses cannot be used to increase the expenditure ceiling or to reduce taxes. They thus lead to a reduction in debt. No upper limit was set for the positive balance of the compensation account. The design of the compensation account is thus asymmetric, intended only for a situation of a negative balance. A surplus in the compensation account can continue indefinitely and there is no obligation to reduce it over time. While the constitutional framework permits symmetrical management of the compensation account, the current Financial Budget Act is more restrictive. Parliament thus gave priority to debt reduction as opposed to spending increases or tax relief.

THE DESIGN OF THE DEBT BRAKE

The Swiss debt brake has two features that we want to describe in more detail because we believe them to be rather unique in international comparison. First, the current Financial Budget Act (FHG) implements the constitutional provision of the debt brake in an asymmetric way. Deficits and surpluses are not treated in the same way. While the former need to be compensated, the later are automatically used for debt reduction. Second, the Swiss debt brake cyclically adjusts revenues but not expenditures. The aim is to stabilize the expenditure path over time. This means that, in contrast to the revenue side, no short-run economic impulses are intended to come from the expenditure side of the federal budget. Tax revenues are supposed to act as automatic stabilizers. In this context, it is important to note that significant expenditure-side automatic stabilizer that react very strongly to economic fluctuations, such as unemployment insurance (as well as other social insurances) have been recorded separately from the federal accounts since 2002. They are therefore not subject to the debt brake rule.[10] Finally, it is important to note that constitutional upper limits to federal taxes make it difficult to adjust tax rates. Changes to tax levels must be accepted by the voters in an optional or even mandatory referendum.

The expenditure ceiling determined by the debt brake corresponds to the cyclically adjusted revenues. During the budget process, the Swiss debt brake is applied twice: first to budget forecasts, then to effective outcomes. It is the second calculation that determines the deviations that must be credited or debited in the compensation account. If the deficit exceeds 6% of expenditures, the excessive amount must be eliminated within the next three annual budgets by lowering the expenditure ceilings.

More formally, the expenditure ceiling required by the debt rule is $G_t = k_t \cdot R_t$, where R are the (budgeted or realized) revenues and k the so-called economic factor that adjusts for economic movements on the revenue side. The economic factor k corresponds to the quotient of the estimated real GDP according to the long-term smoothed trend and the expected real GDP in the forecast year: $k_t = Y_t/Y_t^*$. For smoothing the GDP series, a modified HP filter is applied. This method has advantages with respect to alternative measures (e.g., production functions) in terms of transparency and symmetry. In addition, it requires only a small number of hypotheses about the future development of output or production factors. The filter method has the further advantage of yielding a symmetrical value of the output gap over time. A disadvantage of the HP filter is that it is known to suffer from a lack of smoothing properties at the end of a series that is to be smoothed. This problem can be handled either by using forecasts, so that the trend calculation does not occur at the end of the series or by a modification of weights within the filter. The latter approach was preferred for the Swiss debt brake, as the use of forecasts magnified the problem. The modified HP filter interprets a (forecasted) change in GDP during the budget year to be around 80% cyclical and 20% structural. The forecasting error regarding the output gap will translate into corresponding errors in both revenue and forecasts of the cyclical adjustment factor k. However, these errors will have opposite signs and generally cancel each other out within the debt brake equation.

In extraordinary circumstances, for example, severe recessions or natural disasters, a debt-financed increase in the expenditure ceiling is possible. Apart from legal restrictions, extraordinary expenditures must be accepted as such by a qualified majority in both houses of parliament (Federal Assembly) and therefore require a larger consensus than ordinary expenditure items. Such expenditures are debited to a special "amortization account" (not to be confused with the compensation account).

The implementation of the debt brake led to several unexpected side-effects that were dealt by introducing new accounts and improving the calculations of revenue forecasts.

REFORMS AND CHALLENGES

Amortization Account: Extraordinary Budget Receipts and Expenditures

Since 2010, the extraordinary budget is also subject to the debt brake. The extended debt brake rule requires deficits in the extraordinary budget to be offset via the ordinary budget in the medium term. Since 2010, extraordinary receipts (without earmarking) and expenditures shown in the federal accounts will be credited or debited to an amortization account held outside the federal accounts. Shortfalls in the amortization account must normally be compensated within six financial years by means of surpluses in the ordinary budget.[11] In the event of foreseeable deficits in the amortization account (and provided that the compensation account does not have a negative balance that needs to be corrected first), the maximum amount of ordinary expenditure may be reduced as a precautionary measure.

Compensation Account: Analysis of Repeated Budget Underruns

The current asymmetric implementation of the debt brake led to an increasing balance of the compensation account and thus to the nominal decrease of Swiss federal debt (figure 4.2).[12] The compensation account is credited (debited) if the actually incurred expenditures are below (above) the maximum permissible expenditures. The expenditure ceiling is recalculated based on the closing accounts for the receipts achieved and the revised economic outlook. Therefore, the balance of the compensation account is not only due to forecasting errors for expenditures but are also influenced by forecasting errors regarding receipts and economic growth, as these lead the estimated expenditure ceiling relevant for the budgetary planning phase to be either too high or too low.

Since 2006, the revenue growth was underestimated and the expenditure growth overestimated. During the period 2004–2019, forecast errors for revenues explained 52% of the inflows into the compensation account (whereof 44% were due forecast errors for "Anticipatory Taxes"). Forecast errors for expenditures explained another 40% while the remaining 8% were due to requirements of the debt brake and estimation errors related to it. According to the expert report on the debt brake (Sturm et al. 2017), civil servants expected the positive bias in the estimation of "ordinary revenues" and especially the revenues from the "withholding tax" to disappear after 2012 when an improved forecasting model was implemented.[13]

Our contribution to the literature relates to the revenue side. We examine for the first time the evolution of revenue forecasts since the introduction of the debt brake. We also evaluate the claim that the positive bias in the forecasting error for revenues was reduced by the introduction of an improved forecasting model implemented by the federal administration in 2012. We provide a systematic evaluation of the differences between the estimates and the realized budget values for the expenditure side (in table 4.1) and for revenues (table 4.2). We present the difference between estimates and the realized values both in nominal Swiss francs and as share of the estimates for two different periods. The period 2004–2019 includes all budget years after the first application of the debt brake in 2003.[14] For the expenditure side, we show average differences for the 2007–2019 period because of the budget sub-item "own expenditures" that has only been available since 2007. In the context of the expert report, civil servants reported their concerns about the estimation of in particular this budget item.

Table 4.1   Difference between the Realized Federal Budget and the Budget Estimate for Ordinary Expenditures

	Million CHF		% of the budget estimate	
	Ø 2004– 2019	Ø 2007– 2019	Ø 2004– 2019	Ø 2007– 2019
Ordinary expenditures	**1,055**	**1,095**	**1.7%**	**1.7%**
	(621)	(664)	(1.0%)	(1.0%)
Transfers to third parties[15]	−194	−199	−2.5%	−2.6%
	(303)	(333)	(3.9%)	(4.2%)
Interest expenditures	292	306	11.4%	12.7%
	(337)	(324)	(13.3%)	(13.6%)
Other ordinary expenditures	956	988	1.9%	1.9%
	(373)	(399)	(0.7%)	(0.8%)
thereof own expenditures[16]		440		4.2%
		(197)		(1.8%)

Notes: Difference between the estimated and the realized expenditures in nominal Swiss francs and this difference relative to the estimated expenditures. A positive (negative) value in the table indicates an underrun (overrun) of the expenditure side of the budget. Standard deviations of the respective realized budget divergences in parentheses.
Source: Swiss Federal Finance Administration.

Table 4.2 Difference between the Realized Federal Budget and the Estimates for Ordinary Revenues

	Million CHF		% of the budget estimate	
	Ø 2004–2011	Ø 2012–2019	Ø 2004–2011	Ø 2012–2019
Ordinary revenues	**2,504**	**267**	**4.4%**	**0.3%**
	(1,934)	(1,469)	(3.3%)	(2.2%)
Withholding tax[1]	1,338	973	43.4%	17.0%
	(993)	(797)	(33.2%)	(13.2%)
Other revenues	1,166	−706	2.2%	−1.2%
	(1,234)	(1,212)	(2.3%)	(2.0%)

Swiss Federal Finance Administration and State Secretariat for Economic Affairs Switzerland.
Notes: Difference between the estimated and the realized revenues in nominal Swiss francs and this difference relative to the estimated revenues. A positive (negative) value in the table indicates a surplus (deficit) of the revenue side of the budget. Standard errors of the respective realized budget deviations in brackets.
Source: Swiss Federal Finance Administration.
[1]Withholding tax (Verrechnungssteuer) refers to the anticipatory tax on the payment of interest and dividends.

Regarding the forecast errors related to expenditures, table 4.1 shows that expenditures incurred during the financial year are consistently lower than those approved by the parliament in the budgetary process. Although some budget items were increased during the financial year, the unused budget lines are more significant. The table shows that the expenditures for interest payments were significantly overestimated for both periods. Since the introduction of the debt brake, the federal level has on average spent about CHF 1 billion less than budgeted. This is about 0.15% of GDP. The largest part of this can be related to ordinary expenditures that are not related to interest expenditure or direct transfers to third parties. Relative to the size of the expenditures, the budget errors regarding interest expenditures have been on average more than 10%. With over 4% of the size of these expenditures, the second largest errors were made for expenditures that are directly related to the administration itself, like personnel costs and other operating expenses. These findings are very similar to what was reported by Sturm et al. (2017).

Table 4.2 shows for the first time the differences between estimated revenues and actual revenues. The average budget error has decreased significantly when comparing the first half of our sample with the second half in which a new forecasting model was used. While up to 2011 there was an average excess of CHF 2.5 billion in revenue, since 2012 it has been only 10% of that. Our main interest, however, is the development of the forecast error of the withholding tax. In this area, an improved estimation method has been in effect since the 2012 budget year. In absolute terms, much of the improved overall revenue budget between these two periods is attributable to all other revenues. Here, a transition from an average underestimation to an overestimation took place. Thus, the overall improvement observed is only partly attributable to the improved forecasting method for withholding taxes.

Relative to the respective revenue stream, however, the reduction in the budget deviation is strongest for the withholding tax: it falls from 43% to 17%. This is partly due to the overall increase in withholding tax revenues. Looking at the absolute values of these estimated and realized revenues, they were still underestimated by almost CHF 1 billion in the second half of our sample (instead of an average of CHF 1.3 billion in the period 2004–2012). Our analysis thus suggests that the expectations of officials in the Federal Finance Administration that forecasting errors for withholding tax revenues would become more symmetrical have partially materialized. Overall, the average forecast error for revenues has remained positive in the budget years 2012–2019 but has decreased significantly compared to 2004–2011.

Compensation Account: Explanations for Repeated Budget Underruns

Regarding the explanations for budget underruns, the government-commissioned report (Sturm et al. 2017) notes four possible reasons: two technical explanations and two hypotheses about the behavior of the administration.

First, the realized costs for the fulfillment of government tasks or the quantitative demand for federal services could be lower than expected. Over the medium to long run, such forecast errors should balance out. The last decade was characterized by economic events with consequences for the federal public finances that are difficult to forecast. Since the financial crisis in 2008–2009, the forecasts for economic growth as well as interest and inflations rates deviated consistently from their realizations. Interest rates on government bonds were lower than expected and the compensation for inflation in the federal financial planning was set too high. Although the compensation for inflation was corrected downward multiple times, unplanned expenditure increases of 7% in real terms were realized from 2009 to 2016.

Second, expenditures might be postponed to the next fiscal year, for example, for technical reasons. The government may carry over budgeted and supplementary credits, delayed disbursements for planned investments, and certain types of other expenditures to the next fiscal year. However, the possibility to carry over the budget is associated with administrative costs and may therefore not be fully exploited, leaving surpluses in the running year.

Third, the precautionary principle may dominate in the public administration. Budgetary hurdles or social and cultural customs may create an asymmetry between the costs occurred for budget overruns and those for underruns. In principle, the credits defined in the budgeting process must not be exceeded. According to Swiss federal budgeting, supplementary credit can only be requested in case of an unforeseen event. Since future needs cannot be forecast accurately and budget overruns are more costly in terms of administrative expenses and reputation than budget underruns, over-budgeting tends to be assumed in the literature as a precautionary motive. Administrative units might implicitly reserve potential savings to avoid supplementary credits, for future additional expenditure, or for future budget cuts. These asymmetries in the budgeting phase can lead to a tendency for administrative units to adopt (over)cautious budgeting practices but also create the intended incentive to use funds economically. Budget residuals resulting from precautionary considerations may well be an expression of an efficient budgeting process, as forecasting expenditures tend to involve uncertainty about costs or demands. To reduce budget underruns related to the precautionary motive, the "costs" of the actors involved in the budget process for exceeding and falling short of the budget would have to be symmetrical.

Fourth, budget underruns can be due to asymmetries in the institutional rules that address the problem of the fiscal commons in the budgeting process and during budget execution. Control mechanisms for budget execution tend to be stricter for practical reasons. To diminish this asymmetry, the role of the finance department during the budgeting process could be further strengthened. Another possibility would be to sanction budget underruns, but this would diminish incentives for an economical budget management and might increase the "December fever" phenomenon of heightened spending at the end of the fiscal year.

Besides technical aspects, reputational consequences and real (administrative) costs on the side of the administration can explain why budgets are systematically underrun by the different federal ministries in Switzerland. Note that this is in sharp contrast to the usual political economy and public finance literature in which because of increasing reelection probabilities, partisan aspects, and common good problems one usually tries to explain why the public sector in many countries are either over-dimensioned, over-indebted, or both. Although it is conceivable that electoral success depends on being able to run a balanced budget or even surpluses, we are not aware of empirical evidence (outside of Switzerland) that prominently shows this to hold true in practice. When analyzing when and why countries break their fiscal rules, Reuter (2019) even concludes that "the probability of compliance with fiscal rules is around 10% lower in years in which a legislative election on the national level is held" and "compliance with fiscal rules seems to play a minor role for election outcomes."

The tradition of having a very stable coalition government in which all major parties have a more or less fixed number of seats might explain why traditional political budget cycles or partisan arguments are less relevant in

Switzerland. This also illustrates that it is probably not only the debt brake that explains the healthy financial situation of the Swiss federal government.

CONCLUDING REMARKS

At the beginning of the SARS-CoV-2 pandemic, Swiss federal public finances were very solid—more than a decade of budget surpluses led to a steady decline in public debt. According to many, the federal debt brake and its asymmetric implementation causing unbudgeted surpluses was key in achieving this. In the years before the pandemic, most discussion surrounding the debt brake involved the budget underruns. This was seen as a potential threat to the reputation of the debt brake and thus ultimately to its support among the electorate.

The resulting low level of debt enabled the federal government to in turn respond quickly and generously to the pandemic and related non-pharmaceutical measures last year without immediately having to worry about future budgetary consequences. As already argued by Sturm et al. (2017), booms and busts are everything but symmetric—having mechanisms in place that generate fiscal space during normal and goods times can turn out to be helpful during clear crisis periods. The pandemic and all its consequences have probably led to an accumulation of the total budget deficit for 2020 to CHF 16 billion or 2.3% of GDP (estimate of March 25, 2021)—of which CHF 15 billion is accounted for by the federal government.

During autumn 2020 and despite the ensuing second wave of COVID-19 infections, the (conservative) Finance Minister Ueli Maurer and part of the economic elite clearly argued that Switzerland could not afford and should not provide similar financial support to the economy as during the first wave in spring 2020. The importance of healthy federal finances is also exemplified by the early start of the discussion about how to respect the debt brake during and after the pandemic.

Nevertheless, the size of the second wave in autumn 2020, the stronger role parliament played at this point in time, and the technical delays in the reaction of tax revenues will lead to substantial debt increases also in 2021. After an estimated increase of CHF 15 billion in 2020, federal debt is forecasted to rise by another CHF 17 billion this year, reaching a level of almost 17% of GDP.[15] The federal debt increase in both years is largely due to extraordinary expenditures and the debt brake law provides for a period of six years for the reduction of this nominal debt. It is hardly realistic that such a reduction that would amount to more than 4% of GDP will materialize until 2027. In accordance with the debt brake, Parliament can, however, decide on an extension of this repayment period. At the time of writing in April 2021 this appears the most likely outcome also because prominent public finance experts in the Swiss-German part of the country as well as important voices within the Federal Department of Finance argue in favor of a reduction of expenditures relative to revenues over a substantially longer period than the technically envisaged six-year period.

Given that the absolute level of federal debt is likely to remain even at the new 2021 peak slightly below the level at the time of the introduction of the debt brake, and quite a few economists argue that the constitution can be interpreted in such a way that maintaining this initial level would be in line with it, there are also voices that argue that the 2020–2021 Corona-induced debt increase should not trigger any austerity measures. Given that the interest rates the Swiss government pays on newly issued debt of basically all maturities has remained negative throughout 2020 makes such a strategy appear relatively cost effective.

To the extent that the COVID-19-related additional debt will be repaid, this will most likely be done through both cuts and lower than planned increases in federal public expenditures. Temporary tax increases, which would require a constitutional amendment subject to a (voluntary) popular referendum, are hardly discussed. This is even though from an international perspective many tax rates, such as VAT and corporate tax rates, are still to be considered low.

Regarding longer-term developments associated with the Swiss debt brake, we believe that proposals to modify the federal debt brake, for example, to a symmetrical management of deficits and surpluses, or other proposals to accumulate debt or increase taxes will most likely not find a majority in the federal executive, parliament, or also the electorate. This is also because there is almost unanimous agreement that, without structural legislative revisions, the federal level will have to expect a sharp increase in expenditures in the coming decades due to past commitments associated with a high level of implicit debt (FFA 2016).

The Swiss setting with direct democracy and strong federalism is unique but other institutional designs with an independent enforcement authority could work equally well. The introduction of debt brakes via popular referendum is constitutionally possible in many jurisdictions. Courts or other government-independent regulatory authorities can also be mandated to monitor and, if necessary, enforce fiscal rules.

NOTES

1. Parts of this chapter draw on Sturm et al. (2017).
2. An important cause for the rapidly growing debt was the economic stagnation phase (1991–1996) and the subsequent costs of the spin-off and financing of pension

funds and federal enterprises (1998–2003). However, deficits were to a considerable degree structural.

3. The yearly average value of the USD in 2019 was about CHF 1. Over time, the CHF tends to nominally appreciate against all other major currencies in the world.

4. In contrast to many cantons, however, the federal government still has no positive equity capital.

5. Detailed descriptions can be found on the website of the Conference of the Cantonal Finance Ministers https://www.fdk-cdf.ch/-/media/FDK_CDF/Dokumente /Themen/Finanzpolitik/Haushaltsregeln/181129_HH_Regeln_18_UPDATE.pdf?la= de-CH (last accessed April 2, 2021).

6. The first debt brake in Switzerland was adopted in the Canton of St. Gallen in 1929. By now, all 26 cantons have a fiscal rule. Numerous studies have provided evidence that cantonal budget rules are associated with lower deficits. Recently, Burret and Feld (2018) analyze the coverage of fiscal rules while Chatagny (2015) analyzes the incentive effects of fiscal rules for finance ministers' revenue projections.

7. Cantons have far reaching autonomy with respect to personal and corporate income taxes and the exclusive competence for property and inheritance taxes. Considering the (rather loose) restrictions of the Federal Constitution, they are free to set their own tax schedules. Municipalities also have their own revenues and can set their own tax schedules within the cantonal rules. While vertical and horizontal redistribution within and between cantons takes place, its extent is limited and guided by clear rules.

8. The following article was inserted into the Federal Constitution by the referendum of May 11, 1958, "Art. 42a. The deficit in the balance sheet of the Confederation shall be paid off. In doing so, the situation of the economy must be taken into account" (translation by the authors).

9. BBI 2000 4653-4686.

10. However, if the debt level of the social security layer of the Swiss government increases above a defined threshold, social security contribution rates are automatically raised. To, for instance, prevent such an automatic increase as a consequence of the Corona crisis, the federal government injected extraordinary funds into the social security system in 2020. Apparently, it is easier to handle the resulting deficit within the federal debt brake than within the social security system.

11. In special cases, the Federal Assembly may extend this six-year limit.

12. Note that Federal Finance Administration reports that "[t]he compensation account was set to zero in 2006 (reduction path), reduced by 1 billion in 2010 (introduction of the supplementary rule), and reduced by around 4.4 billion and 1.9 billion in 2016 and 2018, respectively, due to accounting changes" (translation by the authors from Table Notes).

13. The FFA (2019) investigates only the evolution of budget underruns on the expenditure side up until 2018.

14. In 2003, the compensation account was not credited with any of the surpluses, that is, we assume that the implementation of the debt brake was not fully realized in this first year.

15. Together with some smaller increases at the cantonal and municipal level, this will increase general public debt from 26% of GDP in 2019 to almost 32% in 2021.

REFERENCES

Burret, Heiko T.; Feld, Lars P. (2018). (Un-)intended effects of fiscal rules, *European Journal of Political Economy* 52, 166–191, https://doi.org/10.1016/j.ejpoleco.20 17.06.002

Chatagny, Florian (2015). Incentive effects of fiscal rules on the finance minister's behavior: Evidence from revenue projections in Swiss Cantons, *European Journal of Political Economy* 39, 184–200, https://doi.org/10.1016/j.ejpoleco.2015.04.012

FFA (2016). Langfristperspektiven der öffentlichen Finanzen in der Schweiz 2016 (no English version available), Federal Finance Administration (FFA), Bern. https:/ /www.efv.admin.ch/efv/de/home/themen/publikationen/oeko_grundlagenarb.html

FFA (2019). Bericht zur Entwicklung der Budgetunterschreitungen (no English version available), Federal Finance Administration (FFA), Bern. https://www.efv .admin.ch/efv/de/home/themen/finanzpolitik_grundlagen/schuldenbremse.html

Reuter, Wolf Heinrich (2019). When and why do countries break their national fiscal rules?, *European Journal of Political Economy* 57, 125–141, https://doi.org/10.1 016/j.ejpoleco.2018.08.010

Sturm, Jan-Egbert; Abrahamsen, Yngve; Abberger, Klaus; Anderes, Marc; Bamert, Justus; Eckert, Florian; Funk, Anne Kathrin; Graff, Michael; Hälg, Florian; Kronenberg, Philipp; Mikosch, Heiner; Mühlebach, Nina; Neuwirth, Stefan; Rathke, Alexander; Sarferaz, Samad; Seiler, Pascal; Siegenthaler, Michael; Streicher, Sina (2020). Konjunkturanalyse: Prognose 2021 / 2022. Fragile Konjunkturerholung, *KOF Analyse* 2020(4), 1–78, https://doi.org/10.3929/ethz-b-000447330

Sturm, Jan-Egbert; Brülhart, Marius; Funk, Patricia; Schaltegger, Christoph A.; Siegenthaler, Peter (2017). Gutachten zur Ergänzung der Schuldenbremse, Expertengruppe Schuldenbremse (no English version available). https://www.res earch-collection.ethz.ch/handle/20.500.11850/235655

Chapter 5

The German "Debt Brake"

Success Factors and Challenges[1]

Lars P. Feld and Wolf H. Reuter

INTRODUCTION

Germany's debt-to-GDP ratio for the general government was at 59.6% in 2019 before the coronavirus pandemic struck (figure 5.1). To tackle the crisis, the government set up massive fiscal support and stimulus packages, including large-scale credit and guarantee programs and pledged to make additional contributions at the European level. The debt ratio is forecast to increase to 70.6% of GDP at the end of 2021. The low initial debt ratio together with the well-established existing fiscal institutions in Germany ensured that, despite the size of the crisis measures, the government has not had to worry about insufficient demand for its government bonds or strong interest rate increases. Rather, there are worries that other countries, especially in the Euro-Area, are more dependent on monetary policy and the availability of external public financing, for example, through the European Stability Mechanism (ESM) or the Recovery and Resilience Facility, to keep interest rates on sovereign bonds low.

Only 10 years ago, after the global financial crisis (GFC) in 2010, the debt-to-GDP ratio in Germany was at 82.3%, the highest ratio since World War II (figure 5.1). Since then, the debt-to-GDP ratio decreased on all levels of government until the coronavirus pandemic hit. In contrast to this development in Germany, during the same time period between 2010 and 2019 debt ratios of the largest economies worldwide increased (figure 5.2). Several factors contributed to the decline in the debt ratio in Germany. The respective years were characterized by steady positive economic growth rates, a booming labor market with an increasing employment ratio, and declining interest expenditures of the government. Furthermore, the old fiscal rule in the German constitution was replaced by the "debt brake" at the beginning of

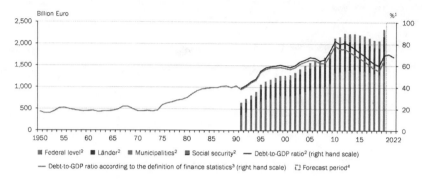

1 - In relation to GDP. 2 - As defined in the Maastricht Treaty. 3 - Deviation from figures according to the definition of national accounts due to methodological differences (Heil and Leidel, 2018). Comparability over time prior to 2010 is limited due to methodological changes. From 1952 including Berlin (West) and from 1960 including Saarland. Since 1991 all-German results. Since 2009 including social security. Data as of 2020: Provisional debt of the general public budget. 4 - Forecast by the German Council of Economic Experts.

Figure 5.1   Public Debt in Germany. Deutsche Bundesbank, Federal Statistical Office, own calculations.

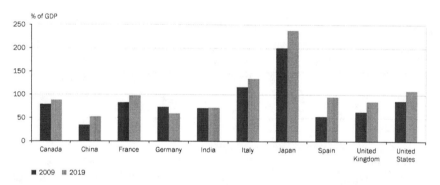

Figure 5.2   General Government Gross Debt in Largest Economies Worldwide. IMF.

this time period in 2009, a fiscal rule which constrains the structural balances of the federal government and the states (the Länder).

In general, fiscal rules are introduced to counteract the deficit bias of governments and politicians. The deficit bias is well documented in the literature and shown empirically (Alesina and Passalaqua, 2016). It causes public deficits to be higher than optimal. This is reflected, for example, in debt ratios which increase during times of economic crisis, but are not reduced again in following years of economic upturn. Politico-economic theories contribute to explaining the long-term trends in public debt ratios worldwide, but also the heterogeneous increases across countries (Feld and Reuter, 2017). A stream of literature shows that fiscal rules actually work in confining the deficit bias, as they are associated with lower or limited fiscal deficits and debt ratios (Burret and Feld, 2014, 2018a, b; Heinemann et al. 2018; Badinger and Reuter, 2017), as well as lower interest rates on government bonds (Heinemann et al., 2014; Feld et al., 2017).

Before Germany introduced the "debt brake," it already had a constitutional fiscal rule constraining the budget balance since 1949. However, the public debt-to-GDP ratio of the general government increased from 17% in 1950 to 61% in 2008. This chapter begins with a brief overview of the history of fiscal rules in Germany. This is followed by a discussion of the features of the "debt brake", and comparison of this rule with previous rules. The "debt brake" is only in force for a few years, in which a transition period followed the introduction, and it has not worked through a full business cycle yet. Thus, it is too early for an econometric assessment of the effects of the "debt brake". However, this chapter highlights some of the factors which, given the experience of the most recent years, might have contributed to a role of the "debt brake" in reducing the debt-to-GDP ratio.

Although Germany seems to be in a strong fiscal position in 2021, maintaining it will be very challenging for its government in coming years. Especially the rapid demographic change in Germany will create a large burden on social security systems and public finances. The chapter concludes with a discussion of the challenges for the "debt brake", which became visible during its first years, and need to be taken seriously. Addressing those could contribute to the sustainability of Germany's public finances and long-term prosperity.

SHORT HISTORY OF FISCAL RULES IN GERMANY

Fiscal rules could already be found in the constitution of the German Empire from 1871 and the Weimar Republic from 1919. Both rules linked the amount of public debt issuance, among others, to the presence of extraordinary necessities. In 1949 a balanced budget rule was introduced in the German constitution. Debt issuance was only allowed for exceptional needs and special purposes. The latter was implemented under customary law as profitable expenditures in a commercial sense, that is, that they finance themselves through higher revenues of the government in the following years (Deutsche Bundesbank, 2007). Both exceptions for debt issuance of this rule were interpreted broadly, such that an effective restraint was not achieved (GCEE, 2007).

A Golden Rule replaced the balanced budget rule in the constitutional reform of 1969. The new rule took business cycle developments into account and was more specific in distinguishing between different types of expenditure, namely between investment and current expenditures. In regular times, net borrowing was allowed to the extent of gross public investment expenditures. However, additional borrowing was allowed to ward off a disturbance of the macroeconomic equilibrium. While there were other parts of the constitution, which suggested that borrowing would have needed to be lower than investment in good times (Deutsche Bundesbank, 2007), the rule had been applied primarily asymmetrically. Thus, higher borrowing was observed in unfavorable economic conditions, but no corresponding consolidation in benign times. This contributed to the positive trend of the debt-to-GDP ratio from 1969 (figure 5.1).

Several characteristics of the rule induced a wide scope for interpretation, uncertainty, and legal challenges, which impaired the effectiveness of the rule (GCEE, 2019). Especially, the interpretation of a disturbance of macroeconomic equilibrium and the classification of expenditures as investment expenditures were often challenged and part of public debates. Only in 1989 a decision of the German Federal Constitutional Court demanded a more systematic explanation of how additional public debt would specifically counteract a macroeconomic imbalance and demanded a more precise definition of investment expenditures in budgetary terms. Nevertheless, the two parts of the rule were subject to public disputes also in the following years. Another problem of the Golden Rule was that it set the maximum debt issuance by using the investment expenditures in the planning, but not in the execution phase. Furthermore, debt issuance was not limited in magnitude other than by investment expenditures. Also special funds and off-budget activities were not included and no sanctions or correction mechanisms were attached to the Golden Rule.

The Golden Rule was replaced by the current "debt brake" as part of Federalism Reform II in 2009. The introduction was gradual, as there was a transition period between 2011 and 2016 for the federal government and until 2020 for the Länder. The fiscal rules at the federal level have to be seen in context with the rules at the state and local levels on the one hand and European fiscal rules on the other hand. The previous Golden Rule was also enshrined in the constitution of the Länder, as is the "debt brake" now. While the state debt brakes are similar to the one at the federal level, the exact implementation in the state constitutions varies across the Länder. Elements that can differ across states are, for example, the method for cyclical adjustment or the design of the adjustment account.

The "debt brake" does not apply to the local level. Municipalities are allowed to issue debt to finance investment and to obtain short-term liquidity. However, there is a structural balanced budget rule in the intergovernmental Fiscal Compact at European level which sets a limit to the structural balance of general government. With a national rule in place for the federal and state governments, this creates a limit for aggregate municipal debt issuance. The rule in the Fiscal Compact is one of the more recent supplements to the set of fiscal rules at European level. The Stability and Growth Pact sets a debt and balanced budget rule for Germany already since 1997. The regulations were modified and additional rules were added in the Two-pack and Six-pack reforms in 2011 and 2013.

Although it is important for German fiscal policy in recent years, the notion of a nominally balanced budget, the "black zero," in non-adjusted headline deficit terms is not codified in a formal fiscal rule. It rather represents a self-imposed political commitment by the then governing parties. It is also mentioned for example in the coalitional agreement of the current German government and often confused with the constitutional debt brake in public debates. While the "black zero" can be a political tool to reign in additional expenditures and reduce debt more strongly in good times, it lacks the countercyclical features of the "debt brake" which takes economic conditions into account.

THE "DEBT BRAKE" IN DETAIL

Article 115 of the German constitution prescribes that a structurally balanced budget should be maintained in consideration of the economic cycle. More precisely, it defines the latter and states that the structural deficit of the central government is not allowed to exceed 0.35% of GDP. The debt brake also applies to the state level. However, for the "Länder" the budget needs to be balanced in structural terms, to comply with the debt brake. The finances of the local level are not constrained by the "debt brake," but the Fiscal Compact at the European level prescribes a maximum for the structural deficit of 0.5% of GDP for the general government. Given the limits set by the "debt brake" for the other levels of government, this leaves 0.15% of GDP for the aggregated local level. In contrast to previous rules, the "debt brake" also applies to newly created special funds, as long as they are legally not independent. Furthermore, financial transactions are excluded such that, for example, selling public assets does not contribute to compliance with the rule.

As the rule constrains the structural balance, it symmetrically takes the cyclical situation and temporary effects into account. The cyclical adjustment of the fiscal deficit is intended to ensure that automatic stabilizers can operate freely. It allows for larger deficits in economically bad times, when generally cyclical public revenues are lower and cyclical expenditures are higher, and lower deficits in good times. The methodology to calculate cyclically adjusted figures is closely related to the method of the European Commission. The cyclical adjustment ensures that there is enough fiscal leeway in downturns of normal economic cycles and that accumulated debt is reduced again in upswings.

However, for special circumstances outside the control of the government like severe economic crises or natural disasters, the "debt brake" is equipped with an escape clause. There have been several events which would count as such special events in the recent history of Germany: the reunification in 1990, the financial crisis in 2008/2009, and the coronavirus pandemic in 2020. The idea is that the "debt brake" increases fiscal space during normal economic cycles such that fiscal policy can forcefully counteract a severe economic shock, which sharply increases the debt ratio within a very short period of time. The existence of circumstances which warrant the activation of the escape clause needs to be decided by the German parliament with an absolute majority of its members. Together with the decision to activate the escape clause, the parliament also decides on the amount of additional debt issuance and a repayment plan.

Deviations arising between planning and execution of the budget are collected in an adjustment account. As soon as the cumulative deficit in the adjustment account reaches 1.5% of GDP, the deficit of the account has to be gradually reduced over time. This reduction has an annual cap and should only happen in cyclically benign times. However, the adjustment account does not work like a rainy day fund. While a deficit needs to be reduced, a surplus cannot be used in the budget. Surpluses only prolong the time until a deficit in the account needs to be reduced.

SUCCESS FACTORS

The "debt brake" has been in force only for a few years, which is why a solid empirical assessment of its effects is not feasible yet.[2] Moreover, until the coronavirus pandemic, those years have been characterized by economically benign conditions and a transition period of the "debt brake" in which different limits applied in the years after its introduction. There is a broad stream of literature showing that fiscal rules go hand in hand with lower public deficits and lower interest rates on government bonds across countries and time (Burret and Feld, 2014, 2018a, b; Heinemann et al., 2018; Badinger and Reuter, 2017). To identify causal effects, a correct construction of the counterfactual is key. When trying to evaluate the effects of the "debt brake" in Germany, it is thus not sufficient to analyze observed fiscal variables, but required to identify which other fiscal policies would have been implemented without the "debt brake" in place. A fiscal rule forces policymakers to choose between different policies, while without a rule more of them might have been implemented at the same time.

The main drivers of the reduction in debt-to-GDP in Germany since the GFC were steady positive growth rates, a steady increase in revenues due to higher employment rates, and a limited increase in expenditures. The growth of expenditures was always lower than the growth of revenues between 2010 and 2018 and both were close to the growth rate of GDP (figure 5.3).

It becomes apparent that the decline in the debt-to-GDP ratio was not driven by any major expenditure cuts or discretionary tax increases, especially as the steady increase in expenditures happened against the background of sharply decreasing interest expenditures during the same period (figure 5.3). Furthermore, although a strong increase in investment expenditures would have been warranted given the low public investment figures in Germany (GCEE, 2019), the increase in expenditure was driven mainly by a strong increase in social spending and only to a smaller extent of investment expenditures. Nevertheless, only such an amount of additional expenditure measures was implemented that growth of expenditures remained lower than growth of revenues. Also on the revenue side, the magnitude of revenue and tax measures was not as large as to push revenue growth below expenditure growth.

Especially during such a longer period of economically good times and steadily increasing revenues, it is fair to assume that politicians would have had further ideas as to which expenditure or tax measures could be implemented. It is impossible to evaluate why those were not taken, but observing the public and political discussions suggests that the "debt brake" played a crucial role. As an example, the coalition of CDU/CSU and FDP had agreed on large tax cuts even in their coalition agreement in 2009, but did not implement them during their term of office with reference to the limits set by the "debt brake" for the following years. Other examples can be found in descriptions of coalition negotiations of consecutive governments or discussions on possible stimulus packages in response to a looming recession in 2019.

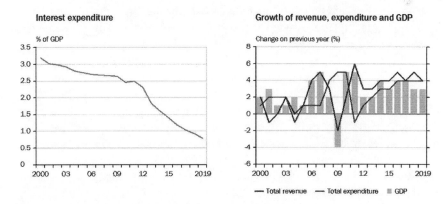

Figure 5.3   General Government Expenditure, Revenue, and GDP in Germany. Federal Statistical Office, own calculations.

However, identifying which measures would have been implemented without the "debt brake," is a tricky task. It is even possible that some measures have not been raised in the public debate due to a limit on public finances being in place, which complicates collecting measures that would have been implemented without the "debt brake."

Against the background of the findings in the literature that fiscal rules have a significant effect on public finances, it is worth discussing which factors might have contributed to a limiting effect of the "debt brake" since the GFC.

Constitutional Legal Basis and Fiscal Framework

The legal basis has been identified as an important design element of fiscal rules in various studies (Asatryan et al., 2017). Rules on a lower legal basis, for example, only in coalition agreements, are easier to abolish or change and thus represent less binding limits with smaller effects. Especially when ruling coalitions change, they might want to change the limits set by previous governments. A stronger legal basis, that is, rules enshrined in statutory law or the constitution, is associated with larger statistical effects (Nerlich and Reuter, 2013). In Germany the "debt brake" was enshrined in constitutional law at the federal level subject to a two-thirds majority, then by votes of the Christian Democratic (conservative) parties (CDU and CSU) and the Social Democratic Party (SPD) in the Bundestag and by states governed by a variety of coalitions in the Bundesrat. The Länder also changed their constitutions, which, for example, required the state of Hesse to hold a constitutional referendum on December 15, 2010, leading to a strong support of 70% of the electorate for the introduction of the debt brake.

Fiscal rules are especially important during benign economic times. When public surpluses and revenues are cyclically higher, interest groups and policymakers are tempted to argue for higher spending and thus a breach or abolishment of fiscal rules. With reference to important tax cuts or investment or social security needs, not a change in priorities but more debt issuance is often demanded. Germany is a prime example for such tendencies. The country had economically benign years between the GFC and the beginning of the coronavirus pandemic with a record high public revenues and a declining debt ratio. Especially in the years right up to the pandemic, a large coalition of politicians and academics argued in favor of abolishing the "debt brake" to allow for higher expenditures. The main argument was to increase public investment expenditures, which were low in Germany during the past 20 years, without wanting to slow the above-mentioned increase of other expenditure items. However, fiscal rules are especially put in place to prevent a circumvention of setting priorities especially in times with high public revenues.

They are introduced to build fiscal buffers during good times, which is only possible if they are in place during good times. Having a fiscal rule enshrined in the constitution helps to prevent an easy abolishment by the ruling parties, especially in economically favorable times.

Public Acceptance and Role in Political Debates

Another factor which restrains the abolishment of fiscal rules is strong public support. In a representative survey of the German population in 2014 two-thirds of 3,575 respondents had a positive view of the "debt brake" and only 15% a negative one (Berger et al., 2017). In a survey conducted in 2013 among 2,042 representatively chosen German citizens, 61% supported the debt brake and only 8% opposed it (Hayo and Neumeier, 2016). This is in line with the outcome of the constitutional referendum on the introduction of the debt brake in the state of Hesse mentioned above.[3] The opinion seems to be similar not only in the general public, but also among economists and financial market experts. In a survey among 120 economists in Germany in 2019, only 28% responded that the debt brake should not be retained for the federal government and the Länder (Blum et al., 2019). Among 198 financial market experts in Germany in 2019 only 12% agreed with the statement that the debt brake should be abolished (Heinemann, 2019).

Studies point out that transparency and public awareness of fiscal rules are crucial for their role in limiting public deficits. A high acceptance of fiscal rules by the public increases reputational and electoral costs of non-compliance for politicians. In contrast, formal sanctions are not as effective, as they lack credibility and are often not implemented or watered down by the governments (Eyraud et al., 2018). Empirically, sanctions associated with rules at the national level also do not seem to increase compliance with fiscal rules (Reuter, 2017). In Germany, the direct sanctions following non-compliance with the "debt brake" seem to be unclear to many politicians. A survey of 669 politicians in regional parliaments of the Länder shows that the uncertainty is high about the consequences of non-compliance (Blesse et al., 2016). Thus, this suggests that the stronger role in the enforcement of fiscal rules is associated with transparency and reputational or electoral costs of rule non-compliance.

Important elements to achieve transparency are the strength of the media reports about compliance with the rules as well as the importance of the fiscal rule for the general public and the political process. If the public does not know about compliance or non-compliance and associated facts, the non-compliance costs, which should enforce compliance with the rules, are lower. The "debt brake" plays an important role in the general media discussions of fiscal policy in Germany. Until 2017, the European Commission published the visibility of fiscal rules in the media in their respective countries in the EU fiscal rules database (European Commission, 2017). The German "debt rule" was categorized in the highest category, category 3 which was defined as "observance of the rule is closely monitored by the media; non-compliance is likely to trigger." For comparison, the average category across all rules and countries for the variable was 1.9.

The "debt brake" also seems to be firmly established in the political process. In a survey of 669 politicians in regional parliaments of the Länder, only 13.7% gave a negative value to the answer for the question "How desirable do you consider it for your state to comply with the provisions of the 'debt brake?'" (Blesse et al., 2016) A share of 45% of the respondents answered with the highest possible positive value. The "debt brake" (or Article 115 in the constitution) is also often cited in plenary protocols and print products of the German Bundestag (figure 5.4). While a spike of mentions were expected around the introduction of the "debt brake," the numbers remained at an elevated level until 2019.

The approval of the "debt brake" in Germany seems to be embedded in more general public support for low public deficits. For many years, the "black zero," that is, a nominally balanced budget, played a key role in German politics. It is not a legal fiscal rule, but a self-imposed political commitment which can be found, for example, in the coalition treaty of the CDU/CSU and SPD from 2017.

Taking the Cycle and Severe Crisis into Account

Worldwide there is a large number of fiscal rules which constrain unadjusted public deficit or expenditure figures. According to the fiscal rules database of the IMF, such rules were in force in 50 countries worldwide in 2015. With this kind of rules, fiscal policy and especially automatic

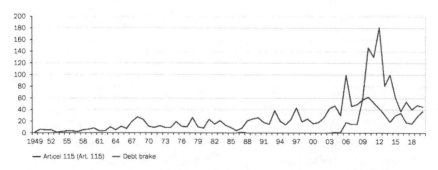

Figure 5.4   Citations in Plenary Protocols and Print Products of the German Bundestag. German Bundestag.

stabilizers can only stabilize the economy in downturns, if governments keep sufficient distance to the limit set by the rules in good economic times. Many of the fiscal rules are indeed introduced as upper limits which should only be reached in some years and not in all years. However, governments do not seem to interpret the limits in the intended way, but rather take them as targets (Reuter, 2015; Caselli and Wingender, 2018; Eyraud et al., 2018). Governments steer their fiscal policy toward those targets and due to the usage as target they comply with the upper limits only in a fraction of years. Fiscal rules in that way still have an effect on fiscal policy, but the limits do not work as intended.

As it seems politically very challenging to keep a distance from the upper limits set by the rules in good times, it becomes advantageous to introduce fiscal rules where the limits are adjusted with the economic cycle. Thereby the rules automatically create more fiscal space through a more restrictive limit in upturns and grants more fiscal leeway in downturns. The "debt brake" is an example for those types of rules that constrain the structural balance, which take cyclical fluctuations and one-off measures into account. In the years since the financial crisis, the structural balance was always equal to or lower than the nominal budget balance, reflecting the economically benign times. For most of the time both the budget balance and the structural balance were both positive, which was higher than the "debt brake" prescribed (structural balance of −0.35%).

The compliance with cyclically adjusted measures—in this case the structural balance—is easier to judge than the provisions of the previous Golden Rule cum disturbance of the macroeconomic equilibrium. The requirement to ward off a disturbance of the macroeconomic equilibrium was too vague and made judgments without clear rules or statistical basis necessary. Furthermore, well-defined escape clauses are an important feature, which provides for a necessary flexibility of fiscal rules. Fiscal space is created in normal times to be available in severe economic crises or with natural catastrophes. In those cases the fiscal rule should not constrain fiscal policy as usually, such that the government can use the built-up fiscal buffers to counteract the economic shock. However, as history with fiscal rules in Germany tells, those escape clauses need to be carefully defined. Otherwise they can be applied too often or not systematically in situations when they are most needed. The "debt brake" has a specific definition related to emergency situations outside the control of the government and the hurdle for its activation is quite high. It is not the Ministry of Finance or other parts of the government which activate the escape clause, but the parliament with an absolute majority of its members. Furthermore, the escape clause is not granted unconditionally, but the government has to present a precise plan as to how it will repay the additional debt issued. Both ensure that the escape clause is not activated lightly and that debt is reduced after the exceptional situation to create scope again for the next crisis.

CHALLENGES

Measurement and Transparency

The "debt brake" is a so-called "second-generation fiscal rule" as described, for example, by Eyraud et al. (2018). Those rules are much more flexible than the first generation and allow fiscal policy to react to cyclical fluctuations as well as severe crises. They allow for automatic stabilizers to operate freely and have clearly defined escape clauses. As with most of the second-generation rules they are an improvement as compared to the first generation; however, this improvement comes at the expense of transparency and with higher complexity and measurement problems.

Calculating the indicator which is constrained by the fiscal rule, that is, the structural balance, requires an estimate of the output gap as well as elasticities which are used to link the output gap and the budget balance. This calculation is associated with large errors. In the EU15, the mean absolute error for the output gap between 2005 and 2015 was larger than 1 percentage point of GDP for estimates within a specific year (in real time) and even above 2 percentage points in two-year ahead forecasts (Reuter, 2020). Moreover, errors do not only seem to be large but also to be biased, as the average error in real time is also close to 1 percentage point of GDP. Across different countries and time samples, studies found similar mean errors of the output gap (Eyraud and Wu, 2015; Kempkes, 2014; GCEE, 2019). The errors imply that given how the economy looked like ex post, for example, a few years after a specific year, the output gap in real time and even more so in forecasts showed a much worse cyclical position than it turned out to be. Translated to the structural balance it follows that the structural balance on average looked better in real time as compared to how the cyclical position turned out to be ex post. Thus, fiscal rules constraining structural balances in hindsight on average were too lax during those time periods. The general conclusions which hold on average, also apply to Germany and the "debt brake." If the ex-post estimates of the output gap were used instead of the real-time estimates during the initial years of the debt brake, that is, from 2011 to 2016, then the allowed maximum debt issuance would have been lower (GCEE, 2019).

Errors of this magnitude render it very difficult to use the structural balance in fiscal planning or decision-making. Various approaches exist that try to reduce the errors of real-time estimates (GCEE, 2019). For example, less revision-prone short-term (business cycle) indicators like surveys can be used to estimate the output gap (GCEE, 2017, 2018; Ademmer et al., 2019; Weiske, 2018). Another possibility would be to change the filtering methods used to identify cyclical fluctuations (Quast and Wolters, 2019), which are especially uncertain at the end of the sample period. Other ways might be to use model-based approaches or structural vector autoregressive models to complement or replace time series methods. Furthermore, the EU added a judgment component and tries to mitigate the implications of uncertainty (Buti et al., 2019). However, so far no comprehensive solution is available for this problem, especially as alternatives would need to cope with other difficulties. Implementing rules without cyclical adjustment would be a step backward in terms of procyclicality and transparency of the inclusion of the cyclical position. Relying on expenditure rules, which do not directly rely on output gap estimates, opens up potentially large errors especially when estimating the effect of discretionary revenue measures.

Quality of Public Finances

If fiscal rules have an effect on public finances, they might also have an effect on their composition and quality. The latter can be discussed in relation to various aspects of fiscal policy, but the most prominent discussion centers around the share of public investment in public expenditures (sometimes augmented by future related expenditures like education). In general, most fiscal rules—also the "debt brake"—do not constrain the amount or share of investment expenditure. Both the amount and the share can be chosen by the government according to its priorities. The rules only set a limit to the amount that can be financed by debt issuance and not by current revenues.

Nevertheless, fiscal rules might have an indirect influence on the amount of investment expenditures. First, investment expenditures often are easier and quicker to cut and sometimes their reduction is politically less costly than, for example, reducing the increase of public wages or social transfers. Thus, they would be reduced first if compliance with a fiscal rule needs to be achieved. However, this argument depends on political priorities of the voters. If they support higher investment and the transparency of fiscal policy is high, reducing investment becomes costlier for governments.

Second, investments often partially or mainly benefit future generations. If investment is not financed by debt, then the current generation needs to bear all costs but receives only parts of the benefits. Thus, if fiscal rules restrict debt financing, the amount of investment expenditures might be too low. This argument is only valid for net investment, as future generations only inherit additional assets such that depreciation of existing assets would need to be subtracted. Furthermore, it is often uncertain whether future generations would have made the same investment choices as the current generation. For example, the current generation might want to invest to support individual mobility such as new roads and the further development of existing technologies, while the future generation might want to restrict individual mobility to reduce carbon emissions and would want to invest in new breakthrough technologies. In addition, if debt issuance is not restricted, the current generation might choose higher debt levels to receive some of the short-term benefits and put less emphasis on the future side-effects.

In Germany total expenditures of the general government increased by 26% from 2010 to 2019. Investment expenditure (gross capital formation) increased by 44% in the same time period and their share in total expenditures increased from 4.9% to 5.5% (figure 5.5). This is the highest share since 1995, that is, the years right after reunification in the early 1990s. It seems that the introduction of the "debt brake" did not lead to decreasing investment expenditures, but to the contrary the government prioritized investment expenditures relative to other spending since the introduction of the "debt brake." In those years, even higher investment expenditures were rather pulled back by barriers such as a high level of capacity utilization in the construction industry and public administration or long planning and approval procedures.

Nevertheless, the question can be raised how fiscal rules can contribute to improving the quality of public finances. The main challenge is measuring investment expenditures and narrowly identifying those which actually lead to benefits for future generations, for example, through higher prosperity or higher revenues. The current statistical definition in the System of National Accounts focuses on physical capital only. Ideally there would be a cost-benefit analysis associated with each project on which the subsequent decision depends, as also within defined categories not every project leads to the same

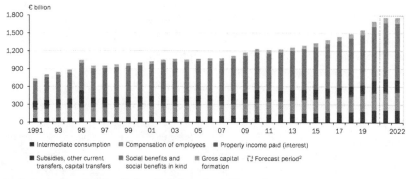

1 - According to national accounts definition.   2 - Forecast by the German Council of Economic Experts.

Figure 5.5 Government Net Lending/Net Borrowing in Germany. Federal Statistical Office, own calculations.

effects. While it is already challenging to identify investment expenditures, it is even trickier to calculate consistent net investment figures which would be necessary if some kind of special treatment of investment expenditures was to be operationalized.

If prioritization of expenditures can work and public opinion is the best tool to achieve compliance with fiscal rules, then pressure by the public on governments might also be the best way to achieve higher quality of public finances. Increasing transparency on the benefits of specific expenditures, like for investment projects or education, compared to other expenditures could contribute to strengthening this channel. Furthermore, cost-benefit analysis and systematically comparing expenditure increases for different items with each other could be put more firmly and central into the political decision-making process. Such analysis could be delegated, for example, to strengthen independent fiscal councils which would have the task to inform and engage the public via various channels.

Fixed Numerical Limit

The "debt brake" sets a fixed numerical limit for the structural balance of 0.35% of GDP at the federal level and 0% at the level of the Länder. This can problematic in two situations: when the debt ratio is already at relatively low levels and after a severe crisis for which the escape clause was activated.

With an average growth rate of nominal GDP of 3% the limit set by the "debt brake" of 0.35% would in the long run lead to a debt-to-GDP ratio of 12% (GCEE, 2019). This level of debt would arguably be too low for Germany and banning almost all public debt would economically not be reasonable. However, the speed of convergence to the long-run point can be quite slow, such that this situation might not materialize. Starting at an initial debt ratio of 60% it would take 20 years to get below 40% and 35 years to get below 30%. If the debt ratio nevertheless reaches very low levels, it might be beneficial to have a laxer limit as long as the debt ratio remains low. The Fiscal Compact at the European level has such a state-dependent limit, which increases from 0.5% to 1% of GDP if the debt ratio is substantially below 60% and there are no risks to the sustainability of public finances.

If only one fixed target is chosen for a fiscal rule, there is a tradeoff between the long-term convergence point and the speed of convergence. Within a very short time period, the debt ratio can jump upward by a lot due to a severe crisis for which the escape clause is activated. Thus, looking only at the long-run value might be misleading, as those crises happen relatively often compared to the long-run convergence. The low convergence points might never be reached as the ratio jumps upward every decade or so. Then the focus when setting the numerical limit is not on the long-run convergence anymore, but on the speed of reduction of debt ratios after those jumps and before the next one.

Public finances are often still stressed in the years following immediately after a crisis and the activation of an escape clause. Thus, going back to the fixed limit right after a crisis can be challenging. To smoothen this transition back to the fixed limit, the government has the possibility to create a kind of rainy day fund in the years before the escape clause is activated. The German government has already used reserves and kind of rainy day funds until recently and creates new reserves in the coronavirus crisis.

CONCLUSION

Germany introduced a new fiscal rule, the "debt brake," after the GFC and since then experienced a strong decline in its public debt-to-GDP ratio until the coronavirus pandemic struck. It was not a period of major expenditure cuts or discretionary tax increases, but of steady positive GDP growth rates, an unusual increase in employment, and decreasing interest expenditures. However, in this environment expenditure increases and revenue decreases remained limited, such that the government kept growth of expenditures below the growth of revenues. The "debt brake" most probably played a role in ensuring that.

The past ten years and the current crisis illustrate the intended effects of fiscal rules very well. Debt ratios are reduced during normal economic times, such that fiscal policy can forcefully counteract a severe crisis. Activating the escape clause of fiscal rules in those circumstances is not equal to abolishing the rules or even a sign that the rules do not work. Rather, the escape clauses are an essential part of the design of fiscal rules. It will be important for Germany and other economies to repeat the reduction in the debt-to-GDP ratio in order to be prepared for the next crisis. Much of the success of fiscal rules depends on the public and political acceptance of the fiscal rules and thus high political costs of not complying with them. Furthermore, the design and framework of the rules among others by restricting cyclically adjusted figures and a strong legal anchoring are important.

The challenges for fiscal policy, especially in Germany, are becoming more important due to rapid demographic change, globalization, and the transformation of the energy system. In such an environment, it is important to create the necessary fiscal buffers to react to sudden and unexpected crises, as exemplified by the coronavirus pandemic. This also means improving the design and framework of fiscal rules, for example, by making the cyclical adjustment less uncertain and susceptible to revisions, improving the transparency of fiscal policy and rule compliance, as well as discussing as to how fiscal rules can contribute to improving the quality of public finances. However, an abolishment of fiscal rules would hamper the ability of fiscal policy to cope with the long-term challenges and prepare for unexpected short-term challenges.

NOTES

1. The authors would like to thank Mustafa Yeter for valuable inputs and discussions, Marina Schwab for excellent research assistance and the staff of the German Council of Economic Experts for data and preparatory support. This paper reflects the personal views of the authors and not necessarily those of the German Council of Economic Experts.
2. Regarding the Swiss debt brake, which faces similar difficulties, there are studies using the synthetic control method to assess its effects. See Pfeil and Feld (2018) and Salvi et al. (2020).
3. This support is similar to that of the Swiss debt brake. In a constitutional referendum on December 2, 2011, 84.7 percent of the Swiss electorate voted for the introduction of the federal debt brake. See Feld and Kirchgässner (2008).

REFERENCES

Ademmer, M., J. Boysen-Hogrefe, K. Carstensen, P. Hauber, N. Jannsen, S. Kooths, T. Rossian and U. Stolzenburg (2019), *Schätzung von Produktionspotenzial und -lücke: Eine Analyse des EU-Verfahrens und mögliche Verbesserungen*, Kieler Beiträge zur Wirtschaftspolitik Nr. 19, Institut für Weltwirtschaft, Kiel.
Alesina, A. and A. Passalacqua (2016), The Political Economy of Government Debt, in J.B. Taylor and H. Uhlig (eds.), *Handbook of Macroeconomics*, Elsevier, Saint Louis, 2599–2651.
Asatryan, Z., C. Castellón and T. Stratmann (2018), Balanced Budget Rules and Fiscal Outcomes: Evidence from Historical Constitutions, *Journal of Public Economics*, 167, 105–119.
Badinger, H. and W.H. Reuter (2017), The Case for Fiscal Rules, *Economic Modelling*, 60, 334–343.
Berger, M., S. Blesse, F. Heinemann and E. Janeba (2017), Föderalismuspräferenzen in der deutschen Bevölkerung, *Perspektiven der Wirtschaftspolitik*, 18, 145–158.
Blesse, S., F. Heinemann and E. Janeba (2016), *Einhaltung der Schuldenbremse und Bewertung von Länderfusionen—Ergebnisse einer Umfrage in allen 16 Landesparlamenten*, ZEW Policy Brief, No. 6, Mannheim.
Blum, J., K. Gründler, R. de Britto Schiller and N. Potrafke (2019), Die Schuldenbremse in der Diskussion, *ifo Schnelldienst*, 72 (22), 27–33.
Burret, H.T. and L.P. Feld (2014), A Note on Budget Rules and Fiscal Federalism, *CESifo DICE Report*, 12 (1), 3–11.

Burret, H.T. and L.P. Feld (2018a), Vertical Effects of Fiscal Rules: The Swiss Experience, *International Tax Public Finance*, 25, 673–721.

Burret, H.T. and L.P. Feld (2018b), (Un-)Intended Effects of Fiscal Rules, *European Journal of Political Economy*, 52, 166–191.

Buti, M., N. Carnot, A. Hristov, K.M. Morrow, W. Roeger and V. Vandermeulen (2019), *Potential Output and EU Fiscal Surveillance*, VoxEU on September 23, 2019, https://voxeu.org/article/potential-output-and-eu-fiscal-surveillance.

Caselli, F.G. and P. Wingender (2018), *Bunching at 3 Percent: The Maastricht Fiscal Criterion and Government Deficits*, IMF Working Papers 18/182, Washington, DC.

Deutsche Bundesbank (2007), *Zur Reform des deutschen Haushaltsrechts*, Monatsbericht, October 2007, Frankfurt a.M.

European Commission (2017), *Fiscal Rules Database*, Archived Version (Old Methodology), Brussels.

Eyraud, L. and T. Wu (2015), *Playing by the Rules: Reforming Fiscal Governance in Europe*, IMF Working Paper WP/15/67, Washington, DC.

Eyraud, L., X. Debrun, A. Hodge, V. Lledó and C. Pattillo (2018), *Second-Generation Fiscal Rules: Balancing Simplicity, Flexibility, and Enforceability*, IMF Staff Discussion Notes 18/04, Washington, DC.

Feld, L.P. and G. Kirchgässner (2008), On the Effectiveness of Debt Brakes: The Swiss Experience, in R. Neck and J.-E. Sturm (eds.), *Sustainability of Public Debt*, MIT Press, Cambridge/London, 223–255.

Feld, L.P. and W.H. Reuter (2017), Wirken Fiskalregeln? Eine Übersicht über neuere empirische Befunde, *Wirtschaftspolitische Blätter*, 64 (2), 179–191.

Feld, L.P.A. Kalb, M.-D. Moessinger and S. Osterloh (2017), Sovereign Bond Market Reactions to Fiscal Rules and No-Bailout Clauses: The Swiss Experience, *Journal of International Money and Finance*, 70, 319–343.

GCEE—German Council of Economic Experts (2007), *Staatsverschuldung wirksam begrenzen*, Occasional Reports, Federal Statistical Office, Wiesbaden.

GCEE—German Council of Economic Experts (2017), *Capacity Overutilisation in the German Economy Continues to Rise*, Chapter 3 in Annual Report "Towards a Forward-Looking Economic Policy", Federal Statistical Office, Wiesbaden.

GCEE—German Council of Economic Experts (2018), *International Economy: Slower Pace of Expansion, High Risks*, Chapter 2 in Annual Report "Setting the Right Course for Economic Policy", Federal Statistical Office, Wiesbaden.

GCEE—German Council of Economic Experts (2019), *The Debt Brake: Sustainable, Stabilising, Flexible*, Chapter 5 in Annual Report "Dealing with Structural Change", Federal Statistical Office, Wiesbaden.

Hayo, B. and F. Neumeier (2016), The Debt Brake in the Eyes of the German Population, *International Economics and Economic Policy*, 13 (1), 139–159.

Heil, N. and M. Leidel (2018), *Der Finanzierungssaldo des Staates in den Finanzstatistiken und den Volkswirtschaftlichen Gesamtrechnungen*, Statistisches Bundesamt, WISTA No. 6/2018, Wiesbaden.

Heinemann, F. (2019), *Schuldenbremse als Investitionshindernis?*, ZEW-Kurzexpertise 19-07, Mannheim.

Heinemann, F., S. Osterloh and A. Kalb (2014), Sovereign Risk Premia: The Link between Fiscal Rules and Stability Culture, *Journal of International Money and Finance*, 41, 110–127.

Heinemann, F., M.-D. Moessinger and M. Yeter (2018), Do Fiscal Rules Constrain Fiscal Policy? A Metaregression-Analysis, *European Journal of Political Economy*, 51, 69–92.

Kempkes, G. (2014), *Cyclical Adjustment in Fiscal Rules: Some Evidence on Real-Time Bias for EU-15 Countries*, FinanzArchiv N.F—Public Finance Analysis, 70, 278–315.

Nerlich, C. and W.H. Reuter (2013), *The Design of National Fiscal Frameworks and Their Budgetary Impact*, ECB Working Paper Series, No. 1588, Frankfurt a.M.

Pfeil, C.F. and L.P. Feld (2018), Does *the Swiss Debt Brake Induce Sound Federal Finances? A Synthetic Control Analysis*, Freiburg Discussion Papers on Constitutional Economics No. 18/08, Walter Eucken Institut, Freiburg.

Quast, J. and M.H. Wolters (2019), *Reliable Real-Time Output Gap Estimates Based on a Modified Hamilton Filter*, IMFS Working Paper 133, Institute for Monetary and Financial Stability, Frankfurt a.M.

Reuter, W.H. (2015), National Numerical Fiscal Rules: Not Complied With, But Still Effective?, *European Journal of Political Economy*, 39, 67–81.

Reuter, W.H. (2017), When and Why Do Countries Break Their National Fiscal Rules?, *European Journal of Political Economy*, 57, 125–141.

Reuter, W.H. (2020), *Benefits and Drawbacks of an "Expenditure Rule", As Well As of a "Golden Rule", in the EU Fiscal Framework*, Study requested by the ECON Committee, European Parliament, Brussels.

Salvi, M., C.A. Schaltegger and L. Schmid (2020), Fiscal Rules Cause Lower Public Debt: Evidence from Switzerland's Federal Debt Containment Rule, *Kyklos*, 73, 605–632.

Weiske, S. (2018), *Indicator-Based Estimates of the Output Gap in the Euro Area*, Working Paper, No. 12/2018, German Council of Economic Experts, Wiesbaden.

Part III

RULES-BASED FISCAL AND MONETARY POLICY IN EMERGING NATIONS

Chapter 6

A Money Doctor's Reflections on Currency Reforms and Hard Budget Constraints[1]

Steve H. Hanke

A STROLL DOWN MEMORY LANE

In this chapter, I take a stroll down memory lane. The sights and sounds reveal important lessons, as well as a few surprises, that I have learned about the connections between currency reforms and hard budget constraints in emerging market countries. These lessons were derived from my experiences in the operating theater, where I have performed as a money doctor. The patients that I have attended to have been afflicted with a wide variety of economic and financial maladies. These have included balance-of-payments, banking, currency, debt, and hyperinflation crises. In all of them, these crises erupted because monetary authorities engaged in discretionary monetary policies with reckless abandon. These policies failed to impose hard budget constraints on fiscal authorities. Without such constraints, the fiscal authorities were left to operate with reckless abandon, too. To cure the patients, my prescription has been the imposition of a hard budget constraint via the removal of the possibility for a monetary authority to engage in discretionary monetary activities. This has been accomplished by putting monetary authorities in a straitjacket, namely a fixed exchange rate regime—either a currency board system or "dollarized" system.

My stroll begins in Hong Kong, where the authorities had allowed the Hong Kong dollar to float in November 1974. The floating Hong Kong dollar became wildly volatile and steadily lost value against the U.S. dollar. The volatility reached epic proportions in late September 1983, after the fourth round of Sino-British talks on Hong Kong's future. It was then that the financial markets and the Hong Kong dollar went into tailspins.

At the end of July 1983, the Hong Kong dollar was trading at HK $7.31 to US $1. By Black Saturday, September 24, it had depreciated to HK $9.55 to US $1, with dealer spreads reported as large as 10,000 basis points. Hong Kong was in a state of panic. People were hoarding toilet paper, rice, and cooking oil. The chaos ended abruptly on October 15, when Hong Kong reinstated its currency board.

I learned the details of Hong Kong's currency crisis and the reintroduction of its currency board from my colleague, close friend, and collaborator Sir Alan Walters, who was operating as Prime Minister Margaret Thatcher's economic guru at the time. Sir Alan conveyed the details to me in real time. The dramatis personae included Sir Alan, Mrs. Thatcher, Milton Friedman, and John Greenwood, the architect of the new currency board (Greenwood 2007). At that time, Hong Kong was still a British Colony, hence Mrs. Thatcher's involvement.

Interestingly, Friedman recounts the importance of the Hong Kong currency crisis of 1983, the installation of the currency board, and the Greenwood-Walters-Friedman involvement in his memoirs *Two Lucky People* (Friedman and Friedman 1998, 326):

> In 1983, when there was an exchange crisis in Hong Kong, John [Greenwood] was the architect of the monetary reform that led to the Hong Kong dollar being unified with the U.S. dollar. He was able to play the crucial role he did because he had analyzed the Hong Kong monetary system in a series of articles in the *Asian Monetary Monitor*, pointed out its defects, and sketched possible reforms. During the course of the detailed negotiations that led to the final reform, John was on the phone almost nightly conferring with Alan Walters, then in London as an adviser to Margaret Thatcher, and with me in San Francisco, getting our comments and suggestions on the details of the proposed reform. After he had succeeded in getting his reform adopted—which incidentally has been a great success and achieved the results he had intended—he had three small silver ashtrays made recording the event as mementos for the three of us.

I recount the Hong Kong currency crisis of 1983 because it was a turning point in the direction of my primary interests and scholarship—a direction that eventually led to many assignments as a money doctor (Hanke 2016). The house calls were numerous and scattered across the globe. Argentina was the first call in 1989. Then came Yugoslavia (1990), Albania (1991), Russia (1991), Estonia (1992), Lithuania (1994), Kazakhstan (1994), Jamaica (1995), Venezuela (1995), Bulgaria (1997), Bosnia-Herzegovina (1997), Indonesia (1998), Montenegro (1999), and Ecuador (2001). Some of the assignments, like Indonesia's, were "big," and some were "small." Some were "long"—lasting the better part of a decade, like Argentina's—while others were "short."

What lessons did I learn from observing Hong Kong's currency crisis and its successful currency board cure? First, if you wish to be a successful money doctor, you must support your prescriptions with research and publishable scholarship, as Greenwood had done. That is why Sir Alan and I began to write about Hong Kong immediately. Some of our findings are contained in the entry "currency boards" in the *The New Palgrave Dictionary of Money and Finance* (Walters and Hanke 1992). Sir Alan and I also wrote many "Point of View" columns in *Forbes* magazine on currency crises and currency boards. My prescriptions have always been preceded with books, monographs, and articles in which the specific ailments of the patients were diagnosed. Many of these were co-authored with my longtime collaborator Kurt Schuler (Strezewski 2020).

The second lesson I learned from studying the Hong Kong crisis is that currency boards are a free-market solution for currency crises. With currency boards, discretionary monetary policies are not possible. The quantity of domestic money in circulation is solely a function of market forces, namely the demand for the local currency issued by a currency board.

The third lesson learned was that effective, high-quality prescriptions are best produced and administered by yourself or in close collaboration with like-minded, trusted colleagues. Indeed, it is usually a small number of people who make things happen.

Lastly, and perhaps most importantly, I observed that, with the reintroduction of a currency board in Hong Kong, the currency crisis was snuffed out and stability was established immediately. Subsequent research has shown that this was not an anomaly. Indeed, currency boards have a perfect record of establishing and maintaining stability (Hanke et al. 1993). And, when it comes to monetary systems, there is nothing more important than stability. As the former German minister of finance Karl Schiller put it: "stability might not be everything, but without stability, everything is nothing" (Marsh 1992, 30).

TYPES OF EXCHANGE RATE REGIMES

So, that's how I started my journey as a money doctor, my initial lessons, and the patients I attended to. But, when considering the types of exchange rate regimes to prescribe, what types are available and what are their characteristics? There are three distinct types of exchange rate regimes: floating, fixed, and pegged—each with different characteristics and different results. These are shown in table 6.1.

Table 6.1 Hanke's Foreign-Exchange Trichotomy

Type of Regime	Exchange Rate Policy	Monetary Policy	Source of Monetary Base	Conflicts Between Exchange Rate and Monetary Policy	Balance-of-Payments Crisis	Exchange Controls
Floating	No	Yes	Domestic	No	No	No
Fixed	Yes	No	Foreign	No	No	No
Pegged	Yes	Yes	Domestic and Foreign	Yes	Yes	Probably

Source: Steve H. Hanke, professor of applied economics at Johns Hopkins University.

Strictly fixed and floating rates are regimes in which the monetary authority is aiming at only one target at a time. Although floating and fixed rates appear dissimilar, they are members of the same free-market family. Both operate without exchange controls and are free-market mechanisms for balance-of-payments adjustments. With a floating rate, a central bank sets a monetary policy but has no exchange rate policy—the exchange rate is on autopilot. As a result, the monetary base is determined domestically by a central bank. With a fixed rate, there are two possibilities: either a currency board sets the exchange rate but has no monetary policy—the money supply is on autopilot—or a country is dollarized and uses a foreign currency as its own. Consequently, under a fixed rate regime, a country's monetary base is determined by the balance of payments, moving in a one-to-one correspondence with changes in its foreign reserves. With both of these free-market exchange rate mechanisms, there cannot be conflicts between monetary and exchange rate policies, and balance-of-payments crises cannot rear their ugly heads. Floating rate and fixed rate regimes are inherently equilibrium systems in which market forces act to automatically rebalance financial flows and avert balance-of-payments crises.

Most economists use "fixed" and "pegged" as interchangeable or nearly interchangeable terms for exchange rates. However, they are "superficially similar but basically very different exchange-rate arrangements" (Friedman 1990, 28). Pegged rate systems are those in which a monetary authority aims at more than one target at a time. They often employ exchange controls and are not free-market mechanisms for international balance-of-payments adjustments. Pegged exchange rates are inherently disequilibrium systems, lacking an automatic mechanism to produce balance-of-payments adjustments. Pegged rates require a central bank to manage both the exchange rate and monetary policies. With a pegged rate, the monetary base contains both domestic and foreign components. It is important to note that pegged rates, in fact, include a wide variety of exchange rate arrangements, including pegged but adjustable, crawling pegs, managed floating, and so on.

Unlike floating and fixed rates, pegged rates invariably result in conflicts between monetary and exchange rate policies. For example, when capital inflows become "excessive" under a pegged system, a central bank often attempts to sterilize the ensuing increase in the foreign component of the monetary base by selling bonds, reducing the domestic component of the base. And, when outflows become "excessive," a central bank attempts to offset the decrease in the foreign component of the base by buying bonds, increasing the domestic component of the monetary base. Balance-of-payments crises erupt as a central bank begins to offset more and more of the reduction in the foreign component of the monetary base with domestically created base money. When this occurs, it is only a matter of time before currency speculators spot the contradictions between exchange rate and monetary policies and force a devaluation, the imposition of exchange controls, or both.

Of note is the fact that, by the 1990s, many countries were practicing what is often termed *managed floating*, in which the monetary authority does not promise to maintain any particular level of the exchange rate but intervenes from time to time to influence the rate. Despite having a fluctuating rate, managed floating falls under what I term pegged exchange rates, because the monetary authority aims at more than one target at a time.

CURRENCY BOARDS

As a matter of both principle and practice, I—like my mentors Friedman, Walters, and Greenwood—embrace free-market, exchange rate mechanisms. But, for emerging market countries, the floating option must be dismissed. In emerging markets countries, floating has never proven to be a solution for a currency crisis and has never offered a stable, sustainable system. So, for this money doctor, the prescription for emerging market countries facing currency crises or those attempting to simply establish stability, I have always prescribed fixed exchange rate systems—either currency boards or official dollarization.

Many controversies in economics stem from ill-defined, vague terminology. Indeed, the debasement of language has gone to such lengths that words—like currency boards—have almost lost their meaning. To avoid any confusion that might be created by problems associated with semantic ambiguity, I present the important features of orthodox currency boards (Hanke and Schuler 1994a).

An orthodox currency board issues notes and coins convertible on demand into a foreign anchor currency at a fixed rate of exchange. As reserves, it holds low-risk, interest-bearing bonds denominated in the anchor currency and typically some gold. The reserve levels (both floors and ceilings) are set by law and are equal to 100%, or slightly more, of its monetary liabilities (notes, coins, and, if permitted, deposits). A currency board's convertibility and foreign reserve cover requirements do not extend to deposits at commercial banks or to any other financial assets. A currency board generates profits (seigniorage) from the difference between the interest it earns on its reserve assets and the expense of maintaining its liabilities.

By design, a currency board has no discretionary monetary powers and cannot engage in the fiduciary issue of money. It has an exchange rate policy (the exchange rate is fixed) but no monetary policy. A currency board's operations are passive and automatic. The sole function of a currency board is to exchange the domestic currency it issues for an anchor currency at a fixed rate. Consequently, the quantity of domestic currency in circulation is determined solely by market forces, namely the demand for domestic currency. Since the domestic currency issued via a currency board is a clone of its anchor currency, a currency board country is part of an anchor currency country's unified currency area.

Several features of currency boards merit further elaboration. A currency board's balance sheet only contains foreign assets. If domestic assets are on the balance sheet, they are frozen. Consequently, a currency board cannot engage in the sterilization of foreign currency inflows or in the neutralization of outflows.

Another particularly important feature of a currency board is its inability to issue credit. A currency board cannot act as a lender of last resort nor can it extend credit to the banking system. A currency board cannot make loans to the fiscal authorities and state-owned enterprises. Consequently, a currency board imposes a hard budget constraint and discipline on the fiscal authorities.

A currency board requires no preconditions for monetary reform and can be installed rapidly. Government finances, state-owned enterprises, and trade need not be already reformed for a currency board to begin to issue currency.

Currency boards have existed in about 70 countries. The first one was installed in the British Indian Ocean colony of Mauritius in 1849. By the 1930s, currency boards were widespread among the British colonies in Africa, Asia, the Caribbean, and the Pacific islands. They have also existed in a number of independent countries and city-states, such as Danzig and Singapore. One of the more interesting currency boards was installed in North Russia on November 11, 1918, during the civil war. Its architect was

John Maynard Keynes, a British Treasury official responsible for war finance at the time (Hanke et al. 1993).

Countries that have employed currency boards have delivered lower inflation rates, smaller fiscal deficits, lower debt levels relative to gross domestic product, fewer banking crises, and higher real growth rates than comparable countries that have employed central banks. Nevertheless, in the aftermath of World War II, many currency boards were replaced by central banks.

Since Hong Kong reinstated its currency board in 1983, currency boards have witnessed something of a resurgence. Indeed, in the wake of the collapse of the Soviet Union, several countries adopted currency boards. In all of these cases, this money doctor was an attending physician and can report that all the new currency boards were installed rapidly and without any preconditions. In most cases, implementation took a month or less.

The reasons for the post-Soviet adoption of currency boards varied. In Estonia in 1992, the overriding objective was to rid the country of the hyperinflating Russian ruble and replace it with a sound currency (Hanke et al. 1992). In 1994, Lithuania desired to put discipline and a hard budget constraint on the government's fiscal operations (Hanke and Schuler 1994b). Hyperinflation was ravaging Bulgaria in early 1997, and the Bulgarians wanted to stop it. As a result, Bulgaria adopted a currency board in July 1997 (Hanke and Schuler 1996, 1997). In Bosnia and Herzegovina, a currency board was mandated in 1997 by the Dayton/Paris Peace Agreement that ended the Balkan Wars (Hanke 1996/97; Hanke and Schuler 1991c).

None of these modern currency boards has failed to maintain convertibility at their fixed exchange rates. Indeed, no currency board has ever failed, and this includes Keynes's Russian currency board in Archangel. For example, the North Russian ruble never deviated from its fixed exchange rate with the British pound, and the board continued to redeem North Russian rubles for pounds in London until 1920, well after the civil war had concluded (Hanke and Schuler 1991b).

At present, the following countries and territories use orthodox currency boards: Bermuda, Bosnia and Herzegovina, Brunei, Bulgaria, the Cayman Islands (Hanke and Li 2019), Djibouti, the Falkland Islands, Gibraltar, Guernsey, Hong Kong, the Isle of Man, Jersey, Macau, and Saint Helena (Hanke and Sekerke 2003). Note that Estonia and Lithuania are not included in the list because both transitioned from currency board systems to the Eurozone, in 2011 and 2015, respectively (Hanke and Tanev 2020). This was done with ease because both countries used the euro as their currency board anchor currencies and were, therefore, already unified with the Eurozone via their currency boards.

THE INDONESIAN CURRENCY BOARD AFFAIR

Even though their performances have been superior, currency boards have been entangled in controversy. Perhaps the most notable episode occurred in Indonesia in 1998, when President Suharto indicated that, on my advice as his chief economic adviser, he was going to adopt a currency board to stop surging inflation and the accompanying food riots. This seemed particularly attractive because the currency boards that I had recently installed in Bulgaria and Bosnia and Herzegovina had worked well to stop inflation and establish stability (Hanke 1996/97; Hanke and Schuler 1991d). Both currency boards had been enthusiastically supported by the International Monetary Fund (IMF), and one had been mandated by an international treaty.

But, in Indonesia's case, the currency board proposal spawned ruthless attacks on the idea and Suharto's chief economic adviser, namely this money doctor (Hanke 2017a). Suharto was told in no uncertain terms—by both the president of the United States, Bill Clinton, and the managing director of the IMF, Michel Camdessus—that he would have to drop the currency board idea or forgo $43 billion in foreign assistance (Blustein 1998; Camdessus 1998a). Economists jumped on the "trash currency boards" bandwagon, too. Every half-truth and non-truth imaginable were trotted out against the currency board idea. For me, those oft-repeated canards were outweighed by full support for an Indonesian currency board from four Nobel laureates in economics: Gary Becker, Milton Friedman, Merton Miller, and Robert Mundell, as well as Sir Alan Walters (Culp et al. 1999).

As for the ad hominem attacks on me, they followed an unoriginal, standard formula, one that contained contradictory claims and false fabrications. On the one hand, I was depicted as an obscure economist who had played a minor, or no, role in the currency board reforms of the 1990s; on the other hand, I allegedly had an enormous and corrupting influence in the currency reform sphere. As he often does, it was Nobelist Paul Krugman who took the prize as the king of ad hominem attacks (Krugman 1998; Ebeling 2020).

Why all the fuss over a currency board for Indonesia? Nobelist Merton Miller understood the great game immediately. As he wrote, the Clinton administration's objection to the currency board was "not that it would not work but that it would, and if it worked, they would be stuck with Suharto" (Tyson 1999, 2). Much the same argument was articulated by Australia's former prime minister Paul Keating: "The United States Treasury quite deliberately used the economic collapse as a means of bringing about the ouster of President Suharto" (Agence France-Presse 1999). Former U.S. Secretary of State Lawrence Eagleburger weighed in with a similar diagnosis: "We were fairly clever in that we supported the IMF as it overthrew [Suharto]. Whether that was a wise way to proceed is another question. I'm not saying

Mr. Suharto should have stayed, but I kind of wish he had left on terms other than because the IMF pushed him out" (Agence France-Presse 1998). Even Camdessus could not find fault with these assessments. On the occasion of his retirement, he proudly proclaimed, "We created the conditions that obliged President Suharto to leave his job" (Sanger 1999, C1).

To depose Suharto, two deceptions were necessary. The first involved forging an IMF public position of open hostility to currency boards. This deception was required to convince Suharto that he was acting heretically and that, if he continued, it would be costly. The IMF's hostility required a quick about-face from its enthusiastic support for Bulgaria's and Bosnia and Herzegovina's currency boards which had been installed in 1997.

Shortly after Suharto departed, the IMF's currency board deception became transparent. On August 28, 1998, Michel Camdessus announced that the IMF would give Russia the green light if it chose to adopt a currency board (Camdessus 1998b). This was followed on January 16, 1999, with a little-known meeting in Camdessus's office at the IMF headquarters in Washington, D.C. The assembled group included IMF top brass, Brazil's finance minister Pedro Malan, and the Banco Central de Brasil's director of Monetary Policy Francisco Lopes. It was at that meeting that Camdessus suggested that Brazil adopt a currency board (Blustein 2001).

The second deception involved the widely circulated story that I had proposed to set the rupiah's exchange rate at an overvalued level so that Suharto and his cronies could loot Bank Indonesia's reserves. This take-the-money-and-run scenario was the linchpin of the Clinton administration's campaign against Suharto. It was intended to "confirm" Suharto's devious intentions and rally international political support against the currency board idea and for Suharto's ouster.

The overvaluation story was enshrined by the *Wall Street Journal* on February 10, 1998 (Pura, McDermott, and Solomon 1998, A13). The *Journal* reported that Peter Gontha had summoned me to Jakarta and that I had prepared a working paper for the government in which I recommended that the rupiah-U.S. dollar exchange rate be set at 5,500. This was news to me. I did not meet, nor know of, Peter Gontha, nor had I authored any such working paper about Indonesia or proposed an exchange rate for the rupiah.

I immediately attempted to have this fabrication corrected. It was a difficult, slow, and ultimately unsatisfactory process. Although the *Wall Street Journal* reluctantly published a half-baked correction on February 19, the damage had been done (*Wall Street Journal* 1998, A2).

The *Journal*'s fabrication (or some variant of it) was repeated in virtually every major magazine and newspaper in the world, and it continues to reverberate to this day, even in so-called scholarly books and journals. For example, in his 2000 memoir, *From Third World to First, The Singapore*

Story: 1965–2000, Lee Kuan Yew asserted that "in early February 1998, Bambang, the president's son, brought Steve Hanke, an American economics professor from The Johns Hopkins University, to meet Suharto to advise him that the simple answer to the low exchange value of the rupiah was to install a currency board" (Lee 2000, 280). Among other things, this bit of misinformation was a surprise, since I have never had any contact with Bambang Suharto. But, it is not just politicians who fail to "fact check" their assertions. Theodore Friend's 2003 tome, *Indonesian Destinies*, misspells my name and then proceeds to say that I "counseled the [Suharto] family to peg the exchange rate at 5000" (Friend 2003, 314).

Setting the record straight was also complicated by the official spinners at the IMF. Indeed, they were busy as little bees rewriting monetary history to cover up the IMF's mistakes, and Indonesia represents one of its biggest blunders. To this end, the IMF issued a 139-page working paper "Indonesia: Anatomy of a Banking Crisis: Two Years of Living Dangerously 1997–99" in 2001 (Enoch et al. 2001). The authors include a "politically correct" version of the currency board episode in which they assert, among other things, that I counseled President Suharto to set the rupiah-dollar exchange rate at 5,000. This pseudo-scholarly account, which includes 115 footnotes, fails to document that assertion. That's because it simply cannot be done. That official IMF version of events also noticeably avoids referencing any of my many published works or interviews based on my Indonesian experience. Nor does it refer to an exclusive interview that I had with Stephens Broening of the *International Herald Tribune* (Broening 1998). That interview should have been of particular interest to the IMF "scholars" since I addressed my preferred procedure for setting an exchange rate for a currency board. That procedure is the one I had employed in Bulgaria. In that interview, I also indicated that no exchange rate had been set for the proposed Indonesian currency board.

ARGENTINA'S CONVERTIBILITY SYSTEM
WAS NOT A CURRENCY BOARD

As if the Indonesian controversy was not bad enough, the currency board idea became engulfed in even more controversy in Argentina. During the 1989–1991 period, at the suggestion of President Carlos Menem, I worked closely with Congressman José María Ibarbia and his colleagues (the so-called Alsogaray faction) in the Argentine Congress to develop a blueprint for a currency board. This blueprint, *Banco Central o Caja de Conversión?*, was published in Buenos Aires, debated in the Argentine

Congress, and presented to President Carlos Menem (Hanke and Schuler 1991a).

To stop a triple-digit inflation, Argentina eventually introduced a Convertibility system in April 1991. Convertibility stopped inflation in its tracks and laid the foundation for an economic boom. Convertibility had certain features of a currency board: (a) a fixed exchange rate, (b) full convertibility, and (c) a minimum reserve cover for the peso of 100% of its anchor currency, the U.S. dollar. However, Convertibility had two major features that disqualified it from being an orthodox currency board and rendered it a pegged exchange rate arrangement. It had no ceiling on the amount of foreign assets held at the central bank relative to the central bank's monetary liabilities. So, the central bank could engage in sterilization and neutralization activities, which it did. In addition, it could hold and alter the level of domestic assets on its balance sheet. So, Argentina's monetary authority could engage in discretionary monetary policy, and it did so aggressively.

In late 1991, I expressed my concerns about the flaws in the Convertibility system and predicted that the system would eventually encounter problems (Hanke 1991). As time passed, my critiques became more pointed (Hanke 2008). But, my critiques were to no avail. In December 2001, Argentina suspended its debt payments and trading of the peso, and, on January 6, 2002, Argentina abandoned the Convertibility system, and the Argentine peso was devalued.

But, that wasn't the only damage associated with the demise of the Convertibility system. Even though Convertibility was not a currency board, most economists failed to recognize this fact. Indeed, a scholarly survey of 100 leading economists who commented on the Convertibility system found that almost 97% incorrectly identified it as a currency board system (Schuler 2005). By mischaracterizing the Convertibility system as a currency board, economists and commentators of all types have been able to spin a false narrative about the so-called failure of Argentina's currency board. The confusion in policy-making circles spawned by this false narrative has been and remains significant.

DOLLARIZATION

A close cousin of the currency board is dollarization. Indeed, both are fixed exchange rate regimes. Dollarization occurs when residents of a country use a foreign currency instead of the country's domestic currency. The term "dollarization" is used generically and covers all cases in which a foreign currency is used by local residents. Even though other foreign currencies, such as the euro, are sometimes used instead of local currencies, it is the U.S. dollar that dominates; hence, the use of the term *dollarization*.

There are different varieties of dollarization. Unofficial dollarization occurs when a country issues domestic currency, but foreign currencies, or assets denominated in foreign currencies, are also used as a means of payment and/or a store of value. Data on the magnitude of total unofficial dollarization are unavailable. However, estimates of U.S. dollar notes held abroad provide a sense of the magnitude. The U.S. Federal Reserve estimates that as much as 72% of all dollar notes are held abroad (Judson 2017). Today, the stock of dollar notes outstanding is $1.99 trillion. So, as much as $1.43 trillion worth of dollar notes are held overseas. And, this is just the tip of the iceberg. Indeed, that number only includes U.S. dollar notes held overseas. It does not include foreign dollar currency bank deposits and foreign holdings of dollar-denominated bonds, nor does it include other dollar-denominated monetary assets. If we add in all the uses of the U.S. dollar as a unit of account and vehicle currency for the execution of foreign trade and capital transactions, a simple fact emerges: the world is unofficially highly dollarized.

Another type of dollarization is semiofficial dollarization. In this case, a country's monetary system is officially multimonetary. Both domestic and foreign currencies are legal tender. Peru is an example. With semiofficial dollarization, foreign currency bank deposits are often dominant, but a domestic currency is still widely used for transactional purposes and mandated for the payment of taxes. Semiofficial systems force local central banks to compete with foreign challengers. Consequently, a domestic central bank in such a system should, in principle, be more disciplined than would otherwise be the case.

Official dollarization occurs when a country does not issue a domestic currency but instead adopts a foreign currency. With official dollarization, a foreign currency has legal tender status. It is used not only for contracts between private parties but also for government accounts and the payment of taxes. Today, the following 37 countries and territories have dollarized systems: American Samoa, Andorra, Bonaire, the British Virgin Islands, the Cocos (Keeling) Islands, the Cook Islands, Northern Cyprus, East Timor, Ecuador, El Salvador, Gaza, Greenland, Guam, Kiribati, Kosovo, Liechtenstein, the Marshall Islands, Micronesia, Montenegro, Monaco, Nauru, Niue, Norfolk Island, the Northern Mariana Islands, Palau, Panama, Pitcairn Island, Puerto Rico, San Marino, Tokelau, the Turks and Caicos Islands, Saba, Sint Eustatius, Tuvalu, the U.S. Virgin Islands, Vatican City, and the West Bank. This list does not include monetary unions, like the European Monetary Union, in which member countries all use a "foreign" currency, namely the euro.

"DOLLARIZATION" IN PANAMA, MONTENEGRO, ZIMBABWE, AND ECUADOR

Panama, which was dollarized in 1903, illustrates the important features of a dollarized economy. Panama is part of the dollar bloc. Consequently, exchange rate risks and the possibility of a currency crisis vis-à-vis the U.S. dollar are eliminated. In addition, the possibility of banking crises is largely mitigated because Panama's banking system is integrated into the international financial system. The nature of Panamanian banks that hold general licenses provides the key to understanding how the system as a whole functions smoothly. When these banks' portfolios are in equilibrium, they are indifferent at the margin between deploying their liquidity (creating or withdrawing credit) in the domestic market or internationally. As the liquidity (credit-creating potential) in these banks changes, they evaluate risk-adjusted rates of return in the domestic and international markets and adjust their portfolios accordingly. Excess liquidity is deployed domestically if domestic risk-adjusted returns exceed those in the international market and internationally if the international risk-adjusted returns exceed those in the domestic market. This process is thrown into the reverse when liquidity deficits arise.

The adjustment of banks' portfolios is the mechanism that allows for a smooth flow of liquidity (and credit) into and out of the banking system (and the economy). In short, excesses or deficits of liquidity in the system are rapidly eliminated because banks are indifferent as to whether they deploy liquidity in the domestic or international markets. Panama can be seen as a small pond connected by its banking system to a huge international ocean of liquidity. Among other things, this renders unnecessary the traditional lender-of-last-resort function performed by central banks. When risk-adjusted rates of return in Panama exceed those overseas, Panama draws from the international ocean of liquidity, and when the returns overseas exceed those in Panama, Panama adds liquidity (credit) to the ocean abroad.

To continue the analogy, Panama's banking system acts like the Panama Canal to keep the water levels in two bodies of water in equilibrium. Not surprisingly, with this high degree of financial integration, there is virtually no correlation between the level of credit extended to Panamanians and the deposits in Panama. The results of Panama's dollarized money system and internationally integrated banking system have been excellent when compared with other emerging market countries (Hanke 2002b).

Since Panama is part of a unified currency area, its inflation rate mirrors, broadly speaking, the rate of inflation in the United States. For example, over the past 16 years, inflation in Panama has averaged 2.8% per year; whereas, the U.S. inflation rate has averaged 2.1% per year. Moreover, Panama's real growth rate in U.S. dollar terms has steadily risen since 2000, increasing much more rapidly than any other country in Latin America during that period.

Whereas Panama has been dollarized for over a century, several countries have dollarized only recently. One is Montenegro. While still part of the rump Yugoslavia, Montenegro, in 1999, dumped the hapless dinar and replaced it with the mighty German mark. President Milo Djukanovic engineered this dramatic, daring, and dangerous move. It will go down as one of the twentieth century's most significant currency reforms, setting Montenegro on a path toward independence, membership in the North Atlantic Treaty Organization, and what might one day be entry into the European Union.

In Montenegro, I served as state counselor, a position that carried cabinet rank, and as adviser to Djukanovic. In that capacity, I determined that the replacement of the Yugoslav dinar with the German mark was both feasible and desirable (Bogetic and Hanke 1999).

In 1999, Montenegro was still, along with Serbia, part of the Federal Republic of Yugoslavia. Strongman Slobodan Milošević was the president of Yugoslavia and had control of the army. On November 2, 1999, Djukanovic made a decisive move that would set Montenegro on a course toward independence: he granted the mark legal tender status. This all but eliminated the dinar from circulation in Montenegro. It also infuriated Milošević. Although he refrained from unleashing the Yugoslav army on Montenegro, he was reported to have given serious consideration to that idea.

Milošević's operatives did, however, engage in a great deal of mischief. For one thing, I became a marked man. Goran Matic, the Yugoslav information minister, produced a steady stream of bizarre stories. These were disseminated through Tanjug, the Yugoslav state news agency. Among other charges, I was accused of being the leader of a smuggling ring that was destabilizing the Serbian economy by flooding it with counterfeit dinars. The most spectacular allegation, however, was that I was a French secret agent who controlled a hit-team code-named "Pauk" (Spider), and that this five-man team's mission was to assassinate Milošević.

In addition to this comedy of the absurd, there was a serious side. I knew this was the case because, although Mrs. Hanke and I were kept in the dark about the specific nature of the threats, Djukanovic's office always assigned us with heavy security when we traveled to Montenegro's capital of Podgorica—a difficult to reach destination that required a flight from Zagreb to Dubrovnik, Croatia and then a long trip through the mountains to Podgorica.

A recent case of dollarization occurred in Zimbabwe. In 2008, Zimbabwe realized the second-highest hyperinflation in world history. The monthly inflation rate in November 2008 was 79,600,000,000% (Hanke and Kwok 2009). Faced with that inflation rate, Zimbabweans simply refused to use

Zimbabwe dollar notes. Consequently, Zimbabwe unofficially and sponta-neously dollarized. In April 2009, the government was forced to officially dollarize. With that, the "printing presses" were shut down, the government accounts became denominated in U.S. dollars, a new national unity govern-ment was installed, and the economy boomed.

That rebound persisted during the term of the national unity government, which lasted until July 2013. During this period, real GDP per capita surged at an average annual rate of 11.2%. And, with the imposition of a hard budget constraint, Zimbabwe's budget deficits were almost eliminated.

Zimbabwe's period of stability was short lived, however. With the col-lapse of the unity government and the return of President Robert Mugabe's Zimbabwe African National Union–Patriotic Front party in 2013, govern-ment spending and public debt surged, resulting in economic instability. To finance its deficits, the government created a "New Zim dollar," and Zimbabwe de-dollarized (Hanke 2017b). The New Zim dollar was issued at par to the U.S. dollar but traded at a significant discount to the U.S. dollar. The money supply exploded in Zimbabwe and so did the inflation rate. On September 14, 2017, Zimbabwe entered its second bout of hyperinflation in less than ten years (Hanke and Bostrom 2017).

Another recent example of dollarization is Ecuador, where I operated as an adviser to the minister of economy and finance. During 1999, the value of Ecuador's currency, the sucre, plummeted, losing 75% of its value against the U.S. dollar. As a result, President Jamil Mahuad announced on January 9, 2000 that Ecuador would abandon the sucre and officially adopt the U.S. dollar. With that announcement, inflation plunged, and Ecuador's economy stabilized.

Ecuador's dollarization is an outstanding example of "The 95% Rule" in action. At least 95% of what was written about the feasibility and pros-pects for currency boards or dollarization is either wrong or irrelevant. The IMF, the Banco Central del Ecuador, leading investment banks, and eco-nomic commentators—including Nobelist Paul Krugman—all warned that Ecuador's dollarization would be a disaster. How wrong they were (Hanke 2003).

Ecuador's dollarization also illustrates the importance of public opinion and public support. Even though many prominent politicians—includ-ing Ecuador's former president Rafael Correa—have found the monetary straitjacket imposed by dollarization to be most uncomfortable, they have not dared to replace it, because the public strongly supports dollarization (Santos 2015). Consequently, dollarization is the longest-lived exchange rate arrangement that has endured in Ecuador since its independence in 1822.

A CURRENCY DOCTOR'S RULES OF THE ROAD

So, for this money doctor, the prescription that, in principle, should work and the one that has worked to introduce hard budget constraints and establish stability has been fixed exchange rate regimes—either currency boards or dollarized systems. While attending to patients, I have made many observations and learned many lessons. Some are narrow and somewhat personal but important. Others are more general. Let's begin with nine somewhat narrow principles and rules.

The 95% Rule

My work as a money doctor confirms an assertion I first heard the late Armen Alchian make during a lecture at the University of Virginia in the summer of 1967: 95% of the material in economics journals and financial press is either wrong or irrelevant. Accordingly, to be right and relevant, you have to think most things through by yourself.

The Plumbing Principle

To develop effective reforms, the late Lord Peter Bauer was fond of counseling me to avoid a curse that afflicts most economists: to float above the detail. I have taken his advice to heart. Consequently, my reform blueprints always contained the details and institutional plumbing required to establish and operate new monetary regimes. They were based on a careful examination of primary documents and data.

The Market Experience Principle

Related to the plumbing principle is the market experience principle. I have had over 65 good years of experience trading currencies and commodities. And, some of those years were notable. For example, in 1995, when I was president of Toronto Trust Argentina (TTA) in Buenos Aires, TTA was the world's best performing emerging market mutual fund (Hanke 2019). There is nothing quite like market experience to assist a money doctor.

The Repetition Rule

At the 1997 Forbes CEO Forum in Los Angeles, the late Prof. Peter Drucker reminded me that the hallmark of great salesmanship is repetition enhanced by incremental product improvement. I have attempted to follow his wise counsel. Indeed, a recent bibliography on currency boards contains 394 entries under my name (Strezewski 2020).

The Patience Principle

Over many enjoyable summer holidays at Palazzo Mundell in Tuscany, I learned an important principle from Nobelist Robert Mundell: the patience principle. Simply stated, a money doctor must develop and circulate his ideas but have the patience to refrain from striking until the iron is hot, namely in times of crisis and stress.

The "Strike While the Iron Is Hot" Rule

When the iron is hot, a money doctor must move. One example will illustrate this rule. Prime Minister Adolfas Šleževičius had visited Estonia in 1993, was impressed by Estonia's currency board, and inquired as to who was the currency board's architect. Upon learning that I had designed Estonia's system, he contacted me in Paris and invited Mrs. Hanke and me for a private lunch in Vilnius. Mrs. Hanke and I caught the next flight from Paris to Vilnius and lunched with Šleževičius on January 26, 1994. Before the dessert was served, Šleževičius had decided that Lithuania would install a currency board and that I would serve as state counselor.

The "Pay Your Own Way" Rule

To retain one's independence and ensure one's speed and freedom of movement, my principal adviser, Mrs. Hanke, advised me to conduct all of my affairs as a money doctor on a pro bono basis, not as a paid consultant. I have strictly followed this rule, and it has paid handsome dividends.

The "Be Prepared to Live Dangerously" Rule

As Machiavelli repeatedly stressed, nothing great could ever be achieved without danger (Machiavelli 1979). How right he was. Some currency reforms of the type proposed by this money doctor have threatened to upset apple carts. That threat has put me in the cross hairs of state-sponsored assassins on three occasions. Fortunately, the attempts failed to hit their intended target.

The first two attempts were in Indonesia. During one of our nightly meetings in his little den at his private residence, President Suharto surprised me by stating that he had good intelligence that I was a marked man. He informed me that two foreign services wanted me out of the picture. As a result,

Suharto assigned part of his personal security detail to look after Mrs. Hanke and me on a 24/7 basis. Two ladies were assigned to Mrs. Hanke and three or four young men usually watched after me. The next time we received this "marked man" treatment was in Montenegro in 1999. As I have recounted earlier in this chapter, that episode was very public.

My memorable episodes of living dangerously would be incomplete without mentioning my work in installing the currency board in Bosnia and Herzegovina. The most memorable part of that episode was the flight Mrs. Hanke and I had from Zagreb to Sarajevo on December 11, 1996. We were packed into a very noisy Dutch military transport with NATO-IFOR troops. This was the only safe means of passage into the war-torn city of Sarajevo, where the snipers were still active. During our stay in Bosnia and Herzegovina, we had heavy security, particularly when we traveled to Pale for meetings with officials from the Serb Republic.

The "Numero Uno" Rule

If possible, listen carefully to counsel from a trusted adviser who is cultured and wise to the ways and art of statecraft. For me, following this rule has been both possible and pleasurable. I have relentlessly relied on sage counsel from Mrs. Hanke, a Parisian and, as Americans would say: my wife, Liliane.

LESSONS LEARNED FROM MILTON FRIEDMAN

Beyond the narrow and somewhat personal lessons that I have learned while practicing as a money doctor, there have been many broader lessons. The broader ones relate to economists. Economists are surprisingly unaware of economic history and the economics literature. They rarely read primary documents and study primary data. They display a tendency toward intellectual laziness. Consequently, they have a great propensity to repeat and echo whatever is in "the wind."

Given the excellent performance of currency boards, one would have thought that economists would have asked the obvious question: What led to the demise of currency boards and their replacement by central banks after World War II? Well, I have found that few have ever bothered to ask the question. Never mind. I posed the question to myself and have concluded that the demise of currency boards resulted from a confluence of three factors. A choir of influential economists was singing the praises of central banking's flexibility and fine-tuning capacities. In addition to changing intellectual fashions, newly independent states were trying to shake off their ties with former imperial powers, including currency boards. And, the IMF and World

Bank, anxious to obtain new clients and "jobs for the boys," lent their weight and money to the establishment of new central banks. In the end, the Bank of England provided the only institutional voice that favored currency boards. That was obviously not enough (Tignor 1998).

So, central banking swept currency boards away in most of the newly independent states. How did that monetary revolution work out? Well, few economists have bothered to ask that question, and even fewer have bothered to produce studies that address it. Perhaps that is because the few studies that have been conducted paint a grim picture of central banking. Indeed, the claims made by the economists who were singing the glories of central banking are refuted (Schuler 1996; Hanke 2002a). With the replacement of currency boards by central banks, fiscal deficits ballooned, debt levels surged, inflation accelerated, economic growth slowed and became more volatile, banking crises became more frequent, and the domestic and international purchasing power of newly issued domestic currencies evaporated. Not a pretty picture, and not a picture on display in standard economics textbooks.

Beyond the failure to ask and answer these basic questions, economists have failed to understand Milton Friedman's works and positions on exchange rate regimes. This is important and has resulted in mountains of misinformation which have generated confusion in policy-making circles (Schleifer 2005, 84–93).

Friedman's first and most famous foray into the exchange rate debate was as much an attack on exchange controls and a case for free trade as anything else. He originally wrote "The Case for Flexible Exchange Rates" (1953) as a memorandum in 1950, when he served as a consultant to the U.S. agency administering the Marshall Plan. At the time, European countries were imposing a plethora of controls on cross-border flows of trade and capital. Friedman opposed these restrictions. He concluded that adopting floating exchange rates across Europe would remove the need for exchange controls and other distortionary policies that impeded economic freedom.

It is important to stress that economic freedom was also a primary motivator for Friedman's advocacy of unified currency regimes for developing countries. Friedman (1973, 47) concluded:

> While the use of a unified currency is today out of fashion, it has many advantages for development, as its successful use in the past, and even at present, indicates. Indeed, I suspect that the great bulk, although not all, of the success stories of development have occurred with such a monetary policy, or rather an absence of monetary policy. Perhaps the greatest advantage of a unified currency is that it is the most effective way to maximize the freedom of individuals to engage in whatever transactions they wish.

Even though the title of Friedman's renowned 1953 article has contributed
to the misperception that he was a dogmatic proponent of floating rates, a
close reading makes it clear that he was not arguing so much in favor of
floating exchange rates as in favor of full convertibility. He simply saw floating exchange rates as the best way to achieve full convertibility quickly in
Western Europe. The overriding "free-trade" motivation is made clear when
Friedman discusses the sterling area: "In principle there is no objection to
a mixed system of fixed exchange rates within the sterling area and freely
flexible rates between sterling and other countries, provided that the fixed
rates within the sterling area can be maintained without trade restrictions"
(Friedman 1953, 193).

Another factor that led people to pigeonhole Friedman as a dogmatic
advocate of floating rates was the fact that Harry Johnson and other economists associated with the University of Chicago were strong, and according to most observers, one-sided, in their advocacy of floating rates. Many
incorrectly concluded that Friedman espoused the same views as some of
his colleagues. Johnson's tendentious views on exchange rates are diagnosed by Richard Cooper. In commenting on a review article by Johnson
(1969) titled "The Case for Flexible Exchange Rates, 1969," Cooper (1999,
8–9) wrote:

> The essay is well-balanced in its overall structure: he states the case for fixed
> rates; the case for flexible rates; and the case against flexible rates. But only
> one paragraph is devoted to stating the case for fixed rates, the remainder
> of the section to why it is "seriously deficient." And the section on the case
> against flexible rates is basically devoted to knocking it down, consisting as it
> does in Johnson's view "of a series of unfounded assertions and allegations."
> It is not a balanced account; Johnson had made up his mind and hoped to
> impose his conclusions on others by a devastating critique of the (unnamed)
> opposition.
>
> Johnson's affirmative analysis is itself based on a series of unfounded asser-
> tions and allegations, an idealization of the world of financial markets without
> serious reference to their actual behavior.

In the 1960s, Friedman turned his attention toward monetary problems in
developing countries, where inflation and exchange controls were pervasive. For many of these countries, Friedman was skeptical about floating
exchange rates because he mistrusted their central banks and doubted
their ability to adopt a rule-based internal anchor (such as a money supply
growth rule). To rid developing countries of exchange controls, his free-
market elixir was the fixed exchange rate (an external anchor). As Friedman
(1974, 270) put it:

The surest way to avoid using inflation as a deliberate method of taxation is to unify the country's currency [via a fixed exchange rate] with the currency of some other country or countries. In this case, the country would not have any monetary policy of its own. It would, as it were, tie its monetary policy to the kite of the monetary policy of another country—preferably a more developed, larger, and relatively stable country.

In many cases, he advocated fixed exchange rates rather than floating. For example, in response to a question during his Horowitz lecture of 1972 in Israel, Friedman (1973, 64) concluded:

The great advantage of a unified currency [fixed exchange rate] is that it limits the possibility of governmental intervention. The reason why I regard a floating rate as second best for such a country is because it leaves a much larger scope for governmental intervention . . . . I would say you should have a unified currency as the best solution, with a floating rate as a second-best solution and a pegged rate as very much worse than either.

It is not surprising that Friedman was clear and unwavering in his prescription for developing countries:

For most such countries, I believe the best policy would be to eschew the revenue from money creation, to unify its currency with the currency of a large, relatively stable developed country with which it has close economic relations, and to impose no barriers to the movement of money or prices, wages, or interest rates. Such a policy requires not having a central bank. (Friedman 1973, 59)

In 1992, I co-authored a book, *Monetary Reform for a Free Estonia*, which carries the following dust jacket endorsement by Friedman: "A currency board such as that proposed by Hanke, Jonung, and Schuler is an excellent system for a country in Estonia's position" (Hanke et al. 1992). On May 5, 1992, I presented our proposal to the Estonian parliament and, on June 24, the Russian ruble was replaced by the kroon, which traded at a fixed rate of 8 per German mark (subsequently 15.65 per euro).

During the Asian financial crisis of 1997–1998, Friedman again entered the fray when he lent his support to my proposed currency board for Indonesia. Shortly after Suharto accepted my proposal, the *Far Eastern Economic Review* (1998) published "The Sayings of Chairman Milton." His thoughts on a currency board for Indonesia were: "If the Indonesians would live by the discipline, it could be a good thing. What else can they do?"

Where did Friedman stand with regard to one of the world's showcase free-market economies? He favored Hong Kong's fixed exchange rate. Friedman wrote in 1994, "The experience of Hong Kong clearly indicates that a particular country like Hong Kong does not need a central bank. Indeed, it has been very fortunate that it has not had one. The currency board system that was introduced in 1983 has worked very well for HK and I believe it is desirable that it be continued" (Friedman 1994, 55). And, I would add, that Hong Kong's currency board system performed very well during the Asian financial crisis and, most recently, during the troubles and political turmoil that have afflicted Hong Kong over the past year (Greenwood and Hanke 2019a; Greenwood and Hanke 2019b).

These examples should put to rest the widespread notion that Friedman exclusively favored floating exchange rates. But, unfortunately, it is clear that most economists have either not read, misunderstood, or chosen to ignore Friedman's works on the subject. Their propagation of misinformation has greatly complicated this money doctor's espousal of hard budget constraints imposed by fixed exchange rate regimes for emerging market countries.

THE CURRENCY BOARD CRITICS' CLICHÉS

With the collapse of the Soviet Union and its satellites, a newfound interest in currency boards and, more broadly, fixed exchange rate regimes rose like a Phoenix. It arose because of a desire to install a monetary regime to which the fiscal regime would be subordinated. By putting the monetary authorities in a straitjacket, currency boards were viewed as a means to impose hard budget constraints and fiscal discipline.

This newfound embrace of fixed exchange rates did not go unchallenged. Indeed, a cottage industry housing passionate opponents of currency boards and fixed exchange rates developed. The works they produced, much like those in development economics, have displayed a "disregard for contrary opinions" (Bauer 1976, 231). Or, as Michael Polanyi phrased it, "the normal practice of scientists to ignore evidence which appears incompatible with the accepted system of scientific knowledge" (Polanyi 1958, 138). The opponents of fixed exchange rate regimes suffer from parasitic citation loops in which like-minded works are often exclusively cited. As for the empirical evidence, it is swept away like flies. The opponents also typically employ "nirvana economics" in which the ideal of central banking is compared to the actual operation of currency boards and dollarized systems. What ended up as a campaign against fixed exchange rates produced a long list of arguments and what are often nothing more than clichés.

The most common cliché that has been propagated by the opponents of currency boards is the notion that certain preconditions must be satisfied before currency boards can be adopted. It was even repeated by the Council of Economic Advisers (CEA): "A currency board is unlikely to be success-ful without the solid fundamentals of adequate reserves, fiscal discipline and a strong and well-managed financial system, in addition to the rule of law" (United States 1999, 289).

This statement is literally fantastic and demonstrates how far off base professional economists can get when they fail to carefully study the his-tory, workings, and results of alternative real-world institutions. After all, none of the successful currency boards of the 1990s was installed in a country that came close to satisfying even one of the alleged preconditions. Interestingly, currency boards (and dollarization) are attractive regimes to employ when the preconditions stated by the CEA are not met. How the CEA, which is armed with an army of fact checkers, could make such an error is remarkable.

The second oft-cited criticism of currency boards is that they are rule bound and rigid. Consequently, it is asserted that countries that employ them are more subject to internal and external shocks than are countries with cen-tral banks. If this were true, the variability of growth measured by the stan-dard deviations in growth rates in currency board countries would be larger than in central banking countries. The facts do not support this thesis (Hanke 1999). Like many things economists assert, the "shock argument" is not based on an examination of primary data. It is little more than an unverified conjecture—a straw man. In reality, the flexibility and discretionary powers enjoyed by central banks in emerging market countries allow them to create and stir troubled waters because they often engage in procyclical, destabiliz-ing policies (Schuler 1996).

The inability of a currency board to extend credit to the banking system constitutes a third criticism. As the United Nations Conference on Trade and Development (2001, 117) puts it, "a currency board regime makes payments crises less likely only by making bank crises more likely." This is yet another straw man. The major banking crises in the world have all occurred in central banking countries in which the lender of last resort function was practiced with reckless abandon (Frydl 1999). In contrast, currency board countries have not only avoided major banking crises, but their banking systems— knowing they would not be bailed out by a lender of last resort—have tended to strengthen over time.

Bulgaria is but one example. The 1999 Organization for Economic Cooperation and Development (OECD) Economic Survey of Bulgaria stated, "By mid-1996, the Bulgarian banking system was devastated, with highly negative net worth and extremely low liquidity, and the government no longer had any resources to keep it afloat" (OECD 1999, 60). However, the OECD also observed, "By the beginning of 1998, [six months after the instal-lation of its currency board], the situation in the commercial banking sector had essentially stabilized, with operating banks, on aggregate, appearing solvent and well-capitalized" (OECD 1999, 59).

It is worth noting that, in 2014, there was a banking scandal in Bulgaria. The Corporate Commercial Bank (KTB) was declared insolvent and shuttered (Hanke and Sekerke 2014). An astounding 76% of its commercial loan portfolio had simply vanished. The KTB apparently never operated as a commercial bank. Unfortunately, the regulators at the Bulgarian National Bank failed to detect this. But, fortunately, the Issue Department (the currency board) at the Bulgarian National Bank could not engage in lender of last resort activities because credits to the KTB would have vanished without a trace. Thanks to Bulgaria's currency board, the country's banking system remained unscathed and stable after the collapse of the KTB.

A fourth cliché states that competitiveness cannot be maintained after the adoption of a currency board. Hong Kong contradicts this conventional wisdom. Since its currency board was installed in 1983, it has retained its rank as one of the most competitive economies in the world (Schwab 2019). Furthermore, countries that adopted currency boards in the 1990s have maintained their competitiveness measured by exports as a percent of GDP.

A fifth assertion made by opponents of currency boards is that currency boards are desirable only in small, if not tiny, economies. It is true that most currency boards today are in relatively small economies. However, Hong Kong is not small. Indeed, Hong Kong ranks as the 35th largest economy in the world (The World Bank 2020).

A sixth concern expressed by economists is that currency boards are not suitable for most countries because most prospective currency board countries are not in an optimum currency area with an anchor currency country. Therefore, currency boards would be inappropriate. Well, an optimum currency area is an artificial construct within which exchange rates should be fixed and between which exchange rates should be flexible. The problem is that the facts on the ground contradict the economists' notion of an optimal currency area. For example, citizens of many countries voluntarily choose to hold bank deposits and make loans in U.S. dollars, and the value of dollar notes (paper money) exceeds the value of the local domestic money issued in those countries. So, citizens have themselves determined that the dollar is the best currency, regardless of what the optimal currency area theorists have concluded.

A seventh argument, the issue of sovereignty, is intended to stir populist ire. It is argued that monetary sovereignty is lost by the adoption of a currency board because an independent monetary policy is given up. True. After all, a currency board has no monetary policy. However, national sovereignty over a country's monetary regime is retained. Indeed, history has shown that many countries that once had currency boards have unilaterally exited from those rule-bound systems, albeit to their peril.

In closing, one final comment merits attention because it reveals just how confusing the debate about the desirability of currency boards has been. Has the IMF been for or against currency boards? Well, it depends on when you ask. Ex ante, the IMF has often been opposed and has employed many of the clichés mentioned above. But, ex post, the IMF has had nothing but praise for the four currency boards installed in the 1990s, as well as Hong Kong's (IMF 2001a, b, c, d, and e). According to the IMF, these currency boards have strengthened fiscal discipline and the banking systems, have motivated reforms, and have been the linchpins for growth.

So, the cacophony about the efficacy of various types of exchange rate regimes coming from economists, as well as established institutions, is deafening. As a result, confusion reigns in the political arena when decisions are made (Schleifer 2005, 84–93). This makes a money doctor's job difficult, to say the least.

CURRENCY BOARDS AND DOLLARIZATION DELIVER HARD BUDGET CONSTRAINTS

There is little doubt that fixed exchange rate regimes, either currency boards or dollarization, impose hard budget constraints. These rein in fiscal authorities, even in countries with weak institutions. Bulgaria, which has had a currency board since 1997, illustrates this point. Table 6.2 contains data for before and after the installation of the currency board in July 1997. All economic indicators improved rapidly and dramatically after the currency board's hard budget constraint was imposed. And, stability has been maintained by various types of governments for over 20 years. Indeed, if we focus only on the fiscal balance, we observe a great deal of fiscal discipline and relatively small deficits. As a result, Bulgaria has the second lowest debt-to-GDP ratio in the European Union: 18.6%. Estonia is the only EU country with a lower debt-to-GDP ratio: 8.4%.

But, the hard budget constraints imposed by exchange rate regimes aren't always guarantors of fiscal probity. For example, Montenegro was dollarized in 1999, and its debt-to-GDP ratio is "high:" 79.3%. And Ecuador, which dollarized in 2001, became so buried in debt that it defaulted in April 2020 (Rapoza 2020).

These two outliers suggest that for greater assurance that hard budget constraints are "hard," fiscal rules should accompany fixed exchange rate regimes. To do this, supermajority voting should be established for fiscal decisions. Many countries require supermajority voting for important decisions. Such a voting rule protects the minority from the potential tyranny of a simple majority. A supermajority voting rule is particularly important for the protection of minorities in countries where the democratic process is not circumscribed by a firm rule of law.

Table 6.2 Bulgaria: Before and After the Installation of Its Currency Board (July 1, 1997)

	1995	1996	1997	1998	1999	2000	2001	2002	2003	2004	2005	2006	2007
Annual Inflation (%)	32.9	310.8	549.2	1.6	7.0	11.3	4.8	3.8	5.6	4.0	7.4	6.1	11.6
Change in Real GDP (%)	-1.6	-8.0	-14.2	4.3	-8.3	4.8	3.8	6.0	5.2	6.4	7.2	6.8	6.6
Interest Rates (Money market rate, % per annum)	52.10	117.66	65.20	2.43	2.87	2.96	3.67	2.42	1.92	1.91	2.02	2.79	4.03
Fiscal Balance (% of GDP)	-5.5	-8.1	0.8	1.1	0.1	-0.5	1.0	-1.2	-0.4	1.8	1.0	1.8	2.0
General Government Gross Debt (% of GDP)	N/A	N/A	N/A	67.3	78.7	73.3	67.1	53.4	45.4	37.8	28.5	22.6	17.6
Foreign Reserves (Millions of U.S. dollars)	1,635	864	2,485	3,056	3,264	3,507	3,646	4,846	6,825	9,337	8,697	11,756	17,544

	2008	2009	2010	2011	2012	2013	2014	2015	2016	2017	2018	2019
Annual Inflation (%)	7.2	1.6	4.4	2.0	2.8	-0.9	-2.0	-0.9	-0.5	1.8	2.3	3.1
Change in Real GDP (%)	6.1	-3.4	0.6	2.4	0.4	0.3	1.9	4.0	3.8	3.5	3.1	3.4
Interest Rates (Money market rate, % per annum)	5.16	2.01	0.18	0.20	0.10	0.02	0.03	0.01	-0.16	-0.20	-0.50	-0.48
Fiscal Balance (% of GDP)	1.6	-4.0	-3.1	-2.0	-0.3	-0.4	-5.4	-1.7	0.1	1.1	2.0	2.1
General Government Gross Debt (% of GDP)	14.7	14.5	14.2	14.4	16.6	17.2	26.4	25.4	27.1	23.0	20.1	18.6
Foreign Reserves (Millions of U.S. dollars)	17,930	18,522	17,223	17,215	20,507	19,883	20,129	22,153	25,176	28,375	28,711	27,900

Sources: International Monetary Fund, European Central Bank, The World Bank.

The arithmetic of the budget shows us that two new fiscal rules would be sufficient to control the scope and scale of the government and protect minority interests. Total outlays minus total receipts equals the deficit, which in turn equals the increase in the total outstanding debt. Rules that limit any two of these variables would limit the remaining variable. Which two variables should be limited?

The easiest way to answer the question about which two variables should be limited by supermajority voting rules is to sketch the outlines of a constitutional amendment (a fiscal rule):

Section 1: The total national debt may increase only by the approval of two-thirds of the members of the Congress (National Assembly, Parliament, etc.).

Section 2: Any bill to levy a new tax or increase the rate or base of an existing tax shall become law only by approval of two-thirds of the members of the Congress.

Section 3: The above two sections of this amendment shall be suspended in any fiscal year during which a declaration of war is in effect.

A CURRENCY DOCTOR PREPARES
FOR HIS NEXT PATIENT

With that, I conclude my stroll down memory lane. For this money doctor, fixed exchange rate regimes—whether they be currency boards or dollarized systems—have always proven to be the proper prescription for countries experiencing economic crises. They have imposed hard budget constraints and stabilized the crisis-torn patients. And, while stability might not be everything, everything is nothing without stability.

NOTE

1. I would like to thank my chief of staff Christopher Arena, deputy chief of staff Cecilia Taylor, and research assistant Spencer Ryan for their comments and assistance in preparing this chapter.

REFERENCES

Agence France Presse. 1998. "US Should Be More Tolerant Toward Indonesia: Japanese Economist." *Agence France Presse*, June 20, 1998.
Agence France Presse. 1999. "Former Aussie PM Says US Used Asia Crisis to Oust Suharto." *Agence France-Presse*, November 11, 1999.

Bauer, Peter T. 1976. *Dissent on Development*. Rev. ed. Cambridge, MA: Harvard University Press.

Blustein, Paul. 1998. "Currency Dispute Threatens Indonesia's Bailout: Clinton Backs IMF in Pressing Suharto Not to Change Country's Monetary System." *Washington Post*, February 14, 1998.

Blustein, Paul. 2001. *The Chastening*. New York City: PublicAffairs.

Bogetic, Zeljko, and Steve H. Hanke. 1999. *Cronogorska Marka*. Podgorica, Montenegro: Antena M.

Broening, Stephens. 1998. "Voice of Suharto's Guru: Q&A/Steve Hanke." *International Herald Tribune*, March 20, 1998, 15.

Camdessus, Michel. 1998a. *Letter From Camdessus to Suharto*. February 11, 1998.

Camdessus, Michel. 1998b. "Press Conference of IMF Managing Director Michel Camdessus." https://www.imf.org/en/News/Articles/2015/09/28/04/54/tr980828.

Cooper, Richard N. 1999. *Exchange Rate Choices*. Harvard Institute of Economic Research Working Paper No. 1877, Cambridge, MA: Harvard—Institute of Economic Research.

Culp, Christopher L., Steve H. Hanke, and Merton H. Miller. 1999. "The Case for an Indonesian Currency Board." *Journal of Applied Corporate Finance* 11 (4): 57–65.

Ebeling, Richard M. 2020. "Paul Krugman's Ad Hominem Defense of Central Banking." *American Institute for Economic Research*. August 3, 2020.

Enoch, Charles, Barbara Baldwin, Olivier Frécaut, and Arto Kovanen. 2001. "Indonesia: Anatomy of a Banking Crisis: Two Years of Living Dangerously, 1997–99." IMF Working Paper No. 01/52, International Monetary Fund.

Far Eastern Economic Review. 1998. "Sayings of Chairman Milton." *Far Eastern Economic Review*, March 26, 1998, 78.

Friedman, Milton. 1953. "The Case for Flexible Exchange Rates." In *Essays in Positive Economics*, 157–203. Chicago: University of Chicago Press.

Friedman, Milton. 1973. *Money and Economic Development*. New York: Praeger.

Friedman, Milton. 1974. "Monetary Policy in Developing Countries." In *Nations and Households in Economic Growth*, edited by Paul A. David and Melvin W. Reder, 265–78. New York: Academic Press.

Friedman, Milton. 1990. "As Good as Gold." *National Review*, June 11, 1990, 28–35.

Friedman, Milton. 1994. "Do We Need Central Banks?" *Central Banking* 5 (1): 55–58.

Friedman, Milton, and Rose Friedman. 1998. *Two Lucky People: Memoirs*. Chicago: University of Chicago Press.

Friend, Theodore. 2003. *Indonesian Destinies*. Cambridge, MA: Belknap Press of Harvard University Press.

Frydl, Edward J. 1999. "The Length and Cost of Banking Crises." IMF Working Paper No. 99 (30), International Monetary Fund.

Greenwood, John. 2007. *Hong Kong's Link to the U.S. Dollar: Origins and Evolution*. Hong Kong: Hong Kong University Press.

Greenwood, John, and Steve H. Hanke. 2019a. "A Lesson in the Virtue of a Stable Currency." *Wall Street Journal*, April 2, 2019, A17.

Greenwood, John, and Steve H. Hanke. 2019b. "Hong Kong's Economy Is Going Strong." *Wall Street Journal*, June 25, 2019, A17.

Hanke, Steve H. 1991. "Argentina Should Abolish Its Central Bank." *Wall Street Journal*, October 25, 1991.

Hanke, Steve H. 1996/1997. "A Field Report from Sarajevo and Pale." *Central Banking* 7 (3, Winter): 36–40.

Hanke, Steve H. 1999. "Some Reflections on Currency Boards." In *Central Banking, Monetary Policies, and the Implications for Transition Economies*, edited by Mario I. Blejer and Mario Skreb, 341–66. Boston: Kluwer Academic Publishers.

Hanke, Steve H. 2002a. "Currency Boards." *Annals of the American Academy of Political and Social Science* 579 (January): 87–105.

Hanke, Steve H. 2002b. "Panama's Innovative Money and Banking System." In *Financial Panama*, edited by N. Barletta, 77–84. Bogotá: Ediciones Gamma.

Hanke, Steve H. 2003. "Money and the Rule of Law in Ecuador." *Journal of Policy Reform* 6 (3): 131–45.

Hanke, Steve H. 2008. "Why Argentina Did Not Have a Currency Board." *Central Banking* 18 (3, February): 56–58.

Hanke, Steve H. 2016. "Remembrances of a Currency Reformer: Some Notes and Sketches from the Field." Johns Hopkins Studies in Applied Economics Working Paper No. 55, Johns Hopkins Institute for Applied Economics, Global Health, and the Study of Business Enterprise, Baltimore, MD.

Hanke, Steve H. 2017a. "20th Anniversary, Asian Financial Crisis: Clinton, The IMF And Wall Street Journal Toppled Suharto." *Forbes*, July 6, 2017. https://www.for bes.com/sites/stevehanke/2017/07/06/20th-anniversary-asian-financial-crisis-clin ton-the-imf-and-wall-street-journal-toppled-suharto/?sh=2ace068f2882.

Hanke, Steve H. 2017b. "Can the Singapore Model Save Zimbabwe?" *The New York Times*, November 30, 2017.

Hanke, Steve H. 2019. "Commodity and Foreign Exchange Trading – Some Notes and High Points." Johns Hopkins Studies in Applied Economics Working Paper No. 133, Johns Hopkins Institute for Applied Economics, Global Health, and the Study of Business Enterprise, Baltimore, MD.

Hanke, Steve H., and Alan Walters. 1992. "Currency Boards." In *The New Palgrave Dictionary of Money and Finance*, edited by Peter Newman, M. Milgate, and J. Eatwell, 558–61. Vol. 1. London: The Macmillan Press Limited.

Hanke, Steve H., and Alex Kwok. 2009. "On the Measurement of Zimbabwe's Hyperinflation." *Cato Journal* 29 (2, Spring/Summer): 353–64.

Hanke, Steve H., and Edward Li. 2019. "The Cayman Currency Board: An Island of Stability." *Cayman Financial Review* 54: 26–27.

Hanke, Steve H., and Erik Bostrom. 2017. "Zimbabwe Hyperinflates, Again: The 58th Episode of Hyperinflation in History." Johns Hopkins Studies in Applied Economics Working Paper No. 90, Johns Hopkins Institute for Applied Economics, Global Health, and the Study of Business Enterprise, Baltimore, MD.

Hanke, Steve H. and Matthew Sekerke. 2003. "St. Helena's Forgotten Currency Board." *Central Banking* 13 (3, February).

Hanke, Steve H., and Matthew Sekerke. 2014. "Bulgaria: Liquidate KTB, Now." *Cato at Liberty* (blog). *Cato Institute*. October 24, 2014. https://www.cato.org/blog /bulgaria-liquidate-ktb-now.

Hanke, Steve H., and Kurt Schuler. 1991a. *Banco Central o Caja de Conversion?* Buenos Aires: Fundación República.

Hanke, Steve H., and Kurt Schuler. 1991b. "Keynes's Russian Currency Board." In *Capital Markets and Development*, edited by Steve H. Hanke and Alan A. Walters, 43–58. San Francisco: ICS Press (Institute for Contemporary Studies).

Hanke, Steve H., and Kurt Schuler. 1991c. *Monetary Reform and the Development of a Yugoslav Market Economy*. London: Centre for Research into Communist Economies.

Hanke, Steve H., and Kurt Schuler. 1991d. *Teeth for the Bulgarian Lev: A Currency Board Solution*. Washington: International Freedom Foundation.

Hanke, Steve H., and Kurt Schuler. 1994a. *Currency Boards for Developing Countries: A Handbook*. San Francisco: ICS Press (Institute for Contemporary Studies).

Hanke, Steve H., and Kurt Schuler. 1994b. *Valiutu Taryba: Pasiulymai Lietuvai*. Vilnius: Lietuvos Laisvosios Rinkos Institutas.

Hanke, Steve H., and Kurt Schuler. 1996. *Currency Board, Beginning or End*. Sofia: Ick "Bard".

Hanke, Steve H., and Kurt Schuler. 1997. *Currency Boards: The Financing of Stabilization*. Sofia: Friedrich Ebert Stiftung.

Hanke, Steve H., and Todor Tanev. 2020. "Bulgaria: Long Live the Currency Board." *Central Banking* XXX (3, March): 140–145.

Hanke, Steve H., Lars Jonung, and Kurt Schuler. 1992. *Monetary Reform for a Free Estonia*. Stockholm: SNS Forlag.

Hanke, Steve H., Lars Jonung, and Kurt Schuler. 1993. *Russian Currency and Finance: A Currency Board Approach to Reform*. New York: Routledge.

International Monetary Fund. 2001a. "News Brief: IMF Completes Final Bosnia and Herzegovina Reviews, Approves US$18 Million Credit Tranche." IMF News Brief No. 01/46, International Monetary Fund.

International Monetary Fund. 2001b. "IMF Concludes Article IV Consultation with Bulgaria." IMF Public Information Notice No. 01/33, International Monetary Fund.

International Monetary Fund. 2001c. "IMF Concludes Article IV Consultation with Estonia." IMF Public Information Notice No. 01/62, International Monetary Fund.

International Monetary Fund. 2001d. "IMF Concludes Article IV Consultation with Lithuania." IMF Public Information Notice No. 01/6, International Monetary Fund.

International Monetary Fund. 2001e. "People's Republic of China—Hong Kong Special Administrative Region: Selected Issues and Statistical Appendix." IMF Country Report No. 01/146, International Monetary Fund.

Johnson, Harry G. 1969. "The Case for Flexible Exchange Rates, 1969." *Federal Reserve Bank of St. Louis Review* 51 (6, June): 12–24.

Judson, Ruth. 2017. "The Death of Cash? Not So Fast: Demand for U.S. Currency at Home and Abroad, 1990–2016." Paper presented at International Cash Conference 2017 - War on Cash: Is there a Future for Cash?, Island of Mainau, Germany, April 25–27.

Krugman, Paul. 1998. "Rupiah Rasputin: A currency board won't solve Indonesia's woes." *Fortune*, April 13, 1998.

Lee, Kuan Y. 2000. *From Third World to First: The Singapore Story: 1965–2000*. New York: HarperCollins Publishers.

Machiavelli, Niccolo. 1979. *The Portable Machiavelli.* Rev. ed. Translated by Peter Bondanella and Mark Musa. Hammondsworth, England: Penguin Classics.

Marsh, David. 1992. *The Bundesbank: The Bank that Rules Europe.* London: Mandarin Paperbacks.

Organization for Economic Cooperation and Development (OECD). 1999. *OECD Economic Surveys: Bulgaria 1999.* Paris: OECD Publishing.

Polanyi, Michael. 1958. *Personal Knowledge.* London: Routledge.

Pura, Raphael, Darren McDermott, and Jay Solomon. 1998. "Suharto Warms to Currency-Board Plan – President's Family Welcomes Plan as Economic Advisers Voice Fears." *Wall Street Journal*, February 10, 1998, A13.

Rapoza, Kenneth. 2020. "The Pandemic Blues: Ecuador Second Latin American Nation To Default In 4 Weeks." *Forbes*, April 21, 2020. https://www.forbes.com/sites/kenrapoza/2020/04/21/the-pandemic-blues-ecuador-second-latin-american-nation-to-default-in-4-weeks/?sh=1ddef05273b8.

Sanger, David E. 1999. "Longtime I.M.F. Director Resigns in Midterm." *The New York Times*, November 9, 1999, C1.

Santos, Tristana. 2015. "The Dollarizers." Johns Hopkins Studies in Applied Economics Working Paper No. 31, Johns Hopkins Institute for Applied Economics, Global Health, and the Study of Business Enterprise, Baltimore, MD.

Schuler, Kurt. 1996. *Should Developing Countries Have Central Banks? Currency Quality and Monetary Systems in 155 Countries.* London, England: Institute of Economic Affairs.

Schuler, Kurt. 2005. "Ignorance and Influence: U.S. Economists on Argentina's Depression of 1998–2002." *Econ Journal Watch* 2 (2, August): 234–278.

Schwab, Klaus. 2019. *The Global Competitiveness Report 2019.* Geneva: World Economic Forum.

Shleifer, Andrei. 2005. *A Normal Country: Russia after Communism.* Cambridge, MA: Harvard University Press.

Strezewski, John. 2020. "On Currency Boards – An Updated Bibliography of Scholarly Writings." Johns Hopkins Studies in Applied Economics Working Paper No. 163, Johns Hopkins Institute for Applied Economics, Global Health, and the Study of Business Enterprise, Baltimore, MD.

The World Bank. 2020. *World Development Indicators.* Washington, DC: The World Bank. https://datacatalog.worldbank.org/dataset/world-development-indicators.

Tignor, Robert L. 1998. *Capitalism and Nationalism at the End of Empire.* Princeton, NJ: Princeton University Press.

Tyson, James L. 1999. "'Dollar Diplomacy' Rises Again as Foreign Policy Tool." *Christian Science Monitor*, February 10, 1999, 2.

United Nations Conference on Trade and Development. 2001. "Trade and Development Report, 2001." United Nations.

United States. 1999. *Economic Report of the President Transmitted to the Congress.* Washington: U.S. Government Printing Office.

Wall Street Journal. 1998. "Corrections & Amplifications." *Wall Street Journal*, February 19, 1998, A2.

Chapter 7

Fiscal Rules and Public Debt

An Emerging Market Perspective[1]

Pablo E. Guidotti

INTRODUCTION

For the past four decades the world has witnessed a steady increase in global public debt. By 2020, Gopinath and Gaspar (2020) estimate that global public debt will reach its highest level ever recorded, at over 100% of GDP. Although public debt of emerging and developing countries has fluctuated more in relation to GDP than that of the advanced economies, today's public debt levels are set to reach record levels in both groups of economies. Therefore, it is fair to say that global public debt levels currently pose one of the most important and urgent challenges for macroeconomic policy around the world.

The recent build-up of debt has reflected quite unusual economic conditions. On the one hand, the world has been hit by two unprecedentedly profound crises: the 2008 Global Financial Crisis and the ongoing COVID-19 pandemic; both have required massive fiscal policy stimulus in response. On the other hand, interest rates in mature bond markets have been reduced to record low—near zero—levels since 2008 and, in some cases, they have even gone into negative territory. Near-zero rates have created conditions favorable for a sustained growth in public debts, as governments privileged the countercyclical role of fiscal policy.

Moving forward, the task of recovering fiscal soundness will take center stage as soon as a new normal for the world economy is reached. In this context, implementation of fiscal rules at supra-national and national levels is seen as a potentially effective instrument to restore fiscal soundness. However, so far, the design of fiscal rules has not produced adequate guidance so as to contain the growth of public debts around the world.

In this chapter, I discuss how existing fiscal rules relate to public debt. A main message of this chapter is to warn that current benchmarks utilized in most fiscal rules in effect around the world are too lax. Especially in, but not limited to, emerging market and developing economies the interaction of fiscal policy with the international capital market is central, and liquidity constraints that translate into sudden stops of capital flows require adoption of public debt ceilings that are significantly lower than those adopted in most fiscal rules and in the debt sustainability guidelines used by the International Monetary Fund (IMF). Moreover, such debt ceilings relate to debt-management policies that governments can adopt—such as the choice of debt maturity—to reduce liquidity risk.

Adoption of tighter public debt ceilings has important implications for the resolution of fiscal problems in emerging market and developing countries and for the design of IMF programs in situations when countries face a significant loss of investors' confidence. In particular, adequate debt sustainability analyses need to include the design of effective rules for debt restructuring.

The chapter is organized as follows. The next section summarizes the current discussion on fiscal rules, the conceptual aspects and the empirical evidence, as well as the importance of domestic politics in determining fiscal outcomes. The following section discusses the notion of debt sustainability for emerging market and developing countries with access to international capital markets and derives numerical safe public debt ceilings. It also discusses the implications for debt restructuring and the international financial architecture. The last section concludes.

THE DEBATE ON FISCAL RULES

Fiscal soundness has long been a central objective of macroeconomic policy. However, for a number of reasons that I will discuss in this chapter, soundness of fiscal policy has often been a rather elusive concept. And especially for developing and emerging market economies the cost of unsustainable fiscal policies has been very high at least on two fronts.

First, high deficits have often led to debt crises, as has been documented by Reinhart and Rogoff (2009). Argentina's long default in the 2002–2016 period and the 2012 Greek debt restructuring, as well as the debt troubles faced by Argentina and Ecuador in 2020 show how difficult it is to achieve fiscal soundness in practice despite its universally recognized importance in theory.

Second, fiscal difficulties can lead to "fiscal dominance," a situation in which central banks and monetary policy become intertwined with fiscal policy and dependent on it. The most obvious consequences of fiscal dominance are loss of central bank independence, loss of confidence in the currency and, eventually, high and persistent inflation. The relationship between fiscal dominance and high inflation can also be related to the presence of large public debts denominated in domestic currency, as have been studied, for instance, by Calvo (1988) and Calvo and Guidotti (1990). It is shown there how time inconsistency of monetary policy, associated with fiscal dominance, can lead to the loss of nominal anchor by the central bank, generating multiple equilibria. The presence of multiple equilibria helps us understand why, under certain conditions, inflation can be very difficult to control, can be extremely variable, and can even result in hyperinflation. The hyperinflation experiences of Argentina and Peru at the end of the 1980s and beginning of the 1990s stand as testimony to the dangers associated with extreme fiscal dominance.[2] One of the best examples of extreme fiscal dominance in recent times is provided by the 1994 Yugoslav hyperinflation, during which the central bank financed over 95% of all government expenditures.[3]

In the end, lack of soundness in fiscal policy results in an increase in the public debt burden. In a recent IMF blog, Gaspar and Gopinath (2020) document the historical evolution of the ratio of gross public debt to GDP in advanced and emerging market economies. Figure 7.1 below, taken from their article, illustrates the evolution of the public-debt-to-GDP ratio in both economic groups of countries from 1880 to 2020.

As can be clearly observed, in the context of the COVID-19 pandemic, the public-debt-to-GDP ratio is set to reach historical heights in both advanced and emerging market economies. Following the policy response to the COVID-19 crisis,[4] advanced economies are expected to reach a public debt-to-GDP ratio of over 130%, piling up on the already very high public debt levels reached in response to the 2008 Global Financial Crisis. In the case of emerging market economies, public debt is also expected to reach a historical record exceeding 63% of GDP.

When considering the evolution of public debt to GDP in the advanced economies one cannot ignore the fact that today's levels exceed the previous historical peak experiences of the post–World War II that had exceeded 120%. Moreover, as can be observed in figure 7.1, public debt in the advanced economies decreased rapidly in relation to GDP in the period following the end of World War II, until reaching a minimum in the mid-1970s.

The behavior of the advanced economies' public debt after World War II mimicked the evolution of the U.S. Federal Debt. This evidence begs the question about the role of fiscal austerity in producing a rapid and consistent—over a 30-year-period—reduction in the public-debt-to-GDP ratio after World War II and whether there are lessons to be learned about fiscal soundness. Unfortunately, the answer to this question is not very encouraging.

Soaring public debt
Global public debt is projected to reach 101.5 percent of global
GDP in 2020 – the highest level ever.
(percent of GDP)

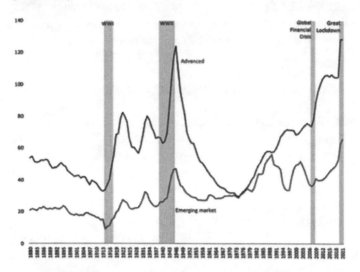

Sources: Historical Public Debt Database, IMF WEO, Maddison Database Project; and IMF staff calculations.
Note: The aggregate public debt-to-GDP series for advanced and emerging market economies is based on debt-to-
GDP data for a constant sample of 25 countries and 27 countries, respectively. The averages are calculated using
weights derived from GDP in PPP terms.

INTERNATIONAL MONETARY FUND

Figure 7.1 Soaring Public Debt. Global public debt is projected to reach 101.5 of global
GDP in 2020—the highest level ever. Adapted from Historical Public Debt Database,
IMF WEO, Maddison Database Project; and IMF staff calculations. Note: The aggregate
public dept-to-GDP series for advanced and emerging market economies is based on
debt-to-GDP data for a constant sample of 25 countries and 27 countries, respectively.
The average are calculated derived in PPP terms.

In an interesting paper, Brown (1990) analyzes precisely which were the
factors that dominated the steady decline in the ratio of the U.S. Federal
Public Debt and GNP from 1945 through 1974. In 1945, the U.S. Federal
Debt amounted to 110% of GNP and fell to 23% of GDP in 1974. In his
paper, Brown studies the relative role played by three factors in the reduction of the U.S.-Federal-Debt-to-GNP ratio between 1945 and 1974 (and two
sub-periods[5]). The three factors are (1) real economic growth; (2) net real
debt repayment (i.e., fiscal policy/austerity); and (3) net price changes (i.e.,
inflation).

Brown's results are highly telling. When considering the period 1945–1974, fiscal policy did not contribute to reducing the U.S. Federal Debt in relation to GNP. On the contrary, fiscal policy contributed to increasing the public debt burden by 10 percentage points—the only sub-period when fiscal policy contributed with a small 3% reduction was the first decade (1945–1955). The 86% fall in the ratio of U.S. Federal Debt to GNP between 1945 and 1974 was due, in similar amounts, to economic growth (a 55% reduction) and to inflation (a 41% reduction). Namely, almost half of the reduction in the U.S. debt burden was due to inflation, its effect being similarly important in all sub-periods.

Interestingly, the above facts are consistent with empirical findings by Calvo et al. (1991) on the evolution of the U.S. Federal Debt and its maturity structure between 1946 and 1988. Especially motivated by the U.S. Federal Debt data, Calvo and Guidotti (1992) characterized the optimal choice of debt maturity in a model where the government is subject to time inconsistency and inflation is therefore a factor that plays an important role in fiscal policy decisions. In particular, the U.S. Federal Debt fell consistently in relation to GDP between 1946 and the mid-1970s and started to increase thereafter. Debt maturity displayed a remarkably similar behavior; it shortened consistently in the period preceding the mid-1970s and lengthened thereafter within the sample period.

Two main results of the Calvo and Guidotti (1992) model are particularly important. First, in a time-inconsistency context, government displays "debt aversion," namely, the government's inability to pre-commit its policies (in particular, inflation) raises the cost of debt and, hence, introduces a bias in the optimal policy toward debt reduction. Second, management of the maturity structure of the public debt is central to the implementation of the optimal policy. The model predicts a positive association between the public-debt-to-GDP ratio and debt maturity. Calvo et al. (1991) find that the stylized Calvo and Guidotti (1992) model conforms with U.S. data.

The discussion so far simply suggests that the debt reduction episode that occurred after World War II may not be useful to deal with the current surge in public debts around the world. In particular, one of the main developments in macroeconomic policy that took place from the early 1980s and especially with the advent of financial globalization in the 1990s has been the defeat of inflation and the concentration of central banks on achieving price stability as its main—and often only—monetary policy goal. Such evolution in monetary policy was supported by theoretical developments; for instance, Barro and Gordon (1983) laid the basis for an extensive literature on the importance of "central bank independence."[6]

With inflation increasingly out of the policy picture, containment of rising public debt ratios was left to just two factors: economic growth and fiscal soundness. Thus, in the 1990s the concept of fiscal rules—and the adoption of numerical constraints on fiscal policy—started to take center stage in the general discussion about fiscal soundness and debt sustainability.

Fiscal rules emerge as instruments to design a fiscal policy that is consistent with low inflation and monetary policy independence and, thus, prevent fiscal dominance. But very importantly, fiscal rules are seen as instruments to force politics to accept the principle of fiscal discipline. Perhaps the most famous example of fiscal rules established to discipline politics is, in the European context, the Treaty of Maastricht signed in 1992, later complemented by the adoption of the Stability and Growth Pact in 1998. These fiscal institutions responded primarily to the perception that fiscal indiscipline had been rampant in Europe during the 1970s and 1980s, prompting high and growing public debts as well as often procyclical fiscal policies in a number of European Union's (EU) members. Therefore, the Treaty of Maastricht and the Stability and Growth Pact were seen as instruments to guide convergence of fiscal policies within the EU, especially because fiscal indiscipline was deemed as inconsistent with the European Monetary Union and, in particular, the creation of the European Central Bank (ECB) and the Euro as the block's single currency.[7] By being supra-national, the European fiscal rules were expected to enjoy strong political support and enforceability at the national level.

In emerging markets, as can be observed in figure 7.1, public debt ratios have increased since the 1980s to reach a historical record under the effects of the current COVID-19 crisis. However, the limited access to the international capital market as well as the occurrence of various sovereign debt crises played central roles in containing the growth of public-debt-to-GDP ratios in the emerging market economies relative to those observed in the advanced economies.

The resolution of the 1980s external debt crisis with the implementation of the Brady Plan at the beginning of the 1990s jumpstarted a process of significant integration of emerging market economies to the international capital market—known as "globalization." The Brady Plan was crucial in fostering financial globalization not only because it put an end to a decade-long series of defaults across Asia, Africa, and Latin America, but also its implementation implied the securitization of large stocks of non-performing loans owed by governments to a set of large international banks. Securitization implied the transformation of illiquid bank loans into Brady bonds that could be widely traded in capital markets.[8]

The Brady Plan allowed risk to be unloaded from the balance sheet of international banks and transferred to a variety of institutional and retail investors in the international capital market. Issuance of Brady bonds by a large number of emerging market economies allowed investors to price and trade risk, which started to be measured by indices such as the Emerging Market Bond Index computed by J. P. Morgan. Once sovereign risk was priced and traded in the capital market, it became easier for governments and corporates to issue additional debt.

As governments recovered access to the international capital market and policy frameworks were strengthened by the reform agenda promoted by the new Washington Consensus, central banks in emerging market economies were able to pursue the, until then, elusive task of winning the battle against persistent high inflation. And, indeed, by the first half of the 1990s, inflation had quickly fallen to single digits in most of the developing and emerging market world.

With inflation out of the picture and with a renewed reliance of governments on external foreign currency debt financing, fiscal indiscipline would rapidly translate into unsustainable public debt levels. And excessive growth in public debt also fueled by an exuberant optimism of international capital markets with the advent of globalization. But market sentiment is known to shift suddenly and without major changes in fundamentals. As a reassessment of risk by investors took hold in the second half of the 1990s, a series of crises rocked emerging markets and some (foreign and domestic) public debts ended up being defaulted and restructured—the most important cases being Mexico, Russia, and Argentina.[9]

Motivated by the financial turmoil in emerging markets, the adoption of fiscal institutions in Europe, and the successful launching of the Euro, the international discussion on fiscal rules picked up steam in the 1990s. Following Schaechter et al. (2012), *fiscal rules* are defined as "a long-lasting constraint on fiscal policy through numerical limits on budgetary aggregates."[10] The so-called first-generation rules started to be adopted in the 1990s, initially in Europe with the Treaty of Maastricht in 1992 and the Stability and Growth Pact in 1998. Adoption of fiscal rules in developing countries started to become popular mostly in the late 1990s in response to the sequence of financial crises that rocked emerging markets.

In terms of design, fiscal rules take various forms that differ from country to country. Some fiscal rules set limits on budget deficits, others on government expenditure or revenues, and some set targets in relation to the public debt. Several countries adopted legislation—often referred to as Fiscal Responsibility Laws—to enforce fiscal rules and make them credible across different political administrations. In some countries, the fiscal framework also comprises the setting up of independent fiscal institutions, known as Fiscal Councils.

As discussed by Eyraud et al. (2018), the growing popularity of fiscal rules in both the advanced and the developing and emerging economies since the late 1990s was also accompanied by the perception that rules were becoming too complex, lacked enough flexibility in the wake of shocks, and were difficult to enforce. This led to the birth of second-generation rules in the aftermath of the 2008 Global Financial Crisis with the emphasis placed at making fiscal rules more flexible and more enforceable albeit, sometimes, at the expense of simplicity. Currently, over 90 countries around the globe have in place fiscal rules of different types.[11]

Before briefly reviewing the existing three-decades-long empirical evidence on the effectiveness of fiscal rules, it is useful to discuss the conceptual justification behind their adoption, as well as the associated trade-offs. The principal conceptual justification for the adoption is the political-economy argument that democratically elected governments often tend to display a "deficit bias" either because the electoral process tends to make governments more myopic as they focus on maximizing their chances of political success, or because governments are unable to commit policies of future administrations.[12]

Moreover, once excessive deficits are in place the political process may make fiscal adjustment more difficult or delayed in time, as argued by the "war of attrition" model of Alesina and Drazen (1991). In turn, political delays in implementing the needed fiscal adjustment may spill over to monetary and exchange-rate instability. Guidotti and Végh (1999) rationalize the interaction of fiscal policy with exchange-rate stability. Combining Alesina and Drazen's (1991) "war of attrition" model with a balance-of-payments crisis model, Guidotti and Végh (1999) characterize "credibility" of an exchange-rate stabilization plan as the probability that a needed fiscal consolidation would be agreed by the political process before the occurrence of a balance-of-payments crisis. Guidotti and Végh (1999) show that credibility displays an inverted-U shape; while credibility increases in the initial stages of stabilization, it will fall if fiscal consolidation is delayed long enough, making the failure of stabilization in the midst of a foreign exchange crisis increasingly likely.

Interaction between fiscal policy and monetary stability is also a major element justifying the adoption of fiscal rules in the context of supra-national institutional frameworks. The most obvious case is provided by Europe, where the adoption of fiscal rules reflected the need to coordinate national fiscal policies in a way that, in the aggregate, they were consistent with the EMU, the single currency, and an independent ECB focused on maintaining price stability. Providing incentives to avoid negative spillovers within the EMU was particularly important in view of the existing heterogeneity in fiscal policy stances and public debt levels across Europe previous to the signing of the Treaty of Maastricht.[13]

Perhaps the most difficult task in designing and implementing fiscal rules relates to the issue of flexibility. The notion that fiscal policy has to be designed to be able to respond flexibly to shocks that affect the economy is central to conventional theory. Based on Barro's (1979) seminal contribution, conventional theory characterizes optimal fiscal policy as one that is characterized by two fundamental principles. First, optimal fiscal policy should seek to raise government revenue through a tax structure that is stable over time—that is, Barro's (1979) "tax smoothing" principle—while meeting an inter-temporal government solvency constraint. Stability of the tax structure seeks to smooth tax distortions over time and, consequently, is optimal by, for instance, facilitating consumption smoothing by individuals.

Second, while meeting inter-temporal solvency, fiscal policy should respond counter-cyclically to shocks affecting the economy. On the one hand, government revenues vary directly with economic activity and, hence, are affected by the economic cycle. In particular, there may be negative shocks affecting economic activity that depress government revenues. In the conventional framework, optimal fiscal policy should let the deficit widen in response to temporary negative shocks while debt should be reduced in the wake of positive shocks.

On the other hand, in addition to their effect on fiscal revenues, shocks that affect the economy affect government expenditures too. As in the case of revenues, government spending is affected automatically by economic activity through programs such as unemployment insurance and social assistance. Such programs expand or contract endogenously in response to economic activity and contribute to the countercyclicality of fiscal policy.[14]

Non-cyclical shocks that affect the economy, or tail events such as the 2008 Global Financial Crisis or the COVID-19 pandemic, require ad-hoc government spending programs in response. To the extent that such programs are designed to be temporary in nature their implementation will be expected to expand the deficit during the duration of the shock and revert when the economy enters the recovery phase, adding to the countercyclicality of fiscal policy.

While countercyclicality is widely recognized as a desirable feature of fiscal policy, it is much less clear how this concept should translate into specific numerical deficit ceilings and the appropriate setting of escape clauses. By characterizing optimal fiscal policy as designed to be consistent with an inter-temporal government budget constraint—thus, assuming solvency—the conventional tax-smoothing model provides little guidance about which levels of public debt in relation to GDP are safe and which are not. In the conventional framework, policy flexibility is large and, for instance, any path that ensures a stable public-debt-to-GDP ratio over time meets the requirement of government solvency. In turn, different stable public-debt-to-GDP ratios relate to combinations of deficits and economic growth rates.

The above-mentioned lack of guidance of the conventional optimal fiscal policy framework is reflected in the international experience about fiscal rules. For instance, rather than being anchored in theory, the numerical targets set in the Treaty of Maastricht were the result of political negotiations to accommodate a quite heterogeneous set of initial fiscal positions while inducing a needed fiscal consolidation in the Euro area.[15] The Treaty of Maastricht set a deficit ceiling of 3% of GDP with a number of escape clauses. Escape clauses allowed the budget deficit to exceed the 3% ceiling in circumstances deemed "exceptional and temporary"—such as a severe economic downturn with a fall in GDP of at least 2%. In addition, the Treaty of Maastricht set a 60% reference value for the ratio of public debt to GDP for member states. For countries where the debt-to-GDP exceeded the reference value, the stance of fiscal policy would be set so as to approach the 60% target over time.

The numerical targets set in the Treaty of Maastricht continue to have significant influence around the world. According to the IMF (2018), 92 countries had fiscal rules in place by 2015, of which more than 60% were emerging market and developing economies.[16] The large majority of countries adopting a public debt ceiling or target set it between 60 and 70% of GDP, mostly reflecting supra-national fiscal rules. The EMU and the East Caribbean Currency Union have a debt target of 60% of GDP, while the Central African Economic and Monetary Community and the West African Economic and Monetary Union adopted a debt ceiling of 70% of GDP. Excluding countries with supra-national rules, most other economies currently adopt a threshold of 60% of GDP. No country has a public debt threshold below 40% of GDP.

The numerical ceilings of the Treaty of Maastricht also continue to be dominant when referring to the budget deficit in relation to GDP. The vast majority of countries with fiscal rules adopted a 3% ceiling on the overall fiscal deficit in relation to GDP.[17]

In sum, absent a clear theoretical guidance about public debt targets, international experience has remained anchored on public debt thresholds initially proposed by the supra-national rules adopted by the EMU. In the next section I will argue that, especially in the case of emerging market and developing economies, debt thresholds in the 60–70% of GDP range are too high. The argument will be based on the relation between a level of public debt and what it implies in terms of access to the international capital market.

Lack of theoretical guidance about what adequate debt-ceiling levels is also present in the IMF's recommendations about how to design fiscal rules. In particular, when discussing the design of a fiscal rule, the IMF (2018) distinguishes between countries where a maximum debt limit is known from those where such a limit is unknown. The maximum debt limit is defined as a public debt level in relation to GDP "beyond which a debt distress episode will occur with heightened probability (for instance, default, restructuring, or large increases in sovereign spreads)."

The notion of an unknown debt ceiling is particularly telling. According to the IMF (2018), this case "is most suitable for advanced economies with unconstrained market access, where considerable uncertainty might exist about how much debt can be sustained." Namely, advanced economies are assumed to conform with the conventional optimal fiscal policy framework discussed above.

The IMF (2013) guidelines for public debt sustainability propose public debt benchmarks of 70% of GDP for emerging market economies and 85% of GDP for advanced economies and that "these benchmarks should not be construed as levels beyond which debt distress is likely or inevitable, but rather as an indication that risks increase with the level of indebtedness." With these benchmarks in mind, assessment of debt sustainability is computed by using a stochastic simulation model—the IMF's Debt Sustainability Analysis (DSA)—so as to ensure that the country does not exceed the maximum limit over the medium term with high probability.[18] Therefore, the maximum debt benchmark or limit plays a central role anchoring the fiscal policy framework.[19] If such limit is set too high, the tension between fiscal policy flexibility and debt sustainability is likely to be resolved in favor of higher public debt levels. As mentioned above, flexibility required by recent global crises has so far resulted in record public debt. In emerging market economies, the recent cases of Argentina and Ecuador are examples of IMF programs where, soon after their signing, events of debt default or restructuring occurred even though performance criteria were largely met.

Before turning to further discussing debt sustainability in the context of emerging markets, it is useful to briefly review the conclusions of recent empirical studies about the effectiveness of second-generation fiscal rules. Given the large variety of national and supra-national fiscal rules in place, setting numerical targets on government expenditure, revenue, budget balance, and debt as well as escape clauses, it is quite difficult to assess their effectiveness in practice.[20]

A recent report prepared by the IMF Staff—see Eyraud et al. (2018)—summarizes the most recent empirical findings regarding the question of fiscal rules' effectiveness. The first observation is that, considering outcomes of fiscal deficit and general government debt observed between 2000 and 2015, on average fiscal rules appear to influence fiscal policy in the right direction, albeit by a limited amount. When comparing the set of countries with fiscal rules with the set of countries that does not have fiscal rules, the improvement in fiscal balances and public debt in the former group, on average, is smaller than 0.2% and 5% of GDP, respectively.

The second important observation relates to the effectiveness of fiscal rules in reducing the "deficit bias." In this respect, more detailed studies that recognize the vast heterogeneity across countries suggest the existence of a "magnet effect"; namely, rules tend to affect low and high deficit countries in opposite direction. For instance, with a numerical limit for the budget deficit set at 3% of GDP, empirical evidence suggests that such a limit tends to work not as a maximum level but as an attractor. Countries with deficits below 3% of GDP tend to increase their deficits while countries with deficits exceeding 3% tend to reduce them.

Additional relevant empirical results are found in the context of the EMU. In particular, compliance with fiscal rules and the excessive fiscal deficits impact financial perceptions. Empirical evidence summarized by Eyraud et al. (2018) suggests that excessive deficits may result in higher bond spreads between 50 and 150 basis points. Also referring to the EMU, Gaspar (2020) shows that compliance has been poor, especially since the 2008 Global Financial Crisis. Since 2009, between 70% and 90% of EMU members did not comply with one or two fiscal rules.

In sum, empirical evidence suggests that fiscal rules have had some impact toward improving fiscal performance, but the effect has not been large, and compliance has not been strong. Moreover, in the absence of a strong theoretical guidance about "safe" public debt levels, the challenges imposed by recent global crises have translated into growing public debts around the world. While advanced economies appear to be in a position to handle large public debts in relation to GDP, emerging market economies remain vulnerable to international capital market volatility. Hence, growing public debts in emerging markets require re-thinking about tighter public debt ceilings or benchmarks, an issue I will discuss in more detail in the next section.

Finally, and especially in emerging and developing economies, it has to be recognized that the empirical assessment on the effectiveness of fiscal rules depends critically on the domestic political environment and dynamics. In fact, adoption of fiscal rules is by definition a political decision that usually involves the Executive Branch as well as Congress. Moreover, in order to be successful, fiscal rules have to be maintained and enforced through different administrations, often of opposite political views.

Rather than discussing this issue at an abstract level, it is useful to briefly compare two contrasting experiences in Latin America: Argentina and Peru.[21] As mentioned above, Argentina and Peru are countries that share similar initial conditions marked by profound monetary and fiscal instability at the end of the 1980s. Between 1989 and 1990, both Argentina and Peru were immersed in hyperinflation and were part of the group of developing countries that had defaulted on their public debt during the 1980s. Moreover, both countries displayed among the highest levels of financial dollarization in the region.[22]

But soon after resolving their debt problems by entering the Brady Plan—Argentina in 1993 and Peru in 1995—both economies entered a period of profound macroeconomic and structural reforms and economic liberalization under the presidencies of Menem in Argentina and Fujimori in Peru. Fiscal consolidation and new budget methodologies to consolidate budget management, accounting, and treasury operations of the government, ambitious privatization in several sectors, trade openness, and monetary stabilization helped turn around both economies after decades of instability. Following the example of Chile, both Argentina in 1993 and Peru in 1992 implemented a wide-ranging reform of their social security systems, moving to an individual-capitalization system anchored in the development of private pension funds.[23] As in other countries in the region, the social security reform was one of the most important drivers of the development of stable and deep domestic capital markets, although its implementation placed significant short-term pressure on fiscal accounts.[24]

In 1999, Congress in both Argentina and Peru passed a Fiscal Responsibility Law, aimed at strengthening fiscal policy and adopting a medium-term framework conducive to fiscal soundness. By the year 2000, both Argentina and Peru displayed similar levels of public debt in relation to GDP at just under 45% of GDP, slightly below the debt ratios observed in South America (at 50.7% of GDP) and emerging market and developing economies (at 47.7% of GDP).[25] Also the fiscal deficit was similar—slightly above 2% of GDP—and largely in line with levels observed in South America (at 2.4% of GDP) and in emerging market and developing economies (at 1.6% of GDP).

The common ground shared by Argentina and Peru ended there, as domestic politics began to interfere heavily with Argentina's economic policy decisions. In the year 2000, under the presidency of Fernando De La Rua, the Argentine government modified the Fiscal Responsibility Law by raising the deficit ceiling, and in 2001 simply violated the new limit, showing lack of political consensus in relation to fiscal rules. At the beginning of 2002, in the midst of a deep political crisis that generated a succession of five presidents in a matter of just a few days, Argentina entered a full-fledged economic crisis. The government devalued the Peso, declared default on the public debt and forced an arbitrary pesification of contracts in the economy.[26]

Since the 2001–2002 crisis, Argentina never re-established fiscal rules. On the contrary, in 2006, the government nationalized the pension system effectively destroying the domestic capital market. As will be discussed in the next section, the default occurred in 2002 and ended only in 2016. After just four years, in 2020, Argentina defaulted again—for the ninth time in its history—and reached a new public debt restructuring in September, the second in just 17 years. As Argentina allowed the return of money printing to finance fiscal deficits high inflation returned. As a result, liability dollarization remained high despite the 2002 pesification experiment. In 2019, 70%

of Argentina's public debt was denominated in foreign currency, mostly the U.S. dollar. A similar level of dollarization remains in place after the 2020 public debt restructuring.[27]

In contrast, Peru stayed the course of fiscal responsibility and passed a new Fiscal Responsibility and Transparency Law in 2003, maintaining a deficit ceiling of 1% of GDP and adopting rules to limit the growth on non-financial government expenditures.[28] Maintaining fiscal responsibility throughout different political administrations was reflected in Peru's economy. Indeed, Peru's fiscal and economic performance in recent years has been impressive. In the 18-year period running between 2002 and 2019 average economic growth in Peru amounted to 5.3% per year, compared to the yearly average growth rate of South America of 2.8% per year. Peru's gross public debt in relation to GDP declined to a level of 27% of GDP in 2019, one of the lowest in the region.

In terms of fiscal policy, Peru was able to sustain a significant improvement in its general government's overall fiscal balance as a percentage of GDP. From a deficit position of 2.1% of GDP in 2000 and 2001, Peru was able to reach a surplus of 2% of GDP in 2006, and 3.3% and 2.7% of GDP in 2007 and 2008. Over the period 2002–2019, Peru maintained on average a deficit of 0.2% of GDP per year compared to an average deficit of 3.6% a year in South America and an average deficit of 2% per year among emerging market and developing economies.[29]

Peru's reputation as a fiscally responsible sovereign also translated into a solid performance in terms of monetary policy. Since recovering from hyperinflation Peru's central bank was able to maintain a low and stable rate of inflation. Over the period 2002–2019, Peru's average inflation stood at 2.8% per year, compared to an average inflation rate of 5.8% per year among emerging market and developing economies. Price stability and fiscal soundness allowed Peru to develop the domestic bond market, and liability dollarization was significantly reduced over time to 37% of the total public debt in 2019.[30]

Peru's success story in terms of its economic management has been reflected in the evolution of Peru's credit ratings over the past two decades. Each of the principal credit ratings agencies determined that Peru's sovereign bonds warranted investment grade status in 2008.[31] Since then, Peru has maintained its investment-grade category and its credit ratings further improved over time.[32]

In sum, the contrasting experiences of Argentina and Peru show the decisive importance of domestic politics in determining the success of fiscal rules, independently of the merits of their design. Political consensus maintained throughout several administrations of differing views is, in the end, perhaps the most important ingredient that separates success from failure.

PUBLIC DEBT AND FISCAL RULES
IN EMERGING MARKETS

A central lesson learned from emerging market economies' integration to international capital markets is that defining fiscal sustainability is a complex task. It involves—as suggested by the IMF's DSA framework—looking at a variety of factors that eventually affect the trajectory of public debt and have significant consequences on investors' judgment about an emerging market country's future capacity to repay its liabilities. Such factors—much less important when considering advanced economies—include the presence of liquidity constraints, of liability dollarization, and of institutional weaknesses and informality that weaken the capacity to raise government revenues.

In a context of potential sudden stops of capital flows, it becomes particularly difficult to define public debt sustainability, as solvency and liquidity considerations become intertwined. Moreover, sudden stops of capital flows often force fiscal policy to behave procyclically, in contradiction with the recommendations of the conventional optimal fiscal policy framework discussed in the previous section.

Guidotti (2007) presented a simple framework to analyze how the interaction of liquidity and solvency considerations impinges on public debt sustainability in emerging markets. In particular, when governments are not fully credible in the eyes of investors—as reflected in risk premia and credit ratings—the notion that fiscal policy can be designed under the assumption that governments meet an inter-temporal budget constraint may lose practical relevance.

In particular, both governments—through their annual budget laws—and investors tend to evaluate a country's capacity to access the capital market over relatively short horizons, most typically on a yearly basis.[33] In this context, as pointed out in Guidotti (2007), the concept of gross public-sector borrowing requirement—measuring the size of the yearly financial program—becomes a highly relevant variable. Over this variable is where both investors and the government's agency in charge of public debt management will focus when designing the borrowing program. In this respect, gross borrowing needs—defined as the sum of the overall budget deficit plus the rollover of maturing debt—are more relevant than the more commonly used ratio of public debt to GDP. However, as I will show next, a limit imposed by the capital market on the size of a government's financing program has strong implications for public debt sustainability.

A simple model illustrates how public debt sustainability is affected by liquidity considerations. The evolution over time of the ratio of public debt to GDP, b, is given by: (1) $b = d - nb$ where d denotes the overall budget deficit as a proportion to GDP, n denotes a (constant) growth rate of GDP, and a dot over a variable denotes its rate of change over time. Similarly, the yearly gross borrowing requirement (net of any pre-funding) as a proportion to GDP, x, can be approximated in the following way: (2) $x = d + b/m$ where m denotes the average maturity of the public debt.[34] Equation (2) simply states that the yearly borrowing requirement is the sum of the budget deficit plus debt amortizations.

Given the above definitions, we are interested in obtaining an enhanced measure of sustainability where fiscal policy—in addition to being consistent with inter-temporal solvency—also satisfies a liquidity constraint of not exceeding a maximum yearly borrowing requirement, x_0. Thus, in this enhanced definition a sustainable fiscal policy satisfies equation (2), where $x \leq x_0$, and the following relationship between long-run growth and the budget deficit implying that the ratio of public debt to GDP, b, is held constant over time:[35] (3) $d = nb$. As a result, the following relationship between a sustainable public-debt-to-GDP ratio, average debt maturity and the maximum gross borrowing requirement in relation to GDP obtains: (4) $b \leq b_{max} = x_0 m/(1+nm)$. For the sake of completeness, assuming equation (4) is binding, namely $x = x_0$, debt dynamics are described by equations (1) and (2), which combined yield: (5) $\dot{b} = x_0 - \alpha b$, where $\alpha \equiv 1/m + n$.

Equation (4) is central to the analysis. The first observation is that, unlike the conventional fiscal policy framework that applies mostly to the advanced economies, the presence of liquidity constraints imposed by the capital market yields a definite ceiling for the ratio of public debt to GDP.[36]

The second observation is that, for given x_0 and n, equation (4) provides a fiscal sustainability criterion that relates the public debt ceiling to the maturity structure of the public debt. In particular, in order to ensure that a country has an adequate liquidity position vis-à-vis the capital markets, as measured by the yearly borrowing requirement, there is an inverse relationship between average debt maturity on the one hand and the sustainable budget deficit and long-run debt-to-GDP ratio on the other. Equations (3) and (4) show that the shorter the maturity of the public debt is, the smaller is the maximum allowable deficit and long-run debt-to-GDP ratio.

The third observation of the above simple framework is that, unlike what would be desirable in the conventional framework, a tightening in the liquidity constraint—that is, a sudden stop in financing as measured by a reduction in x_0—will make the fiscal response to the shock procyclical, as discussed in detail by Guidotti (2007). Moreover, the procyclicality of fiscal policy in a sudden stop situation may be reduced by a lengthening of debt maturity, m. However, a significant change in m over a short time period can only be achieved through voluntary debt exchange operations or through a debt restructuring process. The main difference between these two alternatives lies in terms of debt reprofiling; voluntary exchanges may result in higher interest costs and may eventually turn out to be counterproductive, while a debt restructuring may result in a reduction in the debt burden, albeit at a potentially significant reputational cost.

In order to bring this analysis closer to practice, it is interesting to explore what values for the public debt ceiling are reasonably suggested by equation (4). In order to undertake this task, it is useful to first consider the recent evolution of capital flows to emerging markets. As reported in the most recent IMF's Global Financial Stability Report (2020), the size of debt inflows to emerging markets has been decreasing since the 2008 Global Financial Crisis. In particular, the cumulative debt inflows to emerging markets during inflow episodes have been decreasing systematically from levels above USD 400 billion before the 2013 Fed's Taper Tantrum, to cumulative inflows ranging between USD 165 billion and USD 60 billion since 2015. Although it is hard to separate between supply and demand factors, this trend points toward a potentially significant reduction in the participation of emerging market debt markets in investors' international portfolios.[37] Such conclusion is consistent with the recent increase in sovereign spreads observed in a number of emerging market economies with significant access to the international capital market. For instance, between January 2018 and April 2020, sovereign risk spreads increased from 210 to 383 basis points in Brazil, from 270 to 393 basis points in Mexico, from 140 to 296 basis points in Russia, from 219 to 732 basis points in South Africa, and from 267 to 833 basis points in Turkey.[38]

Liquidity considerations appear to have played a role in shaping debt management in emerging markets, especially in the context of near-zero international interest rates developed since the 2008 Global Financial Crisis. The average maturity of public debt among emerging market economies has lengthened since 2009, increasing from an average of 5.2 years over the period 1995–2008 to 6.9 years in 2019.[39] However, averages disguise significant heterogeneity across countries. Average debt maturity ranges from lows of 1 and 3.5 years in Pakistan, Egypt, Hungary, respectively, to highs between 10 and 13 years in Chile, Peru, and South Africa.[40] At the same time, governments in several emerging market economies sought to develop domestic bond markets. Examples of such strategy in Latin America notably include Brazil, Chile, and Peru.

These considerations suggest that "safe" public debt ceilings can be computed using ranges of debt maturity and borrowing requirements exemplified in table 7.1. In particular, I consider ranges of average debt maturity from 3 to 9 years and a maximum size of the yearly financing program—as measured by the government's borrowing requirement—in a range from 5% to 9% of GDP. In this respect, it is important to take these values as levels that can be sustained over time under various market conditions, and not values

Table 7.1 Implied Public Debt Ceilings

		Maximum Borrowing Requirement (in % of GDP)		
		5%	7%	9%
	3	13.6%	19.0%	24.4%
Average Debt	5	21.3%	29.8%	38.3%
Maturity (in yrs.)	7	28.1%	39.4%	50.6%
	9	34.2%	47.9%	61.6%
Average		**24.3%**	**34.0%**	**43.7%**

Source: Compiled by author.
Note: Computations are performed using a 3.5% growth rate (*n*).

that can be reached occasionally during periods of high investors' optimism. In its recent DSA for Argentina, for instance, the IMF (2020a) reaches the conclusion that—based on the experience of a number of emerging market economies that suffered debt restructuring events—government gross financing needs should not exceed 5% of GDP on average over the medium term (i.e., after 2024) and 6% of GDP on any given year.[41]

The main lesson that emerges from this numerical exercise is that safe public-debt-to-GDP ratios are much lower than those currently embedded in fiscal rules across the world (and emerging markets in particular). For instance, a 7-percent-of-GDP borrowing requirement and a 3- to 9-year average debt maturity yield, on average, a public debt ceiling in the order of 35% of GDP. Such a level is half the size of the benchmark used by the IMF in its debt sustainability guidelines discussed in the previous section.

Figure 7.2 shows current levels of public debt in relation to GDP in Latin America and in selected countries in the region in 2019. As can be observed, in 2019 the region as a whole displayed a public debt level that amply exceeded the implied safe ceiling, *previous* to a further deterioration occurring in 2020 as a result of the COVID-19 pandemic. Latin America's notable exceptions are Chile and Peru with public debt levels in relation to GDP well below 30%.

Interestingly, a 35%-of-GDP safe public debt ceiling for emerging market economies is consistent with Reinhart, Rogoff, and Savastano's (2003) conclusions from their empirical analysis on what they have named "debt intolerance." Empirical "safe" debt ceilings suggested by their study lie below the 35% of GDP threshold. Reinhart, Rogoff, and Savastano's study is highly illustrative about how significant the challenge is for Latin American governments in the future, as history suggests that very few countries have been successful in implementing significant debt reductions without resorting to defaults or other forms of involuntary restructuring processes.[42]

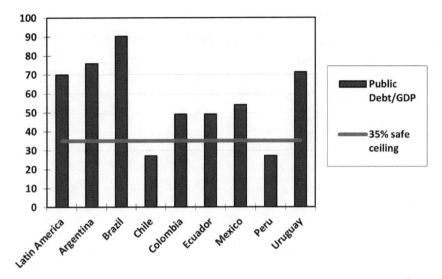

Figure 7.2   Public Debt in Latin America, 2019 (in % of GDP). Congressional Budget Office 2020.

The main conclusion from the above discussion is both straightforward and important. Once liquidity constraints deriving from countries' interaction with international capital markets are considered, sustainable public debt levels are likely to be significantly lower than those recommended by the IMF (2018) guidelines, as well as those embedded in most current fiscal rules in place.[43] Hence, the introduction of liquidity constraints in the conventional tax-smoothing model delivers a stricter notion of debt sustainability than when those considerations are not accounted for. Especially in the case of emerging market economies, it provides a realistic argument in favor of the adoption of low debt ceilings when designing fiscal rules. Moreover, it is useful to define such ceilings in relation to variables such as the average maturity (or duration) of the public debt so as to induce governments to have the right incentives to reduce liquidity risks.

The above simple model suggests that governments in emerging market economies should strive toward lengthening the maturity structure of their public debts. However, although this objective has been greatly facilitated by the long period of low international interest rates initiated since the 2008 Global Financial Crisis, experience shows that governments often resort to issuing debt denominated in foreign currency when they attempt to develop long-term debt markets. A tradeoff then arises, as the sustainable development of long-term domestic currency debt markets is often made prohibitive by weak credibility of monetary policy.

Having argued in favor of safe public debt ceilings in the 35% of GDP range, a *fourth* important observation follows from the analytical framework presented above. What happens when a country that enjoys high investors' credibility faces a sudden loss of confidence?

As I have discussed above, economies that are credible vis-á-vis the capital market may operate (at least for some time) under the conventional optimal fiscal policy framework and, therefore, consider inter-temporal solvency as the relevant criterion to be met, without consideration to liquidity constraints. This is the framework that currently appears as the most relevant to characterize fiscal policy in the advanced economies. And in such a world we have seen that public debt may increase without a clear bound; by 2020, advanced economies' public debt has reached an average of 122.4% of GDP and 137.7% of GDP among the G-7 countries.[44]

Therefore, when a country transitions from a high credibility scenario to a liquidity constrained scenario, the sudden drop in what is perceived as a sustainable debt-to-GDP ratio may be very large—say, from a 100% of GDP to a 35% of GDP ratio—and effectively impossible to implement through fiscal austerity alone. In such cases, debt restructuring becomes the only possible alternative to regain debt sustainability.

Although there are numerous examples of sudden stops across emerging markets, even some advanced economies have been subject to the situation described above. The best example is provided by the 2012 European sovereign debt crisis. In such crisis, a large and unsustainable build-up of public debt had forced Greece into a debt restructuring under the auspices of the ECB, the European Community, and the IMF. The Greek restructuring was the first event of this type in the Euro area and, in particular, had to be undertaken without any role for monetary policy as what was referred to as the Grexit option was not legally available within the EMU and, eventually, was perceived as an even costlier alternative by the Greek authorities.[45]

In any event, the Greek debt restructuring was deemed by the European authorities to be a "unique and non-repeatable" case, in a clear effort to avoid financial contagion to other EMU economies. However, by the end of 2011 and in 2012, contagion could no longer be contained and sovereign spreads in Ireland, Portugal, Italy, and Spain surged to levels comparable to those observed in emerging markets during the financial crises of the 1990s. The difference this time was that sovereign spreads spiked in a context of record very low international interest rates.

The European policy response was decisive and successful in containing a further escalation of financial contagion. It implied major changes in the context of the EMU. First, the ECB modified its policy and was allowed to intervene in bond markets so as to prevent financial conditions to differ significantly across member states.[46] Second, the European Stability Mechanism

(ESM) was created with the ability to also intervene in bond markets to assist economies under contagion, and impose adjustment programs in exchange for its intervention, with the participation of the IMF.

Anchored on the analytical framework discussed above, my conclusion from the 2012 European sovereign debt crisis is that, faced with a loss of investors' confidence, it would have been impossible to restore stability in Europe without further debt restructurings in a number of countries. And the occurrence of additional credit events would have probably expanded contagion even more. Instead, Europe had the possibility, and created the instruments to avoid new debt restructurings within the EMU by choosing to socialize the public debt problem and restore financial stability.

Of course, the type of policy response that was possible in the EMU is not available in emerging markets. If unsustainable public debts exceed significantly safe ceilings, the likelihood of defaults and restructurings will increase significantly. Contrary to what occurred in the 1990s, when the world was surprised by financial contagion and responded treating the crisis as a liquidity problem, the notion of debt sustainability is better understood today, as is the need for debt restructuring when public debt accumulation becomes excessive.

Interestingly, Argentina's 2018 exceptional access stand-by program with the IMF is a reminder of the fact that once investors' confidence and market access is lost, liquidity assistance only postpones the final day of reckoning. Despite implementing a massive fiscal adjustment—mostly through government expenditure cuts—and nearly restoring primary fiscal balance in 2019, Argentina was headed for default even before the outbreak of the COVID-19 pandemic.

The above discussion suggests that, as the introduction of safer—and tighter—debt ceilings is adopted in debt sustainability analyses, new IMF programs may increasingly rely on a combination of liquidity-assistance -and-debt-restructuring. Hence, adoption of standards that ensure efficiency, and equitable and fair treatment in sovereign debt restructuring processes will become a necessary component to be taken into account in the design of fiscal rules. Such standards will affect the conduct of fiscal policy and may provide strong incentives toward fiscal soundness and restraint in excessive debt buildups.

Since the 1990s, the international community has made significant progress in improving the resolution of international sovereign debt crises. In the absence of agreement on a formal sovereign debt resolution formal framework such as Krueger's (2002) Sovereign Debt Restructuring Mechanism (SDRM) proposal—the international community focused on introducing innovations to international bond debt contracts so as to facilitate eventual restructurings and limit the role of holdout creditors in debt exchanges.

An agreement was reached on the adoption of enhanced Collective Action Clauses (CACs) in international sovereign bond contracts allowing a majority of bondholders to bind all bondholders to the financial terms of a restructuring or debt exchange offer.[47] Although legal discussions are still taking place with regard to the practical implementation of enhanced CACs, there is significant optimism about their effectiveness following the debt restructurings of Argentina and Ecuador.[48]

Adoption of enhanced CACs in foreign-law sovereign bond contracts is anchored on a set of best practices over which the international community has reached consensus. The set of best practices (or, the Principles) that guide sovereign debt restructurings include that (1) the debtor should attempt to maintain payments to creditors while a workout is being negotiated; (2) creditors and the debtor should negotiate in good faith; (3) creditors of equal standing should be treated equally; and (4) in order to ensure transparency and sustainability, the negotiation process should involve the IMF.[49]

Notwithstanding the adoption of enhanced CACs in emerging markets and the consensus reached about best practices, the issue of sovereign debt crisis resolution is complex and, when credit events take place, they become highly contentious and politically charged and have profound consequences on the debtor country's economy and welfare.

On the one hand, issuing debt governed by the law of a foreign jurisdiction, especially in a major financial center, has important benefits for the issuer. By issuing debt governed by the law of the major financial centers, sovereigns seek to tap a larger demand for their bonds and, most importantly, "borrow" the credibility enjoyed by the legal systems of those jurisdictions. The effect of this is clear; the issuing State seeks to receive better terms on its debt and to enjoy a larger volume of financing than would otherwise be the case if it issued debt under its own domestic law.[50]

On the other hand, issuing debt governed by foreign law in principle reduces significantly a government's discretion for restructuring its foreign obligations—this limit on government discretion is what makes these assets more credible and desirable in the eyes of investors. But limiting government discretion comes at a cost; that is, sovereigns (as opposed to corporations) do not enjoy the protection typically given by bankruptcy law. And here is where CACs enter into action, as a mechanism to facilitate sovereign debt restructurings by limiting the role of holdouts in debt exchanges.

However, the emphasis placed by the international community on the effectiveness of the enhanced CACs is implicitly based on the assumption that sovereigns will abide by the best practices mentioned above. Unfortunately, this may be not always the case.

Argentina's debt saga between the 2002 default and its resolution in 2016 shows that it cannot be taken for granted that sovereign debtors will abide by best international practices. As its 2005 unilateral debt exchange offers received limited support by bondholders, Argentina decided to openly defy foreign courts and international tribunals.[51] In March 2014, the Argentine Supreme Court decided that a ruling obtained in a foreign court could be brought to enforcement in Argentina.[52]

The possibility that a sovereign may choose to defy foreign courts to which they had originally submitted when issuing bonds may weaken the credibility offered by international financial centers—such as New York—and, hence, generate negative externalities on other emerging market issuers. Moreover, by ignoring rulings of foreign courts, rogue debtors may have negative effects on the functioning of the international capital market. This discussion suggests that, short of adopting a formal sovereign debt resolution framework, the future international reform agenda should promote the adoption of a specific debt restructuring protocol by which sovereigns agree to submit to the ruling of foreign courts and, for this purpose, renounce the immunity currently enjoyed by their international reserves (present and future).[53]

Finally, signing of the proposed debt-restructuring protocol should be made a condition for issuing bonds under foreign jurisdiction. Countries that opt not to be signatories of the protocol would only be able to issue debt under domestic jurisdiction.

CONCLUDING REMARKS

This chapter has discussed the interaction between fiscal rules, the public debt, and the capital market. It has been emphasized that the presence of liquidity constraints that emerge from the interaction with the capital market has important implications for the adequate design of the fiscal policy framework and, hence, of fiscal rules.

In particular, it has been shown that, especially in emerging and developing economies, fiscal policy should be designed to include safe public debt ceilings that are significantly lower than those imbedded in current debt sustainability analyses. Moreover, at current high levels of public debt, it may be increasingly difficult to avoid debt restructuring as part of the multilaterals' effort to restore financial stability in situations where governments lose the confidence of investors. In this context, further innovations may be needed in the international financial architecture to make sovereign-debt-crisis resolution more efficient.

NOTES

1. I wish to thank Guillermo Calvo, Ricardo López Murphy, Steve Hanke, Gabriel Lopetegui, and Barry Poulson for their insightful comments.

2. Argentina experienced hyperinflation in 1989 and 1990, with inflation reaching almost 4924% in 1989 and 1344% in 1990; data accessed from www.indec.gob.ar/indec/web/Institucional-Indec-InformacionDeArchivo-1. Peru experienced hyperinflation between 1988 and 1990, with inflation reaching 1722% in 1988, 2775% in 1989, and 7650% in 1990; data accessed from www.imf.org/external/datamapper /PCPIEPCH@WEO/OEMDC/ADVEC/WEOWORLD/PER. See Hanke and Krus (2013) for a precise characterization of each hyperinflation episode.

3. See Hanke (1999).

4. According to Gaspar and Gopinath (2020), the fiscal response (both higher spending and lost revenue) to the COVID-19 pandemic has reached, on average, about 9 percentage points of GDP in the advanced economies and about 3 percentage points of GDP in emerging market economies. In addition, advanced economies deployed an additional 11% of GDP in loans, equity, and guarantees, compared to an additional 2% of GDP in these same items across emerging market economies.

5. The sub-periods analyzed by Brown (1990) are 1945–1955 and 1945–1965.

6. Cukierman (1992) contains an excellent discussion about the theoretical underpinnings of central bank independence.

7. See Buti and Giudice (2004).

8. The Brady Plan resulted in a massive securitization of previously illiquid bank assets. This eventually led to the emerging market crises of the second half of the 1990s and beginning of the 2000s. A decade later, a similar process occurred in the advanced economies, when the securitization of sub-prime mortgages in the United States became a central cause of the 2008–2009 Global Financial Crisis.

9. Russia and Argentina defaulted in 1998 and 2002, respectively. Mexico did not suffer a full-fledged default because it was rescued by the U.S. Treasury in 1995 to resolve a short-term debt (Tesobonos) crisis.

10. *Fiscal rules* were first defined by Kopits and Symansky (1998) as "a permanent constraint on fiscal policy, typically defined in terms of overall fiscal performance."

11. See Schaechter el al. (2012) and Eyraud et al. (2018).

12. See, for instance, the discussion in Persson and Tabellini (1990).

13. See Buti and Giudice (2004).

14. Factors that affect government revenues and established expenditure programs through changes in economic activity are called "automatic stabilizers."

15. As reported by Buti and Giudice (2004), the Treaty of Maastricht induced a 3.5 percentage point fiscal consolidation between 1993 and 1997 in the Euro area, starting from an historical initial budget deficit of 5.5% of GDP. By 1997, all member countries except Greece had a budget deficit below the ceiling of 3% of GDP.

16. By 2017, according to the IMF Fiscal Rules Database, the total number of advanced, emerging market, and developing economies employing fiscal rules had increased to 96.

17. See IMF (2018).

18. In addition to the debt benchmark, the IMF (2013) guidelines and the IMF's DSA analysis take into account a number of other relevant benchmarks such as bond spreads, external financing requirements, the change in short-term public debt in% of total debt, and the share of public debt held by non-residents.

19. In the midst of the COVID-19 pandemic, the IMF (2020b) has initiated a review toward reforming its Public Debt Limits Policy (DLP) in Fund-supported programs. The reform proposals aim at improving measurement, transparency, and disclosure of public debt information, as well as increasing flexibility in the design of debt conditionality so as to "strike the right balance between providing space for public investment to support inclusive growth and maintaining debt sustainability."

20. Schaechter et al. (2012) contains a detailed discussion of the different types of fiscal rules adopted by countries around the world.

21. When discussing fiscal rules in the Latin American context, the most obvious example that comes to mind is Chile—see, for instance, Frankel (2011) and Marshall (2003). Chile pioneered fiscal rules in the region adopting a structural fiscal balance target—accounting not only for the economic cycle but also for the evolution of the price of copper—that has been very successful over time. I focus here on the comparison between Argentina and Peru because they share fundamental similarities before diverging in terms of fiscal outcomes.

22. See Guidotti and Rodriguez (1992).

23. While Argentina moved from a pay-as-you-go regime to a private individual-capitalization system, in Peru's reform envisaged a coexistence of both the public and the private pension system.

24. Guidotti (2006) analyzes in detail the impact of Argentina's 1993 pension reform on its fiscal dynamics.

25. Data from the IMF's Data Mapper.

26. *Pesification* refers to the compulsory conversion of U.S.–dollar contracts into domestic currency. In the banking system, pesification was "asymmetric," as bank assets were converted into pesos at a lower exchange rate than that applied to the conversion of deposits. For an in-depth analysis of the 2001–2002 Argentine crisis, see Guidotti and Nicolini (2016).

27. As discussed in Guidotti (2020), Argentina's latest debt restructuring may not solve the country's debt woes. The structure of the 2020 restructuring has not reduced the significant debt burden; it has only postponed payments into the next administration. Moreover, fiscal dominance remains significant, as the 2021 budget contemplates a monetary financing of 60 % of the budget deficit.

28. See Rossini, Quispe and Loyola (2011) and Liendo (2015) for an analysis of fiscal rules in Peru.

29. Data from the IMF Data Mapper.

30. See Peru's Ministry of Finance, Estrategia de Gestion Integral de Activos y Pasivos 2019–2022, 2019.

31. In April and July 2008, respectively, Fitch and S&P raised Peru's credit rating to BBB−, in the investment-grade category. Moody's followed suit in December 2009 when it assigned Peru the investment-grade rating of Baa3.

32. Peru's public debt is currently rated A3 by Moody's and BBB+ by Standard & Poor's and Fitch. On April 16, 2020, in the midst of the COVID-19 crisis, Peru issued debt with 11 years maturity at an annual interest rate of 2.8%.

33. Greenspan (1999) and Guidotti (2000 and 2003) pointed out the necessity of linking the concept of fiscal sustainability to the development of adequate liquidity management strategies in emerging market economies.

34. It is assumed for simplicity's sake that amortizations are uniformly distributed over time.

35. The overall budget deficit, d, is related to the primary balance, s, by $s = rd - d$, where r denotes the rate of interest on the public debt. Together with equation (3), it yields the commonly used requirement for achieving a stable debt-to-GDP ratio; that is, $s = (r - n)b$.

36. The maximum borrowing requirement referred in the present context, although exogenous to the government, is not an arbitrarily fixed number. As discussed in Guidotti (2007) it depends on a number of characteristics, such as the economic growth rate (n), the extent of liability dollarization, the government's credit history, and a number of additional considerations such as those taken into account in the IMF's (2018) debt sustainability guidelines.

37. See Lane and Milesi-Ferretti (2017) for an in-depth analysis of recent trends in international financial integration.

38. See IMF Fiscal Monitor (2020).

39. See IMF Fiscal Monitor (2020).

40. In some cases, such as Argentina, a long public debt average maturity reflects events of debt restructuring rather than the result of an active debt management strategy.

41. See IMF (2020a).

42. The quality of fiscal austerity measures is very important. Alesina, Favero and Giavazzi (2019) provide extensive evidence comparing fiscal adjustment programs based on expenditure reductions with those anchored on tax increases.

43. Most public debt sustainability analyses rely on the concept of gross public debt in relation to GDP. However, the precise definition of public debt to be used may be important when assessing risks in specific cases, as gross public debt includes intra-government debts as well as debt owed to multilaterals. At the same time, in some cases it is important to add central bank debt—usually not included in the gross public debt definition—to the relevant aggregate used to assess debt sustainability.

44. See IMF Fiscal Monitor (2020).

45. Grexit referred to the possibility of Greece abandoning the Euro area.

46. Corsetti and Dedola (2016) discuss how the type of backstop for government debt provided by the ECB in the midst of the 2012 European sovereign debt crisis may be successful in preventing sovereign defaults while being consistent with the monetary policy objective of maintaining price stability.

47. See, for instance, IMF (2014), Sobel (2016), IMF (2019).

48. See discussion in Buchheit and Gulati (2020).

49. Variations of these principles have been proposed in different international fora; see, for instance, IIF (2013) and IMF (2014).

50. There is ample evidence that emerging market bonds governed by foreign law trade at tighter spreads than similar bonds issued under domestic law.

51. In 2010, Argentina reopened the 2005 debt exchange. However, the new offer still left a significant number of holdout creditors.

52. Argentine Supreme Court Ruling C. 462 XLVII, "Claren Corporation c/ E.N.-arts. 517/518 CPCC exequatur s/ varios," March 2014.

53. Other aspects of this proposal are discussed in Guidotti and Hamilton (2015). In particular, in order to foster enforcement of the protocol, the BIS should be required to provide no immunity protection with respect to international reserves deposited by non-complying countries.

REFERENCES

Alesina, Alberto and Alland Drazen. 1991. "Why Are Stabilizations Delayed?" *American Economic Review*, 81: 1170–88.

Alesina, Alberto, Carlo Favero, and Francesco Giavazzi. 2019. *Austerity: When it Works and When it Doesn't.* Princeton University Press.

Barro, Robert. 1979. "On the Determination of the Public Debt." *Journal of Political Economy*, 87: 940–971.

Barro, Robert and David Gordon. 1983. "A Positive Theory of Monetary Policy in a Natural Rate Model." *Journal of Political Economy*, 91: 589–610.

Brown, Cary. 1990. "Episodes in the Public Debt History of the United States." In *Public Debt Management: Theory and History*, edited by Rudiger Dornbusch and Mario Draghi. MIT Press, 229–254.

Buchheit, Lee and Mitu Gulati. 2020. "The Argentine Collective Action Controversy." Working Paper (July).

Buti, Marco and Gabriele Giudice. 2004. "EMU's Fiscal Rules: What Can and Cannot Be Exported." In *Rules-Based Fiscal Policy in Emerging Markets: Background, Analysis, and Prospects*, edited by George Kopits. Palgrave-Macmillan, 97–113.

Calvo, Guillermo. 1988. "Servicing the Public Debt: The Role of Expectations." *American Economic Review* 78 (September): 647–661.

Calvo, Guillermo and Pablo E. Guidotti. 1990. "Indexation and Maturity of Government Bonds: A Simple Model." In *Public Debt Management: Theory and History*, edited by Rudiger Dornbusch and Mario Draghi. MIT Press, 52–82.

Calvo, Guillermo and Pablo E. Guidotti. 1992. "Optimal Maturity of Nominal Government Debt: An Infinite-Horizon Model." *International Economic Review* 33 (November): 895–919.

Calvo, Guillermo, Pablo E. Guidotti and Leonardo Leiderman. 1991. "Optimal Maturity of Nominal Government Debt: The First Tests." *Economic Letters* 33 (April): 415–421.

Corsetti, Giancarlo and Luca Dedola. 2016. "The "Mystery of the Printing Press" Monetary Policy and Self-fulfilling Debt Crises." Working Paper (July).

Cukierman, Alex. 1992. *Central Bank Strategy, Credibility, and Independence: Theory and Evidence*, MIT Press.

Eyraud, Luc, Xavier Debrun, Andrew Hodge, Victor Lledó and Catherine Pattillo. 2018. *Second-Generation Fiscal Rules: Balancing Simplicity, Flexibility, and Enforceability*, IMF Staff Discussion Note SDN/18/04. Washington, DC: (April).

Frankel, Jeffrey. 2011. "A Solution to Fiscal Procyclicality: The Structural Budget Institutions Pioneered by Chile." NBER Working Paper 16945 (April).

Gaspar, Vitor. 2020. "Future of Fiscal Rules in the Euro Area." Workshop on Fiscal Rules in Europe: Design and Enforcement, DG ECFIN, Brussels: (January).

Gopinath, Gita and Vitor Gaspar. 2020. "Fiscal Policies for a Transformed World." IMF Blog (July 10th).

Greenspan, Alan. 1999. "Currency Reserves and Debt." Remarks Before the World Bank Conference on Recent Trends in Reserves Management, Washington, DC. (April).

Guidotti, Pablo E. 2000. "On Debt Management and Collective Action Clauses." In *Reforming the International Monetary and Financial System*, edited by Peter Kenen and Alexander Swoboda. Washington: International Monetary Fund, 265–276 .

Guidotti, Pablo E. 2003. "Toward a Liquidity Management Strategy for Emerging Market Economies." In *Latin American Macroeconomic Reforms: The Second Stage,* edited by José Antonio Gonzalez, Vittorio Corbo, Anne Krueger, and Aaron Tornell. The University of Chicago Press, 293–323.

Guidotti, Pablo E. 2006. "Argentina's Fiscal Policy in the 1990s: A Tale of Skeletons and Sudden Stops." In *Challenges to Fiscal Adjustment in Latin America: The Cases of Argentina, Brazil, Chile and Mexico.* The Organization for Economic Co-Operation and Development (Chapter 3): 69–92.

Guidotti, Pablo E. 2007. "Global Finance, Macroeconomic Performance, and Policy Response in Latin America: Lessons from the 1990s." *Journal of Applied Economics* X (2, November): 279–308.

Guidotti, Pablo E. 2020. "Argentina on the Brink, Again." OMFIF, (October 7th). https://www.omfif.org/2020/10/argentina-on-the-brink-again/.

Guidotti, Pablo E. and Jonathan Hamilton. 2015. "Sovereign Debt Restructuring and the Global Financial Architecture." In *Bretton Woods: The Next 70 Years*, edited by Marc Uzan. New York: Reinventing Bretton Woods Committee: 135–144.

Guidotti, Pablo E. and Juan Pablo Nicolini. 2016. "The Argentine Banking Crises of 1995 and 2001: An Exploration into the Role of Macro-Prudential Regulations." Prepared for the *Riksbank Macroprudential Conference.* Stockholm: (June).

Guidotti, Pablo E. and Carlos Alfredo Rodriguez. 1992. "Dollarization in Latin America: Gresham's Law in Reverse?" *IMF Staff Papers* 39 (3, September): 518–544.

Guidotti, Pablo E. and Carlos A. Végh. 1999. "Losing Credibility: The Stabilization Blues." *International Economic Review* 40 (February): 23–51.

Hanke, Steve. 1999. "Yugoslavia Destroyed Its Own Economy." *The Wall Street Journal* (April 28th).

Hanke, Steve and Nicholas Krus, 2013. "World Hyperinflations." In *The Handbook of Major Events in Economic History*, edited by Randall Parker and Robert Whaples. London, UK: Routledge, 367–377.

Institute of International Finance. 2013. *Principles for Stable Capital Flows and Fair Debt Restructuring*, Report on implementation by the Principles Consultative Group, Washington, DC: (October).

International Monetary Fund. 2013. *Staff Guidance Note for Public Debt Sustainability Analysis in Market-Access Countries.* Washington, DC: (May).

International Monetary Fund. 2014. *Strengthening the Contractual Framework to Address Collective Action Problems in Sovereign Debt Restructuring.* Washington, DC: (October).

International Monetary Fund. 2018. *Fiscal Policy: How to Calibrate Fiscal Rules, A Primer.* How To Note 8. Washington, DC: (March).

International Monetary Fund. 2019. *Fourth Progress Report on Inclusion of Enhanced Contractual Provisions in International Sovereign Bond Contracts.* Washington, DC: (March).

International Monetary Fund. 2020a. *Technical Assistance Report-Staff Technical Note on Public Debt Sustainability.* Country Report 20/83. Washington, DC: (March).

International Monetary Fund. 2020b. *Reform of the Policy on Public Debt Limits in IMF-Supported Programs.* IMF Policy Paper. Washington, DC: (November).

International Monetary Fund. 2020c. *Global Financial Stability Report.* Washington, DC: (April).

International Monetary Fund. 2020d. *Fiscal Monitor.* Washington, DC: (April).

Kopits, George and Steven Symanski. 1998. *Fiscal Rules.* IMF Occasional Paper 162. Washington, DC: 1998.

Krueger, Anne. 2002. *A New Approach to Sovereign Debt Restructuring*, International Monetary Fund. Washington, DC: (April).

Lane, Philip and Gian Maria Milesi-Ferretti. 2017. "International Financial Integration in the Aftermath of the Global Financial Crisis." IMF Working Paper WP/17/115 (May).

Liendo, Cesar. 2015. "Evolution of Fiscal Rules in Peru." In *Peru: Staying the Course of Economic Success,* edited by Alejandro Werner and Alejandro Santos. Washington: International Monetary Fund (September): 85–98.

Marshall, Jorge. 2003. "Fiscal Rule and Central Bank Issues in Chile." In *Fiscal Issues and Central Banking in Emerging Economies,* BIS Papers no. 20 (October).

Persson, Torsten and G. Tabellini. 1990. *Macroeconomic Policy, Credibility and Politics,* Harwood Academic Publishers.

Reinhart, Carmen and Kenneth Rogoff. 2009. *This Time Is Different: Eight Centuries of Financial Folly*, Princeton University Press.

Reinhart, Carmen, Rogoff Kenneth and Miguel Savastano. 2003. "Debt Intolerance." *Brookings Papers on Economic Activity* 1 (Spring): 1–74.

Rossini, Renzo, Zenón Quispe and Jorge Loyola. 2011. "Fiscal Policy Considerations in the Design of Monetary Policy in Peru." BIS Papers no. 67.

Schaechter, Andrea, Tidiane Kinda, Nina Budina and Anke Weber. 2012. "Fiscal Rules in Response to the Crisis-Toward the "Next-Generation" Rules. A New Dataset." IMF Working Paper WP/12/187 (July).

Sobel, Mark. 2016. "Strengthening Collective Action Clauses: Catalysing Change-The Back Story." *Capital Markets Law Journal* 11 (1): 3–11.

Chapter 8

Populist Economic Thought

The Legacy of Juan Domingo Perón

Carlos Newland and Emilio Ocampo

INTRODUCTION

During a recent official visit of Argentina's president Alberto Fernandez to Germany, Chancellor Angela Merkel asked him what was the ideology of Peronism, the political party founded by Juan Perón in the 1940s. Since a transcript of their conversation was not made available, we don't know Fernandez's exact answer. A blogger from *The Economist* provided an imaginary version of their conversation that sounds plausible (Bello 2020). Outside Argentina, Peronism is an enigma to sociologists and political scientists. The categories they apply in most countries don't seem appropriate. It is not fascism but draws many elements from it; it is not socialism but appeals to class struggle and leads to similar results. Extremists from the right and the left claim to be Perón's true heirs and still cohabit, not without conflict, in the party he created. According to *New York Times* columnist Roger Cohen,

> [T]o give expression to its uniqueness, Argentina invented its own political phi-
> losophy: a strange mishmash of nationalism, romanticism, fascism, socialism,
> backwardness, progressiveness, militarism, eroticism, fantasy, musical, mourn-
> fulness, irresponsibility and repression. The name it gave all this was Peronism.
> It has proved impossible to shake. (Cohen 2014)

Peronism has also been defined as the quintessential Latin American version of populism. That may not help much to understand it, since political scientists, economists, and sociologists cannot agree on a definition of the latter (see Ocampo 2019). In their classic study on the macroeconomics of Latin American populism, Dornbusch and Edwards (1991) defined it as a set of policy measures that emphasized income redistribution and ignored economic or financial constraints. They also described the typical populist experiment as having three phases: an initial boom followed by bottlenecks, inflationary pressures and foreign exchange shortages followed by a crisis and a period of austerity. The idea that deficit financing through monetary expansion can lead to high inflation is anathema to populist policymakers (and their voters). Instead, they believe it stimulates domestic consumption and an expansion of real output. In reality, as Dornbusch and Edwards pointed out, it leads to shortages, high inflation and, eventually, a financial crisis. At the end of the populist cycle, orthodoxy prevails and real wages are always lower. The paradox of populism is that those who are meant to benefit from its policies end up suffering the most. According to Edwards (2019b), Perón's economic policies during 1946–1949 were the archetype of this economic policy paradigm.

In the last decade, both left- and right-wing populism have spread beyond Latin America. Although both versions present a threat to liberal democracy, they have a different approach to economic policy. Right-wing populism favors protectionism and crony capitalism, whereas left-wing populism adds income and wealth redistribution and extensive state intervention to the mix (Ocampo 2019). In recent years, some elements of the Latin American populist policy paradigm have surfaced in the United States in the form of what is called "Modern Monetary Theory" (MMT). As Edwards (2019a) has explained, the types of policies advocated by MMT supporters have been tried in several countries in Latin America with disastrous results. Argentina is in fact a prime example of what happens to a country that consistently applies those policies. In fact, we argue in this chapter that Perón was a precursor in the implementation of the MMT policy paradigm (see Ocampo 2020).

Four decades ago, Samuelson (1980) argued that Schumpeter's prediction that socialism would inevitably replace capitalism was still valid. In his view, the problem with the original version was that the definition of socialism proposed by Schumpeter was incorrect. According to Samuelson, the biggest threat to Western-mixed advanced economies was not the Soviet or Maoist version of socialism, the one proposed by Oskar Lange in the 1930s, the one advocated by Jan Tinbergen and Joan Robinson in the postwar era, or the 1970s Scandinavian variety, but the type of populism prevalent in South America, particularly Argentina since Juan Perón. Given the growing number of countries governed by populists in recent years and the emergence of policy prescriptions such as those offered by MMT, it may be worth delving into the economic ideology behind Peronism, a subject that has not received the attention it deserves from economists and historians (exceptions are Di Tella and Dubra 2010; Llach and Gerchunoff 2007, and Sowter 2015). Peronism not only determined Argentina's economic trajectory since 1945 but also influenced the policies of many other countries in Latin America, such as Peru and Venezuela.

This chapter is organized as follows. The second section analyzes the main features of the Peronist economic policy paradigm. The third section describes the consequences of applying this paradigm. The final segment offers some concluding remarks.

THE PERONIST ECONOMIC POLICY PARADIGM

According to Edwards (2019b), the Latin American populist policy paradigm is best condensed in a letter sent by Perón in 1952 to the newly elected president of Chile, Carlos Ibáñez del Campo:

> Give the people, especially to the workers, all that is possible. When it seems to you that you have already given them too much, give them more. You will see the results. Everybody will try to frighten you with the specter of an economic collapse. But all of this is a lie. There is nothing more elastic than the economy, which everyone fears so much because no one understands it.

It is ironic Perón would give such advice when those policies had given him such poor results. By the end of 1951, the Argentine economy was on its knees, having endured four years of stagflation and growing social unrest. It was evident by then that the economy was not "elastic," as Perón had just launched his "Austerity Plan." In 1952, Argentina's GDP per capita ended up roughly at the same level as in 1946. When comparing these years, the level of real wages remained constant (Newland and Cuesta 2017).

Perón was an unknown army colonel until June 4, 1943, when together with a group of fiercely nationalist army officers he staged a coup d'état. Even after his death in 1974, he has remained the dominant figure of Argentine politics. Although Perón gave himself airs of a profound thinker and pretended to be deeply knowledgeable about most public policy issues, his economic ideas were a contradictory mishmash representative of past and contemporary zeitgeists with an Argentine flavor. Perón exemplifies well Keynes's dictum about the power of the ideas of economists and political philosophers on both statesmen and practical men. He claimed that he had learned economics during his two-year stay in Italy, a country that, in his opinion, had "the best economists" (Luna 1971, 59). Italy certainly had great economists, but most of them in fact opposed fascism (see Ocampo 2020a). One exception is Franco Modigliani who in his youth was an enthusiastic supporter. In 1936, Modigliani even received "an award for economics writing from the hand of Benito Mussolini himself" (Klein and Daza 2013, 472). Modigliani was by no means the guru of fascist economics, but in several articles he wrote in 1937 and 1938, before racist laws forced his emigration, he succinctly described its essence. In one of these articles he explained that the goal of a fascism was to prevent "the exploitation of the weak by the strong," which he considered the inevitable result of a free market economy, and promote the advent "of a higher social justice" (Klein and Daza 2013, 477). The same could be said about Peronism (or *Justicialismo*, as Perón liked to call it). Social justice is one of its key tenets of Peronism. The other two were being economic independence and political sovereignty, also common to fascism.

Perón's economic policies were predicated on two assumptions, which he also shared with fascist economic policies. First, a communist revolution was an imminent and existential threat to Argentina. Second, communism originated in the injustices engendered by unfettered capitalism. A third important assumption was that foreign interests allied with a local oligarchy had imposed a capitalist system in Argentina to exploit "the people." From a policy perspective, his solution to this problem was the "Third Way," which entailed creating a "Corporate State" along the same lines as the one Mussolini imposed in Italy during the 1920s and 1930s.

From 1944 until 1949, Perón was very influenced by José Figuerola, a Spanish exile who became one of his key economic advisers and collaborators. Trained as a lawyer, Figuerola had been a government official in Spain under the right-wing dictatorship of General Primo de Rivera. After the latter's downfall, he moved to Italy where he studied the fascist labor legislation that was embodied in the *Carta del Lavoro*. In the early 1930s, he moved to Argentina and joined the National Labor Department (NLD) where he was responsible for compiling statistics. Shortly after the 1943 *coup d'état*, Perón took over the NLD and turned it into a ministry with the intention of making it the springboard of his political career. Perón took an immediate liking to Figuerola, who authored the first five-year economic plan announced in October 1946.

Ramon Cereijo, who Perón appointed as his first minister of finance, was also influential in giving a theoretical patina to Peronomics. Cereijo was a finance professor who had been greatly influenced by the Catholic Church's social doctrine, Roosevelt's New Deal, and Keynesianism, particularly as articulated by Alvin Hansen. Above all, Cereijo emphasized that *Justicialismo* had "perfected" economic theory with its rejection of liberal and free-market ideas (Cereijo 1947, 1950). A useful document to understand Peronist thought is a manual written to indoctrinate the regime's cadres (Apuntes 1954). The starting point of *Justicialismo* is the existence of a central conflict between workers and capitalists. Although it recognized the Marxist notion of class struggle, as in Mussolini's fascism, it rejected the annihilation of the private sector proposed by communism. Instead, it proposed that the government (Perón), the state (public officials), and the "organized community" would determine a fair distribution of income among workers and businessmen.

Basically, government had to regulate market forces when demand or consumption exceeded supply by imposing price controls or rationing. In line with Perón's speeches, Cereijo argued that foreign companies in general did not operate in a market of perfect competition, but instead sought to "exploit" the countries in which they operated. Once again, an active state intervention was necessary, particularly in foreign trade. Supposedly, bulk purchases and sales through a state export-import monopoly would increase Argentina's negotiating power in world markets. An active government intervention and planning was necessary to achieve "economic independence," another key tenet of Peronism. Perón felt that the "revolutionary doctrine" that he had developed with his collaborators had refuted "the old capitalist truth that is struggling in retreat, persecuted by those people it exploited for centuries" (Perón 1951, 230).

The strong role in economic affairs Perón granted to the state was not new in Argentina. In fact, the idea of the paternalistic state preceded Perón. In 1942, Francis Herron, an American journalist who spent a year visiting Argentina, observed the following:

> I am at last beginning to appreciate government is important, important beyond anything which North Americans can imagine. Argentine society depends upon governmental paternalism. Government, not individuals or individual Enterprise, creates the great utilities of the nation, influences the educational system, and directs the development of the country. Enterprise in the Argentine is something which the people believe must be "fomented" by government. Because of the nature of Argentine society, this view of things is natural. The force of private capital is not known in the Argentine as it is in the United States . . . Foreign capital is regarded as predatory, and whether it be of English, United States or German origin it is not popular . . . In a country where individual enterprise is uncommon and where success is difficult to achieve, wealth can most easily be obtained by a quick stroke at the expense of others. Hence a capitalist is not esteemed. He is considered to be a schemer, an opportunist, at times even a thief. A capitalist is not admired; he is more hated than admired. A capitalist is not regarded as one who promotes civilization; he is thought of as a plunderer. If he does good, it is regarded as a simulation, and the good he does is presumed to be for the ulterior purpose of placing himself in a position so that he can make another profitable deal at the expense of others. This conception of the capitalist has been inherited from the Spanish colonial system. (Herron 1943, 155–156)

One can go back to the colonial era to find the roots of these ideas. At that time, Juan Bautista Alberdi, Argentina's most prominent liberal thinker, argued that one of the greatest obstacles to the development of Argentina and Spanish America was a deeply ingrained negative attitude toward business and businessmen. As Alberdi pointed out, all of Argentina's heroes were generals who had victoriously led its armies during the wars of independence. Entrepreneurs were ignored at best and despised at worse (Gómez and Newland 2013). Perón viewed himself as the successor of General San Martin, who in Argentina was and is still widely considered "the father of nation" and the "Liberator of South America." He promoted the notion that he waged a war for Argentina's economic independence against foreign interests and was thus completing San Martin's epic.

THE ECONOMIC CONSEQUENCES OF PERONISM

When analyzing the economic policies of the first Peronist experiment, it is essential to distinguish four phases, the last three of which follow exactly those described by Dornbusch and Edwards (1991) as typical of Latin American populism. The first phase started at the end of October 1943 when Perón appointed himself Secretary of Labor and started to exert a growing influence on the military regime's social and economic policies. He consolidated his power by early 1944, accumulating the titles of Vice President, War Minister, Labor Minister, and Head of the National Postwar Council (NPC). This was the militaristic authoritarian phase of Peronism. The second phase started at the beginning of 1946 when Perón won the presidential election and ended in January 1949, when after a long crisis he fired Miguel Miranda, his "finance czar." It was during this period that the economic policies of Peronism that are considered the archetype of populist economic policies were defined and implemented. A "muddling through" phase followed during which Perón avoided taking any drastic measures to correct the imbalances generated by his policies in the previous phase for fears that they could jeopardize his reelection. Shortly after he won the presidential election in November 1951, the last phase started. In early 1952 Perón launched an "Austerity Plan" that emphasized increasing productivity and private-sector investments, particularly foreign. This "quasi-orthodox" phase ended in September 1955 when Perón was overthrown by a military coup. When Perón returned to power in 1973, his economic policies were almost identical to those of the 1946–1949 period.[1]

During the 1930s, increased government intervention was the norm in Europe and North America. In Argentina, it involved greater control of monetary policy, exchange rates, and international trade. This trend deepened during World War II. Argentina was no exception. Although, after the war there was a trend toward liberalization, particularly in foreign trade, government intervention continued to grow in many economies through the nationalization of public utilities, the increase in public employment, and the implementation of national development plans. The UK under the Labor Party was a typical example, which may have been an inspiration for Perón. Some of his biographers claim that after returning from Italy, he read works by Harold Laski and the 1942 Beveridge Report as well as the welfare program developed by Leonard Marsh for Canada (Pavón Pereyra 2018).

Perón's first five-year plan compared itself favorably to the Beveridge plan with respect to pensions. However, the government that emerged from the 1943 military coup led by Perón took government intervention to a higher level.

Between 1946 and 1955 Perón closed the economy to foreign competition and intensified state intervention. The measures he took during his presidency included the nationalization of the railways and utilities, as well as some industrial and shipping companies. In the banking sector, he eliminated Central Bank independence, created new public financial institutions to finance industrial development, allocated credit on a discretionary basis to benefit mostly the urban industrial sector, and nationalized deposits as well as mortgage credit. Foreign trade was put under the control of IAPI, a state monopoly which was presided by the president of the Central Bank.[2]

The Peronist regime also increased government bureaucracy. Between 1943 and 1955, the number of public employees doubled while population grew by only 25%. Public expenditures grew 60% between 1946 and 1955. Compared with the rest of Latin America, by the end of the period, Argentina had the largest public sector (CEPAL 1958, 134, 139). The growth in government expenditures was unchecked by a Congress dominated by Peronist legislators who obeyed Perón's orders to a tee. The constitutional reform that Perón enacted in 1949 reduced the role of the Legislative power by allowing the Executive to replace annual budgets with bi-annual or tri-annual ones.

On average between 1945 and 1955, fiscal spending exceeded public revenues by 14% (CEPAL 1958, 149). Although tax pressure increased markedly from 10% of GDP in 1946 to 17% in 1951 (Bellini 2014, 124), revenues did not match growing expenditures, which led to persistent and growing deficits. In addition, the government incurred off-budget expenditures that on average represented half of total budgeted expenditures (Reutz 1991). The fiscal gap was partly covered by the issuance of low-yielding bonds that were forcibly placed in state-controlled pension funds (leading to their actuarial bankruptcy). The off-budget deficits were indirectly financed with increases in credit from state-owned banks. At least during the first years of the Perón presidency, monetary and credit expansion were not a concern for the government, since the underlying assumption was that it would lead to increases in output and therefore not generate inflationary pressures.

In line with Keynesianism, Minister Cereijo argued that sometimes it was necessary to resort to deficit financing. In his view, if properly implemented, this policy would inject "vitality" into the economy (Cereijo 1947, 37). Anticipating MMT, Juan De Greef, a leading Peronist legislator who was in charge of presenting the Executive's budget in Congress, explained that according to the "Peronist Theory" of public spending, the notion of a balanced budget was irrelevant. "No other ghost frightened our rulers so much as that of the invincible financial deficit . . . but the advice was thrown on deaf ears, and the State began to spend." De Greef proudly boasted that in 1948 public spending had tripled in comparison to 1946. Against demands for greater fiscal austerity, he advocated the principle of "spending well," which he deemed more appropriate to the management of a "modern" state (Degreef 1950, 34–35).

In many regards, Peronism can be considered a precursor in the application of MMT-like policies. The general idea was that deficits did not matter and that an increase in the monetary supply would have real effects on the economy and no impact on inflation. Perón himself articulated these ideas in many of his speeches (Perón 1953, 861), and government officials in charge of formulating and implementing economic policy followed his lead.

Apparently, it was Miguel Miranda, a wily unscrupulous businessman, who convinced Perón about the "wonders" of using "other people's money." In 1944, Perón had called in the Central Bank's economic experts to help him find a way to finance an ambitious five-year development plan. They replied that the plan was not viable given that the government was already running a substantial deficit. Perón then turned to Miranda. Many years later, he recounted the story of their meeting:

> I told him [Miranda] about the exchange with the experts and he said: "General! Do you think that if they were capable of something they would be earning a miserable salary as advisers [at the Central Bank]?"—"But Miranda," I said, "we have to spend a lot and we don't have any money!"—"That's the way to buy anything, without money," he replied. "Only fools buy with their own money!"—This is my man, I thought to myself . . . Miranda was a true genius. His intuition, his great capacity for synthesis and his acute business acumen earned the Argentine Republic in one year more than what its economists, who are no more than dilettantes and generalizers of routine and inconsequential methods and systems, had earned in fifty years. (Perón 1956, 37)

In May 1946, Perón, who was not yet president, had Miranda appointed as president of the Central Bank and IAPI, a newly created state agency that had as its mission to control Argentina's foreign trade. The following year he was elevated to the role of chairman of the National Economic Council, the supreme authority on economic matters. Until January 1949, Miranda was the all-powerful "finance czar" of Argentina.

Miranda had a very particular vision of monetary policy: he maintained that as currency issuance returned to the nationalized banking system in the form of deposits, which the Central Bank controlled, there was no cost to the government (Brennan and Rougier 2013, 80). The government faced no financial constraint. It was possible to create wealth by simply expanding the money credit. As evidenced in a speech to provincial finance ministers in 1947, Perón clearly shared Miranda's unorthodox views on monetary policy:

> We must not forget that we have an annual currency circulation that is much higher than what we had when we took over the government. The old banking system had managed to produce an annual turnover of fiduciary circulation equivalent to four times the issuance: that is, about 16 billion pesos, considering that the value of the issuance was 4 billion. Now we are turning over eight times the value of the issuance, so that the annual wealth in circulation has become 32 billion pesos. And we have to take it to ten times, so that we have an annual turn-over of approximately 40 billion. This increase in wealth will mean an increase in inflation, but also increased economic activity, which is what matters. In any case, the resulting inflation will always be kept 20% below that of the country with the lowest inflation. We cannot abandon the natural relationship that must exist in international trade. I have always thought that, in the economic sphere, we were going to live without any crisis during the six years of my government. Today, as a result of new studies being carried out, I believe that we will have sixty years without crisis. (Perón 1947, 29)

According to Antonio Cafiero, a rising star in the Peronist movement who was minister of trade (1952–1955), the quantity theory of money had to be discarded. Money could not be an "insurmountable obstacle to the strengthening of the national economic capacity" but instead a tool to promote the country's industrialization (Cafiero 1974, 206, 208). Central Bank independence was anathema and monetary policy had to be subordinated to the government's development plans. Alfredo Gómez Morales, who was president of the Central Bank (1949–1952) and Minister of Economy (1952–1955), expressed similar ideas. In his view, the main objective of the monetary authority was not to safeguard the value of the currency or to dampen macroeconomic fluctuations but to finance the government's development plans and "promoting, guiding and carrying out . . . the appropriate economic policy to maintain a high degree of activity "(Gómez Morales 1949a, 352). The Central Bank also had to allocate banking credit according to the "superior interests of the community" (Gómez Morales 1949, 355). Essentially, Peronist policymakers believed that monetary expansion accompanied by an "equivalent creation of wealth" would not generate inflation (Gómez Morales 1949b, 430).

Reality soon refuted these notions. In a very short period of time expansionary monetary and credit policies led to higher inflation. Between 1946 and 1949, the money supply grew at a 25% annual rate. In the same period, overall credit grew by 36% per annum while credit to public-sector entities by almost 100% per annum. From 1900 until 1945, Argentina's inflation rate had averaged 2.1% per annum, slightly below that of the United States. Five years later, it had increased almost twentyfold. The rise in consumer prices between 1946 and 1955 was at least 500% despite strict price and rent controls. This sustained increase in consumer prices was a direct consequence of the increase in the money supply, facilitated by the gradual abandonment of minimum gold reserve backing behind paper issuance that Perón decreed in 1949.

As mentioned earlier, the experience of Peronism between 1946 and 1955 closely follows the three stages of populist economics described by Dornbusch and Edwards (1991). After an uncontrolled fiscal expansion and monetary issuance, the development of an inflationary process, bottlenecks, and FX shortages, an external crisis and recession followed. In Argentina the crisis broke out in mid-1948 when the country ran out of dollars to finance its growing trade deficit. In January 1949, Perón fired his "finance czar" and appointed Gómez Morales to lead his economic team. But Perón dithered as he faced a reelection in 1951 and feared that following Gómez Morales's recommendations could jeopardize his chances of victory. In 1949, the annual inflation rate reached 34% and GDP fell by 1.6%. The following year the National Economic Council, which had overall authority on all economic policy matters, provided Perón with a diagnosis of the macroeconomic situation that went against everything the government had done in the past:

> Given the importance that the amount of public expenditures has in the inflationary process, it is important to continue with the policy followed to date, even though it would be difficult if not impossible, to make greater reductions than those introduced to date without running the risk of paralyzing some essential services. (cited in Bellini 2014, 124)

It was in 1952, a few months after securing a second mandate, that he launched an "Austerity Plan" that sought to limit public spending and reduce the deficit.[3] In the first year of adjustment, GDP fell by almost 5% while accumulated inflation reached almost 50%. However, the fiscal deficit was reduced to half its level in previous years (Bellini 2014, 127). According to Gómez Morales, it was no longer possible to continue with what he described as the "Keynesian policies" initiated by Miranda because the economy had already reached full employment (Vercesi 1995, 48). The application of a more restrictive monetary policy was also effective. Overall credit fell 36%

in real terms between 1950 and 1953 (Bellini 2014, 121). These measures, coupled with strict price controls, managed to reduce inflation to 16% in 1954 and half that level in 1955.

But as Dornbusch and Edwards (1991) pointed out, politicians and societies with a populist culture have limited memory. When Perón returned to the presidency in 1973, he followed the same economic policy cycle. This time, however, the consequences were a lot more serious. Public spending increased from 37% of GDP in 1972 to almost 50% in 1975. The result was a growing fiscal imbalance that reached 13% of GDP in 1975, leading to the first hyperinflationary bout in Argentine history. This is not surprising since the deficit was financed primarily through money creation (Newland 2017). The story did not end there. It is an accepted dogma among contemporary Peronist policymakers that there is no direct link between monetizing deficits and inflation. For example, during Cristina Kirchner's government, both the economy minister and the president of the Central Bank publicly denied that an increase in the money supply would lead to higher inflation:

> It is totally false to say that [monetary] issuance generates inflation. Only in Argentina prevails that idea that an expansion in the quantity of money generates inflation . . . . We rule out that financing the public sector is inflationary, because according to that view, price increases are due to excess demand, something that we do not see in Argentina. In our country the means of payment adapt to the growth in demand and price tensions are on the supply side and the external sector. (Zaiat and Lukin 2012)

Given the above, it is not surprising Argentina continues to have persistent and high fiscal deficits, recurrent sovereign defaults, and one of the world's highest inflation rates. Given the permanence of these phenomena and the way policymakers interpret their causes, their explanation must surely be sought in deeper cultural and/or psychological causes (see Ocampo 2018).

DIGRESSION: RULES AND MONETARY STABILITY

It is clear that if there had been legal or institutional restrictions on the issue of currency and if these were accepted by the political power, the inflation would have been different. An example was given by the Gold Standard, fully in force in Argentina between 1899 and 1914. During this period, the country enjoyed monetary stability and economic growth that placed it among the most prosperous nations on earth. Although the Gold Standard was suspended with World War I and was only reinstated in a brief period between 1927 and 1929, Argentina did not abandon an orthodox monetary policy that implied remarkable price stability until the arrival of Perón to the government after 1943. Another historical moment should also be noted, the "Convertibility" policy applied between 1991 and 2000. This scheme applied a simple rule: the government would not issue currency that was not backed by foreign reserves or public securities in foreign currency. This rule that was applied during the government of Peronist Carlos Menen and implemented by his minister of economy, Domingo Cavallo, was very successful in drastically reducing inflation. One of its most beneficial effects of the Convertibility plan was the resurgence of a domestic capital market. But the system eventually failed because it was not compatible with growth in public spending financed by domestic and external debt. Fiscal inconsistency led to a run on bank deposits. With internal convertibility in doubt, external convertibility became unsustainable.[4]

A related topic is the issue of public debt: Argentina holds the world record in defaults and restructuring. Successive governments have raised debt abroad to fund unsustainable fiscal and current account deficits. The same can be said for domestic debt, leading to the gradual disappearance of the domestic capital markets. These irresponsible policies have inevitably led to recurrent crises and the intervention of the International Monetary Fund. In many instances, the IMF's financial assistance has paradoxically contributed to fiscal irresponsibility and economic stagnation. The typical IMF recipe has been to raise taxes in an economy already overburdened with taxes. Predictably, this has led to lower private investment and lower growth.

CONCLUSION

Until the turn of the twenty-first century it seemed that the reformulation of Schumpeter's prediction that a "populist democracy" similar to Peronism would became dominant was too pessimistic. However, the resurgence of populism in Europe and North America in the last decade and its persistent appeal in Latin America suggest otherwise. Many of the ideas that took Argentina down the path of decadence have become standard fare in progressive platforms. Although right-wing populism may seem more innocuous from an economic standpoint, it can be as harmful. Populism is essentially chameleonic and opportunistic. It not only degrades institutions but also leads to lower economic growth.

At the time these words are written, the COVID-19 pandemic hit Argentina. The administration led by President Alberto Fernández followed the Peronist "Manual of Economic Policy" to a tee. In recent months, the government has vastly expanded public expenditures exacerbating the fiscal deficit, which is being mostly financed by a massive expansion of the money supply. If history is any guide, Argentina will graduate from having a high inflation to having extreme inflation, and maybe even hyperinflation.

NOTES

1. The Kirchners did the same during 2007–2011. In all three cases, a boom in international agricultural commodity prices helped finance a "Peronist party," which entailed confiscating income and wealth from farmers and savers to urban workers and protected manufacturers. The Kirchners' main innovation was to secure the support of a growing portion of non-workers through clientelism.
2. A comprehensive description of Perón's economic reforms and be found in Cavallo and Cavallo Runde 2017, 118–125.
3. On the stabilization Plan of 1952 see Cavallo and Cavallo Runde (2017), 128–129.
4. On the convertibility scheme see Cavallo and Cavallo Runde 2017, 195–199. On why convertibility cannot be called a Currency Board see Hanke 2008.

REFERENCES

Belini, Claudio. 2014. "Inflación, recesión y desequilibrio externo. la crisis de 1952, el plan de estabilización de Gómez Morales y los dilemas de la economía peronista." *Boletín del Instituto de Historia Argentina y Americana "Dr. Emilio Ravignani"*, 40: 105–148.

Bello. 2020. "What is Peronism?" *The Economist*. Feb 13.

Brennan, James, and Marcelo Rougier. 2013. *Perón y la Burguesía Argentina*. Buenos Aires.

Cafiero, Antonio. 1974. *De la Economía Social-Justicialista al Régimen Liberal-Capitalista*. Buenos Aires.

Cagan, Phillip. 1956. "The Monetary Dynamics of Hyperinflation." In *Studies in the Quantity Theory of Money*, edited by Milton Friedman, 25–117. Chicago: University of Chicago Press.

Cavallo, Domingo, and Sonia Cavallo Runde. 2017. *Argentina's Economic Reforms of the 1990s in Contemporary and Historical Perspective*. New York: Routledge.

CEPAL. 1958. *El desarrollo económico de la Argentina: anexo: algunos estudios especiales y estadísticas macroeconómicas preparados para el informe*. México: CEPAL.

Cereijo, Ramón. 1947. "La política económica-financiera del Gobierno." *Hechos e Ideas*, VII:44: 32–44.

Cereijo, Ramón. 1950. "La evolución económica y financiera argentina." *Hechos e Ideas*, XI:80–81: 207–274.

Degreef, Juan. 1950. "La política económica y financiera del Gobierno." *Hechos e Ideas*, XI:79: 29–60.

Di Tella, Rafael, and Juan Dubra. 2010. "Peronist beliefs and interventionist policies." NBER Working Paper Series.

Dornbusch, Rugider, and Sebastián Edwards, editors. 1991. *The Macroeconomics of Populism in Latin America*. Chicago: University of Chicago Press.

Edwards, Sebastian. 2019a. "Modern Monetary Theory: Cautionary Tales from Latin America Economics." Working Paper, Hoover Institution.

———. 2019b. "On Latin American Populism, and Its Echoes around the World." *Journal of Economic Perspectives*, 33:4: 76–99.

Gómez, Alejandro, and Carlos Newland. 2013. "Alberdi, sobre héroes y empresarios." *Cultura Económica*, i: 30–37.

Gómez Morales, Alfredo. 1949a. "La función del Estado en la vida económica del país y en el manejo de la administración de la hacienda pública." *Hechos e Ideas*, X:68–69: 341–361.

———. 1949b. "La emisión de moneda en la nueva Ley Bancaria." *Hechos e Ideas*, X:68–69: 413–433.

Hanke, Steve H. 2008. "Why Argentina did not have a Currency Board." *Central Banking Journal*, 18:3: 56–58.

Klein, Daniel, and Ryan Daza. 2013. "Franco Modigliani." *Econ Journal Watch*, 10:8: 3.

Llach, Lucas, and Pablo Gerchunoff. 2007. *El ciclo de la ilusión y el desencanto: un siglo de políticas económicas argentinas*. Buenos Aires.

Newland, Carlo,. and Martín Cuesta. 2017. "Peronismo y salarios reales. Otro mirada al período 1939–56." *Investigaciones y Ensayos*, 64: 75–98.

Ocampo, Emilio. 2018. "Las raíces psicológico-culturales del populismo argentino." In *El populismo en la Argentina y el mundo,* edited by Roque Fernández and Emilio Ocampo. Buenos Aires: Ediciones UCEMA.

———. 2019. "The Economic Analysis of Populism: A Selective Review of the Literature." *Serie Documentos de Trabajo-Working Papers UCEMA*, No. 694 (May).

———. 2020a. "The Populist Economic Policy Paradigm: Early Peronism as an Archetype." *Serie Documentos de Trabajo-Working Papers UCEMA*, No. 731 (June).

———. 2020b. "MMT: Modern Monetary Theory or Magical Monetary Thinking." *Serie Documentos de Trabajo-Working Papers UCEMA* No. 762 (November).

Pavón Pereyra, Enrique. 2018. *Yo Perón*. Buenos Aires: Sudamericana.

Perón, Juan Ddomingo. 1947. "Palabras pronunciadas en la conferencia de ministros de hacienda provinciales." In Ministerio de Hacienda. *Segunda Conferencia de Ministros de Hacienda*. Buenos Aires.

———. 1951. "La obra realizada en cinco años de gobierno." *Hechos e Ideas*, XII:56: 201–230.

———. 1953. "Palabras ante delegados de la Confederacion General Economica." 1 de diciembre de 1953, in Perón, Juan Domingo. 2000. *Obras completas*, XVII, Vol. 2, Buenos Aires: Fundación Universidad a distancia "Hermandarias".

———. 1956. *La fuerza es el derecho de las bestias*. Panamá: Editora Volver.

Sowter, Leandro. 2015. "¿Pragmatismo vs. Planificación? Del proyecto peronista, las ideas económicas de Perón y la industria." *H-industri@*, 9:16: 165–194.

Unknown. 1954. "Apuntes de economía peronista." *Hechos e Ideas*, XV: 124–125, 215–277.

Vercesi, Alberto. 1995. "Influencia del pensamiento keynesiano en la política económica peronista (1946–1955)." *Estudios Económicos*, 11:25/25: 33–56.

Zaiat, Alfredo, and Tomás Lukin, Tomas. "Reportaje a Mercedes Marcó Del Pont." March 25. In Pagina 12 [Online]. https://www.pagina12.com.ar/diario/economia/2 -190369-2012-03-25.html [Accesed on 15 March 2020].

Part IV

IS NON-CONVENTIONAL MONETARY POLICY SUPPORTING OR UNDERMINING FISCAL STABILIZATION POLICY?

Chapter 9

Monetary Policy and the Worsening U.S. Debt Crisis

Norbert J. Michel

In the face of the coronavirus pandemic, the U.S. Congress, with the support of the administration, has so far enacted four major bills that will increase the federal deficit by $2.1 trillion during fiscal year (FY) 2020.[1] Combined with the economic and fiscal effects of the economic lockdowns, the Congressional Budget Office (CBO) currently projects that the FY 2020 deficit will increase to $3.3 trillion.[2] On May 15, the House passed an additional bill that is estimated to necessitate an additional $3 trillion in federal borrowing, heightening the possibility that even more will be added to the federal deficit and debt in the near future.[3]

The Federal Reserve is absorbing much of this new debt, but their new operating framework means that the traditional economic implications of central bank asset purchases have to be modified. The new framework separates the Fed's monetary policy stance from the amount of assets it buys, thus blurring the distinction between fiscal policy and monetary policy. Consequently, the Fed has abruptly enlarged its balance sheet by nearly $3 trillion—an increase of more than 70% in the space of three months—as part of the government's efforts to offset the economic consequences of the lockdown orders.[4] Combined, these operations have put the U.S. government in fiscal circumstances that few other highly developed countries have ever experienced during peacetime. They also heighten the political pressure for the Fed to fund elected officials' favored projects directly, thus subverting the congressional appropriations process.

During the past several years, especially, many advocates have been seeking to fund infrastructure projects (broadly defined) through central banks. For instance, in January 2020 the Bank of International Settlements (BIS) published a book titled *The Green Swan: Central Banking and Financial Stability in the Age of Climate Change*. Although it tends to equivocate on exactly how central banks should help stave off climate change, the book does call for central banks to be more proactive in coordinating new policies and supporting sustainable investments. The book fits squarely within the goals of the proponents of the Green New Deal and Modern Monetary Theory (MMT), two groups who see the central bank as pivotal in their efforts to increase government spending through creating and/or borrowing more money.[5] For many of these advocates, fiscal crises—or even fiscal problems—are of no concern.

While it is true that one-time spikes in federal borrowing are not worrisome by themselves, high growth in federal debt unrelated to business cycles does raise substantial concerns. Moreover, growth in entitlement spending—which already accounts for roughly two out of every three dollars of federal spending—is the principal source of rising U.S. debt. Elected officials should heed the warning of the recent downgrade in the U.S. credit outlook: the current trajectory of U.S. federal debt is unsustainable. Fixing this problem would be difficult enough had the Federal Reserve not altered its operations in a way that makes it easier to accommodate profligate fiscal behavior. Now, changing course will require a herculean effort on the part of elected officials and the leaders of the central bank.

Importantly, the Federal Reserve can no longer rely on its price-stability mandate to fend off congressional attempts to engage in massive spending programs. This new era of monetary policy poses the following dangers:

SUBSIDIZED FINANCIAL REPRESSION

The Fed has created a new risk-free investment choice (interest on excess reserves, or IOER) for banks and other favored financial firms, and it literally administers the rate it pays on these investments. This arrangement is the equivalent of the federal government directly paying favored constituents to keep funds out of the private sector.

DECREASED PRIVATE INVESTMENT

The Fed's new operating policies encourage banks to park funds at the Fed instead of investing funds in private securities and loans. Each dollar of excess reserves held at the Fed represents a dollar that banks fail to invest in the private market, thus detracting from economic growth.

CREDIT MARKET DISTORTIONS

The Fed's policies have eliminated the federal-funds market as a source of bank liquidity. They have also allocated credit directly to (among others) the housing and government sectors. The Fed now holds more than $7 trillion in total assets, with $1.98 trillion of that total in mortgage-backed securities (MBS). To put this figure in perspective, the entire commercial banking sector holds $2.3 trillion in MBS.[6] Neither prices of MBS nor the federal-funds rate convey economic information as they have traditionally, a situation that will only worsen as the Fed expands its holdings of government and agency debt obligations.

INCREASED POLITICAL RISK FOR THE FED

The Fed's large interest payments to banks pose an increasing political threat to the Fed's operational independence.[7] To deal with the COVID-19 crisis, the Fed lowered the interest rate it pays on excess reserves to just 0.10%. However, in 2018, the rate was as high as 2.4%.[8] In 2013 and 2014, the Fed paid banks $5.2 billion and $6.7 billion, respectively, and the amount increased to more than $10 billion in 2016.[9] In 2018 and 2019, the amount paid fell to $1.3 billion and $0.95 billion, respectively.[10] These payments reduce funds flowing to the Treasury and give the obvious appearance of providing generous government subsidies to large banks, especially when the IOER rate is greater than the basic deposit rate available to the public (as it has been for years). If the Fed has to raise the IOER rate to control inflation as market interest rates increase, these subsidies will also increase.

MORE ACCESSIBLE MONEY SPIGOT

The new framework divorces the Fed's monetary policy stance from the size of the Fed's balance sheet. It is designed to allow the Fed to purchase as many assets as it would like, all while paying firms to hold on to the excess cash that these purchases create. This framework can all too easily allow the Fed to be a pawn of the Treasury (or Congress), enabling the government to run larger deficits. It also opens new opportunities for political groups to pressure the Fed for direct funding.

WEAKENED MONETARY POLICY EFFECTIVENESS

Because the new framework replaces market forces with bureaucratically administered rates, it prevents private markets from allocating credit without (potentially massive) ongoing government interference. This arrangement distorts prices and jeopardizes the Fed's ability to maintain monetary control.

That is, it endangers the Fed's ability to regulate the economy's overall liquidity so that it can meet its broader economic goals with respect to the general course of spending, prices, and employment.

After the Great Recession ended, the Fed failed to normalize monetary policy by both shrinking its balance sheet and getting rid of its IOER framework. That failure heightened the risk that this framework would still be in place when a new crisis occurred, and the COVID-19 pandemic was that crisis. The pandemic has worsened the near-term fiscal outlook, with ever-larger entitlement spending problems looming, thus further cementing the new operating framework and amplifying the risk and severity of the above-listed problems. The Federal Reserve is now further entrenched in credit allocation and outsized involvement in financial markets than prior to the Great Recession, and its new endeavors endanger the legitimacy of both fiscal and monetary policy.

THE FEDERAL RESERVE'S PRE-2008 OPERATING FRAMEWORK

A central bank implements monetary policy by regulating the economy's overall liquidity (the availability of liquid, or cash-like, assets) to indirectly influence the economy's general course of spending, prices, and employment. Prior to the 2008 financial crisis, the Federal Reserve exercised monetary policy mainly through open market operations, that is, the buying and selling of short-term Treasury securities on the open (public) market.[11] Many economists focus on the relationship between open market operations and interest rates, but that focus ignores the underlying mechanics of the Fed's traditional operating framework.

The Fed conducted these operations with the specific intent of increasing or decreasing the amount of reserves—a highly liquid asset—in the banking system, thereby increasing or decreasing the amount of money that banks could lend. This system worked because banks need reserves to make new loans,[12] and only the Federal Reserve can increase (or decrease) the total amount of reserves in the banking system. While the Federal Reserve decided the total amount of reserves in the banking system, private banks ultimately determined how those reserves were allocated throughout the system.

Traditionally, banks regularly lent and borrowed reserves to satisfy their legal (and precautionary) reserve requirements in the federal-funds market, so named because banks hold reserve balances at the Federal Reserve. The interest rate in this lending market, the federal-funds rate, was a market-determined rate. In other words, private banks' lending negotiations—not the Federal Reserve—determined the federal-funds rate.[13] While the Federal Reserve did not set the federal-funds rate itself, it did set a target for the federal-funds rate based on ensuring that overall liquidity was consistent with its broader macroeconomic goals.

In such a system, the target federal-funds rate is merely a means to an end—it is a policy instrument but it is not a policy objective. This policy framework depends on the Fed keeping a minimal footprint in the market for reserves, causing some economists to refer to the traditional framework as a reserve-scarcity regime.[14] All else constant, a scarcity of reserve balances (relative to demand for reserves) results in a larger volume of reserve lending between banks. In that operating environment, the federal-funds rate conveys information based largely on conditions in private credit markets, as perceived by the private lenders and borrowers putting their capital at risk.

Naturally, the Fed's open market operations would have very little influence on the federal-funds market if holding reserves is regularly more attractive versus other uses of funds. In such an environment, with plentiful reserves that have little opportunity cost, banks would find it unnecessary to borrow reserves and the federal-funds rate would no longer be the result of the same market process. In fact, the enormous buildup in reserves during the 2008 crisis ultimately caused interbank lending markets to break down and contributed to the Fed abandoning its traditional operating procedures.

INTEREST ON EXCESS RESERVES: THE FED'S POST-2008 OPERATING FRAMEWORK

In late 2007, the Federal Reserve began various emergency lending programs, such as the Term Auction Facility, that increased reserves in the banking system. In 2008, the Federal Reserve implemented the first of several quantitative easing (QE) programs, purchasing large quantities of long-term financial assets. These operations left the Fed with more than five times the amount of securities it had prior to 2008. In particular, the Fed was left with $4.5 trillion in assets, consisting mainly of long-term Treasuries as well as the debt and the MBS of Fannie Mae and Freddie Mac.

According to Ben Bernanke's memoir of the crisis, at the first signs of trouble in 2007, he quickly ordered the New York Fed to buy "large quantities of Treasury securities on the open market" to flood the federal-funds market with reserves.[15] These initial actions were appropriate in that they provided system-wide liquidity. Soon after, however, the Fed began allocating credit directly to certain firms, operations that also increased reserves in the system.[16] Some of these efforts may have kept several large financial firms afloat, but the Fed hamstrung its overall efforts by sterilizing its liquidity operations. Specifically, the Fed sold Treasury securities from its portfolio, thus taking reserves out of the system at the same time it was injecting reserves into the system.

To the extent that there was an increased demand for liquidity, the sterilization process hindered the Fed from meeting that demand. Ben Bernanke provides the following account of the Federal Open Market Committee's (FOMC's) decision during its August 2008 meeting:

> We were facing what might prove to be a critical question: Could we continue our emergency lending to financial institutions and markets, while at the same time setting short-term interest rates at levels that kept a lid on inflation? Two key elements of our policy framework—lending to ease financial conditions, and setting short-term interest rates—could come into conflict . . . . Since April, we had set our target for the federal funds rate at 2%—the right level, we thought, to balance our goals of supporting employment and keeping inflation under control. We needed to continue our emergency lending and at the same time prevent the federal funds rate from falling below 2%.[17]

Thus, the Fed was officially worried about meeting its overall macroeconomic goals and maintaining what control it had over the federal-funds rate. Regardless of whether this was the right approach, by the time the Fed conducted the rescue of American International Group (AIG) in September 2008, they had exhausted the ability to sterilize their emergency lending by selling Treasuries. From August 2007 to September 2008, the Fed's holdings of Treasury securities had fallen from approximately $791 billion to $480 billion. Given the size of its operations, the Fed believed it was nearly out of short-term Treasuries to sell.[18]

At the same time, the traditional interest rate targeting approach was coming apart. In late 2007, the federal-funds rate began to collapse, leaving the Fed no choice but to begin lowering its target federal-funds rate. In little more than one year, the Fed had to lower its target from 5.25% to 1%. By the end of 2008, the Fed was still having difficulty hitting its target, so it scrapped the idea of a single target rate in favor of a target range (from 0% to 0.25%).[19] Ultimately, the Fed created a new policy framework that relied on bureaucratically administered interest rates rather than the traditional approach that depended on market forces and targeting a market rate.

This new approach required the Fed to pay interest on reserves, something which it had not previously done. Initially, Fed officials believed this change would help the Fed hit its interest rate target, and that the rate they paid on reserves would serve as a floor for the federal-funds rate.[20] In other words, their original intent had been to create a corridor system, whereby the interest rate on reserves is set below the central bank's policy rate (the target federal-funds rate in the case of the Federal Reserve).[21]

Economists have long recognized that requiring banks to hold non-interest-bearing reserves acts as a tax on bank deposits and, therefore, on bank depositors. However, in 2008, the Fed asked Congress for the authority to pay interest on reserves for reasons that went well beyond merely offsetting the cost of reserve requirements. Congress subsequently granted the Fed the authority to pay interest on reserves by amending legislation that was passed in 2006.[22] In his memoir, former Fed Chair Ben Bernanke explained the request as follows:

> We had initially asked to pay interest on reserves for technical reasons. But in 2008, we needed the authority to solve an increasingly serious problem: the risk that our emergency lending, which had the side effect of increasing bank reserves, would lead short-term interest rates to fall below our federal funds target and thereby cause us to lose control of monetary policy. When banks have lots of reserves, they have less need to borrow from each other, which pushes down the interest rate on that borrowing—the federal funds rate.

Until this point, we had been selling Treasury securities we owned to offset the effect of our lending on reserves (the process called sterilization). But as our lending increased, that stopgap response would at some point no longer be possible because we would run out of Treasuries to sell. At that point, without legislative action, we would be forced to either limit the size of our interventions or lose the ability to control the federal-funds rate, the main instrument of monetary policy. So, by setting the interest rate we paid on reserves high enough, we could prevent the federal-funds rate from falling too low, no matter how much lending we did.[23]

This new approach also required the Fed to pay IOER so that banks would hold their excess reserves—of which the Fed had created an enormous quantity—at the Fed rather than lend them in the federal-funds market.[24] As Bernanke reasoned, the only possible way to accomplish this task was to offer banks a higher rate of IOER than they could earn by lending those reserves in the federal-funds market.[25] Thus, the IOER rate could not serve as a floor for the federal-funds rate and sterilize the Fed's operations. As a result, the Fed did not create a traditional corridor system due to its conflicting goals.

When it began paying IOER in October 2008, the Fed set the IOER rate at 0.75%, well below the federal-funds target rate of 1.5%. In approximately two weeks, the Fed increased the IOER rate to 1.15%, reducing the spread between that rate and the prevailing federal-funds target rate to 0.35%. By November 2008, both the federal-funds target rate and the IOER rate were 1%. The Fed held the IOER rate above the effective federal-funds rate—the actual rate charged in the federal-funds market—from the end of October 2008 through 2017. In fact, for roughly the entire period it has paid IOER, the

Fed has set this overnight interest rate above virtually all short-term low-risk rates available on the market.

This operating framework provides banks with a new risk-free investment choice, one for which the Fed can increase the rate in order to induce banks to hold excess reserves rather than make new loans. Naturally, the more banks hold in reserve, all else constant, the less money they create in the broader economy. Thus, this aspect of the new operating framework—the decision to pay interest on reserves—has at least as far-reaching implications as the QE programs themselves.[26]

Perhaps the most important repercussion of the framework is that it divorces the Fed's monetary policy stance from the size of its balance sheet: Federal Reserve asset purchases no longer automatically translate into expansionary monetary policy. Put differently, the framework is designed to allow the Fed to purchase as many assets as it would like regardless of its monetary policy stance because it allows the Fed to pay firms to hold the excess cash that these purchases create. While Federal Reserve asset purchases were traditionally tied to inflationary pressure, this relationship is no longer a given.[27]

The payments on excess reserves are critical to the Fed's ability to maintain control of monetary policy, but they create several potential problems for the central bank. By paying billions of dollars in interest to large financial institutions to make it more attractive to place funds with the Fed rather than to lend in short-term markets, this framework gives the Fed an abnormally large presence (by historical standards) in credit markets. Moreover, it requires the Fed to pay interest to large private financial institutions to maintain its policy stance, a political problem that will worsen if interest rates rise, thus threatening the viability of the operating framework.

The new policy structure also makes it very difficult for the Fed to adequately regulate the overall availability of credit in private markets without allocating credit to specific groups. Good monetary policy, of course, requires the Fed to conduct policy in a neutral fashion, rather than allocate credit to preferred sectors of the economy. As the coronavirus epidemic drags on and the entitlement spending problems remain unresolved, the Fed's new framework, along with its recent actions, makes it more likely that Congress (or Treasury) will call on the Fed to further blur the lines between monetary and fiscal policy.

THE FED'S NEW FRAMEWORK, FISCAL POLICY, AND COVID-19

The new framework has stark implications for expansionary fiscal policy, because the Fed can buy more government debt without regard to its monetary policy stance. Therefore, it is much easier for the Fed to become a pawn of the Treasury (or Congress), enabling the government to run larger deficits and take on higher levels of debt. Furthermore, it opens new opportunities for political groups to pressure the Fed for direct funding, a fact that has not gone unnoticed by Congress. For instance, House Financial Services Chairwoman Maxine Waters (D–CA) released a statement calling for the Fed to provide more than liquidity, "Unfortunately, the Fed appears to be using its old playbook in trying to calm funding markets by flooding them with liquidity. During this time of economic turbulence, it is critical that the Fed go beyond these steps and provide much-needed support to those who are on the front lines of this pandemic."[28]

In many ways, the Fed's (and Congress') response to the COVID-19 pandemic is a test case for the new operating framework and the Fed's foray into fiscal policy. Between March 2020 and April 2020, the Fed injected trillions of dollars into short-term credit markets, announced a new $700 billion QE program (the Fed will purchase $500 billion in Treasuries and $200 billion in MBS), and created more than 10 new lending facilities.[29] The Fed will use these facilities to lend directly to commercial firms, and to lend indirectly by supplying funds for banks to lend to small and medium-sized businesses.

One of the early facilities marked a troubling departure from the norm, because the Fed uses this facility to lend directly to private companies.[30] Specifically, the Fed will buy newly issued corporate bonds directly from commercial companies through the Primary Market Corporate Credit Facility. Although the stated purpose of this facility is to provide liquidity to the corporate bond market, even the promise of such "support" undermines market forces and potentially distorts prices. The facility represents subsidized lending to distressed companies and politicizes credit allocation. While the facility could induce private investors to purchase additional corporate bonds, the debt-issuing companies could simply use those funds to pay down existing debt rather than invest in productive capital. If losses continue, investors will have a vehicle for offloading their debt, effectively socializing their losses.[31]

The Fed also created several facilities that indirectly provide credit to private markets. For instance, through the Paycheck Protection Program Liquidity Facility, the Fed will provide loans to banks that make loans to small companies under the Small Business Administration's Paycheck Protection Program (PPP).[32] Separately, the Fed will use the Main Street New Loan Facility (MSNLF) and the Main Street Expanded Loan Facility (MSELF) to supply up to $600 billion to private banks that make loans to medium-sized businesses (those with no more than 10,000 employees or $2.5 billion in 2019 annual revenues).[33] The Fed also created a similar facility for the state and local government debt market named the Municipal Liquidity Facility (MLF). The MLF allows any district Federal Reserve Bank to buy

state and municipal bonds (up to an aggregate total of $500 billion), opening
it to political pressure to bail out profligate state and local governments.

While it is true that Treasury took an "equity stake" in most of these
lending facilities, doing so was not required by the Federal Reserve Act.
Moreover, it was not necessary as a matter of economics. The Fed is not
a private bank, it does not have to meet capital requirements, and it does
not have to redeem any of its liabilities. If the Fed loses money, it actually
can just "print" more. The economic constraint on the central bank printing
more money is how much of its excess money creation the public is willing
to tolerate, an amount that has nothing to do with Treasury's equity stake in
the Fed's operations. This quantity is not precisely knowable ex-ante, but it
is most likely one that will be reached only in limited circumstances, such as
if the Fed creates an inflation problem or if citizens revolt against profligate
bailouts and spending.[34]

On the legal side, the question essentially comes down to who has the
power of the purse, and the U.S. Constitution gives Congress that responsibility.[35] To help create the current funding arrangement between Treasury
and the Fed, Congress did not amend the Federal Reserve Act. Instead, the
Coronavirus Aid, Relief, and Economic Security (CARES) Act authorized
a somewhat murky arrangement between the U.S. Treasury and the central
bank.

For instance, the CARES Act appropriates up to $454 billion to the
Treasury to "make loans and loan guarantees to, and other investments in,
programs or facilities established by the Board of Governors of the Federal
Reserve System for the purpose of providing liquidity to the financial system
that supports lending to eligible businesses, States, or municipalities."[36]

The CARES Act leaves many of the details for those "other investments" up
to the Fed and Treasury, but it does require that all of the applicable requirements of the Federal Reserve's emergency lending authority (Section 13(3) of
the Federal Reserve Act) apply to any "program or facility" established under
the CARES Act.[37] Using this authority, Treasury then took equity stakes in
the various special purpose vehicles (SPVs) that the Fed used to establish the
lending programs. The specific intent (at least among Treasury and the Fed)
is for the Fed to "leverage" these equity stakes to provide loans that exceed
the amount Congress appropriated.[38] For instance, Treasury has a $75 bil-
lion stake in the SPV that established the two Main Street lending facilities,
and the Fed will use these two programs to provide up to $600 billion in
loans.[39]

It is currently impossible to know precisely in how much lending the Fed
will engage through all of its new facilities, or how large its balance sheet will
grow. According to *The Wall Street Journal*, "Economists project the central
bank's portfolio of bonds, loans and new programs will swell to between $8

trillion and $11 trillion from less than $4 trillion last year. In that range, the portfolio would be twice the size reached after the 2007–09 financial crisis and nearly half the value of U.S. annual economic output."

If the lending facilities lose the money that Treasury provided as an equity investment, then there is no problem in the sense that Congress explicitly appropriated those funds.

However, if the losses exceed the appropriated funds, the additional money to cover those losses has to come from a new congressional appropriation or the Federal Reserve. If the latter, then the Fed would be spending more than Congress appropriated for a specific purpose. The fact that the Federal Reserve is not an on-budget federal agency is only a technical matter, and its action would still be in direct conflict with the underlying structure of the U.S. government—the Constitution gives the power of the purse to the elected members of Congress. Naturally, the same critique applies to any Fed lending program that does not include a congressional appropriation, as well as to any fiscal QE program the Fed undertakes on its own.

The fact that the Fed's new operating framework divorces their monetary policy stance from the size of the Fed's balance sheet means that, in theory, covering losses from such activities could have smaller monetary effects than asset purchases in traditional monetary policy operations. The new framework is designed to allow the Fed to purchase as many assets as it would like, or spend new base money for any particular reason, all while paying firms to hold on to the excess cash that these actions create. Still, the fact that the Fed can cover any such expenditures—or consequent losses—via creating new base money only gives the appearance that this arrangement is fiscally sound. The situation is ripe for allowing the Fed to be a pawn of Congress (or the Treasury), enabling the government to paper over larger and larger deficits, a trick that cannot continue indefinitely.

EXOTIC MONETARY POLICY AND SYSTEMIC FISCAL IMBALANCES

As of this writing, most of the Fed's existing QE programs can be viewed as quasi-fiscal QE programs because they have been used to serve the central bank's monetary mandates as well as various fiscal ends.[40] The Federal Reserve's purchases of Fannie and Freddie MBS, for example, are part of a QE program designed to increase aggregate investment by reducing longer-term interest rates (a monetary function), and also to support the housing market (a fiscal function). Yet, this breaching of the traditional boundaries between the monetary and fiscal authorities makes it easier for the Fed to engage in strictly fiscal QE operations, the type of financing favored by supporters of MMT, large-scale infrastructure projects, and helicopter money proposals (QE for the people).[41]

Proponents of MMT effectively argue that governments can run unlimited deficits because they have control over their sovereign currencies. This position, which Cato's George Selgin has referred to as "an especially naïve sort of Keynesianism," essentially assumes that monetary expansion can costlessly finance unlimited projects because real resource constraints are not a problem.[42] In truth, the federal government's spending can only be financed if it raises funds through taxation or borrowing. Although the Federal Reserve can help the U.S. Treasury by purchasing more Treasury securities, it cannot magically erase resource constraints.

While proponents sometimes offer Japan as a positive example of MMT being put into practice, such assertions are based on neither empirical nor historical evidence.[43] Nonetheless, MMT advocates see the central bank as pivotal in their efforts to increase government spending, and they will likely try to convince Congress to force the Fed to engage in fiscal QE operations to implement large spending programs.[44] Indeed, proponents of the Green New Deal, large-scale infrastructure projects, or any other large spending proposals could similarly pressure Congress (and the Executive branch) to rely on the Fed to implement their preferred policies.

Aside from any specific fiscal QE proposals, the Fed could face increasing pressure to address the systemic fiscal imbalances caused by entitlement spending.[45] Federal debt is now largely driven by entitlement spending and, if left unchecked, will continue to necessitate massive new borrowings well into the future. Research shows, for instance, that less than 2% of the nearly 1,800 spending accounts that fund all government activities drive the long-run unsustainability of the federal budget.[46] Spending from just those accounts is equivalent to 60% of gross spending projected over the next 10 years, with spending on government-funded health-care programs contributing the largest component to fiscal unsustainability.[47]

Separately, the CBO recently projected that the Social Security Old Age and Survivors Insurance fund faces insolvency in less than a decade, and that the Social Security Disability Insurance program could run out in 2026.[48] Faced with possible sharp benefit cuts, some members of Congress will be tempted to call on the Federal Reserve. The risk of such an occurrence appears especially heightened given Congress's recent raiding of the Fed's capital surplus to pay for a highway bill, the Fed's recent foray into quasi-fiscal QE programs, and the central bank's novel responses to the COVID-19 crisis.[49] At the very least, the Fed will no longer be able to point to its price stability mandate as a reason that it cannot help fund larger payouts and debt absorption. The Fed's new operating framework separates its monetary policy stance from its asset purchases, so it is more likely than ever that calls will mount for the Fed to engage in more fiscal/quasi-fiscal operations.[50]

CONCLUSION

Good monetary policy ensures that the economy does not stall due to an insufficient supply of money or overheat due to an excessive supply of money. To achieve this balance, the Federal Reserve needs to conduct policy in a neutral fashion, passively providing liquidity for the economy. Similarly, the Fed must maintain a minimal footprint in the market so that it does not create moral hazards, crowd out private credit and investment, or transfer financial risks to taxpayers. Many of the Federal Reserve's recent actions, along with its post-2008 operating framework, make it increasingly unlikely that they will achieve sound monetary policy in the near future. Indeed, it is clear that the Fed no longer engages in pure monetary policy, more so now than at any other point in the post–World War II era.

The Fed is now on the brink of being a mere pawn of Congress, forced to finance government expenditures in a manner that endangers the legitimacy of both monetary and fiscal policy. At minimum, this situation runs the risk of grossly distorting credit markets. It boosts the likelihood that the Fed will not be able to maintain monetary control, and risks both decreased private investment and above-average capital outflows. The idea that a government can run unlimited deficits with no real economic consequences is a dangerous fantasy. The federal government can finance spending only if it raises funds through taxation or borrowing. The fact that the Federal Reserve can buy Treasury bonds or "print" the sovereign currency does not erase real resource constraints or enable to the Fed to "fine tune" the economy to meet macroeconomic goals.

Many of the Fed's actions during the COVID-19 crisis have further blurred the lines between monetary and fiscal policy, but U.S. monetary policy would remain in unchartered territory even without these recent policy changes. Prior to the coronavirus pandemic, the U.S. government's finances were in poor shape due to pre-existing structural deficits (in all but five of the past 50 years, the U.S. budget was in cash deficit) and unfunded obligations in entitlement programs. The continuous level of deficit spending has increased public debt which, during the same period, rose from 32% to 79% of GDP. Prior to the onset of the novel coronavirus, the CBO estimated that the 2020 federal budget deficit would be $1.1 trillion.[51]

Now that Congress has passed several coronavirus spending bills, the CBO expects the 2020 deficit to reach at least $3.3 trillion, the largest (as a share of the economy) since World War II. The CBO projects the combined deficits for 2021 through 2030 at just under $13 trillion. Given that the current gross debt is $26.7 trillion, the per-household share could stand at approximately $275,000 in just ten years. While one-time spikes in federal borrowing are not worrisome by themselves, high growth in federal debt unrelated to business cycles does raise substantial concerns, and entitlement spending—which already accounts for roughly two out of every three dollars of federal spending—is the principal source of this rising debt.

The recent downgrade of the U.S. credit outlook is a warning signal that the trajectory of federal debt is unsustainable. If left unchecked, the debt will continue to necessitate massive new borrowings well into the future, and the Fed already holds 21% of all federal debt held by the public (as of October 30, 2020).[52] Still, many elected officials are clamoring for enormous new spending programs that would require even more debt, and some of them want to rely on the Federal Reserve for funding support. There is no doubt that the Fed *can* facilitate government borrowing and new spending programs, but this fact does not change the true economic costs of such undertakings. Moreover, these new endeavors come with additional risks that endanger the legitimacy of both fiscal and monetary policy to a greater degree than they would have prior to 2008.

Largely by accident, the Fed now finds itself with an operating framework that makes it much easier to facilitate new federal debt and spending. The Fed created the new framework in the midst of the 2008 crisis to maintain monetary control by placing a check on the excess reserves their emergency operations had created. However, after the Great Recession ended in 2009, the Fed decided against systematically normalizing monetary policy in a timely fashion. Instead, they maintained an abnormally large balance sheet for much longer than necessary and kept the crisis-era operating framework in place, thus heightening the risk that a new economic shock would shrink their policy options. Before the Fed fully normalized, the coronavirus pandemic and subsequent government lockdowns caused major economic difficulties, and now the Fed is even further entrenched in credit allocation and outsized involvement in financial markets. They are also less able to maintain their operational independence because they can no longer rely on their price stability mandate to fend off congressional attempts to finance profligate spending.

Currently, elected officials do not appear to be considering any viable plan to curb rising U.S. debt and entitlement spending, thus leaving the nation's fiscal health on an unsustainable trajectory. To remedy this situation, now more than ever, the Federal Reserve will have to play a major role in developing such a plan. One option is for the Fed to take its own stance against fiscal-QE-type programs and announce that it will revert to its traditional (pre-crisis) operating framework over a specific period. Alternatively, the Fed will have to work with congressional leaders to develop legislation that restores the Fed's traditional operating framework and that restricts the Fed's ability to engage in fiscal operations. The immediate prospects for either solution appear rather remote, but the longer policymakers delay, the more severe the consequences become.

NOTES

1. Congressional Budget Office estimates of H.R. 6074, https://www.cbo.gov/system/files/2020-03/hr6074.pdf (accessed May 15, 2020); H.R. 6201, https://www.cbo.gov/system/files/2020-04/HR6201.pdf (accessed May 15,2020); H.R. 748, https://www.cbo.gov/system/files/2020-04/hr748.pdf (accessed May 15, 2020); and H.R. 266, https://www.cbo.gov/system/files/2020-04/hr266.pdf (accessed May 15, 2020).

2. Phill Swagel, "An Update to the Budget Outlook: 2020 to 2030," *Congressional Budget Office*, September 20, 2020, https://www.cbo.gov/system/files/2020-09/5651 7-Budget-Outlook.pdf (accessed October 26, 2020). In early October, the CBO also announced that the federal government "ran a budget deficit of $3.1 trillion in fiscal year 2020…more than triple the shortfall recorded in 2019." The same publication states "2020 was the fifth consecutive year in which the deficit increased as a percentage of GDP," and that this measure (15.2% of GDP) was the highest it has been since 1945. See Congressional Budget Office, "Monthly Budget Review for September 2020," October 8, 2020, https://www.cbo.gov/publication/56661 (accessed October 26, 2020).

3. H.R. 6800, The Health and Economic Recovery Omnibus Emergency Solutions Act, https://www.congress.gov/bill/116th-congress/house-bill/6800/text (accessed May 15, 2020).

4. Current deficits and debt are insufficient measures of the U.S. government's financial sustainability because of the impending problems with entitlement spending. See Norbert J. Michel, Paul Winfree, and Doug Badger, "Potential Long-Term Economic Consequences of the Federal Response to the COVID-19 Lockdowns," *Heritage Foundation Backgrounder No. 3498*, June 4, 2020, https://www.heritage.org/sites/default/files/2020-06/BG3498.pdf (accessed September 1, 2020).

5. Warren Coats, "Modern Monetary Theory: A Critique," *Cato Journal*, Vol. 39, No. 3 (Fall 2019), https://www.cato.org/sites/cato.org/files/2019-09/cj-v39n3-4.pdf (accessed September 1, 2020). Also, the first broad fiscal-QE proposal was from a British economist who referred to the plan (in 2009) as "Green QE2." See George Selgin, *The Menace of Fiscal QE* (Washington, DC: Cato Institute, 2020), 13.

6. These figures are as reported by Federal Reserve Economic Data (FRED), Federal Reserve Bank of St. Louis as of September 30, 2020. The data series are: Assets: Total Assets: Total Assets (Less Eliminations from Consolidation): Wednesday Level (WALCL); Assets: Securities Held Outright: Mortgage-Backed Securities: Wednesday Level (WSHOMCB); and, Treasury and Agency Securities: Mortgage-Backed Securities (MBS), All Commercial Banks (TMBACBW027SBOG).

7. For more on how the Fed's new operating framework endangers their operational independence, see Jerry Jordan and William Luther, "Central Bank Independence and the Federal Reserve's New Operating Regime," *Quarterly Review of Economics and Finance* (October 2020), https://www.ncbi.nlm.nih.gov/pmc/articles/PMC7554479/ (accessed October 27, 2020).

8. See Federal Reserve Economic Data (FRED), Federal Reserve Bank of St. Louis, Interest Rate on Excess Reserves (IOER), https://fred.stlouisfed.org/series/IOER (accessed October 26, 2020).

9. "Is the Federal Reserve Giving Banks a $12bn Subsidy?" *The Economist*, March 18, 2017, http://www.economist.com/news/finance-and-economics/21718872-or-interest-fed-pays-them-vital-monetary-tool-benefits (accessed June 23, 2017).

10. The totals for 2018 and 2019 are the "Interest payable to depository institutions and others" line item from the Federal Reserve's consolidated income statement. See Federal Reserve Banks Combined Financial Statements, "As of and for the Years Ended December 31, 2019 and 2018 and Independent Auditors' Report," March 6, 2020, 3, https://www.federalreserve.gov/aboutthefed/files/combinedfinstmt2019.pdf (accessed October 26, 2020)

11. Norbert J. Michel, "The Fed at 100: A Primer on Monetary Policy," *Heritage Foundation Backgrounder No. 2876*, January 29, 2014, http://www.heritage.org/report/the-fed-100-primer-monetary-policy (accessed November 12, 2020), and George Selgin, "A Monetary Policy Primer, Part 7: Monetary Control, Then," *Alt-M*, September 20, 2016, https://www.alt-m.org/2016/09/20/monetary-policy-primer-part-7-monetary-control/ (accessed September 29, 2017).

12. Whether banks find additional reserves before or after they arrange to make new loans is irrelevant. When a bank makes a loan, it credits the borrower's account with newly created money. The borrower then withdraws money and pays another individual (the payee), who places the funds in his own bank. This transaction requires a transfer of reserves from the lending bank to the payee's bank. Thus, the effect of making the loan is the same as if the lending bank simply lent its reserves.

13. What is commonly referred to as *the* federal-funds rate actually refers to an average measure called the effective federal-funds rate. Norbert J. Michel, "Fascination with Interest Rates Hides the Fed's Policy Blunders," *Heritage Foundation Issue Brief No. 4500*, December 15, 2015, http://www.heritage.org/report/fascination-interest-rates-hides-the-feds-policy-blunders (accessed November 12, 2020).

14. Alexander Kroeger, John McGowan, Asani Sarkar, "The Pre-Crisis Monetary Policy Implementation Framework," Federal Reserve of New York *Staff Report* No. 809, March 2017, 15, https://www.newyorkfed.org/medialibrary/media/research/staff_reports/sr809.pdf?la=en (accessed September 29, 2017).

15. Ben Bernanke, *The Courage to Act: A Memoir of a Crisis and Its Aftermath* (New York: W.W. Norton & Company, 2015), 144. The first sign of trouble that Bernanke is referring to is when France's largest publicly traded bank, BNP Paribas, suspended withdrawals from three of its subprime mortgage funds. Sudip Kar-Gupta and Yann Le Guernigou, "BNP Freezes $2.2 Bln of Funds Over Subprime," *Reuters*, August 9, 2007, https://www.reuters.com/article/us-bnpparibas-subprime-funds/

bnp-freezes-2-2-bln-of-funds-over-subprime-idUSWEB612920070809 (accessed September 30, 2017).

16. The Fed provided additional credit through open market purchases and various new lending programs, both of which have the same (positive) effect on reserves in the banking system. U.S. Government Accountability Office, "Federal Reserve System: Opportunities Exist to Strengthen Policies and Processes for Managing Emergency Assistance," *GAO–11–696*, July 2011, http://www.gao.gov/new.items/d11696.pdf (accessed September 30, 2017).

17. Bernanke, *The Courage to Act*, 236 and 237.

18. Bernanke, *The Courage to Act*, 325. This figure ($480 billion) is the lowest reported balance since 2002, the first year in the full series reported by the Federal Reserve.

19. Federal Reserve Board of Governors, Transcript of the joint Federal Open Market Committee and Federal Reserve Board of Governors meeting, held December 15–16, 2008, 22 and 23, https://www.federalreserve.gov/monetarypolicy/files/FOMC20081216meeting.pdf (accessed June 23, 2017).

20. In 2005, Fed Governor Donald Kohn testified to Congress that "[i]f the Federal Reserve was authorized to pay interest on excess reserves, and did so, the rate paid would act as a minimum for overnight interest rates." Donald Kohn, "Regulatory Relief," testimony before the Subcommittee on Financial Institutions and Consumer Credit, Committee on Financial Services, U.S. House of Representatives, June 9, 2005, https://www.federalreserve.gov/boarddocs/testimony/2005/20050609/default.htm (accessed September 30, 2017).

21. John Taylor, "Reserve Balances and the Fed's Balance Sheet in the Future," *Economics One*, June 24, 2017, https://economicsone.com/2017/06/24/reserve-balances-and-the-feds-balance-sheet-in-the-future/ (accessed September 30, 2017).

22. Title II of the Financial Services Regulatory Relief Act of 2006, 120 Stat. 1966 Public Law 109–351, authorized the Fed to pay interest on reserves, beginning October 1, 2011. Section 128 of the Emergency Economic Stabilization Act of 2008, 122 Stat. 3766 Public Law 110–343, amending 12 U.S. Code § 461, accelerated the start date to October 1, 2008.

23. Bernanke, *The Courage to Act*, 325 and 326.

24. The same economic justification for paying interest on required reserves does not apply to banks' decisions to hold *excess* reserves, and it is long-standing bank management practice to minimize excess reserves. Timothy Koch, *Bank Management*, 3rd ed. (Orlando, FL: The Dryden Press, 1995), 462. The idea of paying interest on *required* reserves was considered, though ultimately rejected, when Congress created the Federal Reserve in 1913. Selgin, testimony Before the Monetary Policy and Trade Subcommittee, 2.

25. Even though the Act (12 U.S. Code § 461 (b)(12)(A)) authorizes the Fed to pay interest on reserves "at a rate or rates not to exceed the general level of short-term interest rates," the Fed has consistently paid rates on reserves higher than the federal-funds rate and other short-term interest rates. George Selgin, "Has the Fed Been Breaking the Law?" *Alt-M*, September 6, 2016, https://www.alt-m.org/2016/09/06/has-fed-been-breaking-law/ (accessed September 3, 2020).

26. For a thorough account of the Fed's interest on reserve policies, see Hearing, *Monetary Policy v. Fiscal Policy: Risks to Price Stability and the Economy*, George Selgin, testimony before the Monetary Policy and Trade Subcommittee, Committee on Financial Services, U.S. House of Representatives, July 20, 2017, https://fi nancialservices.house.gov/uploadedfiles/hhrg-115-ba19-wstate-gselgin-20170720.pd f (accessed September 14, 2017). Also see Norbert J. Michel, "The Crisis Is Over: It Is Time to End Experimental Monetary Policy," *Heritage Foundation Backgrounder No. 3265*, November 9, 2017, https://www.heritage.org/sites/default/files/2017-11/BG3265.pdf (accessed November 12, 2020); and, George Selgin, *Floored!: How a Misguided Fed Experiment Deepened and Prolonged the Great Recession* (Washington, DC: Cato Institute, 2018).

27. See Donald Dutkowsky and David VanHoose, "Interest On Reserves, Regime Shifts, And Bank Behavior," *Journal of Economics and Business*, Vol. 91 (2017):1–15, https://www.sciencedirect.com/science/article/abs/pii/S0148619516 301047 (accessed October 27, 2020); and Donald Dutkowsky and David VanHoose, "Breaking Up Isn't Hard To Do: Interest On Reserves And Monetary Policy," *Journal of Economics and Business*, Vol. 99 (2018):15–27, https://ideas.repec.org/a/ eee/jebusi/v99y2018icp15-27.html (accessed October 27, 2020).

28. Waters Statement on Federal Reserve Response to Coronavirus, Washington, DC, March 16, 2020, https://financialservices.house.gov/news/documentsingle.aspx ?DocumentID=406435 (accessed May 11, 2020).

29. For a complete list of policy actions, see Norbert J. Michel, "The Federal Reserve Should Not Help Congress Duck Its Responsibilities," *Forbes.com*, March 23, 2020, https://www.forbes.com/sites/norbertmichel/2020/03/23/the- federal-re serve-should-not-help-congress-duck-its-responsibilities/#5b143d17610c (accessed September 3, 2020), and Norbert J. Michel, "The Federal Reserve Should Not Help Congress Duck Its Responsibilities: Part 2," *Forbes.com*, April 27, 2020, https://ww w.forbes.com/sites/norbertmichel/2020/04/27/the-federal-reserve-should-not-help-congress-duck-its-responsibilities-part-2/#662d4b1ec5a3 (accessed September 3, 2020).

30. Michel, "The Federal Reserve Should Not Help Congress Duck Its Responsibilities: Part 2."

31. James Dorn, "The Fed's Corporate Lending Facilities: A Case of Pseudo Markets," *Alt-M*, May 25, 2020, https://www.alt-m.org/2020/05/25/the-feds-corporat e-lending-facilities-a-case-of-pseudo-markets/ (accessed October 29, 2020); and James Dorn, "Fed's Intervention in Corporate Credit: A Risky Venture," *Alt-M*, July 13, 2020, https://www.alt-m.org/2020/07/13/feds-intervention-in-corporate-credit-a -risky-venture/ (accessed October 29, 2020).

32. Businesses with more than 500 employees can be eligible for these loans provided that they meet the existing statutory and regulatory definition of a "small business concern" under section 3 of the Small Business Act, 15 U.S. Code 632. See U.S. Treasury, "Paycheck Protection Program Loans Frequently Asked Questions (FAQs)," May 27, 2020, https://home.treasury.gov/system/files/136/Paycheck-Pro tection-Program-Frequently-Asked-Questions.pdf (accessed May 29, 2020).

33. Ibid.

34. Nick Timiraos and Jon Hilsenrath, "The Federal Reserve Is Changing What It Means to Be a Central Bank," *The Wall Street Journal*, April 27, 2020, https://www .wsj.com/articles/fate-and-history-the-fed-tosses-the-rules-to-fight-coronavirus-dow nturn-11587999986 (accessed May 7, 2020).

35. For a broader analysis, see George Selgin, "The Constitutional Case for the Fed's Treasury Backstops," *Alt-M.org*, April 13, 2020, https://www.alt-m.org/2020 /04/13/the-constitutional-case-for-the-feds-treasury-backstops/ (accessed September 3, 2020).

36. 15 U.S. Code 9042(b)(4). Section 4027 of the CARES Act (15 U.S. Code 9061) appropriates this amount from the Exchange Stabilization Fund, the fund established under section 5302(a)(1) of title 31, United States Code.

37. 15 U.S. Code 9042(c)(3)(B).

38. Jeanna Smialek, "How the Fed's Magic Money Machine Will Turn $454 Billion into $4 Trillion," *New York Times*, March 26, 2020 https://www.nytimes.com /2020/03/26/business/economy/fed-coronavirus-stimulus.html (accessed September 8, 2020).

39. Federal Reserve Board of Governors, "Main Street New Loan Facility," April 9, 2020, https://www.federalreserve.gov/newsevents/pressreleases/files/monetary 20200409a7.pdf (accessed September 3, 2020).

40. Selgin, *The Menace of Fiscal QE*, 9.

41. Ibid., 14–18 and 22–26.

42. George Selgin, "The Modern New Deal That's Too Good to Be True," *Alt-M*, February 8, 2019, https://www.alt- m.org/2019/02/08/the-modern-new-deal-tha ts-too-good-to-be-true/ (accessed October 29, 2020). For a more detailed dissection of the subtleties of the MMT arguments, see George Selgin, "On Empty Purses and MMT Rhetoric," *Alt-M*, March 5, 2019, https://www.alt-m.org/2019/03/05/on-empt y-purses-and-mmt-rhetoric/ (accessed October 29, 2020); and, George Selgin, "The Nice Limits of Modern Monetary Theory," *Alt-M*, May 10, 2019, https://www.alt-m.org/2019/05/10/the-nice-limits-of-modern-monetary-theory/ (accessed October 29, 2020).

43. John Greenwood and Steve H. Hanke, "Magical Monetary Theory," *The Wall Street Journal*, June 4, 2019.

44. Selgin, *The Menace of Fiscal QE*, 22–26.

45. Michel, Winfree, and Badger, "Potential Long-Term Economic Consequences."

46. Paul Winfree, "Causes of the Federal Government's Unsustainable Spending," *Heritage Foundation Backgrounder No. 3133*, July 7, 2016, https://www.heritage .org/budget-and-spending/report/causes-the-federal-governments- unsustainable-spending (accessed November 12, 2020).

47. The trust fund for Medicare Part A (hospital insurance) will be depleted by 2024. See David Ditch and Rachel Greszler, "New Report Shows Why Congress Must Address National Debt," *Heritage Foundation*, Forthcoming.

48. Megan Henney, "Social Security Benefit Cuts Could Be Coming—Here's Who It Will Affect First," *Fox Business*, September 4, 2020, https://www.foxbusin ess.com/economy/social-security-benefit-cuts-could-be-coming-heres-who-it-will-a ffect-first (accessed September 6, 2020).

49. For more on Congress using the Fed's capital surplus to pay for the highway bill, see Norbert J. Michel, "Banks Should Not Be Forced To Buy 'Stock' in the Federal Reserve," *Forbes*, December 21, 2015, https://www.forbes.com/sites/ norbertmichel/2015/12/21/banks-should-not-be-forced-to-buy-stock-in-the-federal-reserve/?sh=5ddb63528d25 (accessed October 29, 2020). For a broader discussion on the heightened risk that Congress might compel the Fed to use its fiscal QE powers to finance new projects, see Selgin, *The Menace of Fiscal QE*, 27–38.

50. Senator Ted Cruz (R–TX), for instance, has already called on the Fed to "provide emergency liquidity for small- and-medium sized businesses that work directly or indirectly with the oil and gas industry." News release, "Sen. Cruz Urges Treasury and Federal Reserve to Ensure Critical Access to Capital for America's Energy Producers," *Senator Ted Cruz*, April 24, 2020, https://www.cruz.senate.gov/?p=press_release&id =5076 (accessed May 11, 2020). Similarly, Bharat Ramamurti, a member of the congressional oversight commission charged with overseeing the federal coronavirus relief efforts, has criticized the Fed's Municipal Liquidity Facility because it *excludes* "certain cities and counties with strong credit ratings and great need—including the 35 cities in America with the highest percentage of black residents, such as Atlanta, Detroit, and Baltimore." Victoria Guida, "Pressure Mounts as Fed Chief Shepherds Massive Economic Rescue," *Politico*, April 20, 2020, https://www.politico.com/news/2020/04 /20/jerome-powell-donald-trump-coronavirus-193377 (accessed May 29, 2020).

51. Michel, Winfree, Badger, "Potential Long-Term Economic Consequences of the Federal Response to the COVID-19 Lockdowns."

52. Federal Reserve, "Securities Held Outright: U.S. Treasury Securities: All: Wednesday Level," FRED Economic Data, Federal Reserve Bank of St. Louis, October 30, 2020 https://fred.stlouisfed.org/series/TREAST (accessed October 30, 2020); and U.S. Treasury, "The Debt to the Penny and Who Holds It," *Treasury Direct*, https://treasurydirect.gov/govt/reports/pd/pd_debttothepenny.htm (accessed October 30, 2020).

REFERENCES

Bernanke, Ben, *The Courage to Act: A Memoir of a Crisis and Its Aftermath*, New York: W.W. Norton & Company, 2015.

Coats, Warren, "Modern Monetary Theory: A Critique," *Cato Journal*, Vol. 39, No. 3 (Fall 2019).

Congressional Budget Office, "Monthly Budget Review for September 2020," October 8, 2020.

Cruz, Ted, "Sen. Cruz Urges Treasury and Federal Reserve to Ensure Critical Access to Capital for America's Energy Producers," *News Release*, April 24, 2020.

Dorn, James, "The Fed's Corporate Lending Facilities: A Case of Pseudo Markets," *Alt-M*, May 25, 2020.

Dorn, James, "Fed's Intervention in Corporate Credit: A Risky Venture," *Alt-M*, July 13, 2020.

Dutkowsky, Donald and David VanHoose, "Interest On Reserves, Regime Shifts, And Bank Behavior," *Journal of Economics and Business*, Vol. 91 (2017), 1–15.

Dutkowsky, Donald and David VanHoose, "Breaking Up Isn't Hard To Do: Interest On Reserves And Monetary Policy," *Journal of Economics and Business*, Vol. 99 (2018), 15–27.

The Economist, "Is the Federal Reserve Giving Banks a $12bn Subsidy?" March 18, 2017.

Federal Reserve Banks Combined Financial Statements, "As of and for the Years Ended December 31, 2019 and 2018 and Independent Auditors' Report," March 6, 2020.

Federal Reserve Board of Governors, Transcript of the joint Federal Open Market Committee and Federal Reserve Board of Governors meeting, held December 15–16, 2008.

Federal Reserve Board of Governors, "Main Street New Loan Facility," April 9, 2020.

Greenwood, John and Steve H. Hanke, "Magical Monetary Theory," *The Wall Street Journal*, June 4, 2019.

Guida, Victoria, "Pressure Mounts as Fed Chief Shepherds Massive Economic Rescue," *Politico*, April 20, 2020.

Henney, Megan, "Social Security Benefit Cuts Could Be Coming—Here's Who It Will Affect First," *Fox Business*, September 4, 2020.

Jordan, Jerry and William Luther, "Central Bank Independence and the Federal Reserve's New Operating Regime," *Quarterly Review of Economics and Finance* (October 2020).

Kar-Gupta, Sudip and Yann Le Guernigou, "BNP Freezes $2.2 Bln of Funds Over Subprime," *Reuters*, August 9, 2007.

Koch, Timothy, *Bank Management*, 3rd ed., Orlando, FL: The Dryden Press, 1995.

Kohn, Donald, "Regulatory Relief," testimony before the Subcommittee on Financial Institutions and Consumer Credit, Committee on Financial Services, U.S. House of Representatives, June 9, 2005.

Kroeger, Alexander, John McGowan, Asani Sarkar, "The Pre-Crisis Monetary Policy Implementation Framework," Federal Reserve of New York *Staff Report* No. 809, March 2017.

Maxine Waters Statement on Federal Reserve Response to Coronavirus, Washington DC, March 16, 2020.

Michel, Norbert J., "The Fed at 100: A Primer on Monetary Policy," *Heritage Foundation Backgrounder No. 2876*, January 29, 2014.

Michel, Norbert J., "Fascination with Interest Rates Hides the Fed's Policy Blunders," *Heritage Foundation Issue Brief No. 4500*, December 15, 2015.

Michel, Norbert J., "Banks Should Not Be Forced To Buy 'Stock' in the Federal Reserve," *Forbes*, December 21, 2015.

Michel, Norbert J., "The Crisis Is Over: It Is Time to End Experimental Monetary Policy," *Heritage Foundation Backgrounder No. 3265*, November 9, 2017.

Michel, Norbert J., "The Federal Reserve Should Not Help Congress Duck Its Responsibilities," *Forbes.com*, March 23, 2020.

Michel, Norbert J., "The Federal Reserve Should Not Help Congress Duck Its Responsibilities: Part 2," *Forbes.com,* April 27, 2020.

Michel, Norbert J., Paul Winfree, and Doug Badger, "Potential Long-Term Economic Consequences of the Federal Response to the COVID-19 Lockdowns," *Heritage Foundation Backgrounder No. 3498,* June 4, 2020.

Selgin, George, "A Monetary Policy Primer, Part 7: Monetary Control, Then," *Alt-M,* September 20, 2016.

Selgin, George, "Has the Fed Been Breaking the Law?" *Alt-M,* September 6, 2016.

Selgin, George, testimony before the Monetary Policy and Trade Subcommittee, Committee on Financial Services, U.S. House of Representatives, July 20, 2017.

Selgin, George, *Floored!: How a Misguided Fed Experiment Deepened and Prolonged the Great Recession,* Washington, DC: Cato Institute, 2018.

Selgin, George, "The Modern New Deal That's Too Good to Be True," *Alt-M,* February 8, 2019.

Selgin, George, "On Empty Purses and MMT Rhetoric," *Alt-M,* March 5, 2019.

Selgin, George, "The Nice Limits of Modern Monetary Theory," *Alt-M,* May 10, 2019.

Selgin, George, *The Menace of Fiscal QE,* Washington, DC: Cato Institute, 2020.

Selgin, George, "The Constitutional Case for the Fed's Treasury Backstops," *Alt-M* .org, April 13, 2020.

Smialek, Jeanna, "How the Fed's Magic Money Machine Will Turn $454 Billion into $4 Trillion," *New York Times,* March 26, 2020.

Swagel, Phill, "An Update to the Budget Outlook: 2020 to 2030," *Congressional Budget Office,* September 20, 2020.

Taylor, John, "Reserve Balances and the Fed's Balance Sheet in the Future," *Economics One,* June 24, 2017.

Timiraos, Nick and Jon Hilsenrath, "The Federal Reserve Is Changing What It Means to Be a Central Bank," *The Wall Street Journal,* April 27, 2020.

U.S. Government Accountability Office, "Federal Reserve System: Opportunities Exist to Strengthen Policies and Processes for Managing Emergency Assistance," *GAO–11–696,* July 2011.

U.S. Treasury, "Paycheck Protection Program Loans Frequently Asked Questions (FAQs)," May 27, 2020.

U.S. Treasury, "The Debt to the Penny and Who Holds It," *Treasury Direct.*

Winfree, Paul, "Causes of the Federal Government's Unsustainable Spending," *Heritage Foundation Backgrounder No. 3133,* July 7, 2016.

Chapter 10

The Federal Reserve and
the Debt Crises

Thomas R. Saving

INTRODUCTION

All the countries in the developed world have been expanding sovereign debt at an alarming rate ever since the 2008 financial crisis. At the same time, their central banks have engaged in unprecedented increases in assets by buying both own country debt and private assets. Traditional monetary theory would have predicted, and many economists did so predict, that the result of these central bank asset expansions would have been raging inflation. What happened that made the combination of rapid sovereign debt expansion and central bank participation in that expansion not lead to inflation? Further, does the reason the first debt expansion did not lead to inflation suggest why the 2020 pandemic debt expansion will not create an inflation crisis? To address the potential for a debt crisis to be controlled through an appropriate central bank response, this chapter concentrates on the Federal Reserve and its actions during two onslaughts of U.S federal debt. The first onslaught of debt was the period from 2008 through 2019. The second debt onslaught came with the deficits due to the 2020 COVID-19 pandemic.

DEBT CRISIS 1: THE GREAT RECESSION

Until the beginning of fiscal year 2009, the first decade of this century was similar to other decades of the past half-century, at least in terms of Federal Reserve behavior. But then came the onset of the Great Recession, and seemingly everything changed. First came an unprecedented increase in federal deficits, both in dollar size and as a share of GDP. This series of deficits followed the also unprecedented series of surpluses of the late 1990s through

2001. Up to fiscal 2009, the annual deficit share of GDP was the same order of magnitude of the previous pre-surplus years. But then with the onset of the Great Recession, the fiscal 2009 deficit ballooned to almost 10% of GDP. Fiscal deficits then gradually declined both in nominal terms and as a share of GDP until beginning a gradual rise in fiscal 2016. Overall fiscal year deficits have averaged 5% of GDP for almost a decade, the longest stretch of deficits at this level in at least a century.

Given the level of post-2008 federal deficits as a share of GDP, it is not surprising that publicly held federal debt as a share of the nation's GDP has also been steadily rising. Further, with the onset of a return to trillion-dollar federal deficits associated with the COVID-19 pandemic, federal deficits as a share of GDP are expected to rise faster than previously estimated by the Congressional Budget Office (CBO). By the end of fiscal year 2020, the fiscal 2020 federal deficit was already $3.1 trillion, 14.9% of GDP, the largest since WWII.

Figure 10.1 shows the path of publicly held federal debt as a share of GDP for the 1992 to 2019 period as estimated by the CBO and a lower path corrected for the fact that the Federal Reserve holds a significant part of the official publicly held debt. The upper line is the share that official publicly held debt is of GDP. The decline of the publicly held debt share of GDP in the early part of the figure is a product of the mid-1990s to 2001 budget

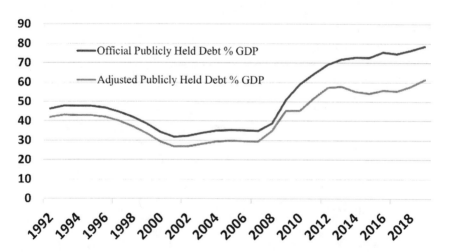

Figure 10.1   Adjusted Debt Held by the Public as a percent of GDP 1992–2019.
Adapted from GDP – U.S. Bureau of Economic analysis – Release Gross Domestic Product Debt Held by the Public- U.S. Department of the Treasury – Fiscal Services Treasury Bulletin Federal Reserve Securities Holdings – Board of Governors of the Federal Reserve System – Factors Affecting Reserve Balances.

surpluses. The GDP debt share was relatively stable until the onset of the Great Recession, fiscal 2009. Then in the next decade, the GDP debt share doubled and reached nearly 80% for fiscal 2019. In the last CBO forecasts before the 2020 pandemic, the CBO suggested that this trend of rising publicly held debt share of GDP would continue into the long future reaching almost 100% by 2030. All that changed with the onset of the government response to the COVID-19 pandemic, so that by April 2020, the CBO was forecasting that the publicly held debt share of GDP would be 100% for 2020 and would reach 110% of GDP in 2021.

The lower line in Figure 10.1 is a corrected measure of the publicly held share of GDP, as the upper line ignores the fact that the usual estimate of the level of publicly held federal debt considers the Federal Reserve as part of the public. That view is consistent with the Government Accounting Office that considers the Federal Reserve as not part of the government. But by law, the earnings of the Federal Reserve must be remitted to the Treasury. In effect then, the Treasury, as the residual income recipient of the Federal Reserve, "owns" the Federal Reserve. In fact, the Treasury might be viewed as a non-voting common stock holder of Federal Reserve assets. All Federal Reserve income earning assets, including Treasury securities and mortgage-backed securities held by the Federal Reserve, are essentially held by the Treasury and not by the public.[1] Thus, these Federal Reserve asset holdings reduce outstanding federal debt on a one-to-one basis.

The difference between the two lines in figure 10.1 is a reflection of the share of the official publicly held debt that is owned by the Federal Reserve. Two things are apparent in that difference. One, it remains almost constant until the 2008 economic meltdown as the federal debt held by the Federal Reserve prior to the 2008 economic meltdown was almost a constant share of GDP. Second, then the tremendous expansion in the Federal Reserve holdings of both mortgage-backed and Treasury securities increased the Federal Reserve's share of the official publicly held federal debt. As a result, the difference between the publicly held debt percent of GDP curves becomes much larger after 2008.

The scale of Federal Reserve holdings of securities as a percent of GDP remained approximately constant from 1992 through 2007. Then, the Great Recession's almost unprecedented increases in the GDP share of federal deficits led to two changes in Federal Reserve behavior. One, the Federal Reserve's securities share of GDP rose from its former equilibrium of about 7% to a peak of 25%. Two, the payment of interest on reserves made reserves essentially negative securities holdings. The total effect of these two events resulted in the significant post-2008 increase in the Federal Reserve net holdings of securities, as is evident in figure 10.1.

FEDERAL RESERVE RESPONSE TO THE 2008 CRISIS

To get a better feel for how dramatic the Federal Reserve's post-2008 change in policy was, consider the period from October 2008 to December 2014. This period was one of massive federal deficits coupled with Federal Reserve unprecedented asset expansions. During that period, the personal consumption expenditure price index (PCE) inflation averaged 1.56% and real GDP growth was 1.8%, both historic lows for any similar length period. Moreover, federal deficits for fiscal years 2009 through 2014 expressed both in terms of absolute dollars and as a share of GDP were post-WWII records.

The levels of fiscal year federal deficits and the corresponding changes in Federal Reserve assets resulted in significant changes in the monetary base. In general, changes in Federal Reserve assets represent either running the money printing press in the case of increasing assets or destroying money in the case of Federal Reserve reducing assets. Based on data from the Federal Reserve for the fiscal years 2009 through 2015, Federal Reserve asset acquisitions financed just over 55% of the Great Recession federal deficits.

Historically, the level of monetary expansion, if measured by the increases in the monetary base, would have resulted in a return to the double-digit inflation of the late 1970s. We know that did not happen and the important question is; why? But before the answer, a more detailed look at Federal Reserve behavior subsequent to the financial breakdown of September 2008 will prove useful.

Except for Federal Reserve responses to the financial crisis in the last four months of 2008, the increases in the monetary base during this period were the result of increases in the Federal Reserve's holdings of securities. But the securities held were not all federal debt. The Federal Reserve was buying assets, principally both Treasuries and Mortgage-Backed Securities (MBSs). But only their Treasury purchases were directly reducing the level of federal debt held outside the government.

An important question is: do Federal Reserve holdings of MBSs and private market assets contribute in any way to the level of Federal Reserve financing of federal debt? To solve this puzzle requires analysis of what happens to all Federal Reserve revenue. By law, profits of the Federal Reserve after all costs revert to the Treasury. Thus, the Treasury is the residual income recipient of Federal Reserve asset holdings, and therefore, in one sense at least, the Treasury owns the Federal Reserve. As a result, all Federal Reserve earnings on Treasuries, MBSs, and other private market holdings accrue to the Treasury and reduce the net servicing cost of the federal debt and as such are equivalent to purchases of federal debt.

In addition to the asset expansion, the Federal Reserve established special facilities to alleviate the financial crisis that began in September 2008. Some of the facilities were already in place at the beginning of 2008, the onset of the Great Recession. The effect of the September 2008 financial crisis resulted in a spike in Federal Reserve loans. These loans were mutual fund and broker assistance. Then, the commercial paper market all but disappeared as money market funds were pressured by customers for liquidity. The Federal Reserve, for all practical purposes, became the commercial paper market. The Federal Reserve also initiated the Term Auction program that provided money to financial institutions at rates of interest determined at auction. All of these special facilities were gone by the end of 2010 and all were very profitable for the Federal Reserve and the Treasury.

FEDERAL RESERVE'S ROLE IN THE GREAT RECESSION DEBT EXPANSION

A common measure of the burden of the federal debt is the share that this debt is of the nation's GDP. At the close of initial debt expansion, 2015, the CBO estimated that the publicly held federal debt was 73.6% of GDP. Presumably, the ratio of debt to a nation's GDP is an indication of a nation's ability to at least pay the cost of servicing that debt. Since taxpayers are on the hook for servicing the federal debt, this federal debt is on the same footing as personal debt. In that sense, the same logic used to value the net debt of any private citizen is also relevant for estimating the ability of the economy to service the federal debt.

But in reporting the publicly held federal debt, the Federal Reserve is considered to be part of the public. And because the Treasury owns the Federal Reserve's net income, debt held by the Federal Reserve is essentially owned by the government and not the public. As a result, the interest payments on that debt accrue to the Federal Reserve and are then turned back into the Treasury. Throughout the period of Federal Reserve expansion, the transfers from the Federal Reserve to the Treasury played a major role in covering the net servicing cost of the federal debt. For the fiscal years 2009 through 2015, transfers from the Federal Reserve to the Treasury rose from $47 billion in 2009 to $99 billion in 2014. By the close of 2014, Federal Reserve transfers to the Treasury were paying for more than 40% of total federal debt servicing costs. Since Federal Reserve holdings of mortgage backed securities (MBSs) create income for the Treasury, these assets offset federal debt, and their purchase is equivalent to the Federal Reserve buying Treasuries.

Returning to the post-2008 federal deficits and Federal Reserve monetization depicted in figure 10.1, as the difference between the official publicly of held debt as a % of GDP and the publicly held debt adjusted for Federal Reserve debt holdings % of GDP widened, it seemed that the Federal

Reserve's asset increases did indeed constitute monetization of a significant share of the massive federal debts of this period. But this simple view of the federal debt ignores the fact that the Federal Reserve increased its liabilities almost in lock-step with its increase in assets. The increase in Federal Reserve liabilities was the result of the introduction of the payment of interest on bank reserves (IOR) in October 2008. Essentially, the obligation to pay IOR made these reserves a short-term debt of the Federal Reserve. Since all earnings of the Federal Reserve offset the servicing cost of the federal debt, and the interest payments on reserves reduce these transfers by the full amount of the payments, bank reserves are the equivalent of short-term federal debt. For all practical purposes, the Federal Reserve, throughout the QEs, was buying long-term federal debt and selling short-term federal debt.

Before interest payments on bank reserves, Federal Reserve actions that increased bank reserves led to an increase in the money supply by a multiple of the increase in reserves. When bank reserves earned nothing, banks moved any excess reserves into market investments, loans, Treasury securities, or other investments. This activity increased the money supply by a multiple of the change in reserves. Then, these money supply increases affected the price level. But now these same bank reserve increases represent member bank income earning assets.

Figure 10.2 shows the level of bank holdings of excess reserves for the period from the beginning of interest payments on bank reserves through the first quarter of 2016. The figure also shows the difference between an

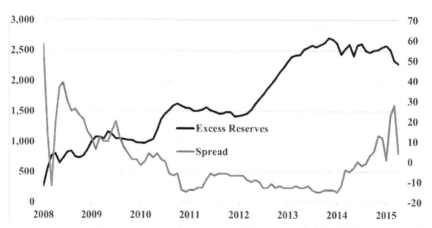

Figure 10.2 1-year Treasury—IOER Spread and Excess Reserves January 2008 to January 2016. Adapted from Excess Reserves: Board of Governors of the Federal Reserve System – H.3 Aggregate Reserves of Depository Institutions and the Monetary Base. IOER: Board of Governors of the Federal Reserve System – Interest on Required Balances and Excess Balances. 1-year Treasury Interest Rate: Board of Governors of the Federal Reserve System – H.15 Selected Interest Rates.

important market rate of interest, the rate of interest on 1-year Treasuries, and the interest rate paid on bank excess reserves measured in basis points.[2] This difference is a measure of the advantage or disadvantage to the banks of holding excess reserves instead of market investments. At the onset of reserve interest payments, the rate of return for holding reserves matched the rate on 1-year Treasury Notes. Then for the period from January 2009 until September 2010, the rate of return on the 1-year Treasury Notes exceeded the return on reserves. From September 2010, the return to holding reserves exceeded the 1-year Treasury interest rate until August 2015. Then in response to rising 1-year Treasury Note rates, the interest rate on reserves was raised to 37 basis points and then to 50 basis points. As is clearly shown in the figure, the tremendous growth in bank holdings of excess reserves occurred when the return on these reserves exceeded the return on 1-year Treasuries.

In effect, the Federal Reserve sterilized the effect of their post-2008 asset increases on the money supply by making reserves a bank asset and a Federal Reserve short-term liability. This sterilization eliminated the normal effect of an increase in bank reserves on the money supply as member banks were paid to hold reserves rather than increase their holdings of economy assets, either loans or securities. Thus, any potential effect of these increased reserves on the money supply was mitigated or eliminated. In fact, excess reserves only contribute to money growth when used to create loans as a result of the concomitant increase in bank demand deposits. Excess reserves only become part of the monetary base when they cease to be excess, that is, become required reserves.

The fact that now bank excess reserves are the equivalent of short-term federal debt requires that the level of Federal Reserve financing of the post-2008 federal deficits must be amended. Now, any increase in Federal Reserve liabilities stemming from member banks excess reserve holdings reduce the level of Federal Reserve financing of federal debt. Essentially, a correct measure of debt monetization must account for the inclusion of the increase in Federal Reserve liabilities, that is, bank reserves, as an offset to Federal Reserve asset growth.

The difference between traditional monetary base growth and the growth in excess reserves for each fiscal year is a measure of the effective monetary base growth. The effective monetary base growth is an estimate of the actual level of monetization of each fiscal year deficit. Using this measure of net Federal Reserve involvement in financing federal deficits for the entire seven fiscal year period, the level of deficit monetization was just over 9%, rather than the 55% estimate when the liability aspect of bank reserves is ignored.

The reported measure of publicly held federal debt includes Treasury debt held by the Federal Reserve and, as of the end of 2015, the debt was $13.11 trillion. However, the Federal Reserve asset holdings belong to the Treasury.

If the Treasury debt and Federal Reserve holdings are consolidated, the publicly held federal is reduced by Federal Reserve holdings of $2.5 trillion of federal debt to $10.6 trillion. There is a further adjustment to the level of publicly held debt that is required due to the income of the Federal Reserve being the property of the Treasury. The other principal assets held by the Federal Reserve are the $1.7 trillion in MBSs; the income of which belongs to the Treasury. In effect, the Federal Reserve holdings of MBSs are Treasury assets that offset Treasury liabilities. When all Federal Reserve Treasuries, MBSs, and other assets are subtracted from reported publicly held debt, the above $10.6 trillion becomes $8.9 trillion.

A final adjustment is required since the introduction of paying IOR has made these reserves short-term liabilities of the Federal Reserve. Further, the Federal Reserve engages in providing non-member financial institutions the ability to earn interest on some of their reserves by buying Federal Reserve reverse repos. Because all these liabilities reduce the level of Federal Reserve transfers to the Treasury, they are the equivalent to publicly held debt. Thus, it is appropriate to add the sum of these liabilities, together they equal $2.8 trillion, to the $8.9 trillion adjusted publicly held debt. The adjusted level of the federal debt taking into account the adjusted Federal Reserve balance sheet is then $11.7 trillion, about 89% of the 2015 measured $13.11 trillion and 63.3% of GDP.[3]

IS THERE AN INFLATION MYSTERY IN THE FEDERAL RESERVE'S RESPONSE TO THE FIRST DEBT CRISIS?

Considering the virtually unprecedented rate of monetary base growth following the onset of the Great Recession, the usual economic projection would have been inflation to match. The natural question then is, what happened? In a simple world of constant currency to deposit and bank reserve ratios, the rate of change in any of the popular definitions of money would equal the rate of change in the monetary base. It is just this growth in the monetary base that represents the Federal Reserve's effect on the economy through its effect on the money supply, however defined. Then in a simple world, the 15.7% rate of growth in the monetary base during the seven years of Great Recession Federal Reserve asset expansion should have, but did not, result in the significant inflation that many economists predicted. There are two reasons why did this not happen.[4]

First, consider the traditional equation of exchange that relates the rate of change in money growth to the rate of change in prices adjusting for both velocity growth and real GDP growth. This equation can be expressed as, $\pi = \mu + v - g$. Essentially the rate of inflation, π, must equal the rate of growth in the money supply, μ, plus the rate of growth in the velocity of money, v, minus the rate of growth in real GDP, g. For this seven-year period, the rate of growth in the expanded definition of the money stock, M2, was 6.3%, much less than the 15.7% rate of growth in the monetary base. For this same period the GDP velocity of M2 fell at a rate of 2.9% and real GDP grew at 1.8%. The result from using the simple equation of exchange is a predicted inflation rate of 1.6%, not significantly different than the measured rate of inflation of the GDP deflator of 1.4%.

Second, what is the reason for the disparity between the 15.7% rate of monetary base growth and the much smaller 6.3% growth in the M2 measure of the money supply? Here the answer lies in the change in the nature of the monetary base, in particular, the reserve component. Traditionally, when the Federal Reserve increases its asset holdings, the proceeds of these purchases became bank reserves and as such became part of the monetary base. Often referred to as "high-powered money," these proceeds can support a multiple of itself in the money supply. But now, all reserves are not high-powered money. In fact, excess reserves are pure bank investments and cannot affect the money supply. As a result, for purposes of bank money creation, only required reserves matter. What must be done is to correct the usual measure of the monetary base by removing excess reserves. Then, the relation between the money supply and this new adjusted monetary base should be unchanged from the before interest on reserves relation between the traditional monetary base and the money supply. Once the base is adjusted for the fact that most reserves are bank investments rather than reserves, the M2 measure of the money stock multiple of that corrected base remained virtually unchanged.

In simplistic terms, what happened to the inflation threat of the tremendous Federal Reserve post-2008 asset expansion was a remarkable reduction in the velocity of money coupled with a reduction in the effect of the monetary base on the supply of money. Understanding what happened brings two perplexing issues into focus. First, did everything we thought we knew about how the monetary system worked become wrong at the beginning of the fourth quarter of 2008? Second, if not, then why did an unprecedented expansion of Federal Reserve assets not have any real effect on the economy?

The answer to both these questions is apparent once we understand the effect of the introduction of interest payments on bank reserves. These interest payments on bank reserves created investment opportunities for banks that did not involve the economy. Simultaneously, interest payments on reserves created liabilities on the Federal Reserve balance sheet.

Prior to these interest payments, the largest official Federal Reserve liability was currency. But currency could not be considered a liability in any real sense. To see this point, consider what you get when you bring currency to the Federal Reserve. You just get replacement currency. The Federal

Reserve gets real resources when it issues currency, just as you would if you issued a personal bond, that is, borrowed money from a bank. The difference is that you would be required to pay back the loan with interest, that is give up something real, while the Federal Reserve never has to pay back anything.[5]

In this new world of interest payments on reserves, the asset purchases of the Federal Reserve have suddenly been financed, at least partially, by issuing debt. Moreover, this new debt has real consequences because all Federal Reserve earnings accrue to the Treasury. Thus, the interest payments on reserves reduce Federal Reserve transfers to the Treasury. These reduced transfers increase the cost of servicing the federal debt and ultimately increase the federal debt burden. In effect, with interest payments on reserves, bank excess reserves are equivalent to federal debt.

THE YEARS BETWEEN THE TWO DEBT CRISES

The Federal Reserve's involvement in the first debt crisis ended at the close of 2014, when it closed down its asset expansion program and essentially ended its role in reducing the level of the relevant measure of federal debt. From that point until the beginning of the second debt crisis, the onset of the COVID-19 pandemic, and the economic shutdown, the Federal Reserve's holdings of securities remained relatively stable.

Before interest on reserves, a long period of stable Federal Reserve assets would have meant little or no monetary growth. Now, monetary growth can happen with asset expansion or liability contraction. During this period, monetary growth matched economic growth as Federal Reserve net assets rose because their liabilities, excess reserves, fell. These net assets belong to the Treasury. As such, increases in Federal Reserve net assets are direct reductions in a correct measure of publicly held federal debt.

From the 1990s until the 2008 financial crisis and the accompanying huge federal deficits, the Federal Reserve held on average about 12% of the outstanding federal debt. Subsequent to 2008, the Federal Reserve share of total federal debt has averaged over 25%, more than double the pre-2008 share. The transfers peaked in 2014 at $99 billion, the year the Federal Reserve ceased its asset acquisitions. In that year, Federal Reserve transfers to the Treasury covered over 43% of total net debt servicing costs. Then, as market interest rates rose, the Federal Reserve had to raise the interest rate on reserves to control the net monetary base. This increase in Federal Reserve payments on their debt with little change in the earnings on their portfolio reduced Federal Reserve transfers to the Treasury. By 2019, the Federal Reserve transfers to the Treasury covered less than 15% of debt servicing cost.

There were three distinct periods of Federal Reserve policy between the two debt crises. The first such period, from the beginning of 2015 until November 2017, Federal Reserve assets were constant but as liabilities in the form of excess reserves fell, net assets rose. Then, a second period of Federal Reserve policy began in November 2017 when the Federal Reserve initiated a program to reduce the assets held in its balance sheet. This asset reduction period was from November 2017 until the close of that program in August 2019. Then, the third period of Federal Reserve policy was the resumption of securities purchases in October 2019 until March 2020, the onset of the second debt crisis.

All three of these periods saw federal deficits. Although in the first, federal deficits as a share of GDP were declining. Even though in the first period the Federal Reserve was not adding to its securities holdings, excess reserves were falling fast enough to allow Federal Reserve holdings of net federal debt to rise. Thus, during this period, net publicly held federal debt as a share of GDP actually fell. In fact, as figure 10.1 shows, during this period, net public debt as a share of GDP remained almost constant while the unadjusted publicly held share continued to rise. The same can be said for both of the remaining periods.

Figure 10.3 shows the path of Federal Reserve net assets, securities holdings plus other investments that contribute to asset earnings and liabilities that use up asset earnings in the forms of interest earning reserves and reverse

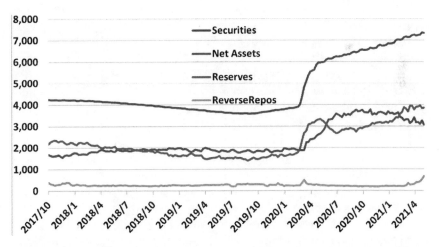

Figure 10.3   Federal Reserve Net Assets January 1, 2015 to March 17, 2021, Billions.
Adapted from Board of Governors of the Federal Reserve System – H.4.1 Factors Affecting Reserve Balances Reserves - Board of Governors of the Federal Reserve System – H.4.1 Factors Affecting Reserve Balances-Liabilities Reverse Repos - Board of Governors of the Federal Reserve System – H.4.1 Factors Affecting Reserve Balances- Liabilities.

repurchase agreements.[6] The figure begins at the end of the 2008 asset expansion period, January 2015, and includes the COVID-19 expansion up to March 2021.

There are four distinct periods presented in the figure. The first period is the time of relatively constant Federal Reserve assets from January 2015 until the onset of asset reductions in November 2017. During that constant gross asset period, reserves fell consistently as the difference between market interest rates and the IOER rose making it profitable for banks to invest their reserve holdings.

The second period was one of asset reduction as the Federal Reserve began to return its asset holdings relative to GDP back toward its long-run equilibrium. Proper management of the relation between the IOER and market interest rates was required for this asset reduction to continue and Federal Reserve net assets to grow enough to allow the money supply to grow with the economy. As the asset reduction period noted in figure 10.3 shows the Federal Reserve succeeded until March 2019, when bank reserve holdings and Federal Reserve net assets stabilized. The failure of net assets to rise and then to actually fall forced the end of asset reductions in August 2019.

The third period is from November 2019 when the Federal Reserve began a new asset accumulation policy until the COVID-19 pandemic. This policy was successful in increasing assets more than the increase in reserves so that net assets rose.

The fourth period begins with the onset of the COVID-19 economic shutdown when assets both gross and net grew rapidly.

As figure 10.3 clearly shows, the Federal Reserve does not have to add to its securities holdings to increase its net assets. In fact, except for the brief period in 2019 when the Federal Reserve failed to decrease the IOER to keep market interest rates above the rate paid on reserves, Federal Reserve net assets rose. The decision in 2008 to begin paying IOR, particularly excess reserves (the IOER), on the path of Federal Reserve net assets has changed the role of the banking system in the determination of the nation's money supply.

Paying IOR essentially turned these reserves into investment opportunities for banks. The effective monetary base is the measured monetary base less the excess reserves held by banks. Now, the effect of an increase in the monetary base on the money supply is reduced by the share of that base increase that is absorbed by bank reserves. As a result, banks are active, rather than passive, players in Federal Reserve monetary policy actions.

The failure of the Federal Reserve to maintain the advantage of holding market assets over holding reserves is the reason for the end of the trend of declining bank reserve holdings. During the period where reserves were falling faster than Federal Reserve asset reductions, the spread was heavily in favor of the market. But by March 2019, the spread between 1-year Treasuries and the IOER was zero and then negative. The failure of the Federal Reserve to adjust the IOER to offset what was happening in the market resulted in its net assets failing to rise and even falling slightly leading to the cessation of the asset reduction program in August 2019. Then, the advantage of holding reserves did not change as the Federal Reserve continued its failure to reduce the IOER as fast as market interest rates were falling. As a result of the falling net assets in October 2019, the Federal Reserve began to expand assets. This asset expansion was enough to offset the advantage of reserves and once again allow net Federal Reserve assets to rise.[7]

The fundamental tool of monetary policy is the control of the monetary base and the nation's money supply. It is clear that the banking system responds to the level of the IOER relative to market interest rates. As a result, we are now in a world where the banking system shares, almost on an equal footing with the Federal Reserve, the control of the money supply.

The Federal Reserve can conduct an expansionary monetary policy by entering the market for securities, but also by reducing the interest rate it pays on bank reserves. As a result, this interest rate, which is wholly determined by the Federal Reserve, is now an important part of monetary policy. But by the same token, market interest rates now play a role independent of the Federal Reserve in monetary policy. An increase in market interest rates, with a fixed Federal Reserve-determined IOER, will increase the effective monetary base and then increase the nation's money supply.

But these changes do not mean that the Federal Reserve has lost its power to control the money supply. But to maintain its ability to control monetary policy, it must be constantly cognizant of financial market interest rates. Thus, the Federal Reserve is more subject to the vagaries of financial markets than at any time in its more than 100-year history.

DEBT CRISIS 2: THE COVID-19 PANDEMIC

While there is some evidence that the onset of COVID-19 might have been even earlier than January 2020, its impact on the world economy was certainly no sooner than January 2020. From figure 10.3 it is clear that the Federal Reserve asset expansion program that began in October 2019 was necessary to allow Federal Reserve net assets to begin to rise, as is required if the net monetary base is to increase. Unfortunately, the Federal Reserve was unwilling to set the IOER enough below market interest rates to incentivize banks to move excess reserves into the market. Thus, by October 2019, the required monetary growth necessitated a significant expansion of Federal Reserve assets.

In the first debt crisis that began in fiscal 2009 with a record $1.4 trillion federal deficit, the Federal Reserve essentially supplied resources to finance

$800 billion of that deficit, just over 56%. But the decision to pay banks to hold reserves resulted in the majority of that $800 billion being offset by Federal Reserve liabilities that, for all practical purposes, were federal debt. So that in the final analysis, the Federal Reserve financed only just over 5% of the monumental fiscal 2009 deficit.

Even before the onset of the pandemic, the Federal Reserve initiated in October 2019, the first month of fiscal 2020, an asset acquisition program. Then, with pandemic economic restrictions multiplying and having a real bite, the rate of asset acquisition virtually exploded. What began in October 2019 as a steady asset purchase of less than $40 billion a week and usually less than $20 billion, quickly exploded. As is clearly shown in figure 10.3, when the pandemic shutdown really took hold, the Federal Reserve from mid-March 2020 to the end of April 2021 added an additional $1.6 trillion in securities to its portfolio. In all of fiscal 2020, the Federal Reserve purchased the equivalent of $2.85 trillion of the $3.13 trillion fiscal 2020 federal deficit, just over 90%. By the close of the first year of the pandemic, the Federal Reserve had added $3.18 trillion to its portfolio.

In addition to the tremendous Federal Reserve securities asset expansion, the pandemic economic shutdown has brought a return to the Federal Reserve operating in private markets and aiding financial institutions. The private market aid for the pandemic includes all of the aids for the 2008 crisis plus several more specific to the characteristics of this broader crisis. Each of these so-called facilities has the characteristics of Federal Reserve investment in the economy and, just as in the 2008 crisis, will be revenue-generating. The total list is: Commercial Paper Funding Facility (CPPF), Municipal Liquidity Facility (MLF), Primary Dealer Credit Facility (PDCF), Primary Market Corporate Credit Facility (PMCCF), Secondary Market Corporate Credit Facility (SMCCF), Term Asset-Backed Securities Loan Facility (TALF), FIMA Repo Facility (FIMA), and Main Street Lending Program (MSLP). The Treasury has an equity position in both the Corporate Credit Facilities and the TALF. The TALF will enable the issuance of asset-backed securities (ABS) backed by student loans, auto loans, credit card loans, loans guaranteed by the Small Business Administration (SBA), and certain other assets.

While many of these facilities were also part of the Federal Reserve response to the Great Recession, there are at least four additional facilities. These recognize that the government-mandated economic shutdown for COVID-19 affected markets much more than a simple recession, which absent the 2008 financial crisis, the 2008 Federal Reserve actions were adequate to handle. The additional facilities for this last crisis include the two corporate facilities, the municipal facility, the TALF, the FIMA, and the MSLP.

The post-pandemic part of figure 10.3 shows the massive Federal Reserve response to the economic shutdown initiated in March 2020. It is clear that while the specialized facilities discussed above were important, the Federal Reserve's major response to the COVID-19 pandemic was in the securities market. The Federal Reserve in the first three months after March 1 increased its holdings of securities by 55% from the February 26 level of $3.848 trillion to a June 3 level of $5.972 trillion. Then by November 11, 2020 securities holdings were $6.555 trillion, up 70% from the last pre-COVID-19 reporting date. Finally, by the end of May 2021, Federal Reserve securities holdings reached $7.208 trillion, 87% greater than the close of February 2020.

In marked contrast to this Federal Reserve COVID-19 securities response, the Federal Reserve's 2008 response in the first five months was a 5% increase in securities holdings. It should come as no surprise then that the money supply responses to the two crises were remarkably different. Figure 10.4 shows the growth of the M2 measure of the money stock relative to the beginning of both the Great Recession and COVID-19 crises for the first 52 weeks of each crisis. The base for the Great Recession is August 27, 2008, the last Wednesday reporting date before the September 2008 financial crisis. The base for the COVID-19 crisis is February 26, 2020, the last reporting date before the onset of the economic shutdown in March 2020. The contrast between the two money supply responses is easily apparent. Not surprisingly, considering the tremendous difference in the securities responses for the two

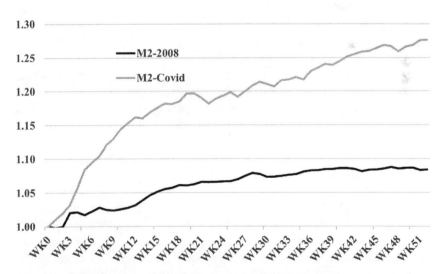

Figure 10.4 M2 Growth—Great Recession versus COVID-19. M2 - Board of Governors of the Federal Reserve System – M2 Money Stock [WM2NS], retrieved from FRED, Federal Reserve Bank of St. Louis.

crises, the money growth in the COVID-19 response is markedly greater than in the Great Recession response. The COVID-19 M2 growth has been more than 27%, while the Great Recession response was under 10%.

Once again, just as in the post-2008 budget crisis, the fear is that the tremendous expansion of the Federal Reserve assets will lead to double-digit inflation. But also, just as in the 2008 budget crisis, the Federal Reserve did much more than expand its securities holdings. All the 2008 non-securities expansion went away within 16 months as shown in figure 10.3. Once the economy opens up fully, the special facilities associated with the pandemic crisis will also disappear. But just as it did in the 2008 crisis, the Federal Reserve will profit from its ability to supply liquidity when others could not. However, even after the special facilities have all disappeared, what will remain is the tremendous increase in Federal Reserve securities holdings. The challenge will be to take actions that will prevent these assets from producing increases in the money supply that will lead to double-digit inflation. The Federal Reserve succeeded in doing just that in the 2008 crisis. The critical question is: Can it do it again?

BACK TO THE FEDERAL DEBT CRISIS

The burden of the debt is essentially the cost to taxpayers of paying the servicing cost of the debt. The debt becomes a crisis when servicing that debt puts such a burden on taxpayers that will prevent the economy from achieving its full potential. From the perspective of the Federal Reserve, the question is: how much can the Federal Reserve absorb of the COVID-19 debt increases without inflation?

The April 28, 2020 CBO projection for fiscal 2020 forecasted a federal budget deficit of $3.7 trillion, more than double the previous record of $1.4 trillion achieved in fiscal 2009. The actual federal budget deficit for fiscal 2020 was $3.132 trillion, more than double the previous record: fiscal 2009 deficit of $1.413 trillion. How much of the fiscal 2020 deficit was financed by the Federal Reserve? In fiscal 2020, the Federal Reserve added $2.847 trillion to its securities holdings, 91% of the entire fiscal 2020 deficit. In addition, the Federal Reserve added another $200 billion in earning assets in the form of loans and facilities holdings. In total, then, in fiscal 2020, the Federal Reserve has added assets covering just over 97% of the fiscal 2020 deficit.

On the surface it would seem that the Federal Reserve has essentially financed the entire fiscal 2020 deficit. If so, then the dire forecasts of the CBO that publicly held debt would exceed 100% of GDP in fiscal 2020, if corrected for the fact that Federal Reserve revenue is owned by the Treasury, will not happen. But, while the Federal Reserve assets have ballooned, its liabilities have ballooned as well. As a result, Federal Reserve net assets for fiscal 2020 have increased by only $1.95 trillion, 62% of the fiscal 2020 deficit. Even when corrected by the increase in Federal Reserve liabilities, publicly held debt will have increased by the difference in the fiscal 2020 deficit of $3.132 trillion and the Federal Reserve financed $1.95 trillion, or $1.12 trillion.

The fiscal 2020 GDP was $21.0 trillion, so the unadjusted GDP share of the official publicly held debt of $21.9 trillion is 101%. But, adjusting for Federal Reserve net asset holdings, at the close of fiscal 2020, the adjusted publicly held debt is $17.3 trillion, 82.5% of fiscal 2020 GDP.

CONCLUSION

All Federal Reserve revenues after costs and payments to bank owners must be transferred to the Treasury. As a result, in the usual meaning of the word "own," the Treasury owns the Federal Reserve. It is the residual income recipient of Federal Reserve revenues. Importantly, the Treasury ownership status does not give Treasury the right to vote on Federal Reserve policy in the way that corporate owners have that right.

Whether or not the Treasury and Federal Reserve are connected in a political way, the Treasury is the residual income recipient of Federal Reserve revenues. Therefore, both Federal Reserve assets and income affect the taxpayer burden of federal debt. The federal debt can and should be adjusted for the Federal Reserve's connection to the Treasury when evaluating the burden of that debt on the taxpayers. Such an adjustment can be done using a balance sheet or an income statement approach.

Using the income statement approach, the level of the federal debt servicing cost must account for the Federal Reserve transfers to the Treasury. In 2014, transfers to the Treasury from the Federal Reserve were $99 billion and accounted for 43% of the net debt service cost. While these transfers have been falling, their fiscal 2020 total was $88.5 billion and covered 25.6% of debt service cost. If the official publicly held debt at the close of 2020 of $21.019 trillion is reduced by the share of the servicing cost that is provided by the Federal Reserve, the adjusted publically held debt for 2020 is $15.6 trillion, 74.4% of 2020 GDP.

An alternate approach is to offset the total federal debt by the assets held at the Federal Reserve. This approach has merit since it is a balance sheet approach given that the flows from Federal Reserve net assets accrue to the Treasury. Essentially, the net assets of the Federal Reserve now stand at $3.7 trillion: the difference between primary asset holdings of $6.63 trillion and $2.95 trillion liabilities composed primarily of bank reserves on which the Federal Reserve must pay interest. After the fiscal 2020 deficit of

$3.132 trillion, the 2020 official publicly held federal debt is $21.019 trillion. Adjusting the close of fiscal 2020 publicly held debt of $21.019 trillion for the close of fiscal 2020 Federal Reserve net assets of $3.76 trillion yields an adjusted fiscal 2020 publicly held federal debt of $17.219 trillion, 82.5% of 2020 GDP. In contrast, the 2019 publicly held federal debt adjusted for Federal Reserve holdings was 60.4% of GDP.

NOTES

1. For a complete analysis of this issue see Thomas R. Saving, "Rethinking Federal Debt: What do We Really Owe?" Private Enterprise Research Center, Texas A&M University, PERC Study No. 1607, August 2016.

2. A 1.00% rate of interest is considered 100 basis points so a basis point is a (1/100)% rate of interest.

3. An alternate way of looking at this issue is to consider the burden of the public debt. That burden is the taxpayer responsibility to pay the interest cost of the debt. Using that criterion for fiscal year 2015, transfers from the Federal Reserve to the Treasury covered 44% of the net federal debt servicing cost. Adjusted for who has to pay the publicly held debt would be 44% of the official 2015 debt of $13.11 trillion, or $7.36 trillion.

4. For a complete analysis of the mystery of the missing inflation see Thomas R. Saving, "The Federal Reserve, the Great Recession and the Lost Inflation," Private Enterprise Research Center, Texas A&M University, PERC Study No. 1604, July 2016.

5. This issue was resolved as long ago as the 1960s. See Thomas R. Saving and Boris P. Pesek, *Money, Wealth and Economic Theory*, 1966, Macmillan.

6. The non-securities assets include repurchase agreements and loans to member banks, and other facilities designed to protect parts of the nation's financial sector. The latter were for all practical purposes zero by 2015 and did not return until the onset of the 2020 COVID-19 crisis.

7. For a complete analysis of the failure of the Federal Reserve's asset reduction plans see Thomas R. Saving, "The Failed Federal Reserve Attempt to Get Back to the Past," Private Enterprise Research Center, Texas A&M University, PERC Policy Study No. 2002, May 2020.

Chapter 11

The High Costs of Fiscal and Monetary Anomie

Argentina since 1945

Emilio Ocampo

INTRODUCTION

Since the late 1980s, the adoption of fiscal and monetary rules became a global trend. This was a major factor behind the global disinflation trend of the last three decades. The primary objective of the former is to avoid deficits and procyclical policy biases by constraining the government's use of discretion (IMF, 2017). In the case of advanced economics, fiscal rules were imposed to comply with supra-national treaties (e.g., Maastricht) and in emerging market economies to commit to fiscal discipline after severe crises (e.g., Argentina) or to ensure sustained stability and growth (e.g., Chile). Monetary rules instead have price stability as their objective and have been associated with currency board regimes, a pre-specified growth rate for monetary aggregates (Friedman, 1960), or inflation targeting regimes (Taylor, 1993). Empirical studies confirm that a rules-based policy framework contributes to price stability, improved fiscal performance, and sustained economic growth (IMF, 2009).

The Global Financial Crisis (GFC) of 2008 seriously tested many governments' commitment to rules and revived the rules versus discretion debate among academics and policymakers (Taylor, 2011). Supporters of discretion argue that "it allows central banks to take advantage of information about the macro-economy that is hard to write into rules" (Kocherlakota, 2016) and that "in an ever-changing world" it is "an unavoidable aspect of policymaking" (Greenspan, 1997). The main arguments in favor of rules are the preservation of individual freedom (Simons, 1948; Friedman, 1948, 1962; Taylor, 2019), incomplete information and limited knowledge of the causes of cyclical fluctuations (Friedman, 1959, 1960), temporal inconsistency of macroeconomic policies (Kydland and Prescott, 1977; Buol and Vaughan, 2003), and policymakers' systematic cognitive biases (Calabria, 2015).

Argentina's history perhaps offers the clearest empirical confirmation of three important propositions: (a) monetary discipline is key to long-run price stability, (b) price stability is the key to sustained economic growth, and (c) monetary discipline is not sustainable without fiscal discipline. Della Paolera et al. (2003) concluded that the best macroeconomic performance in the twentieth century occurred between 1899–1904 and 1991–1999 and was strongly associated with a hard-currency regime and an inter-temporally consistent fiscal stance. Based on a statistical analysis of the period 1915–2006, Ávila (2011) concluded that persistent fiscal deficits were a significant restriction on economic growth. Argentina's history also provides strong empirical support for another hypothesis: although initially engendered by populism, monetary and fiscal anomie is reinforced by the interaction of recurrent crises, entrenched interests, pernicious cultural beliefs, and flawed political institutions.

From 1900 until 1939, when the country mostly followed the rules of the gold standard, its inflation rate and fiscal balances were in line with those of Australia, Canada, the United States, and the United Kingdom, while its GDP per capita growth rates were similar. Something happened after World War II, and its effects proved persistent: since 1945, inflation averaged 143% a year—with three bouts of extreme and hyperinflation—with persistent and high fiscal imbalances and low growth. During this period, Argentina restructured or defaulted on its sovereign debt several times. The country's position in global GDP per capita rankings fell from 10 in 1945 to 72 in 2019.

Argentina probably offers the clearest empirical evidence in support of three important propositions: (a) monetary rules are key to price stability in the long run, (b) price stability is a necessary condition for sustained economic growth, and (c) monetary rules are not sustainable without fiscal discipline.

The country exhibits what may be described as fiscal and monetary anomie.[1] The term *anomie* dates back to Ancient Greece but was popularized in the late nineteenth century by French sociologist Emile Durkheim (Defiem, 2015, 719). Etymologically, it is derived from the Greek *anomos*, which means lawlessness. More generally, it describes a situation where laws or norms of interaction are not followed or respected. Argentine jurist Carlo Nino (1992) introduced the concept of "institutional" anomie to describe a situation in which the Executive power at all levels of government does not generally abide by constitutional rules. He proposed Argentina as a typical example of this condition. One can view fiscal and monetary anomie as a manifestation of institutional anomie. This is the meaning used in this chapter. This is the main legacy of populism. Recurring crises, an institution-ally weak political system with perverse incentives, and certain predominant cultural beliefs have contributed to reinforce this condition.

The remainder of the chapter is organized as follows. The second section traces the historical roots of Argentina's fiscal and monetary anomie and examines the disfunctionality of the budgetary process and the functional subordination of the Central Bank to the Executive power. The third section explains the key role Peronism played in the development of this condition. The fourth section compares the experience of Argentina with that of Chile and Uruguay to investigate whether a common regional pattern exists. The last section presents some tentative conclusions.

THE RELEVANCE OF THE ARGENTINE CASE

As mentioned above, from 1900 until 1939, a period during which Argentina mostly abided by the rules of the gold standard, its inflation rate and fiscal balances were in line with those of Australia, Canada, the United States, and the United Kingdom, while its GDP per capita grew at comparable rates (see table 11.1).

In a comparative study of Argentina and Australia, Harvard's Arthur Smithies concluded that in the postwar era "another period of parallel advance seemed likely" but a "*diabolus ex machina* appeared in Argentina" (Smithies, 1965, 23). He was referring to Juan Perón, who ruled Argentina from mid-1943 until September 1955 and between 1973 and 1974 and whose political party governed during most of the period since 1983, when democracy was reestablished. There is probably no other country

Table 11.1   Argentina before and after 1945

Country	Primary Fiscal Balance	Net Fiscal Balance	Average InflationRate	GDP per capita Growth Rate
		1900–1939		
Argentina	0.4%	−1.6%	1.6%	0.9%
Australia	0.4%	−1.0%	2.0%	1.0%
Canada	0.0%	−1.8%	1.7%	0.9%
UK	3.0%	−1.9%	1.4%	0.7%
US	−0.8%	−1.4%	1.6%	1.1%
		1945–2019		
Argentina	−2.4%	−4.5%	143.0%	1.1%
Australia	0.0%	0.0%	5.5%	1.9%
Canada	0.7%	−2.0%	3.9%	1.9%
UK	−0.3%	−3.0%	5.0%	1.9%
US	−0.7%	−2.7%	3.7%	1.9%

Source: Adapted from IMF Public Finance Database, IMF World Economic Outlook, and Ferreres (2010).

comparable to Argentina at the start of World War II, in which contemporary political developments had such a lasting impact on current affairs. In fact, none of Perón's contemporaries had such a lasting influence on their own countries as he did on Argentina. Peronism dominates its politics, culture, and economy.

Although economics is a very useful tool to understand the shortcomings of the "Argentine disease" and to quantify its dismal results, it is less useful to understand its origins. As Paul Samuelson once explained, Argentina's sickness "is political and sociological rather than economic . . . It has to do with the breakdown of social consensus. It has to do with the workings out of the logic of populist democracy" (1980, 69). Given this conclusion and the observable fact that Argentina's macroeconomic performance is an outlier (even among countries with comparable levels of development), one may wonder what is the usefulness of trying to understand the nature of its monetary and fiscal anomie. After all, it would seem the risk of contagion to other countries appears negligible.[2]

However, this presumption may not be entirely accurate. In recent decades, right- and left-wing populism emerged in Europe and the United States. Also, since the GFC, proponents of Modern Monetary Theory (MMT) have gained ascendance in the U.S. Democratic Party and challenged the established fiscal and monetary policy paradigm (Mankiw, 2020). As Edwards (2019) has pointed out, in recent decades several Latin American countries have implemented policies that are predicated on the same assumptions as MMT with dismal results. Argentina is probably the best example of what happens to a country that consistently follows such policies (Ocampo, 2020).[3]

ARGENTINA'S FISCAL AND MONETARY ANOMIE IN HISTORICAL CONTEXT

The origins of Argentina fiscal and monetary anomie can be traced back to the wars of independence (1810–1820) that required large military expenditures. A war with Brazil over the possession of what is now Uruguay (1825–1828) put public finances under stress and led to deficits and inflation. In 1827, Argentina played a leading role in the first global emerging markets crisis by defaulting on its first ever issued foreign bond.

From its institutional organization in the early 1860s until 1889, the Argentine economy experienced rapid growth that was punctuated by severe financial crisis in 1876, 1885, and 1890 (see Amado et al., 2005). During this period, lack of fiscal and monetary discipline was the norm and adherence to the gold standard was sporadic. Following the 1890 crisis, which was one of the deepest in the country's history and the one that provoked the collapse of Baring Brothers, Argentina embarked on a series of structural reforms. By 1899 the country had returned to the gold standard and quickly became one of its most disciplined members. For the following 15 years, the economy grew rapidly, inflation remained in check, and the country risk premium declined (Della Paolera and Taylor, 2001, 122–124). Argentina abandoned the gold standard on August 1914, and until 1927, when it rejoined it at the prewar parity, followed a "dirty" convertibility. The gold parity was abandoned again at the end of 1929 to avoid the deflationary impact of Wall Street's crack.

During the early 1930s, a mix of expansive monetary policies and fiscal austerity allowed the economy to weather the Great Depression relatively well, but the economy never regained its former dynamism. Without external discipline and with a flawed financial architecture, fiscal and monetary anomie gradually started to rear its head. Following the creation of the Central Bank in 1935 and the advent of World War II, monetary discipline gradually started to wane. However, thanks to favorable trade balances during World War II, by 1945, Argentina had the fifth largest gold reserves in the world at US$1.2 billion (UN, 1951, 462). At that time, more than 160% of Argentina's monetary base was fully backed by reserves and the Treasury could borrow long term in pesos at an interest rate of 4–5% a year.

With respect to fiscal discipline, Della Paolera et al. (2003) concluded that it was "a transitory phenomenon from the 1850s to the 1930s, when budget deficits came to rule Argentine public finances." From 1935 onward, governments relied on monetary expansion to finance recurrent and high fiscal deficits "which led to inflation and allowed the government to repudiate some of its liabilities" (72–73). Another study (Araoz et al., 2007) found that during the 1865–2002 period, fiscal sustainability was either weak or non-existent.[4] However, it was relatively stronger during 1865–1914 and 1990–2002 when the economy was open to trade and capital flows. In contrast, there was no sustainability in 1951–1989, a period during which the economy was relatively closed. This study also concluded that the common explanatory factor behind all major financial crises in Argentine history was a lack of fiscal sustainability. Most of them happened after 1946 (Reinhart, 2010).

Despite a tendency toward fiscal profligacy from 1871 until 1944, the budgetary process was timely and transparent. Every single year, the Executive sent an annual budget to Congress before the start of the calendar year and Congress approved it within the timeframe specified by law (Ministerio de Hacienda, 1945, 217–219). From 1945 onward, the quality of budgetary institutions deteriorated markedly. Since then, the timely presentation and approval of the annual budget has been the exception rather than the norm, even under democratic rule. The evidence suggests that the quality of a country's budgetary institutions, which include procedural rules, have a significant positive influence on fiscal discipline and stability (Alesina et al., 1996; Alesina and Perotti, 1996; Von Hagen, 2002).

During the Perón regime (1946–1955), the government also used an off-budget scheme involving the Central Bank and IAPI to finance large military expenditures and massive increases in public employment, an ambitious public works program, and the nationalization of foreign-owned companies.[5] As Reutz (1991) noted, during 1946–1955 off-budget expenditures, of which the most significant were the losses incurred by IAPI, amounted to almost half of budgeted expenditures (120). The Central Bank extended special credit lines to state-owned banks with which they financed those deficits. Between 1946 and 1949 IAPI's borrowings increased eight times in nominal terms and in the latter year represented 16% of GDP. With this financing scheme, the government didn't have to report almost half of its expenditures and the Central Bank avoided statutory limits on financing them. Given that IAPI didn't publish balance sheets until 1949, financing gimmicks allowed the regime to "hide under the rug" almost a third of total government expenditures. IAPI closed the loop by financing the government directly with loans.

After 1945, the Treasury started using "creative" accounting methods to disguise growing fiscal imbalances. The annual report for that year indicated that the government had a deficit equivalent to 0.9% of GDP. In reality, it was ten times higher. The trick was simply to count the increase in public debt as a source of revenue. The following year, the clarity and quality of the information provided by the Treasury about Argentina's public finances deteriorated further.[6] In 1946, total government expenditures increased by almost 70% in real terms due to increases in off budget items while revenues declined slightly (Reutz, 1991, 122). However, official statistics showed a slight surplus for the year equivalent to 0.1% of GDP. This accounting legerdemain didn't seem particularly troubling given that starting in 1946, a significant portion of the budget deficit was "borrowed" at artificially low interest rates from the state-run pension fund. In 1949, Perón boasted that "we have our budget fully balanced; we have closed our budgets with a surplus" (Perón, 1949, II, 191). In fact, the previous year, the Treasury had reported a slight surplus in fiscal accounts (Ministerio de Hacienda, 1949). However, the government's actual cash deficit had reached almost 16% of GDP and would reach 13% in 1949 (Reutz, 1991, 136). Transparency also suffered as the Treasury delayed 18 months the publication of its annual reports.

On the monetary side, there was also a clear break after 1946 when Perón nationalized the Central Bank and the entire deposit base of the banking system. The expansion of credit to finance budget and off-budget deficits increased 28 times in only three years. Between December 1945 and September 1955, monetary and credit aggregates grew at unprecedented rates. In August 1948, when the Argentine economy started to show signs of an impending external crisis, the Central Bank stopped publishing its monthly bulletin, which included detailed monetary and financial information. By the end of the Peronist regime, the debasement of the Argentine currency was almost complete: reserve backing of the monetary base had dropped from 160% in 1945 to 4% in 1955.

According to official statistics, total public debt decreased from 63% of GDP in 1945 to 45% in 1955. However, if off-budget debt is taken into consideration, the ratio actually increased to 74% of GDP. More importantly, given that public debt was forcibly placed on state-managed pension funds at yields significantly below the inflation rate, the "real" public debt burden was almost double (the difference was obviously borne by savers, mostly the pension fund system). A perverse consequence of this method of financing was the destruction of the domestic capital market. As a result, Argentina became an "original sinner" as defined by Eichengreen, Hausmann, and Panizza (2005): the public sector was never able again to borrow long term in pesos. Successive governments were forced to resort to increasingly devious mechanisms to finance recurrent fiscal deficits. Without a local capital market and limited access to international capital markets, the only option left was monetization.

Besides reshaping Argentine politics, Peronism also had a profound economic impact. During 1945–2019, Argentina experienced the period of highest macroeconomic instability in its history, which included, among other things, three hyperinflationary bouts (1975–1976, 1989, and 1990), six banking crises (1980, 1982, 1995, 2001, 2008, 2019), five balance of payments crises (1958, 1962, 1981–1982, 1989, 2018–2019), four external public debt defaults (1982, 1989, 2001, 2020), and three local public debt defaults (1989, 2007–2009, and 2019). A recent study of Argentina's monetary and fiscal history since 1960 concluded that this endless string of crises showed "symptoms of the same disease: the government's inability to restrict spending to genuine tax revenues" (Buera and Nicolini, 2019, 23).

Argentina's recurrent and high fiscal deficits in the last seven decades reflect the persistent inability (or unwillingness) of Argentine society to live within the constraints imposed by economic reality (see table 11.2). Peronism has been the main (but not exclusive) "enabler" of this fantasy, promising greater equality and prosperity without ever tackling the structural barriers that prevent both. Predictably, Perón never fulfilled his promise. Instead, his policies led to secular stagnation and high inflation with greater inequality and growing poverty. Peronism also turned fiscal and monetary anomie into a chronic disease with no easy cure in sight.

Over the course of the last 200 years, the fundamental cause of Argentina's fiscal imbalances changed. In the first years after independence, it was military expenditures due to continued wars; from 1860 until 1939, bailouts of

Table 11.2 A History of Fiscal Profligacy (1956–2019)

Period	Primary Fiscal Balance (% GDP)	Interest on Public Debt (% GDP)	Net Fiscal Balance (% GDP)	Gross Public Debt (% GDP)	Inflation Rate	Real GDP pc Growth Rate
1956–72	−3.5%	0.1%	−3.5%	15.1%	30.5%	2.1%
1973–75*	−9.4%	−1.0%	−8.4%	19.6%	89.0%	−0.9%
1976–81	−5.2%	1.4%	−6.6%	20.3%	193.3%	−0.4%
1982–91*	−3.6%	4.0%	−7.6%	62.0%	793.7%	−1.0%
1992–01	0.1%	2.0%	−1.8%	34.7%	5.0%	0.5%
2002–05	3.4%	1.9%	1.5%	119.9%	13.3%	7.6%
2006–15*	−0.1%	2.2%	−2.2%	50.6%	23.2%	1.7%
2016–19	−2.8%	2.5%	−5.3%	72.4%	41.0%	−2.5%

Source: Compiled by author using BCRA, IMF World Economic Outlook (2019), Ferreres (2010), and Mauro et al (2013).
Note: * indicates a period during which populist economic policies were in place.

an over-extended financial sector; during the Perón years, the growth of the populist welfare state; in the 1960s and early 1970s, the losses of inefficient state-owned companies; in the late 1970s, again military expenditures and war; in the 1980s, the cost of excessive foreign and local debt (partly generated by bailouts of the private sector); in the 1990s, the profligacy of provincial governments and state-owned banks; and in the first decade of twenty-first century, again the growth of the populist welfare state.

Remarkably given this history, after two consecutive hyperinflationary bouts, in April 1991 the Argentine government, a Peronist one to boot, resorted to a rules-based policy framework to regain price and economic stability. Congress enacted as laws fiscal and monetary rules that reflected global "best practices." The best known was the Convertibility Law approved in March 1991, which created a convertible peso and legalized the use of the dollar and any other convertible currency in any kind of transaction or contract.[7] In the following decade, Congress also approved a Public Financial Management Law (1992) and a Fiscal Convertibility Law (1999) to a) provide transparency and accountability and b) limit the growth of primary expenditures and recurrent fiscal deficits (see Appendix B for a list of major legislation connected with fiscal and monetary rules approved during this period).

Compliance with these rules, which was sporadic even during 1991–1999, almost vanished in the twenty-first century. During 2006–2017, *The Open Budget Index* (OBI), an independent global assessment of budget transparency, consistently placed Argentina near the middle of its global ranking, with scores ranging between 40 and 60 points on a 100-point scale (Diaz Frers, 2017). In 2017, the last year for which there is data, the country occupied the

46th position in global rankings, between Ghana and Namibia. More importantly, an examination of the Congressional record shows a national proclivity to amend and repeal fiscal and monetary rules that restrained the power of the Executive branch with "Emergency Laws" also approved by Congress, always with the excuse that an imminent or ongoing financial crisis requires giving the former ample discretionary powers. Argentine politicians don't seem (or want) to understand that the point of having rules is precisely to prevent such scenarios.

Two recent instances exemplify the extent and nature of Argentina's fiscal and monetary anomie. At the end of 2017, Congress approved a Fiscal Responsibility law that capped the rate of growth of primary expenditures and public employment. At the same time, the National Government reached an agreement with provincial governments to limit spending and reduce taxes. The stated objective of both measures was to gradually reduce the weight of public spending on GDP and create "the fiscal space to also lower the tax burden and improve the tax system" (Galiani, 2018). Months later, in October 2018, as part of an agreement with the IMF, the Central Bank replaced the existing inflation targeting regime with a simple rule that limited monetary base growth to zero and allowed the exchange rate to float within a pre-specified band. The goal was to reduce inflation and let inflationary expectations push down the interest rate gradually.

Simultaneously, to ensure public debt sustainability, the government committed itself to achieving a primary fiscal balance in 2019 and modest surpluses starting in 2020 (IMF, 2018). Twelve months later, both rules were abandoned after a victory of the Peronist candidate in the presidential election triggered a severe currency crisis. By December 2019, the remnants of Central Bank independence had completely disappeared and Congress approved an "Emergency Law" that gave "super powers" to the incoming president, Alberto Fernández. And so ended another experiment with fiscal and monetary rules. In Argentina, "Emergency Laws" are a euphemism for undermining the constitutional separation of powers. They allow the Executive to arbitrarily intervene in markets and impose taxes or exactions and confiscate resources (usually from savers or exporters) without the prior approval of (or debate by) Congress. Their ultimate objective is to find creative ways of financing an ever growing fiscal deficit.

THE ARGENTINE DISEASE:
A BRIEF HISTORICAL BACKGROUND

In their classic analysis of populism, Dornbusch and Edwards (1991) argued that the Latin American economic policy paradigm could be summarized as ignoring the existence "of any type of constraints" and relying on macroeconomic policy "to redistribute income, typically by large real-wage increases that are not to be passed on into higher price" (9–10). They also identified four phases in the typical Latin American populist experiences: 1) a short-lived economic boom driven by consumer demand fed by higher wages, 2) a slowdown provoked by internal and external bottlenecks, 3) accelerating inflation due to monetary and fiscal expansion, capital flight, and foreign exchange shortages, and 4) an "orthodox stabilization" under a new government. As Dornbusch and Edwards pointed out, after the whole cycle was finished, real wages were usually lower, that is, those who were supposed to benefit ended up being the most hurt. Dornbusch and Edwards also noted that populist governments repeatedly implement self-destructive policies "in spite of abundant historical evidence on their harmful consequences" and wondered, "whether countries have an economic and political memory that allows them to learn from their own mistakes" (8). This is clearly not the case in Argentina. When it comes to designing stabilization plans, policymakers seem to pay no attention to recent history (see Ocampo, 2017). One possible explanation for Argentina's persistent inability to learn is the predominance of a flawed ideology that proposes spurious causality.

Another distinctive feature of populism in Argentina is that it has been fueled by the price cycles of agricultural commodity (Ocampo, 2015). There is a simple economic and political explanation behind this relationship. First, rising food prices have a negative impact on real urban wages while they generate extraordinary profits in the land-intensive agricultural sector. Second, the policy of redistributing those profits to urban consumers and manufacturers has an obvious electoral appeal. In the Peronist narrative, farmers are an "oligarchy" that, allied with foreigners, "exploits" the Argentine "people." This conspiratorial and paranoid narrative feeds and supports populist policies. Its effectiveness is beyond dispute, since the Kirchners and Fernández revived it in 2008 and 2021. This "cultural factor" is not present in Brazil, Chile, Paraguay, or Uruguay even though they are also large producers and exporters of agricultural commodities and have similar land ownership concentration ratios.

Argentina under Peronism

Sociologists and political scientists outside Argentina have a hard time defining Peronism. The usual categories don't seem appropriate. It is not fascism but draws many elements from it; it is not socialism but it appeals to class struggle and leads to similar results. Extremists from the right and the left claim to be the true heirs of Perón and still cohabit, not without conflict, in the movement he created. According to *New York Times* columnist Roger Cohen

(2014), *Peronism* is "a strange mishmash of nationalism, romanticism, fascism, socialism, backwardness, progressiveness, militarism, eroticism, fantasy, musical mournfulness, irresponsibility and repression" that has proved "impossible to shake."

To understand Peronism it is critical to understand what drove Perón, an army colonel, to enter politics. His overriding objective was to neutralize what he believed was an imminent existential threat to Argentina: a communist revolution. Perón's ideas were greatly influenced by a sojourn in Italy as a military attaché in 1939–1941. He believed communism was engendered by the unfairness of the capitalistic system. Therefore, to prevent the former, it was necessary to reform the latter by introducing "social justice."[8] Unlike Hitler or Mussolini, Perón never managed to seduce the business establishment and therefore he increasingly relied for political support on the leaders of the labor movement, the Catholic Church, and the Army. It was a modified version of Mussolini's corporatism system. Ironically, although his original intention was to prevent a revolution, he incited one with his policies and rhetoric that turned out to be more detrimental to long-term prosperity.

At the beginning of the twentieth century, Poland's GDP per capita was half of Argentina's, and by 2018 it doubled it. Even after 50 years of communist rule, Poland's political and economic institutions are also more advanced than those of Argentina.[9]

Waisman (1987) has argued that Peronism institutionalized two policies that transformed the structure of Argentine economy and society: a corporatist strategy toward labor, supported by the church and the military, and radical protectionism (136–137). One could not survive without the other. Their main consequence was to divorce wage levels from productivity and domestic from international prices. It essentially "politicized" the allocation of economic resources. The industrial sector was willing to go along with this system in exchange for protection and subsidies.

The "populist bash" required across the board wage increases and subsidies, financed at the expense of farmers and savers, and loose credit and monetary policies (Diaz Alejandro, 1970). As Smithies (1965) pointed out, any sophomore could have told Perón that this system was not viable. In fact, after a short-lived boom, starting in mid-1948 the economy experienced a severe external crisis. Three years of stagnation and indecision followed. Finally, in 1952, after having secured his reelection, Perón launched an austerity plan. He toned down his anti-Yankee rhetoric and emphasized in his speeches that wage increases had to be linked to productivity. In a counterfactual scenario, Perón could have cured Argentina of the virus that he had inoculated it with. However, a confrontation with the Catholic Church, one of his erstwhile allies, led to his overthrow in September 1955. Another key element of the Peronist system was merging the labor unions with the Peronist party. Therefore, corporatization of labor meant Peronism remained relevant even after Perón's ouster.

Even though Perón was exiled for 18 years, the military and civilian governments that succeeded him were unable or unwilling to reform the essence of the Peronist economic system. Part of the problem was that the inefficient and highly protected industrial sector that grew under the Peronist regime had become the economy's largest employer and the business sector grew accustomed to guaranteed profits. Union leaders and crony capitalists forged a lasting alliance. The only novelty added during the 1960s was foreign investment, which helped the economy to recover some of the ground lost during 1946–1955. However, political uncertainty remained high as Perón continued to pull strings from his exile in Madrid.

When Perón returned to Argentina in mid-1973, the world was experiencing another boom in commodity prices. Thanks to high taxes on agricultural exports, the coffers of the Argentine treasury again swelled. It seemed as if the old dictator had learned nothing and forgotten nothing. The country experienced another "populist bash," but it was more short-lived than the first. After Peron's death in July 1974, the country sank into political instability and violence while inflation spiraled out of control and the economy stagnated. A military coup in 1976 brought chaos to an end but at a very high cost. The new regime brutally repressed a left-wing insurgency and tried to stabilize the economy. However, the military feared labor unrest and their innate nationalism prevented cuts in public spending and the privatization of highly inefficient state-owned enterprises. A tight monetary policy was combined with an expansive fiscal policy and lower trade barriers. The result was predictable: currency overvaluation with growing fiscal and current account deficits, followed by a sudden stop when it became obvious that the situation was unsustainable. Although the military regime managed to survive the crisis that ensued, it could not survive a defeat in the Malvinas War.

In the 1983 presidential election, a center-left coalition led by Raul Alfonsín defeated the Peronist party. However, the new administration adopted the same policies that had led to the stagnation of the Argentine economy: protectionism, fiscal profligacy, and political wages. However, unions remained loyal to Peronism. Another fiscal crisis and hyperinflation followed. In the 1989 election, a Peronist candidate, Carlos Menem, won by a landslide. To everybody's surprise he abandoned the classic Peronist economic recipe. In January 1991, he appointed Domingo Cavallo as economy minister. A few months later, Cavallo launched the Convertibility Law, which established a fixed parity between the peso and the dollar and prohibited the Central Bank from financing the treasury. The plan also contemplated the deregulation of the economy, lower tariffs, and the privatization of all state-owned companies. For a decade, it seemed as if Argentina had been finally cured of its disease: from 1992 until 2000, it had one of the lowest inflation rates in the world and the economy boomed. But cumulative fiscal imbalances at the provincial level, a heavy debt load, and the effect of several international crises undermined confidence in the Convertibility program. In December 2001, the IMF withdrew its financial support even though Argentina had complied with the fiscal targets that had been set in the Stand-by Agreement signed months earlier. A political and economic crisis ensued. President De la Rúa and Cavallo resigned, and a new government controlled by the Peronist party repealed the Convertibility Law, devalued the peso, and defaulted on the public debt.

By early 2002, thanks to China's extraordinary growth, a new commodity super-cycle started. The rise in the price of soybeans and its by-products, which accounted for more than a third of total exports, enlarged tax revenues and supported a strong economic recovery. Nestor Kirchner became president in 2003. Although he resorted to traditional Peronist rhetoric, initially he maintained fiscal and current account surpluses. However, at some point he and his wife, Cristina Fernandez, who succeeded him in 2007, convinced themselves, just like Perón did in 1946 and 1973, that agricultural commodity prices would remain high forever. After several years of net fiscal surpluses, an anomaly in Argentina's history, the Kirchners increased primary expenditures at the national level from 13% to 24% of GDP. Coincidentally, Vito Tanzi, one of the world's foremost fiscal experts, argued at that time that Argentina needed a structural reduction in spending of at least 10% of GDP (2007, 47).

Most of the increase in spending was in social programs and subsidies to utility companies forced to keep rates below operating costs. The classic Peronist recipe of redistributive fiscal profligacy and monetary expansion lasted until mid-2012, when commodity prices started to decline. Overburdened by a high level of public expenditures and growing fiscal deficits, the Argentine economy veered rapidly toward a new crisis that was staved off by the widespread expectation of an imminent regime change.

In 2016, Mauricio Macri, a former businessman, won the presidency with the promise of change. Optimism was high in Argentina and abroad that he would be able to steer the country in a different direction. However, his "gradualist" economic policy not only shunned structural reforms but also led to increased spending financed with foreign debt. As a result, during the first two years of Macri's presidency, the primary deficit increased while the Central Bank attempted to impose an "inflation targeting" regime. The inconsistency between monetary and fiscal policy came to the fore at the end of 2017 and ended whatever independence the monetary authority still had. A severe drought significantly reduced agricultural export revenues and fueled uncertainty about the government's ability to continue to finance its deficits with foreign borrowings. A "sudden stop" in April 2018 put an end to Macri's gradualist experiment. A few months later, the IMF came to Argentina's rescue with the largest financing package in its history. In exchange for this support, it imposed a fiscal austerity program that pushed the economy into a recession. The crisis that followed was compounded by the results of the 2019 election, which brought Peronism back to power with Cristina Kirchner as Vice President (and the decision maker on key policy issues).

The fourth Peronist revolution started on December 10, 2019. It is unclear how President Alberto Fernandez will fulfill his campaign promises given that the Argentine economy is literally on its knees. As usual, the likely candidates for confiscation are farmers and local and foreign savers. In early 2020, for the third time in three decades, the Argentine government defaulted on its external debt and started negotiations with bondholders. It also imposed higher taxes on agricultural exports and publicly criticized farmers for not being "good patriots." The COVID-19 crisis compounded the severity of the crisis. A strict lockdown led to the biggest GDP drop in Argentine history. The Central Bank doubled down with a massive monetary expansion.

POPULISM, ANOMIE, CULTURE, AND INSTITUTIONS

Rules or institutions are ink on paper. As Simons (1948) explained, to the extent they limit the action of government and prevent special interests groups from imposing policies that benefit them at the expense of the majority, they help preserve individual freedoms. Institutions that preserve freedom are critical to sustained economic growth. The critical question is: why certain societies adopt institutions that are inimical to growth? The history of Argentina raises another important question that is even more difficult to answer: Why does a society that experienced extraordinary economic growth thanks to the adoption of certain institutions at some point willingly choose to abandon them? Theories that claim institutions are all that matters cannot explain the secular economic decadence of one of the most institutionally advanced countries in the world in the early twentieth century. Theories that claim that education precedes institutional development, cannot explain the institutional degradation of one the most educationally advanced countries in Latin America. Theories that assert that culture is the determinant factor cannot explain what changed in Argentina's culture after World War II that pushed the country into a secular decline.

The literature on the causes of Argentina's decline is vast, and a summary is beyond the scope of this chapter. However, understanding why this experience is relevant requires at least an outline of an explanation. The compliance and effectiveness of institutions requires not only enforcement but also supportive cultural values and beliefs. One of the main conclusions Tocqueville (1838) drew from his study of the United States was that customs were more important than written laws. Mill (1862) also stressed that "a philosophy of laws and institutions not founded on a philosophy of national character is an absurdity" (104).[10] More recently, Hayek (1973) argued that the institutions a society chooses to govern itself are the result of a long evolutionary cultural process. Because culture is, in Hayek's description, the product of spontaneous evolution, the rules that restrict power are shaped by a "spontaneous order." If a society's cultural norms do not require limited government, constitutional restrictions on the Executive branch will prove useless. North argued that "it is culture that provides the key to path dependence" (1994, 364). In his view, culture provides a cognitive model that allows society to evaluate the costs and benefits of different forms of social organization over time (North, 1996). There is a close relationship between a society's predominant ideology and its institutions. In certain cases, to the extent it is predominant, the former can condition, or even hinder, a society's learning process and institutional development.

Even if we accept that culture and institutions mutually reinforce each other, the key question is how and when Argentina went from being an institutionally developed and prosperous society to a decadent one. To the extent Peronism reflects an imperfection (or failure) of the collective "cultural" learning process, explaining its origin requires understanding a) how certain values and beliefs that hamper collective learning became predominant, and b) in which way these values and beliefs "filter" the impact of social, demographic, and/or economic exogenous shocks that eventually generate a frustration gap. Ocampo (2018) identified four deeply rooted cultural traits that significantly contributed to the rise of Peronism: *caudillismo* (fealty and attachment to strong leaders), anomie (non-compliance with formal and informal rules of social interaction), entitled indolence (a belief that having a high standard of living without having to work for it is an unalienable right), and malignant collective narcissism (an unwarranted feeling of national superiority coupled with xenophobia). The first two traits are common to Latin America. The third is also widespread but without the entitlement dimension. The last is unique to Argentina. It was not only the consequence of particular historical circumstances, but also the indoctrinating efforts of successive governments in the earlier part of the twentieth century. These four cultural traits/beliefs mutually reinforced each other, in particular, *caudillismo* and anomie: the authority of a strongman always prevailed over the rule of law.[11]

Perón was a narcissistic strongman who embodied cultural traits and beliefs that were predominant in Argentina in the 1930s and 1940s. His policies and rhetoric appealed to national pride, and the system of social and economic organization he imposed promoted anomie (by requiring absolute obedience to his authority and disregard for written laws) and entitled indolence (social justice ensured that a good standard of living would be guaranteed by the state, i.e. Perón). The special economic interests engendered by Perón's economic policies also fostered, and benefited from, these cultural traits. By establishing a web of mutually reinforcing interests and beliefs, Peronism became path dependent. The status quo became tyrannical.

There was another important mechanism at work that reinforced path dependence. Peronism's dismal economic results did not lead to its electoral defeat but the opposite. In the worldview proposed by Peronism, Argentina's failure can only be explained by a foreign conspiracy led by the United States. From this notion derives another equally pernicious belief: only another strong leader can save the country from this foreign conspiracy. Populist politicians have a strong interest in promoting the "wrong" ideology. This is one of the reasons why once in power, they give so much importance to propaganda and control of the media.

ARGENTINA, CHILE, AND URUGUAY IN COMPARATIVE PERSPECTIVE

Argentina shares with Chile and Uruguay a similar colonial, religious, ethnic, and cultural background. Between 1960 and 1990, they all exhibited the same symptoms: political instability, high inflation, and low growth. This was one of the arguments Samuelson used to exonerate Perón for Argentina's decline. However, the situation changed after 1990, when all three had a well-functioning electoral democracy. Chile and Uruguay recovered from their past populist spells and in the last three decades were able to develop institutionally and economically. At the end of 2019, both countries had the highest GDP per capita, HDI, and institutional quality indices in Latin America as well as the lowest poverty rates (although Chile exhibited higher levels of inequality). As table 11.3 shows, during the last decade, the divergence between Argentina and its neighbors deepened as Chile and Uruguay reinforced their commitment to fiscal and monetary discipline:

The most obvious explanation for this divergence is Argentina's lack of fiscal sustainability. Ironically, although the country was one of the pioneers in establishing fiscal rules in Latin America, its government was never able to consistently comply with them. Whereas the IMF (2017) recommends that developing countries that are exporters of commodities should design fiscal rules that reduce and/or eliminate the procyclicality of the fiscal stance "by delinking expenditure from volatile revenue sources," Argentina has done exactly the opposite. Among developed and emerging economies, between

Table 11.3   Growth, Inflation, and Volatility in Argentina, Chile, and Uruguay (2010–2019)

Country	Average Monthly Inflation Rate	Monthly Inflation Volatility	Average GDP Growth Rate	GDP growth Volatility	% of Years in Recession
Argentina	2.0%	1.2%	0.2%	340%	50.0%
Chile	0.3%	0.3%	2.1%	52%	0.0%
Uruguay	0.6%	0.6%	1.6%	74%	0.0%

Source: Adapted from INDEC (Argentina), Banco Central de Chile and Instituto Nacional de Estadisticas (Uruguay).
Note: Inflation volatility is measured as the standard deviation. GDP growth volatility is measured as the coefficient of variation.

1980 and 2016, it had the highest correlation between output and both total primary and discretionary expenditures (Izquierdo, Pessino and Vuletin, 2019, 23, 27).

Argentina's problem is not only fiscal unsustainability but also economic unsustainability, given the distortive effects of a large, expensive, and inefficient public sector. In the last decade, it not only had significantly larger deficits than Chile and Uruguay but also significantly higher public revenues and expenditures. A recent IADB study of Latin America and the Caribbean revealed that Argentina had the highest levels of government spending, both at the national and subnational level (Izquierdo, Pessino and Vuletin, 2019, 49, 91).

The cost of Argentina's welfare state is comparable to that of OECD countries with much higher GDP per capita. Public-sector employees represent 20% of the labor force and their remuneration, at 14% of GDP, is the highest in Latin America (Ibid., 56–57). The IADB study also estimated that losses due to waste and inefficiencies in government spending amounted to 7.2% of GDP in Argentina (the highest in the region), compared to a 4.4% average for Latin America, 3.7% for Uruguay, and 1.8% for Chile (Ibid., 63-64) (see table 11.4).

Table 11.4   Fiscal Discipline in Argentina, Chile, and Uruguay (2010–2019)

Country	Total Revenues	Primary Expenditures	Primary Fiscal Balance	Net Fiscal Balance	Gross Public Debt
Argentina	33.9%	36.8%	-2.8%	-4.4%	51.1%
Chile	23.1%	23.9%	-0.8%	-1.0%	16.3%
Uruguay	29.3%	28.8%	0.4%	-2.0%	55.7%

Source: Adapted from IMF WEO October 2019.

In contrast, since the beginning of the twenty-first century, Chile has been a "poster child" for fiscal and monetary rules. Central bank autonomy is enshrined in the Constitution and has been strictly respected. Under a floating exchange rate system, monetary policy has loosely followed an adapted Taylor rule (Claro y Opazo, 2014). As to fiscal policy, since the early 2000s, it has also been guided by a rules-based framework with the objective of achieving a structural surplus for the Central Government equal to 1% of GDP (García et al., 2005). This rule has achieved high credibility and has reduced procyclicality. It has also contributed to a reduction in public debt, easier access to international capital markets at favorable conditions, greater macroeconomic stability, and a more effective countercyclical use of both fiscal and monetary policy (Larrain et al., 2019). Chile has had for several years the highest credit rating in Latin America (A+ by Standard & Poor's), which has lowered the cost of capital for the private sector. Over the last decade, this rules-based fiscal and monetary policy framework served Chile well even in the face of seriously negative external shocks. Unfortunately, there is not insignificant risk that the political crisis that started in October 2019 may end up undermining it, particularly if an upcoming referendum favors a constitutional reform.

In the case of Uruguay, although successive governments have eschewed a rules-based framework, they have consistently maintained a primary surplus (even those of a leftist persuasion). The deterioration of the country's fiscal position in recent years is explained by a growing deficit of the public pension fund system. Uruguay's Central Bank has also remained autonomous from the Executive branch with the sole statutory mandate of price stability. Thanks to fiscal and monetary discipline, Uruguay enjoys an investment grade rating and has been able to tap international bond markets in favorable terms.

The different level of fiscal and monetary discipline of the three countries is partly explained by differences in the quality of their respective institutions. Argentina significantly lags behind Chile and Uruguay in several indicators of institutional development, as shown in table 11.5.

Compliance and enforceability of existing institutions is weaker in Argentina. That is, the country exhibits a higher degree of anomie. *Latinobarómetro*'s annual surveys during the period 1996–2011 confirm this hypothesis. On average, 84% of respondents in Argentina believed that their compatriots did not observe the law, whereas in Chile and Uruguay these percentages were 62% and 44%, respectively.

Not surprisingly, these institutional differences also seem to be positively correlated with certain beliefs regarding the advantages and disadvantages of a liberal democracy. Argentina and Chile exhibit significantly lower levels of support for this system than Uruguay. In the case of Chile, these results may

Table 11.5   Comparative Indicators of Institutional Quality

	Average Value (2006–2018)		
Indicator	Argentina	Chile	Uruguay
Economic Freedom	49.7	77.8	68.9
Liberal Democracy	61.8	82.6	82.7
High Court Independence	68.3	79.2	82.0
Legislative Constraints on the Executive	76.1	94.6	89.4
Rule of Law	38.3	75.6	62.8
Control of Corruption	42.5	77.3	75.7
Voice and Accountability	57.9	71.0	72.2
Political Stability	50.7	59.3	68.2

Source: Adapted from Heritage Foundation (1), V-Dem Institute (2-4), and World Bank (5-8).

Table 11.6   Percentage of Respondents That Have Beliefs Inimical to Free Markets

Country	Don't Believe a Market Economy Is Good for the Country (1)	Don't Believe Free Trade Is Good for the Economy (2)	Believe One Can Only Get Rich at the Expense of Others (3)	Average
Argentina	29.6% (100%)	9.1% (100%)	42.2% (100%)	27.0% (100%)
Chile	26.1% (88%)	3.8% (42%)	39.2% (93%)	23.0% (74%)
Uruguay	21.5% (73%)	2.2% (24%)	31.1% (74%)	18.3% (57%)

Source: Adapted from Latinobarometro (2000-2018) and World Values Survey (2010-2014).

help explain its recent political crisis and are grounds for some pessimism about its future (see Newland and Ocampo, 2020, and Newland, 2019). However, Argentina exhibits the highest level of skepticism about the aims of the government: a significantly larger percentage of respondents believe that government policies are designed to benefit powerful interest groups (see table 11.6).

There is also a positive correlation—strongest in the case of Uruguay—between these beliefs and the predominant economic ideology. The following table shows the results of two surveys—*Latinobarómetro* and *WVS*—that assess the level of support for the free enterprise system. Interestingly, although relatively fewer Argentines identify themselves as having a left-wing ideology than Chileans and/or Uruguayans, they exhibit a stronger anti-capitalist and anti-free trade mentality.

The bias against capitalism in Argentina, and particularly foreign capitalists, is not new. In fact, it preceded Perón, as confirmed by the observations made in 1942 by Francis Herron, an American journalist who spent a year visiting the country (Herron, 1944). Herron also noted two other cultural traits that distinguish Argentina from Chile and Uruguay: first, an extreme national pride based on a strong belief of superiority, and, second, a profound dislike of the United States. Both subsist today. In the annual

Latinobarometro surveys since 2000, on average, Argentina exhibits the strongest negative view of the United States among 18 Latin American countries.[12] National pride and anti-Americanism figured prominently in Perón's rhetoric and dictated his economic and foreign policies from 1943 until 1953. Argentina's continued decadence during the Kirchner administration intensified xenophobic feelings, which were also fueled by government propaganda.

CONCLUSION

Argentina's history offers perhaps the clearest empirical confirmation of three important propositions: (a) monetary discipline is key to long-run price stability, (b) price stability is the key to sustained economic growth, and (c) monetary discipline is not sustainable without fiscal discipline. Argentina's history also provides empirical support for another hypothesis: although initially engendered by populism, monetary and fiscal anomie are reinforced by the interaction of recurrent crises, entrenched interests, pernicious cultural beliefs, and flawed political institutions.

Although fiscal and monetary discipline delivered good macroeconomic results in certain periods, it was almost impossible to maintain, particularly after the 1930s. Anomie cannot be solely explained by political economy considerations. In this and other dimensions, it seems to be related to culture, which, in turn, explains path dependence. No matter how well designed, monetary and fiscal rules will not be complied with under a dysfunctional political system beholden to special interest groups and supported by certain predominant cultural traits and beliefs. Macroeconomic instability has also contributed to its fiscal and monetary anomie. It is unclear whether Argentina will be able to escape this negative feedback loop. If history offers any guidance, there is not much room for optimism.

The GFC and the COVID-19 pandemic have tested the fiscal and monetary discipline of most nations. Like individuals, societies rarely learn from the experience of others. Otherwise, the history of Argentina could serve as a powerful antidote to the idea that fiscal and monetary profligacy is a viable long term solution to economic recovery, or at worst, innocuous.

NOTES

1. Argentina's anomie extends well beyond fiscal and monetary matters (see Nino, 1992).
2. Only Venezuela seems to have developed and adopted its own version of Peronism, with equally dismal results.

3. MMT presupposes that a country is not an "original sinner" (see Eichengreen et al., 2003), which means that it can issue foreign bonds or long-dated domestic bonds at fixed rate in its own currency. Until 1945, Argentina did not suffer from "original sin" and was able to borrow abroad and domestically in its own currency.

4. Fiscal deficits are sustainable if the current market value of government debt equals to the discounted sum of expected future surpluses.

5. IAPI was a government agency created by Perón in 1946 that monopolized foreign trade, particularly involving exports of agricultural commodities.

6. In 1946, the Treasury pushed back the discussion of public finances to the back of its annual report instead of starting with it as it had been the tradition for decades. The quality and clarity of the information included in the *Memorias del Ministerio de Hacienda* deteriorated markedly after 1944.

7. As Steve Hanke observed in a previous version of this paper, the system implanted by Cavallo in 1991 was not an orthodox currency board since it allowed for much fiscal and monetary discretion. See Hanke (2002).

8. Hayek pointed out that "almost every claim for government action on behalf of particular groups is advanced in its name, and if it can be made to appear that a certain measure is demanded by 'social justice', opposition to it will rapidly weaken" (Hayek, 1976, 65). In Argentina, social justice has meant higher salaries and social benefits for urban workers and higher profits for crony capitalists. The former divorced from productivity and the latter from efficiency, both financed by exactions on the agricultural sector.

9. This comparison in no way seeks to minimize other aspects of communist rule in Poland such as political persecution and incarceration. Interestingly, Poland's institutional quality indicators deteriorated markedly after 2016 when the populist Law and Justice won parliamentary elections.

10. Argentina copied the U.S. constitution in 1853 but its author, Juan B. Alberdi, who had read De Tocqueville, warned that 100 years would be necessary to eradicate customs shaped by centuries of Spanish colonial rule. It only lasted 77 years. In 1949 Perón replaced it with a constitution inspired by Mussolini's corporatist state.

11. There is a subtle difference between anomie and anarchy. The former denotes non-compliance with existing rules and norms whereas the latter describes the absence of such rules.

12. Even higher than in Colombia, Dominican Republic, Guatemala, Mexico, and Panamá, countries which were occupied by the U.S. military.

REFERENCES

Alesina, Alberto, Hausmann, Ricardo, Hommes, Rudolf and Stein, Eduardo. 1996. "Budget Institutions and Fiscal Performance in Latin America." NBER Working Paper 5586.

Alesina, Alberto and Perotti, Roberto. 1996. "Fiscal Discipline and the Budget Process." *The American Economic Review*, 86, No. 2, Papers and Proceedings of the Hundredth and Eighth Annual Meeting of the American Economic Association San Francisco, CA, January 5–7, (May), 401–407.

Amado, Néstor A., Cerro, Ana María and Meloni, Osvaldo. 2005. "Making Explosive Cocktails: recipes and costs for 26 Crises from 1823 to 2003." *Economic History 0510001*, University Library of Munich, Germany.

Aráoz, Florencia, Cerro, Ana María, Meloni, Osvaldo and Soria Genta, Tatiana. 2008. "Fiscal Sustainability and Crises: The Case of Argentina." In *Fiscal Imbalances and Sustainability: Concepts and Country Experiences,* edited by Alagiri, Dhandapani, 170–194. Hyderabad: Icfai University Press.

———. 2009. "Empirical Evidence on Fiscal Policy Sustainability in Argentina". *The IUP Journal of Monetary Economics*, Vol. VII, Nos. 3 & 4, (August–November), 116–127.

Ávila, Jorge C. 2011. *Fiscal Deficit, Macro Uncertainty, and Growth in Argentina.* Working Paper, No. 456 (July), UCEMA.

Buera, Francisco and Nicolini, Juan Pablo. 2019. "The Monetary and Fiscal History of Argentina, 1960–2017." Federal Reserve Bank of Minneapolis, Staff Report 580 (December).

Buchanan, James M. 2005. *Why I Am Not a Conservative: The Normative Vision of Classical Liberalism.* Cheltenham: Edward Elgar Publishing Limited.

Buol, Jason J. and Vaughan, Mark D. 2003. "Rules vs. Discretion: The Wrong Choice Could Open the Floodgates." *The Regional Economist*, Federal Reserve Bank of St. Louis, issue Jan, 10–11.

Cagan, Philip. 1956. "The Monetary Dynamics of Hyperinflation." In *Studies in the Quantity Theory of Money*, edited by Friedman, Milton, 25–117. Chicago: University of Chicago Press.

———. 1987. "Hyperinflation." In *The New Palgrave's Dictionary of Economics*, edited by Eatwell, John, Milgate, Murray and Newman, Peter. London: Macmillan.

Calabria, Mark A. 2015. "Rules versus Discretion: Insights from Behavioral Economics." Cato at Liberty (August 7). https://www.cato.org/blog/rules-versus-discretion-insights-behavioral-economics.

Cerro, Ana María and Meloni, Osvaldo. 2005. "Crises in Argentina: 1823–2002: The Same Old Story?" Paper presented at the XXXVIII Annual Meeting of the AAEP, Mendoza.

———. 2014. "Making Explosive Cocktails: Recipes and Costs of 20 Argentine Crises from 1865 to 2004." *Investigaciones de Historia Económica - Economic History Research*, Vol.10, No. 2 (June): 104–114.

Claro, Sebastián and Opazo, Luis Aníbal. 2014. "Monetary Policy Independence in Chile." In *The Transmission of Unconventional Monetary Policy to the Emerging Markets*, Vol. 78, 111–123. Basle: Bank of International Settlements.

Cohen, Roger. 2014. "Cry for Me Argentina." *The New York Times*, 27 February 2014. https://www.nytimes.com/2014/02/28/opinion/28iht-edcohen28.html

Defiem, Mathieu. 2015. "Anomie: History of the Concept." International Encyclopedia of the Social & Behavioral Sciences, 2nd edition, Volume 1, 718–721.

Della Paolera, Gerardo and Taylor, Alan 2001. *Straining at the Anchor: The Argentine Currency Board and the Search for Macroeconomic Stability, 1880–1935.* Chicago: University of Chicago.

Della Paolera, Gerardo, Irigoin, María Alejandra, and Bozolli, Carlos. 2003. "Passing The Buck: Monetary and Fiscal Policies in Argentina: 1953–1999." In *A New Economic History of Argentina*, edited by Gerardo Della Paolera and Alan Taylor, 46–86, Cambridge: Cambridge University Press.

De Tocqueville, Alexis. 1841. *Democracy in America.* 4th edition. New York: J. & H.G. Langley.

Diaz Alejandro, Carlos F. 1970. *Essays in the Economic History of the Argentine Republic.* New Haven: Yale University Press.

Diaz Frers, Luciana. 2017. "The Road to Budget Transparency in Argentina." *Case Study*, International Budget Partnership (September).

Dornbusch, Rudiger and Edwards, Sebastián. 1991. "The Macroeconomics of Populism." In *The Macroeconomics of Populism in Latin America*, edited by Rudiger Dornbusch and Sebastián Edwards, 7–14. Chicago: University of Chicago Press.

Dornbusch, Rudiger, Sturzenegger, Federico and Wolf, Holger. 1990. "Extreme Inflation: Dynamics and Stabilization." *Brookings Papers on Economic Activity*, Vol. 21, No. 2, 1–84.

Eichengreen, Barry, Hausmann, Ricardo and Panizza, Ugo. 2005. "The Pain of Original Sin." In *Other People's Money*, edited by Barry Eichengreen and Ricardo, Hausmann, 13–47. Chicago: University of Chicago Press.

Ferreres, Orlando. 2010. *Dos siglos de economía argentina, 1810–2010.* Buenos Aires: Fundación Norte y Sur.

Friedman, Milton. 1948. "A Monetary and Fiscal Framework for Economic Stability." *American Economic Review*, Vol. 38, No. 3 (June), 245–264.

———. 1959. "Statement and Testimony." In U.S. Congress, Joint Economic Committee, Employment, Growth, and Price Levels, Part 4, *The Influence on Prices of Changes in the Effective Supply of Money*, 86th Congress, 1st Session, 25 May 1959 Washington, D.C.: Government Printing Office, 605–648.

———. 1960. *A Program for Monetary Stability.* New York: Fordham University Press.

———. 1975. "Can Inflation Be Cured... before It Ends Free Society?" In *Milton Friedman in Australia*, 45–80. Sydney: Constable & Bain and the Graduate Business School Club.

———. 1981. "Taxation, Inflation, and the Role of Government." In *Taxation, Inflation and the Role of Government*, edited by Friedman, Milton, 1–12. CIS Occasional Paper, no. 4. St. Leonards, N.S.W., Australia: Centre for Independent Studies, 1981.

Friedman, Milton and Friedman, Rose. 1982. *The Tyranny of the Status Quo.* New York: Harcourt Brace Jovanovich.

Friedman, Milton and Heller, Walter. 1969. *Monetary vs. Fiscal Policy. A Dialogue.* New York: William Norton and Co. Inc.

Galiani, Sebastián. 2018. "Stabilising Argentina's Public Expenditure." *Development Matters*, OECD, 26 March 2018. https://oecd-development-matters.org/2018/03/26/stabilising-argentinas-public-expenditure/

García, M., García, P. and Piedrabuena, B. 2005. "Fiscal and Monetary Policy Rule: The Recent Chilean Experience." Central Bank of Chile Working Papers, N° 340 (December).

Greenspan, Alan. 1997. "Rules vs. Discretionary Monetary Policy." Remarks at the 15th Anniversary Conference of the Center for Economic Policy Research, Stanford University, Stanford, California, 5 September 1997. https://www.federalreserve.gov/boarddocs/speeches/1997/19970905.htm

Hanke, Steve H. 2002. "Argentina: Caveat Lector." Prepared for the Cato Institute's 20 Annual Monetary Conference cosponsored with *The Economist*, October 17, 2002, New York City, https://www.cato.org/publications/white-paper/argentina-caveat-lector

Hanke, Steve H. and Krus, Nicholas. 2013. "World hyperinflations." In *Routledge Handbook of Major Events in Economic History*, edited by Randall E. Parker and Robert Whaples, 367–377. New York: Routledge.

Hayek, Friedrich A. 1973. *Rules and Order: A New Statement of the Liberal Principles of Justice and Political Economy*. London: Routledge and Kegan Paul.

———. 1976. *Law, Legislation and Liberty. A New Statement of the Liberal Principles of Justice and Political Economy, Volume II: The Mirage of Social Justice*. London: Routledge.

Herron, Francis. 1943. *Letters from the Argentine*. New York: G.P. Putnam.

International Monetary Fund. 2009. "Fiscal Rules —Anchoring Expectations for Sustainable Public Finances," *IMF Policy Paper*. www.imf.org/external/np/pp/eng/2009/121609.pdf

———. 2017. *Fiscal Rules Dataset* (March). http://www.imf.org/external/datamapper/fiscalrules/map/map.htm

———. 2018a. "How to select fiscal rules: A Primer." Technical Note, Fiscal Affairs Department.

———. 2018b. "Second-Generation Fiscal Rules: Balancing Simplicity, Flexibility, and Enforceability." Staff Discussion Note.

Izquierdo, Alejandro, Pessino, Carola, and Vuletin, Guillermo. 2019. *Better Spending for Better Lives: How Latin America and the Caribbean Can Do More With Less*. Washington, DC: Inter-American Development Bank.

Kiguel, Miguel Ángel. 1989. "Budget Deficits, Stability, and the Monetary Dynamics of Hyperinflation." *Journal of Money, Credit and Banking*, Vol. 21, No. 2 (May), 148–157.

Kocherlakota, Narayana. 2016. "Rules Versus Discretion: A Reconsideration." *Brookings Papers on Economic Activity* (Fall), 1–54.

Kydland, Finn and Prescott, Edward. 1977. "Rules Rather than Discretion: The Inconsistency of Optimal Plans." *Journal of Political Economy*, Vol. 85, No. 3 (June), 473–492.

Larrain, Felipe, Ricci, Luca and Schmidt-Hebbel, Klaus. 2019. "Enhancing Chile's Fiscal Framework Lessons from Domestic and International Experience." Washington, DC: International Monetary Fund.

Lucas, Robert E. 1980. "Rules, Discretion, and the Role of the Economic Advisor." In *Rational Expectations and Economic Policy*, edited by Fischer, Stanley, 199–210. Chicago: University of Chicago Press.

Mankiw, Gregory. 2020. "A Skeptic's Guide to Modern Monetary Theory." NBER Working Paper No. 26650.

Mauro, Paolo, Romeu, Rafael, Binder, Ariel and Zaman, Asad. 2013. "A Modern History of Fiscal Prudence and Profligacy." IMF Working Paper No. 13/5, International Monetary Fund, Washington, DC.

Meloni, Osvaldo and Tommasi Mariano. 2013. "Instituciones y Politica Fiscal." In *Progresos en Economía Política de la Política Fiscal*, edited by O. Meloni, 15–36. Buenos Aires: Temas Grupo Editorial.

Mill, John Stuart (1838. "Bentham." In Mill, John Stuart (1897) *Early Essays by John Stuart Mill*. London: George Bell and Sons.

Ministerio de Hacienda 1945. *Memoria del Departamento de Hacienda Correspondiente al Año 1944*, Tomo I. Buenos Aires: Gerónimo J. Pesce y Cia. Impresores.

Naipaul, Vidia S. 1974. *The Return of Eva Perón, with the killings in Trinidad*. New York: Vintage Books.

Newland, Carlos. 2019. "Pese a su modelo, en Chile persiste la mentalidad anti-capitalista." *La Nación*, 31 de octubre de 2019. Available en https://www.lanacion.com.ar/el-mundo/pese-a-su-modelo-en-chile-persiste-la-mentalidad-anticapitalista-nid2302263.

Newland, Carlos and Ocampo, Emilio. 2020. "La crisis chilena de 2019 desde una perspectiva argentina." In *El octubre chileno. Reflexiones sobre democracia y libertad*, edited by Benjamin Ugalde, Felipe Schwember, and Valentina Verbal, 283–298. Santiago de Chile: Ediciones Democracia y Libertad.

Nino, Carlos. 1992. *Un país al margen de la Ley. Estudio de la anomia como componente del subdesarrollo argentino*. Buenos Aires: Emecé.

North, Douglass C. 1994. "Economic Performance Through Time." *The American Economic Review*, Vol. 84, No. 3 (June), 359–368.

———. 1996. "Economics and Cognitive Science." Paper provided by Economics Working Paper Archive at WUSTL in its series Economic History.

Ocampo, Emilio. 2015. "Commodity Price Booms and Populist Cycles An Explanation of Argentina's Decline in the 20th Century." UCEMA Serie Documentos de Trabajo. Nro. 562 (May).

———. 2017. "Fighting Inflation in Argentina: A Brief History of Ten Stabilization Plans." UCEMA Serie Documentos de Trabajo. Nro. 613 (July).

———. 2018. "Las raíces psicologico-culturales del populismo argentino" en Fernández, R. y Ocampo, E. *El Populismo en la Argentina y el Mundo*. Buenos Aires: Editorial Claridad.

———. 2019. "The Economic Analysis of Populism: A Selective Review." UCEMA Serie Documentos de Trabajo. Nro. 694 (May).

———. 2020. "MMT: Modern Monetary Theory or Magical Monetary Thinking? The Empirical Evidence." UCEMA Serie Documentos de Trabajo. Nro. 762 (May).

Perón, Juan Domingo. 1949. *Discursos, mensajes, correspondencia y escritos: 1949*. Buenos Aires: Biblioteca del Congreso de la Nación, 2016.

Reinhart, Carmen. 2010. "This Time is Different Chartbook: Country Histories on Debt, Default, and Financial Crises." NBER Working Paper No. 15815, March.

Reutz, Ted. 1991. "Ilusiones fiscales, dimensión y método de financiamiento del deficit fiscal del gobierno, 1928–1972." *Ciclos*, Año 1, Vol. 1, No.1 (2do Semestre), 117–147.

Samuelson, Paul Anthony. 1973. *Economics*. 9th Edition. New York: Mc Graw-Hill.

———. 1980. "The World at Century's End." In *Human Resources, Employment and Development*, edited by Shigeto Tsuru, Volume 1, The Issues, 58–77. London: Macmillan, 1983.

———. 1981. "The World Economy at Century's End." *Bulletin of the American Academy of Arts and Sciences*, Vol. 34, No. 8, 35–44. This is shorter and slightly different version of the 1980 article.

———. 1984. "Japan and the World at the Century's End." NEXT Magazines, In Samuelson, P. A. (1986) *The Collected Scientific Papers of Paul A. Samuelson*, edited by Kate Crowley, Volume 5. Cambridge: MIT Press, 496–510.

Smithies, Arthur. 1965. "Argentina and Australia." *The American Economic Review*, Vol. 55, No. 1/2 (Mar. 1, 1965), 17–30.

Tanzi, Vito. 2007. *Historia Fiscal Argentina. De Perón al FMI*. Buenos Aires: Edicon.

Taylor, John B. 1993. "Discretion Versus Policy Rules in Practice." Carnegie Mellon-Rochester Conference Series on Public Policy 39, 195–214.

———. 2011. "The Cycle of Rules and Discretion in Economic Policy." *National Affairs*, Spring, 55–65.

———. 2019. "Monetary Institutions and Policy in a Free Society" at the Dallas-Fort Worth meeting of the Mont Pelerin Society, May 20, 2019.

Von Hagen, J. 2002. "Fiscal Rules, Fiscal Institutions, and Fiscal Performance." *The Economic and Social Review*, Vol. 33, No. 3, Winter, 263–284.

Von Mises, Ludwig. 1923. *On the Manipulation of Money and Credit*. New York: Liberty Fund, 1978.

Waisman, Carlos H. 1987. *Reversal of Development: Postwar Counterrevolutionary Policies and Their Structural Consequences*. Princeton: Princeton University Press.

Part V

THE ULTIMATE CHALLENGE
FOR FISCAL SUSTAINABILITY

ENTITLEMENT REFORM

Chapter 12

The Failure to Establish Effective Rules for Financing U.S. Federal Entitlement Programs

Charles Paul Blahous

INTRODUCTION: THE CENTRALITY OF ENTITLEMENT REFORM TO FISCAL REFORM

Understanding the fiscal practices of the U.S. government requires in turn an understanding of how its federal mandatory spending programs, otherwise known as entitlements, have largely eluded effective financial controls.[1] The U.S. federal government's structural budget deficit has grown persistently over the past several decades, driven principally by spending growth in these entitlement programs. While other aspects of federal budgeting ranging from tax policy to discretionary appropriated spending are frequently a focus of political debate, non-partisan examinations of the federal fiscal imbalance consistently conclude that its primary cause is the growth of entitlement program spending, with the largest amounts occurring in Social Security, Medicare, and Medicaid (Congressional Budget Office 2019, 20; Riedl 2018; Blahous 2013).[2]

Figure 12.1 shows Congressional Budget Office (CBO) projections for federal deficits, published just prior to the onset of the COVID-19 crisis (Congressional Budget Office 2020).[3] Figure 12.1 as well as other figures in this chapter are based on CBO's pre-COVID projections for the following reasons. First and foremost, this study was conducted in 2020 before the budgetary effects of COVID-19 were fully known, including both direct budgetary effects of the economic downturn, as well as the effects of multiple economic relief bills, which continue to move through Congress at the time this article is going to press. These various economic relief bills have both worsened and complicated the near-term budget outlook. However, irrespective of this ongoing legislation, the long-term story remains one of spiraling

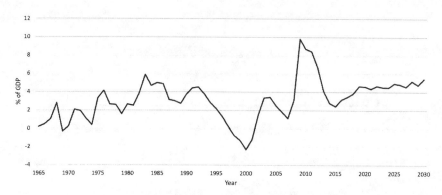

Figure 12.1   Historical/Projected Federal Budget Deficits. Congressional Budget Office, Historical Budget Data, January 2020, and Congressional Budget Office, Long-Term Budget Projections, January 2020, https://www.cbo.gov/about/products/budget-economic-data#2.

federal deficits and debt, with the situation deteriorating dramatically over the last decade and projected to grow out of control in the years to come. With the exceptions of a brief period of fiscal consolidation in the late 1990s, and surges in annual deficits during two recent recessions, the picture looks remarkably consistent across time. Deficits in individual years rise and fall, but the midpoint of the fluctuations has persistently grown faster than Gross Domestic Product since the 1970s. As a consequence, federal debt has been accumulating faster than growth in U.S. economic output, again excepting a brief period in the late 1990s and mid-2000s (Congressional Budget Office 2020).

The federal policies that have led to these results have not evolved according to any particular fiscal rule, whether automatically implemented or otherwise. The accumulation of red ink has transpired in good economic times and bad, in periods of market declines and recoveries, and during both Democratic and Republican control of the presidency and of Congress.[4] The imbalance directly reflects the collective unwillingness of lawmakers to limit federal spending to amounts more closely approximating federal revenue collections.

More specifically, the imbalance derives from the growth of federal entitlement spending. Figure 12.2 illustrates a counterintuitive reality, that the growth of federal deficits has coincided with relative declines in total annually appropriated (discretionary) spending, including both defense and domestic discretionary spending. In contrast, the growth of entitlement spending, also shown in figure 12.2, corresponds closely to the concurrent growth of federal deficits and debt (Congressional Budget Office 2020; Blahous 2012).[5]

Trends in federal tax collections contrast markedly with the patterns displayed in figure 12.2. Unlike entitlement spending, tax collection levels have no clear relationship to the persistent rise in federal debt. To the contrary, federal tax collections as a share of GDP have remained remarkably stable across the decades, neither rising nor falling with consistency nor to large degrees

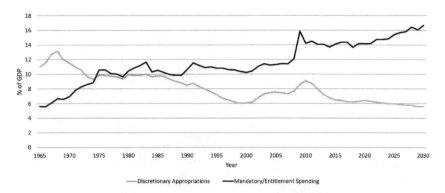

Figure 12.2 Historical/Projected Federal Spending, by Type. Source: Congressional Budget Office, Historical Budget Data, January 2020, and Congressional Budget Office, 10-Year Budget Projections, January, 2020, https://www.cbo.gov/about/products/budget-economic-data#2.

(Congressional Budget Office 2020). Indeed, federal deficits and debt are projected to increase through the late 2020s despite projected tax collections also increasing relative to the size of the economy and relative to historical norms (Congressional Budget Office 2020). The conclusion is straightforward and inescapable: the federal fiscal imbalance is not primarily rooted in either annually appropriated spending or tax policy, but is predominantly a consequence of uncontrolled entitlement spending growth.[6]

Federal mandatory (entitlement) spending is defined as spending that is automatically authorized under continuing statute, without requiring an intervening vote by lawmakers, whether on a new budget resolution, budget reconciliation bill, or any other new authorizing legislation. Because such spending continues on autopilot unless a vote is held to discontinue or reduce it, it creates a powerful procedural bias toward rising spending relative to government restraint. If in addition the spending is indexed to automatically increase relative to economic growth and/or to tax collections, as is the case under current law, there results a powerful impetus toward escalating deficits and debt.

As long as current budgetary processes persist, it is difficult to posit that an enduring solution to the federal fiscal shortfall is even reasonably likely. Without fundamental restructuring of federal entitlement programs, fiscal improvements can only be episodic and temporary, after which the budget must return to its persistently destabilizing trajectory. Lasting fiscal corrections are unlikely until federal finances are placed on a course that is sustainable without requiring repeated legislative interventions.

Additional political economy factors only accentuate the unworkability of leaving automatic entitlement spending growth mechanisms in place, while relying perpetually on periodic legislation to ameliorate the resulting fiscal problems. Legislators' policy views span a wide spectrum of preferences with respect to deficit-reduction strategies, ranging from reliance entirely on tax increases to reliance entirely on spending restraints.[7] As long as a critical mass of diverse legislators must agree on new legislation to stabilize federal budgets, a worsening fiscal imbalance remains the most likely outcome.

In addition, lasting fiscal improvements are precluded under current law unless legislators overcome the powerful psychological force of "loss aversion" (Kahneman 2011, 282–286). That is, as long as the no-action scenario appears to provide that Americans will receive benefits without the necessity of financing them, then legislation to correct federal finances will be perceived by voters as an income loss, and resisted accordingly.[8] Only if the baseline scenario is one in which the budget is in balance or in surplus are legislators likely to find common ground on future adjustments that can receive public support. Hence, a one-time, permanent correction of the federal fiscal trajectory could have an enormously powerful effect in enabling future bipartisan cooperation and problem solving. Such a correction would itself face formidable political obstacles, but it is more realistic to overcome them a single time than repeatedly.

A lasting correction to federal budget policy and processes could be achieved by making mandatory spending programs subject to automatic corrections that ensure their continued financial balance without requiring repeated rescues by federal legislators. The following sections of this chapter present an abbreviated history of the largest such programs, and how they have come to lack such automatic correction mechanisms.

THE HISTORICAL ROOTS OF SOCIAL SECURITY'S FINANCING SHORTFALL

Social Security, the federal government's largest and costliest program, pays old-age, disability, and survivor benefits to qualifying workers and their dependents. The program is funded primarily by payroll taxes collected from participating workers' wages, which are credited to a pair of trust funds (one for old-age and survivor benefits, the other for disability benefits), from which all benefit payments must be made. Social Security's costs are persistently growing faster than its revenue base and thus contribute significantly to the federal government's structural fiscal imbalance described in the previous section. This section provides an historical overview of how Social Security came to lack effective financial controls.

Because Social Security's spending authority is limited to the resources held by its trust funds, there is a widely shared perception that corrections to its financial operations must occur automatically. That is to say, if benefit obligations grow beyond what the program's dedicated revenues can finance, then either legislators will realign benefit and tax schedules before the trust funds run dry, or else benefit payments will be restrained automatically to affordable levels. However, a closer examination of Social Security's history reveals a more complicated and less reassuring picture. Historically, no Social Security trust fund has been allowed to be depleted in a manner that limited benefit payments, and the few instances of legislative action to correct a programmatic financial imbalance are sufficiently rare that it remains unclear whether they are operative precedents or were instead outlier political events. Additionally, previous financial corrections were enacted in an era when the program's annual operations were not nearly as imbalanced as they will be when trust fund depletion nears again (Social Security Administration Office of the Chief Actuary 2020, Table VI. G2).

Perhaps most importantly, the few historical instances of lawmakers successfully addressing a Social Security financing imbalance reflected the policy scruples of a handful of influential policymakers of an earlier time, who were personally invested in the principle of Social Security self-financing. As the following paragraphs will detail, there is reason for skepticism that the principles that animated prior corrections still receive the allegiance of a critical mass of lawmakers.

Social Security's current trust fund system was essentially created in the 1939 Social Security amendments pursuant to the recommendations of a 1938 Social Security Advisory Council (Social Security Advisory Council 1938). Per the language of the Social Security Act as later amended in 1956, disability benefit payments "shall be made only" from Social Security's disability insurance (DI) trust fund, and all other program benefits "shall be made only" from the old-age and survivors' (OASI) insurance trust fund (Social Security Administration 2021). The most common legal interpretation of this language is that the Social Security Administration cannot send benefit payments in amounts exceeding the assets credited to Social Security's trust funds (Social Security Board of Trustees 2020, 65). This can be, and often is, thought of as a mechanism that both requires and enforces financial corrections; specifically, if lawmakers fail to maintain the alignment of Social Security's dedicated revenues with its benefit obligations, then when the eventual trust fund depletion occurs, outgoing benefit payments will be halted until sufficient revenue arrives to finance them, effectively reducing total benefits via the mechanism of delay.

This mechanism for ensuring financial balance is, however, surprisingly weak, easily circumvented, and is proving inadequate to prevent future Social Security obligations from far surpassing its projected revenues. As figure 12.3 shows, the growth of Social Security benefit obligations has persistently outstripped growth in the U.S. economy that provides its revenue base. Lawmakers have facilitated this cost growth in various ways, most significantly by automatically indexing initial benefit levels so that per-capita benefits grow in real (inflation-adjusted) terms, and by paying them over

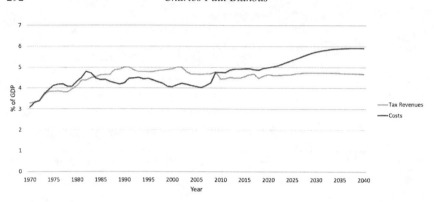

Figure 12.3 Historical/Projected Social Security Costs and Tax Revenues. Social Security Office of the Chief Actuary, Single-Year Tables Consistent with the 2020 OASDI Trustees Report, Table VI. G4, Table VI. G5, https://www.ssa.gov/OACT/TR/2020/lr6g4.html, https://www.ssa.gov/OACT/TR/2020/lr6g5.html.

more years as program eligibility ages have not been adjusted sufficiently to reflect trends in population aging. Under the trustees' most recent projections, the combined Social Security trust funds will be depleted in 2035, and the gap between annual income and obligations in that year will be more than twice as large, relative to the U.S. economy, than lawmakers have ever successfully closed with short-term actions in the past (Social Security Administration Office of the Chief Actuary 2020, Tables VI. G4 and VI. G5, Social Security Board of Trustees 1982).[9]

Social Security's financial imbalance has been repeatedly documented for over three decades, most notably in the annual reports of the program's trustees, and yet lawmakers have conspicuously declined to correct it. This is not because the last rescue enacted in 1983, when the trust funds were last on the verge of depletion, can be readily duplicated in 2035, when they are next projected to be. The trustees and other experts have repeatedly advised lawmakers that by the time the trust funds are nearing depletion in the 2030s, the short-term adjustments required to preserve solvency will be prohibitively severe. As the public trustees warned in their annual message in 2015, "continued inaction to the point where the combined trust funds near depletion would—unlike the situation in 1983—likely preclude any plausible opportunity to preserve Social Security's historical financing structure" (Social Security Board of Trustees 2015).[10]

For example, even if 100% of new benefit claims are eliminated when 2035 arrives, this extreme measure would still be insufficient to prevent Social Security's combined trust funds from being depleted. Consider also that federal lawmakers have never permitted sudden across-the-board benefit cuts as a result of trust fund depletion, let alone the immediate 21%

reductions that would be required in 2035 (Social Security Board of Trustees 2020, 13).[11] Hence, the mere requirement that all benefits be paid from Social Security trust fund assets is not necessarily a sufficient spur to preserve Social Security's financial integrity. Under current law, realistic financial corrections depend on lawmakers taking it upon themselves to act while there is still time and space for success, which is far earlier than a trust fund's impending depletion compels by itself.

A closer examination of Social Security policy history reveals that to date, the program has operated without automatic, effective, durable financial correction mechanisms, its finances instead depending on key lawmakers acting upon particular policy principles. President Franklin D. Roosevelt strongly favored a funded Social Security system, and personally intervened to ensure that his legislative proposals to Congress anticipated no future deficits requiring future lawmakers to enact future revenue increases, even after 1980, which was then more than four decades into the future (Schieber and Shoven 1999, 36–37). The original 1935 Act largely conformed to FDR's wishes in projecting to collect substantially more in taxes than would be needed to pay benefits in the program's early years, which would have led to a buildup of trust fund assets, and interest earnings thereupon, to be drawn upon in later decades to finance benefit payments that significantly exceeded payroll tax collections.

The 1935 Social Security financing framework was almost immediately dismantled under simultaneous pressure from both the political left and the political right. The left was concerned that the schedules contained in the 1935 law would have Social Security paying only very small benefits in its early years, relative to the tax burdens it was imposing and relative to the more generous pension benefits paid in the private sector. The political right for its part was also troubled by the original 1935 design, as it envisioned the federal government completely buying down the public debt and managing a massive accumulation of savings through Social Security. As Sylvester Schieber and John Shoven have put it, in such a circumstance the government would either "have to create added debt just to accommodate the Social Security funding," or would have to invent new spending projects in which the trust fund would be invested (Schieber and Shoven 1999, 53). Conservatives disliked either option.

The concerns shared by left and right led to amendments enacted in 1939 to convert Social Security to a largely pay-as-you-go system—that is, a system in which current participants' benefits were financed by tax contributions of younger workers, rather than having been funded previously by the beneficiaries themselves. Accordingly, near-term benefit payments were increased, and previously scheduled payroll tax increases were delayed. Thereby turning away from fully funding Social Security, the 1939 amendments attempted to enforce the opposite: that its trust fund be inhibited from growing to exceed three years' worth of benefit expenditures. Known as the "Morgenthau Rule" after the then-Secretary of the Treasury, it was reflected in a provision in the 1939 legislation requiring that the program's trustees immediately report to Congress whenever the trust fund breached this ceiling.

The 1939 amendments placed Social Security on a course whereby future promised benefits were likely to exceed future program revenues over the long term. The 1942 trustees' report presented two projection scenarios lasting through 1990; under both of them the growth of benefit payments would surpass the growth of tax collections, and in one scenario the deficits would become so large that the trust funds would be depleted circa 1970 in the absence of further legislation (Social Security Board of Trustees 1942). Thus, virtually from its inception, Social Security was constructed to require legislators to intervene periodically to maintain its financial stability.

Social Security's finances would probably have destabilized earlier than they did historically were it not for certain judgments made by particularly influential individuals. One of them was Robert Myers, who was a central player throughout Social Security's history, working with the Committee on Economic Security that developed the initial legislative proposals, becoming a Social Security actuary in 1936, serving as chief actuary from 1947 to 1970, and later being the executive director of the 1981–1983 Greenspan commission (Social Security Administration 2010). The 75-year projection window the Social Security trustees use today was developed by Myers, who also favored the inclusion of "infinite horizon" projections, which are currently provided in the annual reports' appendices (Social Security Administration 2021).[12]

Throughout Myers's tenure as chief actuary, SSA's actuarial estimates did not project future wage growth, instead assuming both that average benefits and average wages would remain constant. This assumption does not align with real-world patterns of economic growth in which, over time, real wage levels rise. The assumptions employed by Myers's actuarial shop came under increasing criticism from outside analysts for underestimating likely future program revenues (and future benefit payments as well, though to a lesser extent), criticism that reached a critical mass by the late 1960s. The 1971 Social Security Advisory Council recommended that the actuarial methodology be revised to reflect projected wage growth, thereby improving the program's reported financial outlook. The 1972 trustees' report accordingly contained two sets of long-term projections, one using the old method and a second using the Council's recommended "dynamic" method. The latter of these showed a considerable long-range surplus, which gave impetus to the passage of a substantial, permanent benefit increase in 1972 (Social Security Board of Trustees 1972, 23–32).

It seems straightforward to hold that Myers's longstanding methodology, which assumed that future earnings would not rise, warranted changing because it was clearly incorrect: over the long term, wages do tend to rise. But it should also be recognized that its use throughout Myers's tenure in effect acted as an automatic financial correction mechanism for Social Security. Each year during that period, the trustees reported on how system finances would evolve if wages did not rise. Then instead, over time, wages did rise, creating a financing surplus, which legislators were then able to spend on benefit increases of their own design. As Schieber and Shoven put it, "The way the Social Security system's cost rate was estimated in combination with the phenomenon of steady wage growth allowed Congress to become a public Santa Claus. It could regularly increase benefits without having to increase the payroll tax rate to do so. If Congress could act like Santa Claus, the Social Security actuaries were the elves that supplied them with gifts to distribute regularly to the voting public" (Schieber and Shoven 1999, 154). But that all changed when SSA's actuarial assumptions were modified, whereupon lawmakers increased benefits beyond the levels future tax collections could finance. Though Myers's actuarial methods' use and abandonment were a mere happenstance of program history, once they were no longer employed there was no longer any effective barrier against Social Security's future cost growth outpacing its affordability.

The change in actuarial methods opened the door to program expansionists overreaching, which occurred almost immediately in 1972. Before 1972, Social Security's revenue growth generally outpaced its cost growth in the absence of further legislation, allowing lawmakers to periodically intervene to increase benefits. But ever since the 1972 amendments were implemented, automatic program cost growth has generally exceeded revenue growth, forcing lawmakers to periodically enact financing corrections, which is proving progressively more difficult to do. Indeed, a significant part of the larger federal government's transition from sustainable to unsustainable budget practices is attributable to changes in how mandatory spending programs grow, with the most significant such change in Social Security occurring in 1972.

The 1972 Social Security amendments instituted an across-the-board benefit increase of 20% and, more significantly for Social Security's financial future, automatic annual Cost-of-Living-Adjustments based on growth in the Consumer Price Index (CPI-W). A technical error in the application of this CPI indexing caused Social Security benefit awards for succeeding cohorts of claimants to grow much faster than lawmakers intended, in turn causing Social Security replacement rates to soar and threatening to plunge the program rapidly into insolvency. The erroneous formula was phased out in the 1977 Social Security amendments, which henceforth tied growth in initial benefit awards, from one cohort to the next, to growth in the national Average

Wage Index (AWI) (Blahous 2010, 33–34, Social Security Administration 2021).[13]

Although the 1977 amendments corrected the major technical mistake in the 1972 amendments, they did not eliminate Social Security's newly created financing shortfall. The program immediately drifted back toward insolvency again, leading to the appointment of the Greenspan Social Security Commission in 1981 and necessitating the passage of the 1983 Social Security amendments, which rescued the program from insolvency with just a few months to spare. The 1983 amendments were intensely controversial, exposing Social Security benefits to income taxation for the first time, delaying annual COLAs by six months, bringing all newly hired federal employees (and thus new payroll tax contributions) into the program, gradually raising the full eligibility age, and accelerating a previously enacted payroll tax rate increase. Passage of the amendments required lawmakers to join forces across party lines, to accept substantial political cost, and to overcome the fierce lobbying pressure of advocacy groups such as the American Association of Retired Persons (AARP).

More significantly for our purposes here, the legislative changes to Social Security in the 1970s produced the near opposite of an automatic financial correction mechanism, in the sense that provisions of law now automatically adjust Social Security operations so that the program remains *out* of financial balance. As previously explained, initial benefit levels are indexed to the AWI, which means that whenever growth in the economy, wages, and tax collections accelerate, this otherwise beneficial revenue growth cannot close Social Security's shortfall because benefit obligations automatically grow faster as well (Social Security Board of Trustees, 2020, 185).[14] A consultant panel informed Congress of this flaw prior to the passage of the 1977 amendments, pointing out that wage-indexing "must commit our sons and daughters to a higher tax rate than we ourselves are willing to pay" (Consultant Panel on Social Security 1976). However, lawmakers failed then to muster the political will to restrain the automatic growth of benefit obligations to levels affordable without future legislative interventions.

PERSISTENT FAILURE TO STABILIZE SOCIAL SECURITY FINANCES

Social Security's 1983 rescue is often held up as a model for bipartisan compromise and for possible future financial corrections, but over time it has become more apparent that the achievement reflected fleeting circumstances, and that the processes that were successful in 1983 are unlikely to work next time around. There are several reasons why the 1983 experience does not embody a reliable precedent for keeping Social Security solvent via similar, repeated legislative interventions in the future.

First, there is the simple empirical fact that the 1983 action has not been replicated, despite repeat warnings from Social Security's trustees of the growing urgency of repairing program finances. As more time passes, legislative gridlock with respect to Social Security is increasingly the established norm, while the bipartisan 1983 reforms become an increasingly exceptional event.

Second, Social Security's long-term shortfall is now substantially larger than the one corrected in 1983, and is growing. This means that enacting financial corrections either today or in the future would require opponents of tax increases to accept far larger tax increases, opponents of benefit restraints to accept far greater restraints, or (more likely) both, than were required in 1983.

Third, although the 1983 rescue required short-term changes that were highly controversial, these were but a small fraction as severe as the immediate, sudden changes that will be required if lawmakers again wait until the brink of insolvency to act. In 1983, legislators only needed to correct a period of relatively surmountable near-term deficits before program operations reverted to surplus, according to projections before the 1983 reforms were enacted (Social Security Board of Trustees 1982). By contrast, in 2034, the year before Social Security's combined trust funds are projected to next be depleted, its annual cash deficit is estimated as being nearly three times as large as it was in 1982 as a percentage of GDP (Social Security Office of the Chief Actuary 2020, Table VI. G4).

Social Security's comparatively surmountable operating deficits in the early 1980s reflected the historical application of the Morgenthau Rule, which previously limited the size of its trust funds' build-up and kept the program operating mostly on a pay-as-you-go basis. That pay-as-you-go financing meant in turn that any downturn that threatened insolvency must be dealt with quickly, before the relatively small trust fund was depleted, but also before annual deficits had grown too large. However, the 1983 amendments banished any lingering effects of the old Morgenthau Rule to the past, as Social Security thereafter ran several years of large surpluses before experiencing increasingly large deficits beginning in 2010. By the time 2035 approaches, Social Security's annual cash deficit will be so large that, as previously mentioned, even zeroing out all new benefit claims would be insufficient to avert insolvency (Committee for a Responsible Federal Budget 2020).

Fourth, while it is difficult to measure the phenomenon with precision, it is widely adjudged that since the 1980s, Congressional behavior has become more partisan and polarized, reducing the likelihood of bipartisan compromise on the scale of 1983 (Blahous 2019, 7–8).

Fifth, federal economic policy has traveled a great distance since the Great Moderation of fiscal and monetary policy that began in the mid-1980s, to which the 1983 Social Security amendments might be seen as a prelude. During that roughly 20-year moderation period, government took recurring actions to reduce public-sector deficits in a manner the United States has not practiced more recently. It is unclear whether and when Social Security policymaking will again transpire in a general policy environment favorable to fiscal consolidation.

Perhaps most importantly, just as early Social Security finances had been kept in check largely via the conservative actuarial assumptions of Robert Myers, the corrections of 1983 were only made possible by subjective policy values ascendant among influential policymakers of that time, but which have experienced declining attachment in subsequent decades. These values may no longer enjoy sufficient support to guide future legislation. Central among them is that Social Security should remain self-financing and funded by participating worker tax contributions, without subsidies from the general fund of the U.S. treasury. Though this reflects an inherently subjective value judgment, it is an essential principle for the analytical purposes of this chapter, because without it, corrections to the finances of a major federal entitlement program such as Social Security might simply come at the expense of the rest of the federal budget without ameliorating the broader fiscal imbalance.

At the time of the 1983 amendments, commitment to Social Security being self-supporting without general fund subsidies was deep, wide, and bipartisan. This principle was viewed as essential to maintaining FDR's vision of Social Security as a contributory insurance program as opposed to welfare. It undergirded shared perceptions that participants (at least in the aggregate) had earned and paid for their benefits, while also providing the basis for the program's financial discipline. Across the decades it was endorsed by countless policy experts, including among many others the 1957–1959 Social Security Advisory Council ("We believe that the experience of the past 22 years has shown the advantages of contributory social insurance over grants from general tax funds") and the 1981 National Social Security Commission ("The primary source of funds to pay Social Security benefits has been, and the Commission believes should remain, the payroll tax") (Social Security Advisory Council 1959, Social Security National Commission 1981, 65). Upholding the principle required, however, that legislators be willing to limit benefit obligations to the levels that workers' tax contributions could finance.

There is substantial evidence that Social Security's self-financing principle no longer receives the same deference today that it long received from policy influencers across the U.S. political spectrum. Increasingly, proposals are floated to use general fund (income tax) revenues to eliminate the Social Security trust fund financing shortfall (Munnell 2016). Policy advocates increasingly express support for abandoning the restrictions of self-financing and allowing Social Security to draw from the general government fund (Social Security Administration Office of the Chief Actuary 2020, Klein 2010). In 2011–2012, lawmakers temporarily reduced the Social Security payroll tax, and granted the program over $200 billion in general revenues to make up the loss, thereby substantially subsidizing Social Security benefits over and above what participant contributions could finance (Blahous 2012).

Lawmakers have also displayed a willingness to enact the fiscal equivalent of a general revenue bailout in parallel situations and via other methods, such as in 2010 when the proceeds of financial corrections to Medicare Hospital Insurance included in the Affordable Care Act were spent—in the very same law—on a new federal health insurance program (Blahous 2012).[15] If these recent trends are more indicative of future events than are the actions of 1983, we should not expect the existence of a trust fund financing structure to, by itself, compel lawmakers to mitigate the federal fiscal imbalance through entitlement program reforms.

For all of the reasons described in the previous paragraphs, it there are now large and growing barriers to repeating the successful 1983 experience of closing Social Security's actuarial shortfall, while simultaneously improving the federal budget outlook.

During the period since 1983 that Social Security's financial imbalance has worsened, there have been episodes when the impending depletion of a trust fund might well have compelled financing corrections. There have also been separate attempts to establish special processes to force or at least expedite such corrections. None have proved effective in stabilizing Social Security program finances.

In the early 1990s, Social Security's DI fund faced impending insolvency. Instead of raising payroll taxes or slowing the growth of disability benefit awards or levels to address the shortfall, lawmakers opted to simply play for time, reallocating taxes from Social Security's Old-Age and Survivors Insurance (OASI) fund to its DI fund, essentially patching the DI problem at the expense of Social Security's retirement benefit program. Social Security's public trustees acquiesced to these dilatory tactics, but cautioned that "this necessary action should be viewed as only providing time and opportunity to design and implement substantive reforms that can lead to long-term financial stability" of disability insurance, also expressing the hope that "Congress will take action over the next few years to make this program financially stable over the long term" (Social Security Board of Trustees 1995). The legislative action urged by the trustees was not taken.

A similar process transpired in 2015. Again, the DI trust fund faced impending insolvency and again, legislators responded by reallocating taxes to DI from Social Security's OASI trust fund (Blahous 2015). This time lawmakers acted with greater prudence, reallocating tax rates only temporarily, and combining the reallocation with other minor reforms of DI benefit awards so that the legislation on balance very slightly improved Social Security's financial outlook (Social Security Board of Trustees 2016). More than in 1994, the 2015 action was in keeping with the historical purpose of the trust fund system to compel occasional financing corrections, although again the principal effect of the 2015 legislation was to postpone the necessity of dealing with the program's persistently worsening financial shortfalls.

Debate over the 2015 DI fix fostered an unfortunate side effect, as policy advocates sought to give cover to procrastinating lawmakers by portraying periodic OASI/DI tax reallocations as the usual method of avoiding imminent trust fund depletion. This was untrue; most previous tax reallocations had been enacted in the context of broader measures to strengthen Social Security program finances (Committee for a Responsible Federal Budget 2015, Blahous 2015). Through an incorrect representation of historical practices, the claim was widely promoted, politically convenient, and thus accepted by many, calling into further question whether henceforth a trust fund's impending depletion will be a forcing event that induces lawmakers to enact meaningful financial corrections.

While federal lawmakers have not heeded the Social Security trustees' increasingly urgent calls for legislative reforms to repair Social Security's finances, there have been countless attempts to set up alternative processes to force corrective action. Most of these were built upon the 1981–1983 model of a bipartisan commission making recommendations, followed by legislation. None have succeeded, suggesting that if Social Security's finances are to be stabilized, it must likely be through adjustments to benefits, taxes, and eligibility ages written directly into Social Security law after a regular process of congressional negotiation and debate, rather than by establishing new correction-forcing processes ostensibly independent of Congress.

The examples of process-based failures to reform Social Security since 1983 are numerous enough that any attempt to list them all risks being incomplete. The Social Security Act itself established multiple quadrennial Social Security advisory councils, whose charges included making recommendations for protecting program finances (Social Security Administration Office of the Historian 2021). The last of these deliberated throughout 1994–1996 and split into three factions, each offering a different solvency plan, none supported by a majority of the council (Social Security Advisory Council 1997). The advisory councils were discontinued and replaced in law with the Social Security Advisory Board, which has generally steered clear of offering recommendations on how to preserve program solvency. President George W. Bush appointed a bipartisan commission in 2001 which reported options for maintaining program solvency, all of which were ignored by Congress (President's Commission to Strengthen Social Security 2001).

Another section of this chapter will review multiple attempts to establish new processes or committees to expedite improvements to the broader federal budget, including the Kerrey-Danforth Bipartisan Commission on Entitlement and Tax Reform (1994, appointed by President Clinton), the Cooper-Wolf SAFE Commission proposal (2009), the Conrad-Gregg Deficit Reduction Commission proposal (2010), the National Commission on Fiscal Responsibility and Reform (also known as Simpson-Bowles, 2010, appointed by President Obama), the Joint Select Committee on Deficit Reduction established in the Budget Control Act (BCA, 2011), and more recently the TRUST Act introduced by Senator Mitt Romney (2019) (Social Security Administration 1994, Cooper 2009, Lightman 2010, National Commission on Fiscal Responsibility and Reform 2010, Barrett, Bolduan and Walsh 2011, Romney 2019). Each of these would facilitate and in some cases require congressional consideration of Social Security financing reforms recommended by a commission, but none have even succeeded in getting such reforms passed even through the commission itself, let alone through Congress.

STRENGTHENING SOCIAL SECURITY'S FINANCES THROUGH AUTOMATIC ADJUSTMENT MECHANISMS

Far more effective than process-based reforms have been indexation and other adjustment factors written into statute through regular congressional order, including both those that gradually strengthen Social Security finances, and those that worsen them. As previously mentioned, prior to 1972, provisions of Social Security law tended to cause program revenues to grow faster than program outlays, in effect serving as an automatic financial stabilization mechanism. By contrast, the benefit indexation mechanisms enacted in 1972 and later revised in 1977 acted as automatic destabilization mechanisms, in that they tended to push Social Security further out of financial balance over time, regardless of national economic performance. Other provisions to gradually adjust Social Security's full eligibility age, enacted in 1983, only removed a small fraction of the actuarial imbalance that would otherwise exist, but they have remained in force over time and have improved program finances as intended. This experience suggests that enduring improvements to Social Security finances might be achieved by enacting automatic, gradually implemented financing correction mechanisms.

Some experts have offered specific proposals to stabilize Social Security finances through such automatic statutory adjustments safeguarding against unanticipated changes in demographic and/or economic conditions. Economist

Jason Furman, for example, proposed "dependency indexing" of either the payroll tax rate or Social Security's benefit formula factors, automatically adjusting these to reflect changes in the ratio of beneficiaries to workers (Furman 2007). Furman's insights included that Social Security finances are governed more by the worker-collector ratio than by virtually any other factor, that uncertainty as to the long-term demographic and economic outlook (specifically, interest groups' fears of overcorrection) is a substantial political barrier to reforms, and that program finances are more likely to remain stable if lawmakers need not repeatedly regenerate legislative majorities to enact corrections. All of these obstacles could be overcome with automatic adjustments designed to maintain Social Security solvency in the event that the future dependency ratio deviates from projections operative at the time of legislation.

The Furman framework was not free of imperfections. It was premised on a few analytical judgments that have not borne out, including the assumption that demographic projection uncertainty is the primary stumbling block to Social Security reform. Social Security's current shortfall actually would have arisen even if the demographic assumptions underlying the 1983 amendments had been perfectly accurate; in fact, demographic projection error in 1983 accounts for none of the actuarial deterioration since then (Chu and Burkhalter 2020).[16] The real problem with the 1983 reforms was that they were insufficient to withstand the passage of time even under the assumptions then in use, primarily because the 1981–1983 Greenspan Commission had embraced a weaker goal of average actuarial balance rather than the stronger one of permanently sustainable solvency (Social Security Administration 2021).[17]

Moreover, while automatic stabilizers may be a policy idea whose time has come, this is not because projection uncertainty is the largest impediment to Social Security reform. To the contrary, political resistance to Social Security corrections has persisted even as the program's impending insolvency has grown closer and more certain. Plus, while it is true that demographic ratios are among the most important variables affecting Social Security's financial balance, it is comparatively easy to anticipate their effects, relative to less-predictable economic growth. Accordingly, there is less need for demographic adjustments to be instituted automatically; lawmakers already have decades of lead time to adjust for demographic change.[18] A final technical note is warranted with respect to the Furman dependency-indexing proposal, which envisions adjusting either Social Security's tax rate or its benefit formula factors as dependency ratios change: it would be more directly responsive to index the eligibility age, which unlike tax and benefit factor changes would alter the dependency ratio itself, and would create savings on both the outlay and revenue sides of the equation.

Eugene Steuerle and Rudy Penner have also embraced the principle of automatic stabilizers in Social Security and other parts of the federal budget, noting that adjusting the retirement age is "a combined spending and revenue reform" (Penner and Steuerle 2016). Steuerle and Penner, as this chapter has done, distinguish between two types of budgetary correction triggers, the first type of which sets in motion a process forcing Congress and/or the president to take action, the second of which "automatically lowers spending growth or increases revenues if some condition is violated and Congress does not respond" (Penner and Steuerle 2016). The evidence cited in this chapter points to the conclusion that the second type of trigger has far greater potential to be effective. Elsewhere, Steuerle, Favreault, and Mermin also suggested that "indexing the NRA (normal retirement age) and EEA (early eligibility age) to changes in life expectancy" is a Social Security (and Medicare) reform worth considering (Papadimitriou 2007). This is certainly true, although it is also true that eligibility age changes alone would likely be insufficient to restore Social Security to long-term balance (Social Security Administration Office of the Chief Actuary 2020).

In summary, Social Security's growing costs and financial imbalance are major contributors to the growing federal budget imbalance, which in turn reflects the lack of automatic financial correction mechanisms within Social Security itself.[19] Correcting Social Security's financing balance under current law requires lawmakers to act repeatedly to overcome formidable political obstacles, an outcome that has not been achieved since 1983. With time, it is becoming clearer that 1983 was a historically atypical event, that legislative action to reduce Social Security benefit obligations and/or increase program taxes is rare, and should be treated as unlikely at any given time. The conclusion is inescapable, that the longer Social Security operates without automatic financial correction mechanisms written into law, the less likely it is that lawmakers will be able to constrain its cost growth to affordable rates.

BUDGET IMPLICATIONS OF MEDICARE TRUST FUND FINANCING

As with Social Security, the lack of effective financial controls in Medicare is a major contributor to a worsening federal budget outlook. Medicare's finances are more complex than Social Security's, and lend themselves less to requiring and enforcing financial corrections. Like Social Security, Medicare is financed from two trust funds: Hospital Insurance (HI) and Supplementary Medical Insurance (SMI). The first of these two trust funds, Medicare HI, is financed in many ways analogous to Social Security. Its funding comes principally from a payroll tax paid by workers, with a small amount of revenue from the income taxation of Social Security benefits as well as interest earnings on trust fund reserves. And, as with Social Security, Medicare HI's finances are monitored by the program's trustees to determine whether projected revenues are adequate to meet program obligations, or whether instead financial corrections are in order.

Medicare's SMI trust fund, which pays for physician services and prescription drugs among other benefits, operates differently. One-quarter of SMI funding comes from premiums paid by or on behalf of participants, the other three-quarters coming from the federal government's general fund. Importantly, these premium assessments and general revenue contributions are automatically adjusted each year, such that SMI is kept solvent by statutory construction. Thus, in one important respect SMI finances are self-correcting; those parts of Medicare can never go insolvent unless the federal government does.

In other important respects, however, the enforcement of financial limits is weaker within SMI than it is in HI or in Social Security. Specifically, SMI outlays are not limited to what particular tax collections can finance; rather, program revenues are automatically adjusted to grow to whatever amounts are needed to meet current spending. This allows SMI spending to absorb a persistently increasing share of federal tax revenues as well as of premium-paying beneficiaries' incomes, which indeed is what occurs (Boards of Trustees of the Federal Hospital Insurance and Federal Supplementary Medical Insurance Trust Funds 2020, 38).

Aside from the political resistance that arises from participants' premiums rising over time, there is little more institutionalized restraint upon Medicare SMI spending growth than there is upon any other part of the federal budget. Nothing strictly requires lawmakers to limit the growth of SMI spending, or even to collect sufficient tax revenue to finance it without running additional debt. To the contrary, SMI spending is automatically authorized to grow in the absence of further legislation, and thus to add by growing amounts to federal indebtedness.

Given that SMI spending growth is less constrained than HI's, we would expect SMI to grow more rapidly of the two sides of Medicare. Indeed, this has also been observed historically (Boards of Trustees of the Federal Hospital Insurance and Federal Supplementary Medical Insurance Trust Funds 2020, 174).

Lacking HI's restraints on the limits of its spending authority, Medicare SMI has grown relatively more rapidly in the past and is projected to continue to do so into the indefinite future. SMI surpassed HI in size in 2006 partly because of the addition of a prescription drug benefit to SMI in 2003 legislation, which became effective in 2006. It was politically easier for legislators to finance the prescription drug benefit from the SMI trust fund than from the HI trust fund, the latter of which would have required a substantial increase in the Medicare payroll tax. However, even separate and apart from the prescription drug benefit, SMI has been the more rapidly growing side of Medicare. As recently as 1985, Medicare HI spending was still more than twice as great as SMI spending, while SMI spending, minus spending on prescription drugs, surpassed HI's in 2015 (Boards of Trustees of the Federal Hospital Insurance and Federal Supplementary Medical Insurance Trust Funds 2020, 174).

The relative lack of restraints upon SMI relative to HI spending sometimes tempts legislators to shift costs between the funds, as occurred in 1997 when the Balanced Budget Act (BBA) shifted home health spending from the HI trust fund to the SMI trust fund. As then-Comptroller General David Walker pointed out, "although this shift extended HI Trust Fund solvency, it increased the draw on general revenues and beneficiary SMI premiums while generating little net savings" (Walker 2003). SMI's open tap on general revenues effectively creates an escape hatch for legislators to improve the apparent finances of Medicare without improving total program or federal finances in any meaningful way.

This said, legislators have periodically enacted cost savings measures in both Medicare trust funds that have not only extended HI trust fund solvency but improved the larger federal budget balance. The 1997 BBA that shifted costs from HI to SMI also contained other SMI cost-containment provisions, such that lower costs were projected for SMI after the BBA than before it (Board of Trustees of the Federal Supplementary Medical Insurance Trust Fund 1997, 32, Board of Trustees of the Federal Supplementary Medical Insurance Trust Fund 1998, 42). Legislators have also enacted cost savings mechanisms within Medicare HI to extend its solvency without transferring costs to SMI, such as the provider payment growth restraints included in the Affordable Care Act (ACA) of 2010.

Though HI's financing basis is theoretically similar to Social Security's, and features tighter restraints than SMI's, it has in practice been operated with looser financial standards than Social Security has. The differences between the two patterns demonstrate how much each program's financial evolution has depended on the subjective judgments of influential lawmakers. Whereas Social Security has been managed in the past with an eye toward maintaining its long-range (75-year) solvency, lawmakers have not been nearly so fastidious with Medicare, despite the two programs' financing bases being essentially similar under law.

There are multiple reasons why Medicare's finances have been managed with a more short-term view than Social Security's have been. One is that the contours of Medicare finances are much more uncertain over 75 years, due to the difficulty of projecting health-care cost inflation over such long periods (Boards of Trustees of the Federal Hospital Insurance and Federal Supplementary Insurance Trust Funds 2004, 64, Congressional Research Service 2020).[20] A second is that Medicare HI is but one part of Medicare as a whole: lawmakers have already—unlike with Social Security—accepted the fact that many Medicare benefits will either be financed by income tax payers or by adding to federal debt. Accordingly, it would represent an extreme disjuncture between one side of Medicare and the other, for lawmakers to require that payroll taxes be adequate to fund HI benefits for the next 75 years, while imposing no such requirements on SMI for even one year. This inevitably relaxes long-term vigilance over Medicare finances relative to Social Security's.

Finally, unlike with Social Security, there is no pervasive sentiment with Medicare that one's benefits should be proportional to one's contributions. It is in the nature of health insurance that net benefits will flow to those with health service needs, irrespective of their own individual contributions. As a result, lawmakers have not traditionally focused on constraining Medicare cost burdens sufficiently to ensure that each generation gets its "money's worth" from the program.

For all of the above as well as other reasons, lawmakers have simply patched Medicare HI finances every few years to maintain its solvency just until the next legislated fix. Unlike with Social Security, the long-term solvency of Medicare is never pursued. In all the trustees' reports since 1990, the average amount of time remaining until HI's projected insolvency has been a mere 13 years (Congressional Research Service 2020, 4). As of this writing, HI is projected to be insolvent in a mere six years, in 2026 (Boards of Trustees of the Federal Hospital Insurance and Federal Supplementary Insurance Trust Funds 2020, 4). Again, it bears mentioning that this projection was made prior to the economic contraction precipitated by the COVID-19 pandemic.

This short-term approach to Medicare HI finances paradoxically carries some financial benefits relative to Social Security's long-term management, because it prevents Medicare HI from developing annual deficits anywhere near as large as Social Security's are currently becoming. The dynamic also permits Medicare benefit payments to be adjusted more frequently than has been the case in Social Security. On the other hand, it also means that very little attention is paid to whether Medicare cost growth is stabilized relative to the growth of the federal government's tax base or to U.S. GDP.

In sum, as the story of worsening federal finances is the story of rising entitlement program costs, Medicare's lack of effective cost controls is a large part of the underlying cause, as figure 12.4 illustrates.

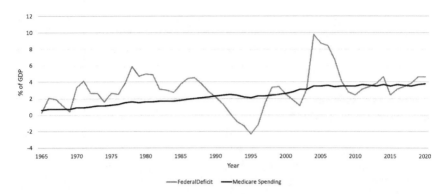

Figure 12.4   Federal Budget Deficits vs. Medicare Spending. Boards of Trustees of the Federal Hospital Insurance and Federal Supplementary Medical Insurance Trust Funds, 2020 Annual Report, and Congressional Budget Office, Historical Budget Data, January 2020.

PERSISTENT FAILURE TO STABILIZE MEDICARE FINANCES

Over the years there have been many efforts to control the growth of Medicare costs and, as with Social Security, these can be divided into process-based reform efforts vs. automatic financial corrections written into Medicare's payment and/or revenue collection formulas. It is fair to say that the approach of automatically adjusting Medicare finances has exhibited occasional successes, although many more such successes would be needed to stabilize Medicare's finances for the long term. Attempts to facilitate reforms by bypassing normal legislative processes, however, have consistently failed.

Among the more successful automatic adjustment mechanisms in Medicare are the provisions enacted in the 1997 Balanced Budget Act indexing Medicare Part B premiums to cover 25% of costs. Prior to 1997 there had been a steady erosion of the share of Part B costs financed through beneficiary premiums, which had started at covering 50% of costs but declined to 23.9% by 1991 (Boards of Trustees of the Federal Hospital Insurance and Federal Supplementary Medical Insurance Trust Funds 2020, 79). A legislative proposal by Congressional Republicans to stabilize the percentage at 31.5%, contained first in the 1995 draft version of the BBA and then in a continuing resolution (CR) later that same year, was one of the reasons cited by President Clinton for his veto of the CR, precipitating a government shutdown (Kahn and Kuttner 1999). Republicans retreated on the premium percentage required of beneficiaries (from 31.5% to 25%) in the 1997 BBA ultimately enacted into law, but the principle of indexing was retained.

The indexing of Part B premiums to hold constant at 25% of total Part B costs is not without its quirks and loopholes, but has proved notably successful in several respects.[21] First and most obviously, it has remained on the books; lawmakers have not acted to shift more costs from beneficiaries to the federal budget by modifying the statute to allow the 25% share to decline. Second, it served as a successful precedent for Medicare's Part D prescription drug benefit, where beneficiaries' premiums are also maintained at a constant percentage of standard drug coverage (25.5%) (Kaiser Family Foundation 2019). Third and perhaps most importantly, it has acted as a rare source of political pressure in the direction of cost containment within a federal entitlement program. Specifically, indexing of beneficiary premiums to overall program costs gives senior advocates a reason to oppose legislative actions (such as increasing provider payments) that raise program costs. The inclusion of beneficiaries among those who feel it when costs rise has proved essential to preventing political pressures on lawmakers from being exerted almost exclusively in a cost-increasing direction.

Similarly durable as an automatic financial maintenance mechanism has been the indexing of Part B deductibles to grow at the same rate as the Part B premiums charged to participating seniors. This indexing was established as part of the 2003 Medicare Modernization Act (MMA), and became effective in 2006 (Centers for Medicare and Medicaid Services 2020).

Other Medicare financing correction provisions that have endured include the income-relating of Part B premiums—that is, requiring higher-income beneficiaries to pay larger premiums for Part B coverage. This income-relating was established in the 2003 MMA, becoming effective in 2007 (Cubanski and Newman 2017). Medicare Part D also has a similar system of premiums, deductibles, and income-relating thresholds, all of which are adjusted annually according to methods set in statute (Kaiser Family Foundation 2019, Centers for Medicare and Medicaid Services 2019).

The unifying principle underlying these various provisions of law is to ensure that the percentage of certain system costs financed by beneficiaries remains relatively constant over time. Such provisions act as a partial brake on federal budget cost growth, even though they are nowhere near strong enough to prevent Medicare from exerting increasing pressure on federal finances. Significantly, these indexing provisions have proved far more durable and successful than simply depending on lawmakers to vote periodically to require additional financial sacrifices of program participants. It is reasonable to surmise that Medicare's as well as Social Security's finances could be further stabilized if additional automatic financing corrections were enacted within each program.

A related approach in recent law, of automatic corrections to the growth of Medicare provider payments, has had mixed results. Among the most notable of these provisions are the provider payment updates under the ACA, currently projected by the Medicare trustees to subtract 1 percentage point each year from the growth of provider payments, compounding to large savings over time (Boards of Trustees of the Federal Hospital Insurance and Federal Supplementary Medical Insurance Trust Funds 2020, 4).

At the time the ACA's provider payment restraints were enacted, some analysts expressed skepticism that they would be upheld over the long term, as they were deemed likely to push rising numbers of health facilities into negative margins (Foster 2011). But the restraints have been upheld over their first decade, even as other controversial provisions of the ACA, such as the Cadillac plan tax and individual insurance purchase mandate, have been repealed (Maurer 2019, Mangan 2018). Even when Congressional Republicans sought to repeal many of the provisions of the ACA in the American Health Care Act in 2017, they did not include the ACA's provider payment updates among those to be repealed (Henry J. Kaiser Foundation 2017). The ACA's provider payment restraints are not by themselves sufficient to stabilize HI costs or prevent HI trust fund insolvency, but they are an example of automatic, gradual adjustments being successfully implemented.

Another provision to gradually constrain provider payment growth, the Sustainable Growth Rate (SGR) formula for Medicare physician payments, is widely regarded as having failed to achieve its cost-containment purposes before it was finally repealed in 2015. Lawmakers began to routinely override the SGR, enacted as part of the 1997 BBA, almost as soon as it began to bite, starting the overrides when the cuts would have been 4–5%, and continuing the overrides past the point where they negated net annual savings of over 25% (Blahous 2019). On the other hand, the Committee for a Responsible Federal Budget has found that SGR successfully forced a nearly equivalent amount of Medicare savings, as lawmakers adopted a habit of legislating offsetting savings whenever SGR was overridden (Committee for a Responsible Federal Budget 2014). In 2015, the SGR was repealed and replaced with an alternative physician payment growth formula under the Medicare Access and CHIP Reauthorization Act of 2015 (MACRA), which eliminated the short-term cuts that would have been required under SGR, but promised even tighter restraints on physician payment growth over the long run (Boards of Trustees of the Federal Hospital Insurance and Federal Supplementary Medical Insurance Trust Funds 2016, 2).

It remains unclear whether a strategy of controlling Medicare cost growth primarily by constraining provider payment growth, without requiring further contributions from beneficiaries, is sustainable over the long term. MACRA's tight long-term restrictions on physician payment growth remain untested. Moreover, the historical pattern of lawmakers offsetting SGR overrides with other payment cuts depended on Congress upholding a policy principle of not simply financing such overrides with federal debt. As these words are being written there is no guarantee that this principle would be upheld in the future, as Congress is currently evincing substantially less concern for debt management than during the years SGR overrides were offset (Congressional Budget Office 2020). In any case, Medicare's financial improvement mechanisms have had their greatest long-term staying power when participating beneficiaries have felt a direct stake in limiting system cost growth.

Automatic adjustments now in place within Medicare are currently insufficient to prevent Medicare HI insolvency or to constrain program cost growth relative to GDP. Accordingly, many experts have developed proposals for additional mechanisms that might stabilize Medicare finances for the long term without relying on perpetually revisited, politically treacherous legislating.

Rudy Penner and Eugene Steuerle have suggested indexing Medicare's eligibility age for changing life expectancy, though savings from this mechanism would be limited unless certain ACA subsidies are simultaneously reformed (Penner and Steuerle 2016).[22] Throughout the years many experts have also voiced support for shifting Medicare to a "premium support" model, in which the federal government would provide a capitated subsidy for each individual as they select from a variety of coverage plans (including privately administered plans), such that the individual faces lower premiums if they opt for a lower-cost plan, and higher premiums if they opt for a higher-cost plan. Variations on the premium support idea have been put forward by former House Speaker Paul Ryan, Senator Ron Wyden, and before them Senator John Breaux and Congressman Bill Thomas (co-chairs of a bipartisan Medicare commission in 1999), as well as by James Capretta (Jacobson and Neuman 2016, Wyden and Ryan 2011, Bettelheim 2018, Nelson 1999, Capretta 2011).

Though for many years premium support was the principle at the core of most bipartisan Medicare financing reform proposals, the concept became intensely politicized in the mid-2010s as opponents equated it with "cutting," "privatizing," or even "killing" or "gutting" Medicare (Kliff 2016, Vinik 2016, Hiltzik 2016). It is unclear whether premium support models can regain the bipartisan support that they once had. It is clear, however, that Medicare's current Fee For Service (FFS) model produces program cost growth that exceeds growth in available financing resources, and further clear that future cost-stabilization mechanisms are unlikely to endure unless they involve participating beneficiaries experiencing at least some of the costs of higher program spending (or put more positively, receiving some of the savings of decelerated program spending).

The enactment, failure, and eventual repeal of the ACA's Independent Payment Advisory Board (IPAB) is emblematic of the failure of the process-based approach to entitlement reform. IPAB was born of policy-makers' mounting frustration with repeated failures to contain the growth of Medicare costs, coupled with the hope that lasting savings could be realized if the process could somehow be moved outside of regular legislative channels. Peter Orszag, an influential advocate for IPAB as Director of the White House Office of Management and Budget when the ACA was enacted, expressed hopeful optimism that IPAB would "take some of the politics out" of necessary efforts to reform Medicare to slow cost growth (Orszag 2011). Similar hopes of transcending politics underpinned the establishments of the Breaux-Thomas National Bipartisan Commission on the Future of Medicare, the Obama administration's Simpson-Bowles commission, and the subsequent Deficit Reduction committee established under the 2011 BCA, which also ended in failure.

There is a contradiction at the heart of all similar efforts, in that they all involve elected legislators seeking to retain credit for preserving the benefits that federal entitlement programs offer, while outsourcing blame for any cost-containment measures required in the course of operating them. What happens instead is that the political pressures, instead of dissipating, are simply transmuted into a different form: into clashes over the rules by which such commissions and boards will operate, and over who will be appointed to them. Consequently, such processes tend to replicate the partisan gridlock within Congress that caused the board or commission to be appointed in the first place. The Breaux-Thomas, Simpson-Bowles, and BCA commissions all failed to report recommendations with the levels of support their respective charters required, while IPAB's membership was never even appointed before its repeal (Spatz 2018).

Long before its demise, the IPAB as enacted into law was hardly untouched by politics. The statutory text establishing IPAB specified that it not make any recommendations that would "increase Medicare beneficiary cost-sharing (including deductibles, coinsurance, and copayments), or otherwise restrict benefits or modify eligibility criteria," even if IPAB's members concluded that such measures were necessary (Patient Protection and Affordable Care Act Text 2010, 372). Thus, from its outset, IPAB reflected the policy and political preferences of its authors, rather than freeing the process of containing Medicare costs from political pressures and considerations.

As a political gambit IPAB failed for many reasons, among them the fact that both Republicans and Democrats feared that IPAB would ultimately embody a fast-track for implementing policies they opposed (U.S. Court of Appeals, Ninth Circuit 2014).[23] These bipartisan fears reinforced one another, even if the specific policies feared may have been entirely different on the Republican and Democratic sides. The intensifying bipartisan opposition to IPAB contrasted with a relative lack of resistance to the provider payment restraints also contained in the ACA. Those restraints, once enacted into law, represented a specific policy choice in which a congressional majority had already invested itself, accepted and had less reason to revisit.

Ian Spatz puts it well in a *Health Affairs* article:

> at their core, "good government" ideas to evade the messiness of the political process in the interest of better and more efficient governance (such as IPAB) are felled by the sharp knives of the political process itself. Powerful interests— whether they be providers or beneficiaries—do not want to relinquish their ability to appeal to political actors for relief. (Spatz 2018)

Moreover, in the case of IPAB, some doubted that Congress could constitutionally outsource these powers in the first place (U.S. Court of Appeals, Ninth Circuit 2014). Regardless of the reasons for opposition, the same fate has met multiple efforts to create channels to bypass political processes in the course of developing and implementing Medicare cost-saving policies, including not only IPAB but also the Breaux-Thomas National Bipartisan Commission on the Future of Medicare, or the recommendations of the Medicare Payment Advisory Commission (MedPac), which Congress "generally ignores" (Penner and Steuerle 2016). In sum, no reliable way has been discovered to remove politics from the administration of government-run health-care programs. The only apparent way to do so is to directly limit the government health program itself.

Another example of a frustrated effort to create an expedited process for producing and implementing Medicare cost savings is the trustees' funding warning. By law, the Medicare trustees must determine whether more than 45% of Medicare's total revenues are projected to come from general revenues in any of the next seven years, with such findings in two consecutive years producing a warning (Blahous 2014). In the event of such a warning, the law specifies that the president must submit a proposal in response, unless Congress enacts legislation to eliminate the excess general revenue funding. Congress must then give expedited consideration to the president's proposal. Despite the trustees repeatedly issuing such warnings—in each of the years of 2007–2013 as well as 2017–2020—only one presidential proposal has been submitted in response (by President George W. Bush in 2007), and presidential administrations have generally ignored them while arguing that requiring such a proposal is unconstitutional (Congressional Research Service 2020, Boards of Trustees of the Federal Hospital Insurance and Federal Supplementary Insurance Trust Funds 2020, 7).

In sum, the lack of fiscal rules governing the larger federal budget is partially reflective of the absence of rules constraining the growth of Medicare. The different sides of Medicare operate under different financing principles, with Medicare HI managed with an eye toward preserving its solvency for only a few years at a time, and almost no meaningful constraints operating on SMI cost growth at all.

Automatic financial correction mechanisms somewhat constrain the growth of Medicare costs, but not nearly enough to stabilize them as a share of U.S. economic output. Some automatic adjustment mechanisms, such as indexing Part B premiums to the growth of program costs, have proved sustainable, while there have been mixed results with provisions to gradually slow the growth of payments to health providers. Efforts to shift political responsibility for cost savings decisions to independent boards and commissions have consistently failed. Unless and until Medicare finances are subject to automatic correction mechanisms written into law, which limit program cost growth so as not to exceed the rate of growth in the U.S. government's revenue base, Medicare will continue to exert a worsening influence on the federal fiscal imbalance.

MEDICAID

Medicaid is a health insurance program covering low-income individuals, established in federal law, administered by the states, and jointly financed by federal and state governments. It is the third largest federal entitlement program after Social Security and Medicare. CBO identifies Medicaid, along with Social Security and Medicare, as one of the leading drivers of the structural federal deficit (Congressional Budget Office 2019, 20).

Unlike Social Security and Medicare HI, spending in Medicaid is not limited to the assets credited to any particular trust fund. As with Medicare SMI, Medicaid spending may exceed the amounts that particular tax collections can finance, meaning that rising Medicaid spending can be (and is) added to federal deficits. Unlike with Medicare, Medicaid's low-income participants are typically exempted from premiums and out-of-pocket costs (Medicaid.gov 2021). Although states make expansion decisions and are responsible for enrollment, the majority of Medicaid costs are borne by the federal government: specifically, the federal government shouldered an average of 57% of the costs of insuring individuals who were eligible before the ACA's Medicaid expansion, and it funds 90% of the costs of insuring the ACA's expansion population (Blahous 2013). This cost-sharing creates enormous incentives for the states to enroll individuals in Medicaid in the manner that maximizes federal support.

These incentives and financing structure have led to a predictable result: Medicaid spending has grown persistently relative to growth in U.S. GDP, and occasional program expansions have only added to that growth (Blahous

2013, 32–33). Because Medicaid spending growth is not generally accompanied by growth in revenues from any particular tax, rising Medicaid spending places intensifying pressure on the federal budget (see figure 12.5).

More specifically, the skewed incentives and complex structure of Medicaid have been shown to be inhospitable to conscientious fiscal stewardship. Administrative costs are much higher in Medicaid than they are in Medicare, while Medicaid history encompasses a long-running battle between the federal and state governments over the techniques states employ to shift costs to the federal ledger (Boards of Trustees of the Federal Hospital Insurance and Federal Supplementary Medical Insurance Trust Funds 2020, 10, Department of Health and Human Services 2018, 13, Blase 2016). The ACA's 90% federal match rate for the expansion population exacerbated many of these incentive problems, leading to per-capita spending on the expansion population exceeding prior projections by more than 50%, and to an estimated 18–27% of those covered under expansion being improperly enrolled, ineligible individuals (Blahous and Amez-Droz 2020, Blase and Yelowitz 2019, 9). These trends result simultaneously in inefficiencies in how well the program serves vulnerable populations, and in rising costs to the federal budget.

These various forces contribute to Medicaid's role in a worsening federal budget picture. No requirement of actuarial balance, no limitation on spending authority, compels Medicaid financing corrections, while elected officials are often reluctant to seek savings from a program that serves the poor. Medicaid spending was already growing at unsustainable rates even before expansion under the ACA but still Congressional Republicans, who had previously opposed the expansion, were unable to muster the votes to repeal it once they gained the congressional majority (Pear, Kaplan and

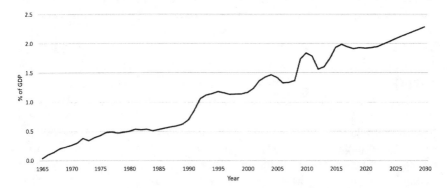

Figure 12.5 Historical/Projected Medicaid Spending. Congressional Budget Office, Historical Budget Data, January 2020, and Congressional Budget Office, 10-Year Budget Projections, January, 2020, https://www.cbo.gov/about/products/budget-economic-data#2.

Cochrane 2017). When Congress and the Obama administration later set up a special Deficit Reduction Committee along with a process to automatically cut ("sequester") federal spending if it could not reach agreement, Medicaid was conspicuously exempted from the sequestration process (Kogan 2012).

This is not to say that legislators have never agreed on the need to control Medicaid spending growth. More typically, they simply disagree on how to do so, with the positions of the political parties often shifting as they assume different responsibilities. During the Clinton administration, congressional Republicans supported converting Medicaid funding to state block grants, which would have provided states a specified amount of funding to provide low-income health insurance, while eliminating the individual entitlement to benefits. The Clinton administration countered with a proposal to cap Medicaid spending per capita, while retaining the individual entitlement to benefits. Both sides agreed on the need to cap the growth of federal Medicaid spending, while they strongly disagreed on how to do it.

By the time of the Obama administration, congressional Republicans had gravitated to supporting per-capita Medicaid spending growth caps, which the Obama administration opposed (Badger 2017). The shift of each party relative to its previous position is reflective of the general political trend of recent years, of declining commitment to containing the growth of federal spending and deficits. In recent months, some have even called for further increasing federal support for Medicaid to help states during the pandemic, treating the federal government's relative lack of fiscal boundaries as a policy advantage (Fiedler and Powell 2020).

As the third largest federal entitlement program, and one which tends to grow significantly faster than U.S. economic output, Medicaid is a major contributor to the worsening federal fiscal imbalance, with even fewer financial constraints upon it than either Social Security or Medicare has. It is unlikely that the federal budget picture can be stabilized without reforms to contain the growth of federal Medicaid costs.

TAX EXPENDITURES AND OTHER ENTITLEMENT PROGRAMS

In principle, the lack of constraints on the growth of spending in any federal entitlement program is a fiscal problem. In practice, mandatory spending apart from Social Security and the major health entitlements has declined relative to GDP in recent years, and CBO projects it will continue to decline in the future. This is primarily because, while many of these other entitlement programs are indexed to grow automatically under current law, they do not tend to grow as rapidly as U.S. economic output. If similar policies governed the larger federal entitlement programs of Social Security, Medicare, and Medicaid, the federal fiscal imbalance would become manageable (Congressional Budget Office 2019, 27).

The growth of tax expenditures (defined as "revenue losses attributable to provisions of the Federal tax laws which allow a special exclusion, exemption, or deduction from gross income or which provide a special credit, a preferential rate of tax, or a deferral of tax liability") also contributes to the federal fiscal imbalance (U.S. Department of the Treasury 2021). Tax expenditures can act as the functional equivalent of spending through the tax code, steering financial benefits to politically favored constituencies and activities, worsening federal deficits, and increasing the tax rates necessary to finance a given level of federal spending. Lawmakers representing constituencies who oppose increases in direct federal spending sometimes find it politically convenient to deliver the same benefits through the tax code. Since the 1986 tax reforms that clamped down on tax expenditures by lowering rates and eliminating loopholes, tax expenditures have grown faster than GDP (Marples 2015, 7–8).

The persistent growth of tax expenditures and their worsening effects on the federal fiscal imbalance have led some budget reformers to propose automatically constraining their growth. Penner and Steuerle suggest that "in addition to applying triggers to spending programs, policymakers can apply them to tax expenditures" (Penner and Steuerle 2016). Regardless of how federal legislators choose to deal with this issue, it is clear that to the extent federal tax expenditures automatically grow faster than GDP in the absence of future legislation, it will become progressively more difficult to stabilize the federal budget. The absence of automatic fiscal correction mechanisms in tax expenditures, as with mandatory spending, is an impediment to a sustainable fiscal policy.

AUTOMATIC STABILIZERS IN THE
GENERAL FEDERAL BUDGET

Although the focus of this chapter is the lack of automatic correction mechanisms in federal entitlement programs, this treatment of the subject cannot be complete without discussing efforts to establish automatic corrections for the larger federal budget, and how these have treated entitlements.

Brian Riedl identifies a "penalty default" (i.e., fiscal corrections that will automatically occur in the absence of new legislation) as a key ingredient in successful budget deals (Riedl 2019). Over the years, various deficit reduction agreements have conspicuously exempted most entitlements from such automatic spending-cut "penalty defaults" that enforce agreed-upon budget targets.

For example, Riedl identifies the 1985 Gramm-Rudman-Hollings (GRH) law as achieving more savings relative to GDP (1.7%) than any other budget deal in the last 40 years. This legislation established an automatic correction mechanism consisting of across-the-board spending cuts (known as "sequestration") which would take effect to hit prescribed budget targets unless legislators enacted other legislation to do the job. The sequestration process exempted most entitlements as well as taxes, which meant that the automatic enforcement mechanism almost exclusively targeted annually appropriated spending. Though GRH was successful in the context of its time, it stands as an example of, rather than a corrective to, current trends in which entitlement spending growth drives federal deficit growth, while annually appropriated spending shrinks in relative terms.[24]

The sequestration required under GRH was eventually terminated pursuant to the 1990 budget deal, which raised taxes (breaking President George H.W. Bush's "no new taxes" campaign pledge) and created new "pay-go" rules requiring that any new tax cuts or entitlement expansions be offset, but which did not enforce prescribed fiscal targets (Riedl 2019). In most subsequent years there has been a similar absence of automatic fiscal corrections, contributing to the mounting budget deficits seen today.

After Republicans assumed control of both chambers of Congress in 1995 for the first time in 40 years, thereupon ensued an unusual effort to enact a BBA, which many of the new officeholders had endorsed during their 1994 election campaigns. Despite its name, and due to constitutional constraints, the BBA as introduced was less a system of automatic corrections to the budget than it was a set of process requirements, and so will be discussed in the next section of this chapter.

Here it is worth noting that when efforts to enact the BBA began, it almost immediately became entangled with Social Security politics. Several Senators who had campaigned in favor of the BBA switched their votes to oppose the version that was introduced, based on the argument that unless Social Security was explicitly excluded, the BBA would tempt Congress to cut Social Security benefits. This led to the introduction of an alternative BBA proposal excluding the Social Security trust fund "from the balanced budget calculation" (Strahilevitz 1998).

In the end, the BBA failed to receive the necessary two-thirds vote in the Senate (Congressional Research Service 2018). It is not important here to settle the issue of whether Social Security should have been included or excluded in the BBA, or whether it is even permissible to reference a specific statutory program in the Constitution. The critical point for our purposes is that the BBA, like so many other attempts at establishing automatic fiscal corrections, foundered in large part on the issue of excluding entitlement programs from enforcement mechanisms.

The peculiar relationship between entitlement program finances and those of the larger federal budget was further reflected in a subsequent echo of the BBA/Social Security debate, when the Clinton administration later proposed to devote an impending federal budget surplus to "save Social Security first" (Clinton 1998). The Clinton proposal was essentially a political maneuver to block congressional Republicans from enacting tax cuts; specifically, the administration proposed to credit federal surplus revenues to the Social Security trust funds. There were a number of substantive flaws in the Clinton approach, one being that it effectively double-credited Social Security for its surplus' role in improving the federal budget balance, another being that it would not have improved the financial operations of Social Security itself (for a fuller explanation, see the contemporaneous testimony of Comptroller General David Walker, which among other things noted that "benefit costs and revenues currently associated with (Social Security) will not be affected by even 1 cent" under the Clinton proposal) (Walker 1999). It was innovative, however, in that it attempted to harness the political sensitivities surrounding entitlement programs, which usually worsen the federal fiscal position, to improve it instead.

The Clinton administration proposal would not have constituted an automatic fiscal correction mechanism of the type explored in this chapter. It was merely a proposal to run federal budget surpluses, reduce publicly held debt, and to issue additional debt to the Social Security trust funds—all discretionary policies that could have been altered or discontinued at any time without triggering automatic alternative fiscal corrections. Most importantly for purposes of this chapter, the Clinton administration proposal would have attempted to improve the federal budget outlook without addressing its underlying stressor in the form of cost growth of the largest federal entitlements.

For several years afterward there was an absence of widely supported proposals for mechanisms to automatically reduce federal budget deficits. The most significant one was the automatic sequestration enacted along with the Joint Select Committee on Deficit Reduction, established as part of the 2011 BCA (House Committee on the Budget 2011). The Obama administration and congressional Republican majorities had been unable to agree on policies to reduce projected federal deficits, so instead they deputized a bipartisan commission to negotiate fiscal corrections. The automatic sequestration mechanism was established as a backup process, a means of ensuring that the deficit reduction would still occur even if the committee failed.

Neither political party hoped or intended that sequestration would actually be the means of achieving fiscal corrections in 2011. Sequestration was developed as a deliberately unpalatable outcome, to motivate the members of the committee to overcome their differences and generate an agreement

(Khimm 2012).[25] Once again, this sequestration largely exempted the entitlement programs that are driving mounting federal deficits (Riedl 2019). For this reason and many others, deficit hawks were largely unenthusiastic about relying on sequestration to improve the fiscal outlook (Committee for a Responsible Federal Budget 2013). Former CBO director Doug Holtz-Eakin, when testifying tepidly in favor of the sequestration mechanism, referred to it as "a bad idea whose time has come" (Holtz-Eakin 2013).

The BCA did succeed in temporarily reducing budget deficits, but given the lack of enthusiasm for the BCA's sequestration mechanism, it is unsurprising that its spending caps were later raised in subsequent budget deals, most notably the Bipartisan Budget Act of 2019 (Committee for a Responsible Federal Budget 2020). No current law compels that spending on entitlements or in other areas of the budget be constrained sufficiently to move the federal budget toward a sustainable trajectory.

These historical episodes serve to remind that analysts confront a difficult "chicken and egg" problem when identifying causes and solutions for the federal government's increasing fiscal imprudence. It is impossible to know with certainty whether the failure to control the growth of entitlement spending is more of a cause or a symptom of federal lawmakers' broader failure to contain mounting federal deficits. These alternative possibilities are not mutually exclusive; indeed, rising entitlement spending is likely both a cause and a symptom of deepening fiscal lassitude.

That said, the history is suggestive that the uncontrolled growth of federal entitlement programs contributes directly to sapping federal lawmakers' commitment to maintaining fiscal balance. For example, lawmakers remained willing to persistently diminish annually appropriated spending, including both defense and domestic spending, as a percentage of both the federal budget and the U.S. economy. Federal deficits nevertheless rose despite these restraints, due to the increasing share of federal spending that transpired automatically through entitlement spending programs.

In addition, multiple attempts to impose overarching budget constraints, such as the sequestration mechanisms in the GRH law, and those which followed the failure of the 2011 Deficit Reduction committee, have largely exempted entitlement spending. Such exemptions led to the temporary fiscal gains under these processes being unraveled later, largely because the mechanisms depended unrealistically on the required cuts all being concentrated within an already shrinking portion of federal spending. A different attempt to impose overarching fiscal targets, the balanced budget amendment initiative of the 1990s, also foundered largely on the issue of whether to exempt the largest federal entitlement program, Social Security. Taken together, this history is highly suggestive that successful entitlement program reforms may be more likely to increase the likelihood of lawmakers setting and maintaining general fiscal policy rules, than that setting global fiscal targets is by itself likely to spur overdue entitlement program reforms.

Some experts have proposed that entitlement spending caps be enacted as part of general budget reform, to be enforced by sequestration if necessary. James Capretta correctly observes that currently "entitlement spending is never held to a firm budget," and that, despite the federal government's successfully holding down spending on appropriated/discretionary spending over the years (see figure 2), the federal budget imbalance is worsening because no similar discipline has been applied to entitlement programs. Because of this, he argues for a new joint budget resolution process which makes "caps on spending binding, including on entitlement spending" (Capretta 2015).[26]

Brian Riedl has proposed the creation of a two-sided automatic fiscal stabilization process—one that automatically generates additional stimulus spending during recessions, coupled with automatic fiscal consolidation provisions that would take effect during good economic times (Riedl 2020). Riedl notes several advantages of such an approach, including lessening temptations for legislators to derail "must-pass" recession relief bills with unrelated spending wants and other policy fights, and locking in deficit reduction during boom times instead of merely hoping that legislators will eventually get around to it.

Irrespective of the advantages and disadvantages of any specific approach, it is clear from this historical review that fiscal correction mechanisms are more likely to be implemented when they occur on autopilot, and when they do not depend on repeated, increasingly elusive success in cobbling together a legislative coalition for deficit reduction. This is likely to be even truer going forward, when our politics are so polarized and when partisan advocates often have louder megaphones on social media than non-partisan budget analysts (Opensecrets.org 2021, Congressional Budget Office 2019). A well-crafted automatic fiscal correction mechanism in law would probably do more to stabilize federal budgets than the sum of all future persuasion by deficit-reduction advocates.

AUTOMATIC PROCESS SOLUTIONS

In recent decades, there have been countless attempts to establish processes to expedite fiscal corrections while bypassing the normal legislative order. These efforts have consistently failed.

The 1983 Social Security amendments are often held up as a process success story, in which a special bipartisan commission paved the way for legislative action to shore up Social Security finances and, as a byproduct, to improve the federal fiscal outlook. Certain caveats must be raised about what the 1983 experience tells us about the utility of process-based solutions. First, the commission's approach has been persistently unsuccessful with respect to the larger federal budget and, as described in an earlier section of this chapter, was only able to facilitate action in 1983 because of the personal policy values of key legislators, and also because Social Security's operating deficits at that time were small enough to be surmountable.

In addition, the 1983 amendments were not enacted by circumventing the normal rules of legislative consideration. The Senate debated the amendments under an "informal rule" imposed by Majority Leader Robert Dole (R-KS, requiring that the pending legislation could only be amended by another plan equally effective in improving long-term solvency (Penner 2014). Apart from such informal restrictions, normal legislative procedures were followed. Thus, even in the 1983 experience, there is nothing to suggest that creating special fast-track legislative procedures will enable the messy process of bipartisan negotiation to be outsourced to a body independent of Congress (Mann 2019).[27]

Efforts to set up expedited processes for deficit reduction have been legion over the last few decades. In 1993, Senator Robert Kerrey (D-NE) extracted a promise from President Clinton to appoint a commission on entitlement and tax reform, when Kerrey voted for President Clinton's budget proposal despite regarding it as omitting critical entitlement reforms (Rosenbaum 1993). The resulting Bipartisan Commission on Entitlement and Tax Reform had no especial legislative authority and required a three-fifths vote to report recommendations (Clinton 1993). The commission, working throughout 1994, was unable to reach agreement on a reform plan (Social Security Bulletin 1995).

As previously mentioned, the BBA that failed of passage in 1995 was less an automatically self-correcting mechanism than an elaborate process for attaining budget balance. It simply declared that federal debt held by the public should not increase, and that outlays should not exceed receipts, except in certain special circumstances (e.g., war) or unless a supermajority (3/5) of each chamber of Congress so voted (Congressional Record 1995). Significantly, the text of the amendment did not specify what kind of corrections would occur to bring the budget into balance; it would simply have established new processes making it more difficult for Congress to run federal deficits. The amendment was defeated when it failed to receive the necessary two-thirds support in the U.S. Senate.

The 1999 Breaux-Thomas National Bipartisan Commission on the Future of Medicare was not a general budget reform commission, and was instead dedicated specifically to Medicare reform. The commission was established by the 1997 Balanced Budget Act and directed to report such recommendations as were supported by 11 of its 17 members (Congressional Research Service 1997). It concluded in failure when the Clinton administration instructed its representatives on the commission to vote against the plan it had developed (Pear 1999).

As deficits mounted during the Great Recession of 2007–2009, proposals arose to establish a bipartisan deficit reduction commission. Congressmen Frank Wolf (R-VA) and Jim Cooper (D-TN) introduced one such proposal, the "SAFE Commission," while in the Senate, Senators Judd Gregg (R-NH) and Kent Conrad (D-ND) proposed their own Deficit Reduction Commission early in 2010 (Committee for a Responsible Federal Budget 2009, NPR 2010). The common denominator of these proposals was to establish a bipartisan commission including members of Congress as well as some representatives of the federal executive branch, whose recommendations would automatically be granted expedited consideration by Congress.

As President Clinton had done in response to coaxing by Senator Kerrey, President Obama appointed a bipartisan commission largely reflective of the Conrad-Gregg approach. The National Commission on Fiscal Responsibility and Reform, co-chaired by former Senator Alan Simpson and Erskine Bowles, needed to garner support from 14 of its 18 members to approve recommendations to Congress (Obama 2010). It failed to do so, with 11 members of the committee supporting the chairmen's proposal on its final vote in December 2010 (Sahadi 2010).

The earlier mentioned Joint Select Committee on Deficit Reduction, created in 2011, also failed to pass a deficit-reduction plan, bringing into effect a fail-safe sequestration of discretionary appropriations that neither Republicans nor Democrats favored (Barrett, Bolduan, and Walsh 2011).

In the current Congress, another bipartisan process approach has been introduced: the TRUST Act, authored principally by Senator Mitt Romney with companion sponsors in both parties and both chambers (Romney 2019). The TRUST act differs from several of its predecessors in focusing specifically on trust fund spending programs such as Social Security and Medicare, whose growth correlates with the growth of federal deficits. It may be that by focusing on the concept of trust fund solvency, the cosponsors of the TRUST Act hope to ward off accusations of balancing the federal budget on the backs of vulnerable beneficiaries of the federal safety net, which have undercut previous fiscal commissions. Regardless, the TRUST Act has not advanced to floor consideration in either chamber of Congress.

A notable feature common to many of the failed commissions is a supermajority vote requirement: such a requirement helped cause the defeat of proposals developed by the Kerrey-Danforth commission, the Breaux-Thomas commission, and the Simpson-Bowles commission.[28] Though undoubtedly included to ensure that any proposal developed by these commissions would have bipartisan support, the result is that it has been even more difficult to move budget proposals through the commissions than it has been through

Congress. On the other hand, the 2011 Deficit Reduction Committee had only a majority-vote requirement, and it also failed.

No lasting corrections to the structural fiscal imbalance can avoid slowing the growth of entitlement programs, which means that there must either be a reliable process for reducing federal deficits that facilitates restraints on entitlement spending growth, or there must be statutory corrections embedded in the laws governing federal entitlement programs themselves. Without one of these two mechanisms in place, it seems apparent that no purely process-based approach to fiscal reform will succeed in correcting the worsening budget imbalance.

CONCLUSION

There is an absence of fiscal rules guiding U.S. federal budget policy. The worsening federal fiscal imbalance reflects no deliberate policy plan to run increasing federal deficits. It is simply an artifact of the asymmetric structure of the federal budget process: specifically, a process in which automatic growth in federal entitlement spending can drive worsening federal budgets without any intervening votes by lawmakers—and does. It is also a process in which there are substantial procedural barriers to reducing federal deficits, barriers that are only becoming taller as politics become more polarized and bipartisan agreements more elusive. It is probably not a coincidence that partisan divisions have become wider as the gap between federal revenues and outlays has become wider. The widening fiscal gap makes bipartisan compromise more difficult.

U.S. budget deficits have worsened as federal entitlement spending has grown, and are projected to become uncontrollable—while at the same time, federal revenue collections are projected to exceed historical norms, and annually appropriated federal spending is shrinking far below historical norms relative to GDP. The only paths to sustainable federal finances involve slowing the growth of the largest federal entitlement programs of Social Security, Medicare, and Medicaid.

At present, there are no guarantees that Social Security and Medicare's trust fund financing structures will by themselves ensure that lawmakers act effectively to stabilize the rising costs of those programs. Medicare's financing construct permits lawmakers to shift rising program costs increasingly to premium-paying beneficiaries and to federal taxpayers, without constraining the worsening pressure Medicare places on federal finances. Social Security's finances have not been corrected in 37 years, and federal lawmakers are showing increased willingness to evade historical restraints on shifting costs from Social Security's payroll tax base to the larger federal budget. Medicaid spending growth is virtually unbound by any meaningful restraints.

The historical evidence indicates that the problem of rising federal entitlement cost growth will likely remain insoluble so long as solutions depend on lawmakers repeatedly cobbling together legislative majorities to enact financing corrections piecemeal. As the historical review in this chapter shows, fiscal corrections are more likely to hold if they are implemented automatically and gradually, such that legislative negotiations henceforth can focus on improving the operations of these programs rather than on the politically difficult tasks of raising taxes and slowing the growth of costs. This approach would flip the "default" outcome to a path of fiscal stability rather than instability, potentially transforming the political economy dynamics governing U.S. budget policy. More specifically, the evidence indicates that corrections are more likely to endure if program beneficiaries as well as taxpayers feel a financial stake in constraining program cost growth (as with, for example, the successful indexation of Medicare Part B and D premiums to overall program cost growth).

Promising approaches to fiscal improvement include enacting automatic stabilizers to index such factors as payroll tax rates, benefit formula growth rates, eligibility ages, and participation criteria so that specific entitlement program costs and revenues remain stable as a percentage of GDP.

Far less promising as an approach are purely process-based reforms, such as outsourcing the task of developing fiscal reforms to independent boards and commissions. The historical evidence suggests that these avenues simply replicate partisan divides in Congress rather than bypassing them.

NOTES

1. The author wishes to thank Brian Riedl, Doug Badger, Keith Hennessey, Barry Poulson, and Marvin Phaup for useful comments on a previous draft of this chapter.

2. Although the three programs of Social Security, Medicare, and Medicaid are the principal drivers of this spending growth, for purposes of simplification certain graphs in this chapter separate federal spending components into the broad categories of mandatory/entitlement spending and discretionary/appropriated spending. As explained later in this chapter, mandatory spending apart from Social Security, Medicare, and Medicaid has declined relative to GDP in recent years, and CBO projects it will continue to decline in the future. In its long-term budget projections, CBO focuses on Social Security and the "major health care programs" as the main drivers of the structural deficit.

3. January 2020 figures have been used in all instances to preserve consistency.

4. Every combination of partisan control of the presidency and Congress (R/R, D/D, D/R and R/D) has resulted in rising debt, such that it would be ill-founded to

assign responsibility to one party more than the other. This said, in the interest of adequately qualifying the statement in the main text about the persistence of debt accumulation, it should be noted that the most recent period during which the federal debt declined substantially relative to GDP was during the second term of the Clinton administration (1997–2001), when a Democratic president worked with a Republican Congress. The last period during which federal debt stabilized as a percentage of GDP (2004–2007) was mostly in the second term of the George W. Bush administration, when a Republican president served with a Republican Congress, before the onset of the Great Recession. Lest one is tempted to derive a pattern from these brief periods of fiscal stability under Republican Congresses, it should be noted that the most recent two years of Republican control of both branches (2017–2019) are among the many periods of rising federal debt.

5. January 2020 projections have been used throughout this chapter to preserve consistency. Mandatory spending shown on the graph represents gross spending, without subtracting offsetting revenues such as Medicare premium collections. Pursuant to congressional scorekeeping practices, CBO projections for the federal budget do not strictly reflect actual law, because they do not incorporate the substantial reductions in Social Security and Medicare spending that would occur upon the projected depletions of their respected trust funds. CBO projections are nevertheless reflective of these entitlement programs' contributions to the federal fiscal imbalance, because they reflect the substantial imbalance between these programs' benefit obligations and their revenues, and also because there is no assurance that these programs' trust fund shortfalls will be closed without recourse to general revenue subsidies or without spending the proceeds of such savings on other programs, as congressional budget rules permit. Indeed, federal budget practice over the last decade exhibits a declining commitment to financing these entitlement programs without recourse to such maneuvers, as for example with the Affordable Care Act of 2010 and the Social Security payroll tax cut of 2011–2012.

6. Short-term increases in annual deficits can and do result from occasional tax cuts or increases in annually appropriated discretionary spending. Examining the long-term trend, however, renders it clear that structural deficit growth is driven by the rise of entitlement spending rather than by discretionary spending or tax policy.

7. The spectrum of legislators' policy views also includes a growing number who question the imperative of addressing fiscal imbalances at all. This adds to the difficulty of repeatedly forging legislative coalitions to achieve deficit reduction.

8. This is even more true for believers in Modern Monetary Theory (MMT), which holds that most deficit-reduction efforts are inherently misguided and literally do result in income losses for individual Americans, relative to the standards of living they could enjoy if the federal government borrowed and spent more. It exceeds the scope of this chapter to settle the escalating argument between MMT supporters and mainstream economists, and the text focuses instead on how any lasting reduction in federal deficits that lawmakers may wish to achieve will require changes in how federal entitlement programs are managed.

9. The 1977 Social Security amendments did eliminate larger annual imbalances that resulted from an error in the indexing formula enacted in 1972, but these were

then projected over a far more distant future than lawmakers would face if they waited until the 2030s to act.

10. The author served as a public trustee at that time.

11. Note that Social Security benefit payments must be made from separate and solvent trust funds, and that Social Security's OASI trust fund is projected to become insolvent in 2034. To simplify, the main text refers to dates and numerical effects for Social Security's theoretical combined trust funds, as is done in the annual trustees' report overview.

12. Myers: "I'm still an 'infinity' guy, because even if you have a 75 year period, every year you do a new valuation, you have some slippage. If conditions were exactly the same, the assumptions were not changed, and the experience was just like the assumptions, the evaluation made later would show, if it was in balance in Year One, by Year Two it would be out of balance by a tiny amount, say .05% of payroll."

13. The formula used to calculate initial Social Security benefit levels, known as the Primary Insurance Amount (PIA), is automatically adjusted each year by statute, proportionally with growth in the national AWI as calculated by the Social Security Administration. As a result of this indexing, a beneficiary who has earned the national average wage income, who is eligible to claim benefits in a particular year, would typically expect to have a benefit that is larger than that of another beneficiary who had also earned the national average wage income, who became eligible to claim benefits the previous year. The difference between these two individuals' respective benefit levels reflects intervening growth in the AWI. For purposes of benefit calculation, SSA indexes an individual's prior earnings to the AWI until two years before they are eligible to claim old-age benefits.

14. There is some improvement in Social Security finances under a faster-growth scenario but it is relatively slight; the program's qualitative shortfall persists mostly unchanged under any realistic growth projection scenario. For example, even if future real wage growth is over 50% faster than the trustees currently project, it would still leave the preponderance of the program's actuarial imbalance in place.

15. Enacting financial corrections to a trust fund while simultaneously spending the resultant unified budget savings on a new program, as was done in the ACA, has fiscal effects equivalent to shoring up a trust fund simply by issuing debt from the general fund, without increasing total revenues, reducing total spending, or improving the unified budget balance. By contrast, entitlement reforms can improve the larger fiscal outlook if trust fund financing corrections are not otherwise spent, a principle that was upheld in 1983.

16. Revisions to demographic data and projections since the 1983 reforms have slightly improved the actuarial balance, by 3% of the current shortfall. Of the existing shortfall, 67% has arisen because Social Security operations under law grow more imbalanced over time, and another 36% because of adjustments in economic projections. These two factors by themselves account for the entirety of the shortfall that has emerged since 1983.

17. Myers: "It wasn't planned. Nobody said let's do it this way. It was just the natural result of saying we'll fix up the long-range situation in 75 years on the average."

18. Social Security's long-range actuarial balance is more sensitive to changes in fertility rates than to nearly any other factor, demographic or economic. The approximate effects of changes in fertility rates upon subsequent tax collections and benefit payments can be anticipated many years, if not decades, in advance.

19. It is sometimes argued that Social Security cannot contribute to the federal budget deficit because of its off-budget self-financing trust fund design. This argument is incorrect, for reasons that go beyond the scope of this chapter to explain, but which can be briefly summarized as follows. First, Social Security's actuarial balance requirement is an average condition over time, and does not speak to Social Security's effects on the federal budget in individual years. Social Security's effects on the federal budget were positive throughout most of the 1980s, 1990s, and 2000s, when the program was running cash surpluses, but have been negative since 2010 when it has been running operating deficits. Federal budget deficits have grown accordingly as Social Security has moved from surplus to deficit. Second, lawmakers can act to subsidize Social Security from the general fund, as was done in 2011–2012 when the payroll tax was cut, and which some have proposed be done in the future to prevent trust fund depletion. Third, the federal fiscal imbalance as projected by the Congressional Budget Office, the White House Office and Management and Budget, and others, includes Social Security's financing shortfall, and so by definition Social Security's own shortfalls contribute to that larger fiscal imbalance.

20. Due to changes in general health-care cost projections, Medicare's financial outlook can change markedly from one year to the next. To take but one example, between the 2003 and 2004 trustees' reports, Medicare HI's actuarial deficit increased by 30%, and its projected insolvency date moved seven years sooner, primarily because of updated assumptions with respect to hospital spending. Since 1997, there have been six different annual reports in which HI's projected insolvency date has moved by five or more years relative to the previous year's projection.

21. Most beneficiaries are held harmless from Part B premium increases that exceed the size of their Social Security COLA, meaning that in zero-COLA years they experience no premium increase at all. But some beneficiaries (those who are subject to income-related premiums, as well as those whose premiums are paid by Medicaid) are not included in these hold-harmless provisions, which means that during low-inflation or zero-inflation years, as aggregate premiums grow to remain 25% of costs, certain beneficiaries' premiums may grow disproportionately.

22. The reason savings would be relatively small is that some of those who would not be eligible for Medicare under revised age criteria would become eligible for other federal subsidies, such as tax credits for those covered under the ACA's health insurance marketplace plans.

23. These concerns included beliefs among some that IPAB was an unconstitutional delegation of legislative authority by Congress. The constitutionality of IPAB was challenged in *Coons v. Lew*, dismissed by the Ninth Circuit U.S. Court of Appeals on the grounds that the challenge to IPAB was "too speculative to satisfy the constitutional requirement of ripeness." Because IPAB was never formed nor took any actions, its powers were never fully subjected to judicial testing.

24. It should be acknowledged that some of the relative decline in annually appropriated spending reflects occasional shifts of spending from the discretionary side to the mandatory side of the federal budget. However, as this chapter documents, rising spending relative to GDP has been driven primarily by the major entitlement programs of Social Security, Medicare, and Medicaid, rather than by other mandatory spending established to evade appropriations spending caps.

25. Khimm: "The indiscriminate pain is meant to pressure legislators into making a budget deal to avoid the cuts."

26. Capretta suggests that certain programs serving very-low-income individuals, such as Supplemental Security Income, be exempt from enforcement cuts, though he argues that Medicaid should be "explicitly included in the enforcement mechanism."

27. The Base Realignment and Closure Commission, or BRAC, is sometimes also cited as a successful example of a bipartisan commission operating outside of standard legislative procedure. Congress established BRAC, restraining its own procedural latitude to amend the commission's recommendations, to achieve politically treacherous local spending cuts. BRAC, however, was not a mechanism for determining the total amount of appropriations provided for national defense, but for deciding which specific military installations should be closed. BRAC helped Congress to manage the parochial politics of specific military base closures, rather than improving the broader fiscal outlook.

28. Both the Breaux-Thomas and Simpson-Bowles commissions were able to generate majority support for recommendations, but not supermajority support. This was not true of the Kerrey-Danforth commission, but the high hurdle of a two-thirds support requirement helped to induce co-chairs Kerrey and Danforth to give up on trying to generate sufficient support for their own proposal.

REFERENCES

Badger, Doug, *Medicaid Per Capita Caps: When Democrats Supported and Republicans Opposed Them, 1995–97,* Mercatus Center, 2017, https://www.mer catus.org/system/files/mercatus-badger-medicaid-per-capita-caps-v2.pdf

Barrett, Ted, Bolduan, Kate and Walsh, Dierdre, "*'Super Committee' Fails to Reach Agreement,*" *CNN,* November, 2011, https://www.cnn.com/2011/11/21/politics/super-committee/index.html,

Bettelheim, Adriel, *Q&A: The Last Time America Tried to Fix Medicare, Politico,* September, 2018, https://www.politico.com/agenda/story/2018/09/12/medicare-bi partisan-commission-hoagland-lemieux-000693/

Blahous, Charles, *The Affordable Care Act's Optional Medicaid Expansion,* The Mercatus Center, March, 2013, https://www.mercatus.org/system/files/Blahous _MedicaidExpansion_v1.pdf

Blahous, Charles, *The End of Social Security Self-Financing,* The Mercatus Center, October, 2012, https://www.mercatus.org/system/files/TheEndofSocialSecurity SelfFinancing_Blahous_v1-1_0.pdf.

Blahous, Charles, *The Fiscal Consequences of the Affordable Care Act*, The Mercatus Center, 2012.

Blahous, Charles, *Future Work Still Needed After Budget's Disability Fix*, e21, November, 2015, https://economics21.org/html/future-work-still-needed-after-budget%E2%80%99s-disability-fix-1501.html

Blahous, Charles, *A Guide to the 2014 Medicare Trustees Report*, e21, August 2014, https://economics21.org/html/guide-2014-medicare-trustees-report-1064.html

Blahous, Charles, *Social Security: The Unfinished Work*, Hoover Institution Press, 2010.

Blahous, Charles, *Thinking Apolitically about Gerrymandering*, The Mercatus Center, July, 2019, https://www.mercatus.org/system/files/blahous-gerrymandering-mercatus-research-v1.pdf

Blahous, Charles, *The Unanswered Questions of Medicare for All*, American Enterprise Institute, February, 2019, https://www.aei.org/wp-content/uploads/2019/02/Single-Payer.pdf

Blahous, Charles, *Warning: Disability Insurance Is Hitting the Wall*, e21, January, 2015, https://economics21.org/html/warning-disability-insurance-hitting-wall-1212.html

Blahous, Charles, *Why We Have Federal Deficits*, The Mercatus Center, 2013, https://www.mercatus.org/system/files/Blahous_WhyWeHaveDeficits_v1.pdf

Blahous, Charles and Amez-Droz, Elise, *Reforming Medicaid Reimbursement before the Next Pandemic*, The Mercatus Center, April, 2020.

Blase, Brian, *Medicaid Provider Taxes: The Gimmick that Exposes Flaws in Medicaid's Financing*, https://www.mercatus.org/publications/healthcare/medicaid-provider-taxes-gimmick-exposes-flaws-medicaid%E2%80%99s-financing

Blase, Brian, and Aaron Yelowitz, *The ACA's Medicaid Expansion: A Review of Ineligible Enrollees and Improper Payments*, The Mercatus Center, November, 2019.

Board of Trustees of the Federal Supplementary Medical Insurance Trust Fund, 1997 Annual Report, https://www.cms.gov/Research-Statistics-Data-and-Systems/Statistics-Trends-and-Reports/ReportsTrustFunds/Downloads/TR1997SMI.pdf

Board of Trustees of the Federal Supplementary Medical Insurance Trust Fund, 1998 Annual Report, https://www.cms.gov/Research-Statistics-Data-and-Systems/Statistics-Trends-and-Reports/ReportsTrustFunds/Downloads/TR1998SMI.pdf

Boards of Trustees of the Federal Hospital Insurance and Federal Supplementary Medical Insurance Trust Funds, *2004 Annual Report*, https://www.cms.gov/Research-Statistics-Data-and-Systems/Statistics-Trends-and-Reports/ReportsTrustFunds/Downloads/tr2004.pdf

Boards of Trustees of the Federal Hospital Insurance and Federal Supplementary Medical Insurance Trust Funds, *2016 Annual Report*, https://www.cms.gov/Research-Statistics-Data-and-Systems/Statistics-Trends-and-Reports/ReportsTrustFunds/Downloads/TR2016.pdf

Boards of Trustees of the Federal Hospital Insurance and Federal Supplementary Medical Insurance Trust Funds, *2020 Annual Report*, https://www.cms.gov/files/document/2020-medicare-trustees-report.pdf

Capretta, James, *The Budget Act at Forty: Time for Budget Process Reform*, The Mercatus Center, March 2015

Capretta, James, *The Case for Reforming Medicare with Premium Support*, e21, December, 2011, https://economics21.org/html/case-reforming-medicare-premium-support-398.html

Centers for Medicare and Medicaid Services, *Medicare Program: Medicare Part B Monthly Actuarial Rates, Premium Rates and Annual Deductible Beginning January 1, 2020*, Federal Register, https://www.federalregister.gov/documents/2019/11/13/2019-24440/medicare-program-medicare-part-b-monthly-actuarial-rates-premium-rates-and-annual-deductible

Centers for Medicare and Medicaid Services, *2020 Part D Income-Related Monthly Premium Adjustment*, September, 2019, https://www.cms.gov/Medicare/Health-Plans/MedicareAdvtgSpecRateStats/Downloads/PartDIRMAA2020.pdf

Chu, Sharon and Burkhalter, Kyle, *Disaggregation of Changes in the Long-Range Actuarial Balance for the Old Age, Survivors and Disability Insurance (OASDI) Program Since 1983*, Social Security Administration, April, 2020, https://www.ssa.gov/OACT/NOTES/ran8/an2020-8.pdf.

Clinton, President William J., *Executive Order 12878*, https://en.wikisource.org/wiki/Executive_Order_12878

Clinton, President William J. *1998 State of the Union Address*, https://www.ssa.gov/history/clntstmts.html#12

Committee for a Responsible Federal Budget, *Analysis of the 2020 Social Security Trustees' Report*, April, 2020, http://www.crfb.org/papers/analysis-2020-social-security-trustees-report

Committee for a Responsible Federal Budget, *Blue Dog Coalition Endorses SAFE Commission Act*, November, 2009, https://www.crfb.org/blogs/blue-dog-coalition-endorses-safe-commission-act,

Committee for a Responsible Federal Budget, *Dispelling Common Myths in the SSDI Debate*, February, 2015, http://www.crfb.org/blogs/dispelling-common-myths-ssdi-debate

Committee for a Responsible Federal Budget, *Economists' Survey: Long Term, Not the Short Term, Should be the Focus*, August, 2013, http://www.crfb.org/blogs/economists-survey-long-term-not-short-term-should-be-focus

Committee for a Responsible Federal Budget, *President Trump Has Signed $4.7 Trillion of Debt into Law,* January, 2020, http://www.crfb.org/blogs/president-trump-has-signed-4-7-trillion-debt-law

Committee for a Responsible Federal Budget, *SGR Continues to Slow Health Care Cost Growth*, March, 2014, https://www.crfb.org/blogs/sgr-continues-slow-health-care-cost-growth

Congressional Budget Office, *CBO's Long-Term Social Security Projections*, December, 2019, https://www.cbo.gov/system/files/2019-12/55914-CBO-Social-Security-Comparison.pdf

Congressional Budget Office, *Historical Budget Data*, January 2020, https://www.cbo.gov/about/products/budget-economic-data#2

Congressional Budget Office, *Long-Term Budget Projections*, January 2020, https://www.cbo.gov/about/products/budget-economic-data#2.

Congressional Budget Office, *Monthly Budget Review for May 2020,* June, 2020, https://www.cbo.gov/system/files/2020-06/56390-CBO-MBR.pdf

Congressional Budget Office, *10-Year Budget Projections*, January, 2020, https://www.cbo.gov/about/products/budget-economic-data#2.

Congressional Budget Office, *The 2019 Long-Term Budget Outlook,* June, 2019, https://www.cbo.gov/system/files/2019-06/55331-LTBO-2.pdf

Congressional Record, U.S. Senate, March 2, 1995, https://www.govinfo.gov/content/pkg/GPO-CRECB-1995-pt5/pdf/GPO-CRECB-1995-pt5-4-1.pdf

Congressional Research Service, *Balanced Budget Amendments,* April, 2018, https://fas.org/sgp/crs/misc/IN10884.pdf

Congressional Research Service, *Medicare: Insolvency Projections,* May, 2020, https://fas.org/sgp/crs/misc/RS20946.pdf

Congressional Research Service, *Medicare Provisions in the Balanced Budget Act of 1997*, August, 1997, https://greenbook-waysandmeans.house.gov/sites/greenbook.waysandmeans.house.gov/files/2011/images/l97-802_gb.pdf

Congressional Research Service, *Medicare Trigger*, February 2020, https://fas.org/sgp/crs/misc/RS22796.pdf

Consultant Panel on Social Security, *Report of the Consultant Panel*, 1976, https://www.ssa.gov/history/reports/hsiao/hsiaoChapter1.PDF

Cooper, Jim, *Cooper, Wolf Reintroduce Safe Commission Long-term Fiscal Reform Bill*, March 2009, https://cooper.house.gov/media-center/press-releases/cooper-wolf-reintroduce-safe-commission-long-term-fiscal-reform-bill

Cubanski, Juliette, and Neuman, Tricia, *Medicare's Income-Related Premiums Under Current Law and Proposed Changes,* KFF, November, 2017, https://www.kff.org/medicare/issue-brief/medicares-income-related-premiums-under-current-law-and-proposed-changes/#:~:text=The%20Part%20B%20income%2Drelated,and%20took%20effect%20in%202007.&text=Beneficiaries%20with%20incomes%20above%20%24160%2C000,costs%2C%20rather%20than%2065%20percent.

Department of Health and Human Services, *2018 Actuarial Report on the Financial Outlook for Medicaid,* https://www.cms.gov/files/document/2018-report.pdf,

Fiedler, Matthew, and Powell, Wilson, *States Will Need More Fiscal Relief. Policy Makers Should Make That Happen Automatically,* Brookings Institution, April, 2020, https://www.brookings.edu/blog/usc-brookings-schaeffer-on-health-policy/2020/04/02/states-will-need-more-fiscal-relief-policymakers-should-make-that-happen-automatically/

Foster, Richard, *Statement of Richard S. Foster, F.S.A., Chief Actuary, Centers for Medicare & Medicaid Services*, The Fiscal Consequences of the Health Care Law, House of Representatives Budget Committee Hearing, January, 2011, https://www.govinfo.gov/content/pkg/CHRG-112hhrg64725/html/CHRG-112hhrg64725.htm

Furman, Jason, *Coping with Demographic Uncertainty,* NYU Wagner, September, 2007, https://www.brookings.edu/wp-content/uploads/2016/06/09useconomics_furman.pdf

Henry J. Kaiser Foundation, *Summary of the American Health Care Act,* May, 2017, http://files.kff.org/attachment/Proposals-to-Replace-the-Affordable-Care-Act-Sum mary-of-the-American-Health-Care-Act

Hiltzik, Michael, *Paul Ryan Is Determined to Kill Medicare,* Los Angeles Times, November, 2016, https://www.latimes.com/business/hiltzik/la-fi-hiltzik-medicare -ryan-20161114-story.html

Holtz-Eakin, Douglas, *Economic Implications of the Budget and Economic Outlook,* Testimony Submitted to the U.S. Senate Committee on Finance, February, 2013, https://www.finance.senate.gov/imo/media/doc/SFC%20DHE%202-26-13%20fin al1.pdf

House Committee on the Budget, *The Joint Select Committee on Deficit Reduction,* https://budget.house.gov/issues-initiatives/joint-select-committee-deficit-recut ion

Jacobson, Gretchen and Neuman, Tricia, *Turning Medicare into a Premium Support System: Frequently Asked Questions,* Kaiser Family Foundation, July, 2016, https:/ /www.kff.org/medicare/issue-brief/turning-medicare-into-a-premium-support-syst em-frequently-asked-questions/

Kahn, Charles III and Kuttner, Hanns, *Budget Bills and Medicare Policy: The Politics of the BBA,* Health Affairs, January/February 1999, https://www.healthaffairs.org/ doi/pdf/10.1377/hlthaff.18.1.37

Kahneman, Daniel, *Thinking, Fast and Slow,* 2011, Farrar, Strauss and Giroux.

Kaiser Family Foundation, *An Overview of the Medicare Part D Prescription Drug Benefit,* November, 2019, https://www.kff.org/medicare/fact-sheet/an-overview -of-the-medicare-part-d-prescription-drug-benefit/#:~:text=Part%20D%20Financ ing&text=The%20monthly%20premium%20paid%20by,for%20their%20expect ed%20benefit%20payments.

Khimm, Suzy, *The Sequester, Explained,* Washington Post, September, 2012, https ://www.washingtonpost.com/news/wonk/wp/2012/09/14/the-sequester-explained/

Klein, Ezra, *The Case against Reforming Social Security*, Washington Post Voices, August 30, 2010, http://voices.washingtonpost.com/ezra-klein/2010/08/the_case _against_reforming_soc .html

Kliff, Sarah, *Republicans Have a Clear Plan to Cut Medicare,* Vox.com, December, 2016, https://www.vox.com/2016/12/6/13817850/republicans-medicare-premium -support

Kogan, Richard, *How the Across-the-Board Cuts in the Budget Control Act Will Work,* Center on Budget and Policy Priorities, April, 2012, https://www.cbpp.org/ research/how-the-across-the-board-cuts-in-the-budget-control-act-will-work

Lightman, David, *Senate Says 'No' to Federal Debt Commission Obama Endorsed,* McClatchy Newspapers, January, 2010, https://www.mcclatchydc.com/news/po litics-government/article24571624.html

Mangan, Dan, *Trump Touts Repeal of Key Part of 'Disastrous Obamacare,' the Individual Mandate,* January, 2018, https://www.cnbc.com/2018/01/30/trump-to uts-repeal-of-obamacare-individual-mandate.html

Mann, Christopher, *Base Closure and Realignment (BRAC): Background and Issues for Congress,* Congressional Research Service, April, 2019, https://www.everycrs

report.com/files/20190425_R45705_9e300ef394d6f4dabc78a7ef8fbbc33ef9bd0 1e7.pdf

Marples, Donald, *Tax Expenditures: Overview and Analysis,* Congressional Research Service, https://fas.org/sgp/crs/misc/R44012.pdf

Maurer, Mark, *Finance Chiefs Relieved after Repeal of Cadillac Tax,* Wall Street Journal, December, 2019, https://www.wsj.com/articles/finance-chiefs-relieved-af ter-repeal-of-cadillac-tax-11577137387

Medicaid.gov, *Keeping America Healthy,* https://www.medicaid.gov/medicaid/cost -sharing/index.html

Munnell, Alicia, *The Problem with Social Security Lies in its History*, The Washington Post, October 6, 2016.

National Commission on Fiscal Responsibility and Reform, *The Moment of Truth,* December, 2010, https://www.aau.edu/sites/default/files/AAU%20Files/ Key%20Issues/Innovation%20%26%20Competitiveness/The-Moment-of-Truth_ Report-of-the-National-Commission-on-Fiscal-Responsibility-and-Reform_2010. pdf

National Public Radio, *Senators Propose Commission to Explore Deficit,* January, 2010, https://www.npr.org/transcripts/122466410

Nelson, Laura, *Medicare Reform,* July 1999, https://web.stanford.edu/class/e297c/ poverty_prejudice/soc_sec/medicare.htm

Obama, President Barack, *Executive Order 13531*, February, 2010, https://obamawh itehouse.archives.gov/the-press-office/executive-order-national-commission-fiscal -responsibility-and-reform

Opensecrets.org, *Social Security Works, Spending by Cycle Split by Party*, https://ww w.opensecrets.org/pacs/lookup2.php?cycle=2018&strID=C00637504

Orszag, Peter, *Medicare Spending Slows as Hospitals Improve Care,* Bloomberg Law, August, 2011, https://www.bloomberg.com/opinion/articles/2011-08-24/m edicare-spending-slows-as-hospitals-improve-care-peter-orszag

Papadimitriou, Dimitri (ed.), *Government Spending on the Elderly,* Palgrave Macmillan, 2007, https://www.google.com/books/edition/Government_Spending _on_the_Elderly/FyqGDAAAQBAJ?hl=en&gbpv=1&dq=steuerle+penner+index +eligibility+age+to+life+expectancy&pg=PA160&printsec=frontcover

Patient Protection and Affordable Care Act, Public Law 111–148, 111th Cong., 2nd sess. (March 23, 2010), 372.

Pear, Robert, *Medicare Panel, Sharply Divided, Submits No Plan,* New York Times, March, 1999, https://www.nytimes.com/1999/03/17/us/medicare-panel-sharply -divided-submits-no-plan.html

Pear, Robert, Kaplan, Thomas, and Cochrane, Emily, *Health Care Debate: Obamacare Repeal Fails as McCain Casts Decisive No Vote,* New York Times, July, 2017, https://www.nytimes.com/2017/07/27/us/politics/senate-health-care -vote.html

Penner, Rudolph, *The Greenspan Commission and the Social Security Reforms of 1983,* Urban Institute, https://www.urban.org/sites/default/files/publication/65126/ 2000323-Myth-and-Reality-of-the-Safety-Net-The-1983-Social-Security-Reforms .pdf

Penner, Rudolph G. and Steuerle, C. Eugene, *Options to Restore More Discretion to the Federal Budget,* Mercatus Center at George Mason University and the Urban Institute, September 2016, https://www.mercatus.org/system/files/penner-federal-b udget-v1.pdf

President's Commission to Strengthen Social Security, *Strengthening Social Security and Creating Personal Wealth for All Americans,* December, 2001, https://www .ssa.gov/history/reports/pcsss/Final_report.pdf

Riedl, Brian, *A Bipartisan Way to Soften Recessions and Address Soaring Debt,* National Review, June, 2020

Riedl, Brian, *A Comprehensive Federal Budget Plan to Avert a Debt Crisis,* Manhattan Institute, September, 2018, https://media4.manhattan-institute.org/sites/ default/files/R-BR-0918.pdf.

Riedl, Brian, *Getting to Yes: A History of Why Budget Negotiations Succeed, and Why They Fail,* Manhattan Institute, June, 2019, https://media4.manhattan-institute.org/ sites/default/files/R-0619BRdl.pdf

Romney, Mitt, *Romney Leads Bipartisan, Bicameral Legislation to Protect Taxpayers, Trust Funds,* October, 2019, https://www.romney.senate.gov/romney-leads-biparti san-bicameral-legislation-protect-taxpayers-trust-funds

Rosenbaum, David, *The Budget Struggle,* New York Times, August, 1993, https://ww w.nytimes.com/1993/08/07/us/budget-struggle-clinton-wins-approval-his-budget -plan-gore-votes-break-senate.html

Sahadi, Jeanne, *Debt Plan Draws Bipartisan Support,* cnn.com, December, 2010, https://money.cnn.com/2010/12/03/news/economy/fiscal_commission_vote/index. htm

Schieber, Sylvester, and Shoven, John, *The Real Deal,* Yale University Press, 1999.

Social Security Act Text, https://www.ssa.gov/OP_Home/ssact/title02/0201.htm

Social Security Administration, *National Average Wage Index,* https://www.ssa.gov /oact/cola/AWI.html#:~:text=The%20national%20average%20wage%20index,th an%20the%20index%20for%202017.&text=When%20we%20compute%20a% 20person's,to%20index%20that%20person's%20earnings.

Social Security Administration, *Myers Oral History,* https://www.ssa.gov/history/my ersorl.html

Social Security Administration, *Remembering Robert Myers,* Social Security Bulletin, Vol. 70, No. 2, 2010, https://www.ssa.gov/policy/docs/ssb/v70n2/v70n2p83.html #:~:text=Myers%20was%20among%20the%20early,Chief%20Actuary%20of%20 Social%20Security.

Social Security Administration, *Report of the Bipartisan Commission on Entitlement and Tax Reform,* https://www.ssa.gov/history/reports/KerreyDanforth/KerreyDan forth.htm#:~:text=On%20November%205th%201993%20President,Danforth %20(R%2DMO).

Social Security Administration Office of the Chief Actuary, *Memorandum to the Honorable John Larson,* Social Security Administration, July, 2020, https://www .ssa.gov/OACT/solvency/JLarson_20200715.pdf

Social Security Office of the Chief Actuary, *Provisions Affecting Retirement Age,* ssa .gov, https://www.ssa.gov/OACT/solvency/provisions/retireage.html

Social Security Administration Office of the Chief Actuary, *Single-Year Tables Consistent with the 2020 OASDI Trustees Report,* Social Security Administration, https://www.ssa.gov/OACT/TR/2020/lr6g2.html

Social Security Administration Office of the Historian, *Research Note #13: Listing of Social Security Advisory Councils and Commissions,* https://www.ssa.gov/history/councils.html

Social Security Advisory Council of 1938, *Report to the Social Security Board,* 1938, https://www.ssa.gov/history/reports/38advise.html

Social Security Advisory Council of 1957–1959, *Final Report,* 1959, https://www.ssa.gov/history/reports/58advise6.html

Social Security Advisory Council of 1994–1996, *Report,* January, 1997, https://www.ssa.gov/history/reports/adcouncil/report/toc.htm

Social Security Board of Trustees, *1942 Annual Report of the Board of Trustees of the Federal Old-Age and Survivors Insurance Trust Fund,* https://www.ssa.gov/oact/TR/historical/1942TR.pdf

Social Security Board of Trustees, *1972 Annual Report of the Board of Trustees of the Federal Old-Age and Survivors Insurance and Federal Disability Insurance Trust Funds,* 1972, p. 23–32, https://www.ssa.gov/oact/TR/historical/1972TR.pdf

Social Security Board of Trustees, *1982 Annual Report of the Board of Trustees of the Federal Old-Age and Survivors Insurance and Federal Disability Insurance Trust Funds,* 1982, https://www.ssa.gov/OACT/TR/historical/1982TR.pdf

Social Security Board of Trustees, *Status of the Social Security and Medicare Programs: A Summary of the 1995 Annual Reports,* 1995, https://www.ssa.gov/history/pdf/1995.pdf

Social Security Board of Trustees, *Status of the Social Security and Medicare Programs: A Summary of the 2015 Annual Reports,* 2015, https://www.ssa.gov/OACT/TRSUM/tr15summary.pdf

Social Security Board of Trustees, *2016 Annual Report of the Board of Trustees of the Federal Old-Age and Survivors Insurance and Federal Disability Insurance Trust Funds,* 2016, https://www.ssa.gov/OACT/TR/2016/tr2016.pdf

Social Security Board of Trustees, *2020 Annual Report of the Board of Trustees of the Federal Old-Age and Survivors Insurance and Federal Disability Insurance Trust Funds,* 2020, https://www.ssa.gov/oact/tr/2020/tr2020.pdf

Social Security Bulletin, *Bipartisan Commission on Entitlement and Tax Reform,* Vol. 58, No. 2, Summer 1995, https://www.ssa.gov/policy/docs/ssb/v58n2/v58n2p74.pdf

Social Security National Commission, *Social Security in America's Future,* March, 1981, https://www.ssa.gov/history/pdf/80chap4.pdf

Spatz, Ian, *IPAB RIP,* Health Affairs, February 2018, https://www.healthaffairs.org/do/10.1377/hblog20180221.484846/full/

Strahilevitz, Lior, *The Balanced Budget Amendment and Social Security,* University of Chicago Law School, https://chicagounbound.uchicago.edu/cgi/viewcontent.cgi?article=1591&context=journal_articles

United States Court of Appeals, Ninth Circuit, Decision, *Coons v. Lew,* August, 2014. https://caselaw.findlaw.com/us-9th-circuit/1674911.html

United States Department of the Treasury, *Tax Expenditures*, https://home.treasury .gov/policy-issues/tax-policy/tax-expenditures

Vinik, Danny, *Can Paul Ryan Actually Privatize Medicare?*, *Politico,* November, 2016, https://www.politico.com/agenda/story/2016/11/paul-ryan-trump-privatize -medicare-000241/

Walker, David, *Medicare: Financial Challenges and Considerations for Reform,* General Accounting Office, 2003, https://www.gao.gov/new.items/d03577t.pdf.

Walker, David, *Social Security: What the President's Proposal Does and Does Not Do, General Accounting Office,* February 9, 1999.

Wyden, Senator Ron and Ryan, Representative Paul, *Guaranteed Choices to Strengthen Medicare and Health Security For All,* December, 2011, https://www .wyden.senate.gov/imo/media/doc/wyden-ryan.pdf

Chapter 13

Fiscal Rules for Social Security and Medicare

Would Accrual Accounting Help?

James C. Capretta

INTRODUCTION

Current U.S. budget processes are inadequate for addressing the nation's increasingly difficult fiscal challenges. A major shortcoming is the absence of effective checks on unfinanced spending commitments that burden future taxpayers. The public perceives eligibility rules for major social welfare programs as approximating binding contractual obligations on the part of the government, and yet the budget process does not ensure that there will be sufficient revenue to cover the commitments that are accruing for program participants. Unanticipated cost increases can force additional public borrowing, tax hikes, or cuts in other government activities.

A potential direction for reform is more extensive use of accrual accounting measures to better inform the public and policymakers of the financial position of the government and to provide a basis for legislated, or automatic, solvency-improving adjustments to key programs. As a practical matter, in the U.S. context, it is Social Security and Medicare that are most central to the nation's fiscal challenge and also the top candidates for revised fiscal rules pegged to their accrued costs and expected receipts across generations.

In recent years, greater use of accrual accounting to help address defects in fiscal processes has been getting more serious consideration in countries with advanced economies. The motivation is to bring forward into decision-making the financial effects of current and previous government decisions which by their nature have substantial long-term implications. State-sponsored retirement programs and pension systems, such as Social Security, are regularly cited as requiring such a long-term focus because they are designed to improve the financial security of multiple generations of participants. Accrual accounting also can be relevant for government-backed loans and insurance programs, as well as for public investments in physical or financial assets that might generate long-term returns or economic benefits.

What follows is an examination of accrual accounting and related fiscal rules and their possible use in the context of improved financial management of Social Security and Medicare, as well as the broader federal enterprise. The discussion begins with a review of why reform is necessary, followed by an overview of current accrual accounting practices in the context of social insurance programs. It concludes with potential reforms that merit further consideration and development.

THE INADEQUACY OF PAY-AS-YOU-GO TRUST FUND ACCOUNTING

The fiscal policy outlook for the United States has become increasingly adverse since 2008. The Congressional Budget Office (CBO) projects federal debt will rise from 98% of GDP at the end of 2020 to 195% in 2050 (see figure 13.1).[1] In 2008, federal debt was below 40% of GDP.[2]

Successive global crises—the financial crash of 2007–2009 and the COVID-19 pandemic of 2020—have exacerbated an already challenging outlook, but the costs of addressing these admittedly destructive events, while substantial, are not by themselves the cause of the nation's fiscal difficulties.

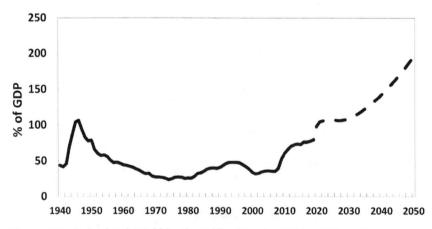

Figure 13.1   Federal Debt Held by the Public. Historical Tables, Office of Management and Budget; "The 2020 Long-Term Budget Outlook," Congressional Budget Office, September 2020.

More important is the steady growth in entitlement spending over past decades and the expected acceleration of that growth in the coming years.

As shown in figure 13.2, the combined spending on Social Security and Medicare was below 4% of GDP in 1970. By 2020, it was above 8% of GDP, and it is projected to exceed 12% of GDP in 2050. With Medicaid and other subsidies for health insurance enrollment included, spending on the major entitlement programs is forecast to exceed 15% of GDP in 2050. Over the period 1970 to 2019, average annual federal revenue collection—intended to cover all government activities, not just these programs—was only slightly higher, at 17.7% of GDP.

Social Security and Medicare use federal trust funds to track their income and outgo over many years, one purpose of which is to ensure their outlays are financed entirely by revenue sources specifically dedicated to these programs. When forecasts indicate the trust funds will run out of reserves and full benefits cannot be paid with the receipts expected over the projection period, it is presumed that, at some point, Congress will act to eliminate the shortfall with legislation that raises revenue or trims expected future costs, or both, to prevent program insolvency.

There are three reasons why trust fund accounting is not sufficient for ensuring these major programs can be sustainably financed over the long term.

First, the use of trust funds to control long-term costs leads to an excessive focus on the date of full depletion of reserves, which encourages the political process to procrastinate in deliberating meaningful reforms. The 2020 trustees' reports for Social Security and Medicare project depletion dates of 2035

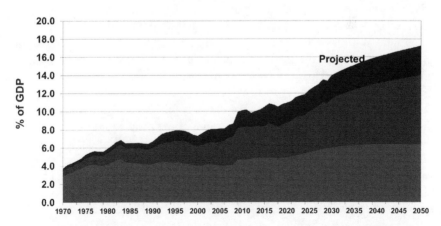

Figure 13.2   Entitlements and Fiscal Pressure. Historical Tables, Office of Management and Budget; "The 2020 Long-Term Budget Outlook," Congressional Budget Office, September 2020.

and 2026, respectively, for the programs' associated trust funds, which leaves the impression that Congress can wait several years before acting.[3] In reality, if Congress were to wait until closer to these depletion dates to act, then the required correction would be more drastic and disruptive than would be the case with a reform enacted more expeditiously.

Delay also creates a bias toward increasing taxes because it is easier to generate added revenue quickly than it is to cut program expenses. Program adjustments often involve complex reforms that need to be phased in slowly to minimize disruption to program participants or other stakeholders, such as medical service providers. In contrast, policymakers may be more willing to impose large near-term tax increases on workers to keep a trust fund solvent because workers are assumed to have more options for adjusting to unexpected financial burdens than retirees.

Second, as Howell Jackson has observed, when program liabilities are growing more rapidly than the program's revenue base, pay-as-you-go trust funds obscure the widening long-term gap.[4] The result could be changes that only temporarily address the problem, and not in a way that gets at the fundamental imbalance.

For instance, if a trust fund has liabilities that permanently outpace growth in revenues, an immediate infusion of resources could delay insolvency but only temporarily because the fundamental cause of the imbalance will not have been addressed.

An example illustrates the problem. If, as is the case today, Social Security's accruing liabilities are growing faster than the revenue base to finance them, then it does not help program solvency to expand the program's reach to new workers. But, over the years, program expansion has been advanced as a solvency improvement step because the immediate revenue increase from new participants occurs well before the benefits owed to them come due. With trust fund accounting, taking this step can appear to be an improvement in the program's financial outlook. However, if, in general terms, liabilities are growing more rapidly than the revenue base for the program, adding more workers to it will only increase the program's unfunded commitments (although it is possible that recognition of these commitments might be obscured by the limited timeframe of the projection).

A third major problem with trust fund accounting is specific to the design of the Medicare program. Medicare has two parts, each with its own dedicated trust fund. The Hospital Insurance (HI) trust fund operates on a pay-as-you-go basis much like Social Security, with payroll taxes on current workers providing most of the revenue used to pay benefits for current retirees. The other trust fund, for Supplementary Medical Insurance (SMI), covers costs for physician services and outpatient care. It is financed by premiums from current retirees covering 25% of program outlays and large payments from

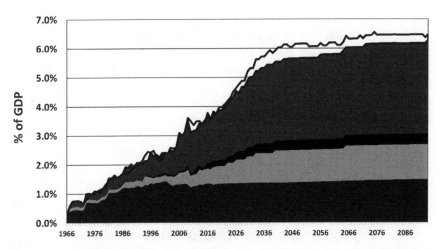

Figure 13.3   Medicare Spending and Revenue Sources. 2020 Medicare Trustees' Report, Intermediate Estimates.

the general fund of the Treasury covering all other expenses. Unlike HI, the SMI trust fund can never be depleted; the general fund payments ensure it will always have sufficient reserves to cover costs.

Figure 13.3 provides a combined view of the outlays and financing sources for the entirety of Medicare spending (HI and SMI). As shown, the program is already heavily dependent on payments from the general fund, and will become much more so in the years ahead. Over the next ten years alone, the general fund will contribute $5.3 trillion to SMI, according to the latest forecast from the trustees.[5] These payments impose a direct burden on U.S. taxpayers, in the form of either foregone spending on other priorities or additional borrowing that will need to be repaid later, but Medicare's trust fund-focused accounting obscures this effect. Because the SMI trust fund is never exhausted of reserves, there is a perception that it is soundly financed, while, in actuality, SMI program spending is a substantial source of the nation's ongoing and impending fiscal challenges.

GROWING USE OF ACCRUAL ACCOUNTING IN GOVERNMENT FISCAL ASSESSMENTS

Budget processes in advanced economies are based primarily on cash accounting. That is, governments' fiscal positions are assessed by examining the income and outgo flows that occur over a fixed period (such as a fiscal year, or sometimes multiple fiscal years).

Accrual accounting has a different focus. Instead of basing financial information on the transactions that liquidate pre-existing financial terms, accrual accounting records changes in the financial position of governments or businesses at the time obligations, or binding requirements of payments from counterparties, are consummated. Expected future payment or revenue streams are converted into present value totals (using discount rates) to allow the sums to be expressed meaningfully in current monetary terms.

Excessive reliance on cash accounting can send misleading budgetary signals. For instance, a government that initiates an insurance plan for property damage from natural disasters might generate a substantial short-term cash flow from premium payments for the program's enrollees. At some point, however, a disaster will occur, and the government will be required to make cash payments to cover the insured losses of eligible participants. Cash accounting would record the premiums when received, and insurance payments when they occur. Accrual accounting provides a more accurate picture of such a program because it would record the present value of all future premium payments and payouts (based on the probability of adverse natural disasters), thus allowing a comparison to reveal whether or not the net position of the program will improve or worsen the government's financial outlook.

In 1990, U.S. policymakers recognized this defect in the federal budget process and inserted the Credit Reform Act (CRA) into a large spending and tax deal that was struck between Republican President George H.W. Bush and a Democratic Congress. The CRA required the use of accrual accounting for certain federally run direct loan and loan guarantee activities, including the large student loan programs run by the Department of Education. Under the CRA, the government calculates a net subsidy cost annually to reflect the expected present value of receipts and outgo for loans issued in that year.[6] In effect, the CRA uses accrual accounting to convert the financial implications of federal loan programs into cash-like terms that can be incorporated into an otherwise cash-based income statement.

While the CRA brought about a major change in federal budget concepts, many programs that might have been covered by its provisions were exempted from it, including major mortgage lending accounts and agencies, the Pension Benefit Guaranty Corporation (insuring private-sector pension funds), federal retiree pension and health benefits, and the Social Security and Medicare programs.

There has been growing interest in recent decades in using more accrual accounting in public budgeting because cash accounting provides a limited, and possibly distorted, view of the true financial condition of an organization. For instance, cash accounting misses the financial effects that may occur from a transaction beyond the time horizon of a budget. Cash accounting also creates a focus on income statements measuring time-limited money flows. Accrual accounting encourages greater use of balance sheet analysis that may provide a broader picture of the financial health of a governmental entity.

THE FINANCIAL REPORT OF THE U.S. GOVERNMENT

While the CRA provides accrual-based budget information for a relatively small subset of federal activities in conjunction with a cash-dominated budget process, broader accrual-like assessments are produced by the federal government, but they garner much less attention among policymakers and in the broader public.

The Financial Report of the United States Government—assembled annually by the Treasury Department and the Office of Management and Budget—is a full, accrual-based look at the entirety of the federal enterprise. While far less prominent than the cash-based president's budget, it is an attempt to use accrual methods to create an income statement and a balance sheet that provide a more comprehensive picture of the overall financial health of all federal activities, taking into consideration income-producing assets and financial obligations that will come due in future years.

Ironically, while Social Security and Medicare constitute the most substantial long-term commitments of the federal government, they are not included in this report in the official income and balance sheet statements. Rather, they are assessed separately, in a "Statements on Social Insurance" analysis that is provided as something of an addendum to the financial statement covering the rest of the government.

Social Security and Medicare receive this special treatment for both understandable and questionable reasons.

On the one hand, the pay-as-you-go design of Social Security and Medicare HI means they do not fit neatly into the accrual-based methodology used to assess private sector, or even state and local government, pension plans. Accrual accounting is focused on assessing the financial consequences of contract-like commitments that have been consummated at the time of the preparation of the financial report. This method does not fit comfortably with the designs of Social Security and Medicare, which are pay-as-you-go systems. They were never set up to have reserves on hand to meet obligations as they accrue. Instead, they rely on the contributions of current workers to finance the benefits obligations that current retirees earned years ago. Thus, the programs have always counted on taxes collected on future earnings to pay for benefits payments that will come due concurrently. In other words, expected future tax receipts are the "assets" that these programs rely upon to meet their accruing benefit commitments.[7]

Still, in a financial report (see table 13.1) that is supposed to inform Congress and the public about the true state of the nation's finances, underplaying the significance of the long-term obligations of Social Security and Medicare, by separating them out from the accrual estimates for the rest of the government, creates the false impression that the outlook is less adverse than it is.

Even with this caveat, however, the financial report serves an important role in presenting in a clear manner information about these programs that is more difficult to ascertain elsewhere (although the trustees' reports do provide similar estimates, as discussed below).

The annual financial report uses an accrual methodology for Social Security and Medicare that takes into account their pay-as-you-go designs. Instead of measuring assets based entirely on contributions in hand, it measures the net liabilities of the programs after calculating the expected future tax and premium receipts of program participants.

The report provides this analysis based on two enrollment constructs. One—for the "closed group"—looks at all future tax receipts and benefit payments associated with participants in the program as of the year of the financial report. The second—for the "open group"—looks at all future tax receipts and benefit obligations both for current and future program participants. Asset and liability calculations are made on a present value basis and confined to projections covering the next seventy-five years (thus excluding even longer-term trends).

As shown in figure 13.2, Social Security is facing substantial unfunded liabilities. On a closed group basis, expected future benefit payments will exceed the tax receipts to pay for them by $37.6 trillion on a net present value

Table 13.1   Financial Report Estimates of Social Security Net Liabilities

	75-Year Net Present Value Amounts By Year of Financial Report ($ Trillions)				
	2015	*2016*	*2017*	*2018*	*2019*
Closed Group:					
Revenue	29.0	30.6	31.6	33.1	35.1
Expenditures	58.1	62.0	64.9	68.1	72.7
Revenue Less Expenditures	−29.1	−31.4	−33.3	−35.0	−37.6
Future Participants:					
Revenue	26.6	29.7	30.5	31.8	35.3
Expenditures	10.9	12.4	12.6	13.0	14.5
Revenue Less Expenditures	15.7	17.3	17.9	18.8	20.8
Total (Open Group):					
Revenue	55.6	60.3	62.1	64.9	70.4
Expenditures	69.0	74.4	77.5	81.1	87.2
Revenue Less Expenditures	−13.4	-14.1	−15.4	−16.2	−16.8

Source: "2019 Financial Report of the United States Government," Department of the Treasury, April 2020.

basis. Not surprisingly, future participants to the program will provide a net surplus over the coming seventy-five years because they are mainly working, and not retired, during this projection period. On an open group basis, Social Security's net unfunded liabilities are still alarming at $16.8 trillion.

Even more troubling is the trend. Since 2015, Social Security's net unfunded liabilities have grown each year, and by a cumulative $3.4 trillion from 2015 to 2019. Put differently, without any change in federal law, Social Security's expected obligations over 75 years have grown by $3.4 trillion more than expected future receipts over the same period. This deteriorating financial outlook has profound implications for the overall fiscal position of the federal government and yet it is almost entirely obscured in today's budget discussions by the dominance of cash-based information covering the next ten years.

The outlook for Medicare is even more adverse than it is for Social Security, in large part because the program's outlays are expected to rise not just because the population is aging but also because health prices are expected to escalate more rapidly than will inflation in the broader economy. As shown in figure 13.3, Medicare has an unfunded liability, measured on a present value basis, of $42.7 trillion for workers and retirees currently participating in the program. When future participants are included (both those born today but not yet working and those expected to be born in future years), the net unfunded liability of the program is slightly lower, at $42.2 trillion.

Like Social Security, the outlook for Medicare is trending in the wrong direction (see table 13.2). Since 2015, the net unfunded liability for the

Table 13.2   Financial Report Estimates of Medicare Net Liabilities

	75-Year Net Present Value Amounts By Year of Financial Report ($ Trillions)				
	2015	*2016*	*2017*	*2018*	*2019*
Closed Group:					
Revenue	17.1	19.5	20.5	22.1	23.9
Expenditures	46.2	52.9	55.5	60.9	66.6
Revenue Less Expenditures	−29.1	−33.4	−35.0	−38.8	-42.7
Future Participants:					
Revenue	10.2	12.2	12.8	13.3	14.6
Expenditures	9.1	11.3	11.3	12.2	14.1
Revenue Less Expenditures	1.1	0.9	1.5	1.1	0.5
Total (Open Group):					
Revenue	27.3	31.7	33.3	35.4	38.5
Expenditures	55.3	64.2	66.8	73.1	80.7
Revenue Less Expenditures	−28.0	−32.5	−33.5	−37.7	-42.2

Source: "2019 Financial Report of the United States Government," Department of the Treasury, April 2020.

program, measured on an open group basis, has risen by $14.2 trillion. It is telling that this data point is not widely cited in budget debates, and very likely not well understood by members of the House and Senate or key officials in the executive branch. And yet it may well be the most important indicator of the precariousness of the nation's fiscal outlook as benefit commitments accruing under current law far outpace the growth in funding dedicated to paying for them.

Critics of the accrual method of assessing Medicare's financial status point out that the unfunded liability calculation omits a crucial additional source of financial support for the program: general fund payments from the Treasury. And, in fact, in the Treasury's annual financial report on the government, the Statements of Social Insurance include a reference to these payments (termed "eliminations"). But, as noted in the financial report, these are payments within the government and are not based on specific receipts collected from individuals or corporations paying taxes. Even so, it is possible to note that this source of funding for Medicare only shifts the economic burden and does not eliminate it without also expecting Medicare to be financed entirely by revenue dedicated specifically and solely for this purpose.

THE ANNUAL TRUSTEES' REPORTS AND THE FEDERAL BUDGET PROCESS

The Treasury and OMB accrual-based financial report gets its data on the unfunded liabilities of Social Security and Medicare from the programs' annual trustees' reports, which examine their financial health over a 75-year period. Those reports have long included comparisons of the estimates of the net present value of accruing liabilities and program receipts. There are reasons, however, to prefer the presentation of the broader financial report as a basis for adjustments to federal budget processes.

Throughout its history, the most used measure of the financial health of Social Security has been its actuarial balance, which is calculated by dividing the excess of the present value of expected expenditures over expected receipts by the present value of the payroll tax base over the same period. In the 2020 Social Security trustees' report, the actuarial deficit from this measure was estimated at 3.21% over 75 years, which can be interpreted to mean that the program's financial deficit could be eliminated by an immediate and permanent payroll tax increase of 3.21% (the current combined employer-employee rate is 12.4%).[8] Similarly, the 2020 HI trustees report estimated its actuarial deficit at 0.76%, which can be compared to the standard employer-employee tax rate of 2.90%.[9]

While these measures can be useful, it is better to direct attention to the dollar estimates of the unfunded liabilities for the programs because those estimates can be put into the larger fiscal context of the rest of the federal enterprise. For instance, the most recent financial report (issued in April 2020) calculated the net financial position of the entire government (excluding the major social insurance programs) at –$23.0 trillion—a staggering sum. This adverse financial position is driven by the government's large and growing outstanding debt obligations. But the size of the unfunded liabilities for Social Security and Medicare—a combined $59.0 trillion—show that the financial pressures from these programs are an order of magnitude more consequential than even the existing debt obligations of the Treasury.

It is also helpful to consider the financial pressures of Social Security and Medicare in the larger fiscal context because of the actual and potential interactions between the two sides of the federal ledger.

As noted previously, the SMI trust fund receives payments from the general fund of the government covering 75% of program expenses. This is one important reason for the government's already large outstanding debt obligations. Examing the full scope of federal fiscal activity in one report and through comparable measures prevents improving the financial outlook for one part of the government at the expense of other parts. In particular, if Medicare's financial outlook is bolstered (as it is under current law) by heavy reliance on transfers from the general fund of the Treasury, then those obligations will show up in time in the outstanding debt obligations for rest of the government.[10]

Highlighting the flows between the general fund and the trust funds points to an important amendment to existing reporting practice. The financial report currently separates out Social Security and Medicare from the base assessment for the rest of the federal enterprise. Further, the assessment of the government's outstanding liabilities does not include a present value calculation of the government's future general fund payments to Medicare. If the financial report continues to exclude the accruing liabilities of Medicare from the base assessment of the government's financial position, it would seem that recognition of the present value of the general fund payments to Medicare as an expected obligation would improve the accuracy of the reported net position of the government. This treatment would also prevent solving the unfunded liability problems for either Social Security or Medicare by simply tapping into future general fund payments.

A REFORM FRAMEWORK

The increased use and reliance on accrual accounting for Social Security and Medicare could be the focal point of a budget process reform aimed at narrowing the long-term gap between projected spending and revenue.

There are many different alternative paths for how to proceed with such a reform. The following framework is but one option.

Establish a Consensus Methodology

Calculating a social insurance program's accrued liabilities and assets requires making choices about a methodology. The construct used in the Treasury's financial report would appear to offer a reasonable approach. It limits the calculation to expected costs and receipts over 75 years (rather than over an infinite horizon), and includes future participants in the calculations as well as those currently taking part in the programs. Once chosen, this method should become standard in reports from the Office of Management and Budget, the Treasury Department, the Social Security Administration, the Centers for Medicare and Medicaid Services, and CBO.

Choose a Level of General Revenue Support for Medicare

Medicare's unfunded liability is staggering in part because the program was never designed to be financed only with dedicated receipts and premiums. At enactment, Congress stipulated that the SMI trust fund should receive half of its revenue from the general fund (the percentage was later pegged to 75%). Moving toward an accrual-based assessment of the program's finances requires specifying a level of general fund support. One option would be to assume that general fund payments in the future are limited to the transfer amount from 2020 after indexing it to a reasonable annual growth rate (which is likely to be less than the expected growth rate of program spending under current law). For instance, general fund support to Medicare could grow after 2020 at either the rate of consumer inflation or, perhaps, growth in GDP.

Medicare's finances should be assessed for the program as a whole rather than for its three parts (A, B, and D). Private insurers do not create completely separate offerings for hospital care, physician services, and outpatient drugs. Rather, they offer single insurance plans that allow providers to deliver the most appropriate care based on the needs of patients. Medicare should move toward integrated coverage as well, starting with how it is financed. While the law will continue to require the use of two trust funds for assigning costs, an accrual-based assessment of the program's overall financial health should ignore this outdated construct.

Refocus the President's Budget

The president's annual budget submission to Congress is often of little consequence today, and that may remain the case even if it is refocused on long-term questions. Still, it is important for the national discussion of the federal government's financial outlook to begin looking beyond this year's borrowing requirements. The use of accrual accounting for Social Security and Medicare in the budget submission would begin to highlight this new way of looking at the nation's fiscal challenges, and may catalyze the development of more reform ideas in Congress.

Reform the Congressional Process

In a similar way, the congressional budget process should require inclusion of accrual estimates for Social Security and Medicare in the annual budget resolution. Instead of focusing on near-term deficit reduction, it should encourage the key committees to bring forth legislation to lower the projected unfunded liabilities of these programs by offering expedited consideration of measures that CBO certifies would meaningfully narrow the shortfall. At the same time, the process should be amended to discourage legislation that would make the problem worse by creating additional vote hurdles to inhibit passage of such measures. To facilitate a focus on the accrued liabilities of Social Security and Medicare, CBO should be required to use the standard methodology used by the executive branch when issuing its reports and when providing cost estimates of bills affecting the revenue and spending provisions of the programs.

Connect Automatic Program Adjustments to Accrued Net Liability Thresholds and Offer Benefit Enhancements When There Are Surpluses

The key to an effective reform is to tie accrual assessments to actual changes in program parameters. When the executive branch estimates a deficit beyond a certain minimal level, the rules governing the accrual of additional benefit commitments should be adjusted to limit the growth in unfunded commitments. This could be done by changing key parameters such as the age of eligibility for full benefits (the normal retirement age), or the rates of return offered for differing levels of average lifetime earnings. In Medicare, payment rates for hospitals and physicians could be adjusted, along with the annual deductibles required by enrollees. The changes should be phased in gradually in future years, and affect only future retirees (not those currently receiving benefits).

As noted previously, such a system of automatic adjustment is not untested. Sweden has been operating under such rules for two decades with impressive results. The nation's pay-as-you-go state pension system is now expected to be in balance over the long term, and the development of any future net liability will be quickly eliminated by changes automatically required in the system's governing law.[11] While implementing such a reform is difficult technically, Sweden has shown it is far from impossible.

The most serious hurdle to building in automatic program adjustments directly into Social Security and Medicare is politics. Any proposed changes to the programs generate intense interest in the United States, and using accrual accounting as the basis for automatic modifications would be sure to meet stiff opposition. Some of the distrust might be assuaged if the reform called for automatic revenue increases as well as benefit adjustments, along with allowing benefits to increase whenever accrual assessments show projected net surpluses.

Even with such amendments, connecting automatic reforms to the accrual process may not be possible during an initial round of legislation. If that is the case, then it would be important to secure adoption of the accrual methodology as a starting point for changing the status quo by injecting into the political conversation information that provides clarity about the scale of the problem and the nature of meaningful remedies.

CONCLUSION

The United States is facing a daunting fiscal outlook. Federal borrowing has risen rapidly over the past dozen years, and will accelerate over the coming three decades based on the aging of the population and rising health-care expenses. Spending for the major entitlement programs—most especially Social Security and Medicare—is the primary source of growing fiscal pressure.

To date, political leaders have not agreed on a plan to lessen the severity of the fiscal challenge, or even on the magnitude of the adjustments that will be necessary to head off an eventual fiscal crisis.

Part of the problem is informational. Today's budget processes are cash focused, which means there is insufficient attention to the persistent and growing gap between new benefit commitments in Social Security and Medicare and the funds that will be required to make good on those commitments. With every passing year, the nation's financial hole becomes deeper because of the program designs embedded in current law.

Moving toward an accrual-based assessment of these major programs may help clarify both the scale of the problem and possible remedies by highlighting the degree to which the problem worsens every year. Further, instead of focusing on near-term fiscal results, policymakers might see that the goal for these programs should be long-term sustainability, measured by ensuring growth in accruing liabilities is matched with expected growth in government receipts to pay for those obligations.

Like all process reforms, accrual-based assessments of Social Security and Medicare will not, by themselves, solve the nation's fiscal challenge. There must be a willingness on the part of elected leaders to use the information such assessments provide to better manage the government's long-term liabilities. Further, there is likely to be substantial debate on technical aspects of such assessments that could increase or lessen their usefulness.

Even with these caveats, however, accrual-based accounting for Social Security and Medicare remains well worth exploring as a potential starting point for a renewed effort at strengthening the sustainability of these programs and ensuring the federal government does not become engulfed in debt.

NOTES

1. "The 2020 Long-Term Budget Outlook," Congressional Budget Office, September 2020, https://www.cbo.gov/system/files/2020-09/56516-LTBO.pdf.

2. "Historical Tables, Budget of the United States Government, Fiscal Year 2020," Office of Management and Budget, February 2020, https://www.whitehouse .gov/wp-content/uploads/2020/02/hist_fy21.pdf.

3. "The 2020 Annual Report of the Board of Trustees of the Federal Old-Age and Survivors Insurance and Federal Disability Insurance Trust Funds," Social Security Trustees, April 2020, https://www.ssa.gov/OACT/TR/2020/tr2020.pdf and "The 2020 Annual Report of the Boards of Trustees of the Federal Hospital Insurance and Federal Supplementary Medical Insurance Trust Funds," Medicare Trustees, April 2020, https://www.cms.gov/files/document/2020-medicare-trustees-report.pdf. The depletion date for Medicare refers to the Hospital Insurance Trust Fund, not the Supplmentary Medical Insurance Trust Fund.

4. "Accounting for Social Security and Its Reform." Howell E. Jackson, *Harvard Journal on Legislation*, Winter 2004, https://papers.ssrn.com/sol3/papers.cfm?abstr act_id=458921.

5. Medicare Trustees, "The 2020 Annual Report of the Boards of Trustees of the Federal Hospital Insurance."

6. "Budgetary Treatment of Federal Credit (Direct Loans and Loan Guarantees): Concepts, History, and Issue for the 112th Congress," James M. Bickley, Congressional Resarch Service, July 2012, https://fas.org/sgp/crs/misc/R42632.pdf.

7. Sweden passed a reform in the 1990s to its pay-as-you-go pension system that explicitly defines future tax receipts as an asset that must be balanced with accruing obligations. See "Automatic Adjustments Within Entitlement Programs: A Look at the Swedish Pension Reform Model," James C. Capretta, *Economic Perspectives*, American Enterprise Institue, March 2018, https://www.aei.org/wp-content/uploads /2018/03/Automatic-Adjustments-Within-Entitlement-Programs.pdf.

8. Social Security Trustees, "The 2020 Annual Report of the Board of Trustees."

9. Medicare Trustees, "The 2020 Annual Report of the Boards of Trustees of the Federal Hospital Insurance."

10. Currently, the financial report separates out the financial reporting for Social Security and Medicare from the base assessment for the rest of the federal enterprise. Further, the assessment of the government outsanding liabilities does not include a present value calculation of the government's future general fund payments to Medicare. If the financial report continues to exclude the accruing liabilities of Medicare from the base assessement of the government's financial position, it would seem that recognition of the present value of the general fund payments to Medicare as an expected obligation would improve the accuracy of the reported net position of the government.

11. Capretta, "Economic Perspectives."

REFERENCES

Bickley, James M. 2012. "Budgetary Treatment of Federal Credit (Direct Loans and Loan Guarantees): Concepts, History, and Issue for the 112th Congress." Congressional Research Service. July. https://fas.org/sgp/crs/misc/R42632.pdf.

Capretta, James C. 2020. "Automatic Adjustments Within Entitlement Programs: A Look at the Swedish Pension Reform Model." American Enterprise Institute. March. https://www.aei.org/wp-content/uploads/2018/03/Automatic-Adjustments -Within-Entitlement-Programs.pdf.

Congressional Budget Office. 2020. "The 2020 Long-Term Budget Outlook." September. https://www.cbo.gov/system/files/2020-09/56516-LTBO.pdf.

Department of the Treasury. 2020. "2019 Financial Report of the United States Government." April. https://fiscal.treasury.gov/files/reports-statements/financial-re port/2019/FR-02272020(Final).pdf.

Jackson, Howell E. 2004. "Accounting for Social Security and Its Reform." *Harvard Journal on Legislation.* Winter. https://papers.ssrn.com/sol3/papers.cfm?abstract_ id=458921.

Medicare Trustees. 2020. "The 2020 Annual Report of the Boards of Trustees of the Federal Hospital Insurance and Federal Supplementary Medical Insurance Trust Funds." April. https://www.cms.gov/files/document/2020-medicare-trustees -report.pdf.

Office of Management and Budget. 2020. "Historical Tables, Budget of the United States Government, Fiscal Year 2020." February. https://www.whitehouse.gov/ wp-content/uploads/2020/02/hist_fy21.pdf.

Social Security Trustees. 2020. "The 2020 Annual Report of the Board of Trustees of the Federal Old-Age and Survivors Insurance and Federal Disability Insurance Trust Funds." April. https://www.ssa.gov/OACT/TR/2020/tr2020.pdf.

Appendix A

CHAPTER 2: THE DYNAMIC SIMULATION MODEL

This appendix summarizes the main components of the dynamic simulation model (more detailed equations are available at the website vetfiscalrules .net).

The central element of the MP rules is an ex ante cap on discretionary spending growth. The two best approximations of a general basis for increased demand for discretionary federal spending are personal income growth and population growth plus inflation. Since our studies of state fiscal stress indicated that personal income growth is too volatile a basis for capping spending growth, the MP rules cap spending growth at a multiple of the sum of population growth and inflation.

A discretionary spending limit (DSP) rises, annually, at a multiple of population growth plus inflation (AFAF) unless the proximity of the deficit or debt to the MP rules' designated deficit and debt threshold levels trigger braking. Countercyclical supplementary spending occurs when revenue declines from one year to the next.

$$DSP_t = IF((1 + ((1 - DEBTBADJ_t - DEFBADJ_t) \times AFAF_t)) > 1, ((DSP_{t-1} - CCYCSP_{t-1})$$

$$\times (1 + ((1 - DEBTBADJ_t - DEFBADJ_t) \times AFAF_t))) + CCYCSP_t, DSP_{t-1})$$

$$(1)$$

Where: DSP = Simulation-revised discretionary spending
AFAF = Allowed Fiscal Adjustment Factor
((Population Growth Rate +Inflation Rate) × MULT)
CCYCSP = Countercyclical General Fund Spending

DEBTBADJ = Debt Brake-based Adjustment of AFAF

$$\text{DEBTBADJ}_t = \text{IF}(\text{DEBTGDP}_{t-1} < (0.8 \times \text{DEBTTOL}), 0,$$

$$((\text{DEBTGDP}_{t-1} \div \text{DEBTTOL})$$

$$\times (\text{DEBTGDP}_{t-1} - (\text{DEBTTOL} \times 0.8))) \times \text{DEBTBRATE})$$

Where: DEBTGDP = National Debt divided by GDP.
DEBTTOL = "Tolerance" level for Debt/GDP ratio.
DEBTBRATE = DEBTBADJ

adjustment factor/rate. $\text{DEFBADJt} = \text{IF}(\text{DEFGDP}_{t-1} < (0.8 \times \text{DEFTOL}), 0,$

$$((\text{DEFGDP}_{t-1} / \text{DEFTOL}) \times (\text{DEFGDP}_{t-1} - (\text{DEFTOL} \times 0.8))) \times \text{DEFBRATE})$$

Where:
DEFBADJ = Deficit Brake-based Adjustment of AFAF
DEFGDP = Deficit divided by GDP
DEFTOL = "Tolerance" level for Deficit/GDP Ratio
DEFBRATE = DEFBADJ adjustment factor/rate

The "0.8" in some of the equations above is there to initiate braking, gradually, as the debt or deficit approaches the threshold levels (80% x .60=.48 for debt); (80% x .03=.024 for the deficit). The not-shown other part of the "IF" in equation (1) bars spending reduction so that zero is the lowest possible growth rate, a constraint not present in each simulation. The braking criteria—capping spending growth below AFAF—are the debt and deficit measures that arise from comparing all revenue to all spending, including interest payments, entitlements, emergency fund and capital fund deposits, and countercyclical spending.

$$\text{RTOTSP}_t = \text{DSP}_t + \text{SSSP}_t + \text{MEDSPA}_t + \text{RINT}_t + \text{KDEP}_t + \text{NEDEP}_t \qquad (2)$$

Where: RTOTSP = Simulation-revised total spending
INT = Simulation-revised interest on the national debt
SSSP = Social Security Spending
MEDSPA = Medicare Part A spending
KDEP = Deposit into Investment Fund

$$NEDEP = IF((EDEPR_t \times DSP_t) + EBAL_{t-1} - EMERG_t)$$

$$> ECAP_t, CAP_t - EBAL_t + EMERG_t$$

$$- EINT_t, (EDEPR_t \times DSP_t) + EINT_t))$$

Where:
EDEPR = Cap on Emergency Fund Deposit Rate
EDEPR = Emergency Fund Deposit Rate (% of General Fund Spending)
EMERG = Emergency Fund Spending
ECAP = Emergency Fund Account Balance Cap
EINT = Interest paid to/by Emergency Fund

$$RGDP_t = ((RGDP_{t-1} + GDPA_t - GDPA_{t-1})$$

$$\times (RMTR \times (FEDTBURD_{t-1} - FEDTBURD_{t-2})))$$

$$+ (OCR \times (RREV_{t-1} - TOTSP_{t-1})) \tag{3}$$

Where: RGDP = Simulation-revised GDP
GDPA = Actual GDP
RMTR = Growth Acceleration Coefficient for Federal Tax
Burden
FEDTBURD = federal tax burden, measured as revenue/GDP.
OCR = growth opportunity cost rate for diversion of resources from private-
sector to public-sector use.

$$RREV = RGFREV_t + RSSMEDREV_t$$

RGFREV = Simulation-revised General Fund Revenue
RSSMEDREV = Simulation-revised Medicare Part A Revenue

Appendix B

Table A1 Chapter 11: Summary of Legislation Involving Fiscal and Monetary Matters Since 1989

Date	Law Number and Title	Brief Description	First Amended by Law		Total Number of Amendments
Sep-1989	23697 Economic Emergency	Gave the Executive branch flexibility and power to deal with the crisis: reformed Central Bank, suspended subsidies and Industrial and Mining Promotion schemes, facilitated foreign investment, consolidated public debt, established emergency budgetary provisions, restricted growth in expenditures of state owned companies, froze public hiring, etc.	M	Oct-1990	106
Sep-1990	23967 Economic Emergency	Repealed article 34 of Law 23697			0
Mar-1991	23928 Convertibility	Established a new peso convertible to the US$ at 1 to 1 exchange rate. Legalized transactions in US$. Central Bank reserves must be equal to 100% of the Monetary Base. Eliminated indexation.	R	Jan-2002	67
Sep-1992	24144 Independence of the Central Bank	Established the Central Bank as an independent entity. President and Board members nominated by the Executive with a term of six years with the consent of the Senate	M	Mar-2012	93
Sep-1992	24156 Financial management of Public Sector	Established criteria for financial management of public sector including budgeting, accounting and treasury.	M	Nov-2003	1054
Feb-1996	24629 Rules for national government's budget	Added the obligation to produce data on expenditures by geographic distribution, In-Year Reports on budget execution, and the Pre-Budget Statement. The law mentions Congress as the direct recipient for these documents.	M	Aug-1999	36
Aug-1999	25152 Fiscal Convertibility	Established (a) that the primary fiscal deficit could not exceed 1.9% of GDP, (b) that primary expenditures could not grow faster than real GDP, (c) 3-year budgeting process, and (d) limits to the growth in public debt.	M	Mar-2002	168

Date	Law	Title	Description		Expiration	
Oct-2000	25344	Economic-Financial Emergency	Allowed the Executive to take extraordinary measures to deal with crisis such as unilateral termination of supply contracts and renegotiation of public debt. Allowed a one-year with a possible extension of another year.	M	Dec-2001	54
Dec-2001	1602	Economic-Financial Emergency	Extended Law 23544 for another year.			0
Jan-2002	25561	Economic-Financial Emergency	Repealed the Convertibility Law. Gave the Executive flexibility to adopt any economic and financial measures to minimize the impact of the crisis.	M	Dec-2003	279
Dec-2003	25820	Public Emergency and Reform of Foreign Exchange Regime	Modified Law 25561 and extended it for another year.	M	Nov-2004	10
Nov-2003	25827	Budget approval and modification	Approved 2004 budget and modified Law 24156 giving significant leeway to the Executive to reallocate expenses at its discretion and raise debt.			168
Aug-2004	25917	Federal Fiscal Responsibility	Imposed transparency and reporting criteria for budgets at all levels of government. Delegates powers on the Executive to restructure budget credits.	M	Dec-2004	49
Nov-2004	25972	Public Emergency and Reform of Foreign Exchange Regime	Modified Law 25820 and extended at the request of the Executive for another year. Prohibited private sector companies from firing employees.	M	Dec-2005	6
Dec-2005	26077	Public Emergency and Reform of Foreign Exchange Regime	Modified Law 25561 and extended at the request of the Executive for another year.	M	Dec-2006	4
Aug-2006	26124	Financial management and control systems for National Public Sector	Allowed Executive branch to make any reallocations in the budget as long as total budget did not change Congress to approve total level of revenues, expenditure, and debt.			1
Dec-2006	26204	Public Emergency and Reform of Foreign Exchange Regime	Modified Law 25561 and extended at the request of the Executive for another year.	M	Dec-2007	8

(Continued)

Table A1 Chapter 11: Summary of Legislation Involving Fiscal and Monetary Matters Since 1989 (*Continued*)

Date	Law Number and Title		Brief Description	First Amended by Law		Total Number of Amendments
Dec-2007	26339	Public Emergency and Reform of Foreign Exchange Regime	Modified Law 26204 and extended at the request of the Executive for another year.	M	Dec-2008	4
Dec-2008	26456	Public Emergency and Reform of Foreign Exchange Regime	Modified Law 26339 and extended at the request of the Executive for another year.	M	Dec-2009	7
Oct-2009	26530	Fiscal Responsibility for Provincial Governments			Nov-2011	7
Dec-2009	26563	Public Emergency and Reform of Foreign Exchange Regime	Modified Law 26456 and extended at the request of the Executive for two years.	M	Dec-2011	3
Dec-2011	26728	National Budget for 2012	Approved 2012 national budget. Modified Law 26530 and 26456.	M	Nov-2012	67
Dec-2011	26729	Public Emergency and Reform of Foreign Exchange Regime	Modified Law 26443 and extended at the request of the Executive for two years.	M	Oct-2013	4
Mar-2012	26739	Reform of the Central Bank	Modified Law 24144. Nominally preserved independent status but established that monetary policies have to "conform" the policies set by the Executive. Allowed the National Government to finance itself with the reserves of the Central Bank.	M		3
Oct-2013	26896	Public Emergency and Reform of Foreign Exchange Regime	Modified Law 26739 and extended at the request of the Executive for two years.	M	Nov-2015	3

Date	Law	Name	Description		Date	
Nov-2015	27200	Public Emergency and Reform of Foreign Exchange Regime	Modified Law 26204 and extended at the request of the Executive for two years.	M	Dec-2016	5
Sep-2016	27275	Right to access to public information	Guaranteed public access to any information produced or held by the government, including specific details about the allocation of public expenditure.			46
Dec-2016	27342	Financial management and control systems for National Public Sector	Modified Law article 37 of Law 24156 granting the Executive Allowed the Executive to rearrange budgetary allocations within the total amount approved up to certain limits that decreased after 2017.	M	Dec-2019	2
Dec-2016	27345	Public Emergency and Reform of Foreign Exchange Regime	Extended Law 27200 until December 31, 2019, created "National Council for the Popular Economy and Complementary Social Wages," and allowed the Executive to fund the expenditures required to implement the law.			6
Dec-2017	27428	Fiscal Responsibility Law	Established financial agreement between National and provincial governments to limit growth in expenditures. Established rewards to provinces with fiscal balance or surplus. Required transparency and performance reports.	M	Jan-2018	2
Jan-2018	27429	Fiscal Consensus	Approval			
Dec-2019	27541	Economic Emergency	Declared the country in a state of economic, financial, and social emergency. Gave "super-powers" to the Executive branch.			26
Jan-2020	27544	Restoration of Public Debt Sustainability	Allowed the Executive to restructure the public debt to achieve sustainability.			2

Source: Infoleg.
Notes: M = modified, R = repealed.

Index

Affordable Care Act, 299
Alberdi, 205
Alesina and Drazen, 178
Alesina and Passalaqua, 118
Alesina and Tabellini, 53
Amador, 53
Amash, 16, 19, 27
American Rescue Plan of 2021, 14
Andersen, 55, 73
Apuntes, 204
Argentina, 4, 148–49
Arrington, 15, 23
Asatryan et al., 124
asset sales, 61
Azzimonti, 53

Badger, 315
Badia, 4
Badinger, 118
bailout: examples, 47–48, 228;
    no bailout rule, 46–48
balanced budget amendment, 16, 27
balanced budget rule, 76
Bank for International Settlements,
    50, 219
Barrett, Bolduan, and Walsh, 322
Barro, 179
Barro and Gordon, 175
Bassetto and Sargent, 54
Bauer, 154, 160

Becker, 146
Beljean and Geier, 55
Bellini, 207
Bello, 201
Berger et al., 125
Bernanke, 223–24
Biden, 14
Blanchard, 54, 89, 93
Blankert, 46
Blesse et al., 126
Blum et al., 125
Blustein, 146
Boccia, 2
Bodmer, 55
Bond rating agencies, 40, 48
Borg, Anders, 77
Brady Plan, 176
Brat, 16, 27
Brennan and Rougier, 209
Brown, 174–75
Budget Control Act of 2011, 13
budgeting: annual balance, 28; full
    structural balance, 27; primary
    balance, 26–27; process, 7, 15, 17,
    23, 28–29, 31, 55–56, 75–76, 101,
    105, 107, 112, 323, 337, 342–43, 346
Buera and Nicolini, 265
Buol and Vaughan, 260
Burchett, 23, 26
Burret and Feld, 118

Cafiero, 209
Calabria, 260
Calvo, 173
Camdessus, 146–47
Capital Investment Fund, 55
capital markets, 8
CARES Act, 228
Carnot, 44
Case, 15, 26
Caselli and Wingender, 127
Caucus Rules, 19
Cavallo, 212, 270
central planning, 220–21, 227, 269
Cereijo, 204, 207–8
Chile, 275–76
China, 4
Chu and Burkhalter, 302
Clarida, 42
Coate and Milton, 54
Cogan, 44
Cohen, 201
Collective Action Clauses, 192
Committee for a Responsible Federal
    Budget (CRFB), 14–15, 25, 27, 300
conference rules, 19
Congressional Budget Office, 5, 8, 14,
    17, 25–26, 37–38, 46, 50, 53, 230,
    287–89
Congressional Budget Reform Act, 17,
    22, 26
Congressional Power of the Purse Act, 23
Congressional Progressive Caucus, 23
Cooper, 158
Couchman, 16, 24, 26–27
Council of Economic Advisors, 161
countercyclical fiscal policies, 3–4, 101,
    121, 171, 179
Covid-19. *See* pandemic
credence capital, 46, 48
Credit Reform Act, 342
Cubanski and Newman, 308
Culp et al., 146

Davig and Leeper, 42
DeBrun, vii–x, 2, 5–6, 41–42

DeBrun and Jonung, 44, 47, 49, 92
debt: anchor, Sweden, 71, 77, 89,
    91; brakes, 47, 54, 101, 105, 117,
    119, 121, 124–25; ceiling, 91, 172,
    181, 183, 187–88, 193; crises, 41,
    212, 241, 256; fatigue, 1, 3, 5–6,
    38–40, 46, 49–50, 63; held by the
    public, 242–43; investor confidence,
    190; maturity structure, 175, 189;
    monetizing, 43, 254; projections,
    56–57; service, 40; special functions,
    vii–x, 50; statutory limit, 4, 25,
    27, 30; tolerance, 50, 180, 188;
    unsustainable, 49, 212, 220, 230–32
default risk, 40, 47, 58, 212
deficit bias, 7, 46, 71, 118, 178, 181
De Greef, 208
deliberation, suppressed, 15
Delong and Summers, 54
dependency indexing, 302
DeSilver, 18
discretionary spending, 58–59
Di Tella and Dubra, 202
Dole, 321
Dornbusch and Edwards, 201, 206
Dowling, 37
Drazen, 178
Drucker, 154

Eagleburger, 146
economic growth, 37
economic ideology, 276–77
Edwards, 202, 262
Eichenbaum, 43
Entrepreneurs, 205–6
Enzi, 15, 22, 28
European Central Bank, 5
European Stability Mechanism, 117
exchange rate, 74, 141–42
Eyraud et al., 125, 127, 177

facism, 201–4
Feld and Kirchgassner, 1, 46
Feld and Reuter, 118
Feldstein, 43

Fernandez, 201
Fiedler and Powell, 315
Figuerola, 204
financial crisis, 39, 87
fiscal cliff, 2–3, 95
fiscal commitment problem, viii
fiscal consolidation, 52, 74, 105
fiscal policy: automatic stabilizers, 7,
    26, 28, 45, 74, 86, 107, 121, 127,
    302, 316; capital market, 172, 185;
    countercyclical, 39; deficit bias, 71,
    206–7, 242; discipline, 46, 69, 71,
    73, 176; discretionary spending,
    13, 21, 29, 44, 49, 55, 59, 62, 73,
    123, 288, 315, 318, 320, 322, 325;
    dynamic scoring, 52; end-of-year
    spending, 112; entitlement reform,
    61, 183, 226, 230–31, 287; off-
    budget, 120, 207, 264–65, 327;
    over-budgeting, 112; pro-cyclical,
    105, 129, 161, 176, 185–86; revenue
    forecasting, 103–9; sequestration, 27,
    315, 318–20; static scoring, 52; tax
    expenditures, 316
fiscal responsibility council, 49, 76–77, 80
fiscal rules: accrual accounting,
    337; automatic fiscal correction
    mechanism, 320, 350; capital
    investment fund of MP Rule, 55;
    debt- and deficit-based braking. *See*
    debt, brakes; design, 6–7, 26, 51,
    53, 75, 91, 119, 128, 165, 180, 337;
    effectiveness, viii, 42, 103, 112,
    117, 129, 178; emergency fund of
    MP Rule, 60; enforcement, ix–x,
    49, 92, 125, 128; escape clause,
    54, 107, 122, 127, 180; investment
    expenditures/loophole, 54, 120,
    123, 130; Merrifield-Poulson, 54;
    motivation, 1, 176, 265; second
    generation, 2, 8, 53–54, 128; surplus
    target, Sweden, 70–71, 75; Taylor, 8,
    276; trade-offs, x
fiscal space, ix, 4, 8, 50, 60, 71, 88, 90
Fiscal Taylor Rule, 44, 49

Friedman, 8, 42, 142, 146, 156, 259
Fujimori, 183
Furman, 302

Galiani, 267
Gallagher, 15
Gaspar and Gopinath, 173
Geier, 55
Gold Standard, 26, 73, 211–12, 260, 262
Gómez and Morales, 209
Gómez and Newland, 206
government, special status, vii
Gramm-Rudman-Hollings, 317
Great Moderation, 38, 43–46, 49–50, 298
Green New Deal, 220, 230
Greenspan, 43, 259, 302
Greenwood, 140

Halac and Yared, 53–54
Hanke and Schuler, 143
Hayek, 273
Hayo and Neumeier, 125
Heinemann, 125
Heinemann et al., 118
Hern, 23
Herron, 205
Hong Kong, 140–41
House Republican Study Committee, 23
House Rules, 16, 18
Hoyer, 17, 23
HP (Hodrick-Prescott) Filter, 107
Huder, 18

inflation, 8–9, 14, 40, 42–43, 50, 56,
    62, 73–74, 80, 105, 111, 145–46,
    149, 151–53, 157, 159, 173–77, 184,
    208–10, 241
interest rates: excess reserves, 220, 223,
    246; federal funds rate, 222–24; low,
    6, 40, 43–44, 48, 50, 62, 71, 74, 93,
    117, 171, 190; savings, 74, 110;
    signals, 80; spread, 4
International Monetary Fund, 4, 51–52,
    93, 146–48, 163, 172–73, 180, 185,
    212, 259, 271

Japan, 5–6, 50, 62–63
Johnson, 158
Joint Select Committee on Deficit
    Reduction, 23, 301, 318, 322
Jonung, 2
Jorda et al., 89

Kahn and Kuttner, 307
Kahneman, 290
Kerrey, 321
Keynes, 73, 86
Keynesian Fiscal Multipliers, 52
Kirchner, 271
Kirk and Mallet, 16
Kleim and Kriwolusky, 44
Klein and Daza, 203
Kocherlakota, 259
Kogan, 315
Krugman, 146
Kumhof and Laxton of 2013, 44
Kydland and Prescott, 259

Lange, 202
Lee, 23
Llach and Gerchunoff, 202
Lledo et al., 54
lockdowns, 219, 232, 252, 272
Lukkezen and Teulings, 44
Lynn and Saturno, 28

Maastricht Treaty, 91, 177, 180, 259
MacGuineas, 25
Machiavelli, 155
Macri, 271
Manchin, 15
Mangan, 309
Mankiw, 262
Maurer, 309
McConnell, 25
Medicaid, 313
Medicare, 344–347
Menem, 183, 212, 270
Merkel, 201
Merrifield and Poulson, 2, 45, 47
Mill, 273

Miller, 146
Miranda, 206–8
Modern Monetary Theory, 202, 209,
    220, 230, 262
Modigliani, 203
monetary policy: base, 248–49;
    commitment problem, viii, 276;
    convertibility programs, 144–45,
    149, 158, 212, 263, 266, 271;
    currency board, 139–41, 143–46;
    direct funding, 226–27; discretionary,
    139, 219; dollarization, 143, 149–52,
    163; fiscal policy connection, 8, 42,
    172, 176, 178, 209, 219, 231, 257,
    260, 263, 270–71; multi-money, 150;
    open market operations, 222–23;
    rules, 42, 139, 154, 259, 265, 276;
    velocity, 248–49
moral hazard, 103
mortgage-backed securities, 244
Mundell, 146, 298
Mussolini, 203–4, 269

National Commission on Fiscal
    Responsibility and Reform, 322.
    See also Simpson-Bowles
national development plans, 207
nationalization, 206–7
Nerlich and Reuter, 124
North, 273

OPEC, 73–74
Organization for Economic Cooperation
    and Development (OECD), 56, 161
Orphanides, 42
Orszag, 311

pandemic, 4, 6, 14, 24, 47, 71, 88, 92,
    113–14, 117, 122, 132, 171, 179,
    212, 219, 221, 226, 254, 272
Papadimitriou, 303
PAYGO, viii
Pear, 322
Pear, Kaplan and Cochrane, 314–15
Penner, 321

Penner and Steuerle, 303
Perdue, 17
Peron, 201, 261–64
Peru, 184
Peters, 15, 23
Peterson, 15, 24
Polanyi, 160
political failure, viii
populist threat, 202, 212
Portman, 24
Poulson and Baghestani, 44
Powell, 43
price control, 205, 210–11
protectionism, 269–70
Puerto Rico, 49

Rachel and Summers, 93
rationing, 205
Reforming America's Fiscal Toolkit
    Act, 26
Reinhart, 41
Reinhart and Rogoff, 41, 172
Riddick and Frumin, 16
Riedl, 287, 316–17
Robinson, 202
Romney, 15, 25, 322
Rosenbaum, 321
rules-based fiscal policy, ix, 13–31

Samuelson, 202, 262
Sanger, 147
San Martin, 206
Schaechter, 52, 177
Schelling, 16
Schick, 52
Schleifer, 157
Select Committee on the Modernization
    of Congress, 23
Selgin, 230
Senate Rules, 16
Shutt, 20
Simons, 259, 272
Simpson-Bowles, 301, 311, 322
Simulation Analysis, 51

Smithies, 261
Snyder, 16
social security, 290–291, 344–347
Sowter, 202
Spatz, 311
Stability and Growth Pact, 91, 120,
    177
stagflation, 203
Strahilevitz, 317
Strezewski, 141, 155
Suharto, 146
Sweden, 69, 349
Swift, 19
Switzerland, 1, 46–47, 51, 54–55, 101

Tanzi, 271
TARP, 56
Tax Cuts and Jobs Act of 2017, 14, 56
Taylor, 8, 42–44, 259, 276
Tea Party, 13
Tignor, 157
Tinbergen, 202
Tocqueville, 273
TRUST Act, 24, 322
Turner and Spinelli, 40
Tyson, 146

unfunded liabilities, 48
unified budgets, 29
United States, 5–6
Uruguay, 275–76

Von Hagen, 75

Waisman, 269
Walker, 318
Walters, 146
Walters and Hanke, 141
Whitehouse, 15, 22, 28
Womack, 23
Wyploz, 52

Yared, viii, 53
Yarmuth, 23

About the Editors

Barry W. Poulson is emeritus professor of economics at the University of Colorado. He has been a visiting professor at several universities, including Universidad Autonomo De Guadalajara, Mexico; University of North Carolina; Cambridge University; Konan University, Kobe, Japan; and Universidad Carlos Tercera, Madrid, Spain. He is the author of numerous books and articles in the fields of economic development and economic history. His current research focuses on fiscal policies and fiscal constitutions. He has served on the Colorado Tax Commission and as vice chair of the State Treasurer's Advisory Group on Constitutional Amendments in Colorado. Professor Poulson is past president of the North American Economics and Finance Association. He is an adviser to the Task Force on Tax and Fiscal Policy of the American Legislative Exchange Council and serves as a consultant on fiscal policy and fiscal constitutions to a number of state and national think tanks.

John Merrifield was a University of Texas at San Antonio faculty member for 32 years. He retired from teaching and faculty meetings to devote additional time to critical research issues, and to have more time with his wife and "high-maintenance" teenage adopted boys. He's the associate editor of the *Nonpartisan Education Review*, and past editor of the *Journal of School Choice*. He has just published *School System Reform: How and Why Is a Price-less Tale*, plus *The School Choice Wars* (second edition, in press), *School Choices, Parental Choice as an Education Reform Catalyst: Global Lessons, Basic Economic Tools*, five edited books (see below), 56 peer-reviewed journal articles, and several chapters in edited books in his primary teaching and research fields of education economics, public finance, urban and regional economics, and environmental and natural resource economics.

Two books are in the works: (1) *Virtuous Language Police: An Essential Semantic Route to Clarity* and (2) *Political Control of K-12 Education.* Dr. Merrifield received a BS in natural resource management from Cal Poly San Luis Obispo in 1977, a MA in economic geography from the University of Illinois in 1979, and a PhD in economics from the University of Wyoming in 1984. Dr. Merrifield is a first-generation German immigrant; born a Hamburger, and raised a Frankfurter (tall—John 6'6"). In 1960, he came to the United States with his mother, (now) Dr. Doris Merrifield-Leffingwell, at the age of 5. He resides in downtown San Antonio, Texas, with his wife, Gayla, and their adopted children, Christopher and Joshua (14 and 13), and their five four-legged children, canines Pete, Nutmeg, Lindsay, and DeLorean, and feline Nike. Additional details are available at: faculty.business.utsa.edu/jmerrifi/.

Steve H. Hanke is a professor of applied economics at Johns Hopkins University and a founder and co-director of The Johns Hopkins Institute for Applied Economics, Global Health, and the Study of Business Enterprise. He is a senior fellow and director of the Troubled Currencies Project at the Cato Institute, a contributor at *National Review*, a well-known currency reformer, and a currency and commodity trader. Prof. Hanke served on President Reagan's Council of Economic Advisers, has been an adviser to five foreign heads of state and five foreign cabinet ministers, and held a cabinet-level rank in both Lithuania and Montenegro. He has been awarded seven honorary doctorate degrees and is an honorary professor at four foreign institutions. He was president of Toronto Trust Argentina in Buenos Aires in 1995, when it was the world's best-performing mutual fund. Currently, he serves as chairman of the Supervisory Board of Advanced Metallurgical Group N.V. in Amsterdam. In 1998, he was named one of the 25 most influential people in the world by *World Trade Magazine*. In 2020, Prof. Hanke was named a "Knight of the Order of the Flag" by Albanian president Ilir Meta. Some of Prof. Hanke's most recent books are *Zimbabwe: Hyperinflation to Growth* (2008), *A Blueprint for a Safe, Sound Georgian Lari* (2010), and Currency Boards for Developing Countries: A Handbook (Revised Edition, 2015). The revised edition of Currency Boards for Developing Countries has been republished in Spanish (2015), Farsi (2018), Turkish (2019), and Arabic (2020). Prof. Hanke and his wife, Liliane, reside in Baltimore and Paris. You can follow him on Twitter @Steve_Hanke.

About the Contributors

Fredrik N. G. Andersson is associate professor at the Department of Economics, Lund University. He holds a PhD from Lund University. In his thesis he developed econometric methods for the study of short- and long-run growth cycles. His recent research covers topics such as the short- and long-run effects of financial crises on economic growth and economic institutions, monetary policy and the credit cycle, and long-run economic growth cycles. He is also engaged in public debate in Sweden on the tension between the Riksbank's inflation targeting and rising private debt levels and property prices jointly with Lars Jonung.

Charles Paul Blahous is the J. Fish and Lillian F. Smith Chair and Senior Research Strategist at the Mercatus Center at George Mason University, and a visiting fellow at Stanford University's Hoover Institution. From 2010 to 2015 he served as one of two public trustees for the Social Security and Medicare programs. Dr. Blahous was deputy director of the National Economic Council under President George W. Bush from 2007 to 2009, previously serving from 2001 to 2007 as a special assistant to the president for economic policy. Prior to that, he served from 1996 to 2000 as policy director for Senator Judd Gregg of New Hampshire. Between 1989 and 1996, Dr. Blahous worked for Senator Alan Simpson of Wyoming, first as a congressional science fellow in 1989–1990, then as a legislative assistant from 1990 to 1994 and as legislative director from 1994 to 1996. Dr. Blahous is the author of the books *Decoding the Debates, Social Security: The Unfinished Work* and *Pension Wise*. He served from 2014 to 2016 on the Bipartisan Policy Center's Commission on Retirement Security and Personal Savings and also with the BPC as a shadow trustee monitoring the finances of Social Security and Medicare. Dr. Blahous has published studies with the Mercatus Center on subjects including the federal budget costs of Medicare for All, the fiscal ramifications of the Affordable Care Act, multiple aspects of Social Security, the origins of federal deficits, gerrymandering, the multiemployer pension solvency crisis, Medicaid expansion, and other issues. Dr. Blahous holds a PhD in computational quantum chemistry from the University of California/Berkeley and also an AB in chemistry from Princeton University.

James C. Capretta is a resident fellow and holds the Milton Friedman Chair at the American Enterprise Institute (AEI), where he studies health care, entitlement, and U.S. budget policy, as well as global trends in aging, health, and retirement programs. Concurrently, Mr. Capretta serves as a senior adviser to the Bipartisan Policy Center and, since 2011, as a member of the Advisory Board of the National Institute for Health Care Management Foundation. He spent more than 16 years in public service before joining AEI. As an associate director at the White House's Office of Management and Budget from 2001 to 2004, he was responsible for all health care, Social Security, welfare, and labor and education issues. Earlier, he served as a senior health policy analyst at the U.S. Senate Budget Committee and at the U.S. House Committee on Ways and Means. From 2006 to 2016, Mr. Capretta was a fellow, and later a senior fellow, at the Ethics and Public Policy Center.

Mr. Capretta is also a contributor to RealClearPolicy, where he regularly publishes commentary on public policy issues. He is the author and co-author of many published essays and reports, including "Toward Meaningful Price Transparency in Health Care" (2019); "Increasing the Effectiveness and Sustainability of the Nation's Entitlement Programs" (2016), and "Improving Health and Health Care: An Agenda for Reform" (2015). In addition, his book chapters include "Medicaid" in "A Safety Net That Works: Improving Federal Programs for Low-Income Americans" (2017) and "Reforming Medicaid" in "The Economics of Medicaid: Assessing the Costs and Consequences" (2014). Mr. Capretta has been widely published in newspapers, magazines, and trade journals, including *Health Affairs* (where he is a member of the Editorial Board), the *JAMA Network*, *National Affairs*, *National Review*, *The New York Times*, and *The Wall Street Journal*. His television appearances include "PBS NewsHour," Fox News Sunday, C-SPAN's "Washington Journal," CNBC, and Bloomberg Television. Mr. Capretta has an MA in public policy studies from Duke University and a BA in government from the University of Notre Dame.

Kurt Couchman is senior fellow, fiscal policy, at Americans for Prosperity. He specializes in budget process, especially constitutional and statutory fiscal targets, as well as helping congressional offices develop a wide range of proposals. Couchman previously advised several members of Congress on budget, tax, financial services, and other policies. He is the author of two innovative, bipartisan balanced budget amendment proposals and numerous other initiatives. Couchman has a master's degree in economics from George Mason University and a bachelor's degree from Indiana University of Pennsylvania.

Xavier Debrun is an adviser in the Research Department of the National Bank of Belgium. He studied economics at the University of Namur and the Graduate Institute in Geneva where he obtained a PhD in international economics. Xavier spent most of his 20-year professional career in the Fiscal Affairs and Research Departments of the International Monetary Fund (IMF). In 2006–2007, he was a visiting fellow at Bruegel and a visiting professor of international economics at the Graduate Institute in Geneva. He has regularly taught in academic institutions, including the University of Geneva, the University of Clermont-Auvergne, and the Catholic University of Louvain (UCL). His research interests include international policy coordination, the economics of currency unions, and macro-fiscal issues, including debt sustainability assessments and the stabilizing role of fiscal policy. His work has been disseminated in peer-reviewed journals, IMF flagship reports, and conference volumes. He led many technical assistance missions for the IMF in relation to the design and operation of fiscal policy rules, macro-fiscal forecasting, and the introduction of independent fiscal institutions.

Vera Z. Eichenauer is a postdoc at KOF Swiss Economic Institute at ETH Zurich. Her research focuses on economic development and growth, emerging donors' activities in developing countries, natural disasters, and the consequences of peaceful secessions. She received her PhD from the University of Heidelberg and her MA from Sciences Po Paris.

Lars P. Feld has been holding a chair of economics, in particular Economic Policy, at Albert-Ludwigs-University of Freiburg since 2010 and is the current director of the Walter Eucken Institute. He is a member of Leopoldina (the German National Academy of Sciences) and the Mont Pelerin Society. From 2007 to 2009, he was president of the European Public Choice Society. Since 2003, Lars P. Feld has been a member of the Scientific Advisory Council to the Federal Ministry of Finance and, from 2011 to 2021, a member and during the last year of his second term the chairman of the German Council of Economic Experts (GCEE). From 2013 to 2021, he represented the GCEE in the Independent Advisory Council of the Stability Council, Germany's construction of a fiscal council. Since 2020, he is also a member of the German minimum wage commission. In 2017, he received an honorary doctorate from the University of Lucerne in Switzerland.

Pablo E. Guidotti is dean of the School of Government at Universidad Torcuato Di Tella. Previously, he has held positions such as counselor at Instituto Torcuato Di Tella from 1997 to 2000; vice president and member of the Board of Directors at Caja de Valores, S.A., from April 1997 to March 2000; deputy minister of the Economy and Secretary of the Treasury, Republic of Argentina, from August 1996 to December 1999; co-chairman, G-22 Working Group on Strengthening Financial Systems, 1998; vice president 2nd and member of the Board of Directors, Central Bank of Argentina, from May to August 1996; director (Member of the Board of Directors), Central Bank of Argentina, from November 1994 to August 1996; member of the Executive Board, Trust Fund for Bank Capitalization, from March to November 1995; adviser to the president of the Central Bank of Argentina, from August 1992 to November 1994; professor of money and banking, University Torcuato Di Tella, from 1995 to present; professor of economics at the Centro de Estudios Macroeconómicos de Argentina, from 1993 to 1999; economist at the Research Department of the International Monetary Fund since October 1988; on leave since August 1992; economist at the European Department of the International Monetary Fund from October 1987 to October 1988; assistant professor of economics at the University of Colorado, Boulder, from September 1985 to September 1987; and visiting research scholar at the Centro de Estudios Macroeconómicos de Argentina.

Lars Jonung is professor emeritus at the Knut Wicksell Centre for Financial Studies, Department of Economics, Lund University, Sweden, since 2010. He served as chairman of the Swedish Fiscal Policy Council 2012–2013. He was research adviser at DG ECFIN, European Commission, Brussels, 2000–2010, working on European macroeconomic issues. Prior to moving to Brussels, he was professor in economics at the Stockholm School of Economics, Stockholm. Jonung served as chief economic adviser to Prime Minister Carl Bildt in 1992–1994. His research covers monetary and fiscal policy, inflationary expectations, the euro, the economics of European integration, and the history of Swedish economic thought. Recently he has published work jointly with Fredrik N. G. Andersson on the inflation targeting regime of the Riksbank. He is the author of several books and articles in English and Swedish. He holds a PhD in Economics from the University of California, Los Angeles, in 1975.

Norbert J. Michel is the director of Heritage's Center for Data Analysis, where he specializes on issues pertaining to financial markets and monetary policy. He edited, and contributed chapters, to two books published by Heritage: *The Case Against Dodd–Frank: How the "Consumer Protection" Law Endangers Americans* and *Prosperity Unleashed: Smarter Financial*

Regulation. Before rejoining Heritage in 2013, Michel was a tenured professor at Nicholls State University's College of Business, teaching finance, economics, and statistics. His earlier stint at Heritage was as a tax policy analyst
in the think tank's Center for Data Analysis from 2002 to 2005. He previously
was with the global energy company Entergy, where he built a logistic regres-
sion model to help predict bankruptcies of commercial clients. His work
allowed Entergy to better monitor monetary losses caused by customers'
delinquent payments. Michel holds a doctoral degree in financial economics
from the University of New Orleans. He received his bachelor of business
administration degree in finance and economics from Loyola University. He
currently resides in Alexandria, VA.

Carlos Newland is professor at ESEADE University and Torcuato Di Tella
University in Buenos Aires. He holds a BA in economics (Universidad
Católica Argentina); a Master of Letters (University of Oxford), and a D.Litt.
in history (University of Leiden). He has been Claude Lambe Fellow (1990),
De Fortabat Fellow at Harvard University (1999), and Guggenheim Fellow
(2000). He has published articles in several journals on economic history
and development, such as the *Journal of Economic History*, *Explorations in
Economic History*, *Desarrollo Económico*, *Revista de Historia Económica*,
Hispanic American Historical Review, and *Journal of Latin American Studies*.

Emilio Ocampo has a Licenciado en Economía degree from Universidad de
Buenos Aires and an MBA from the University of Chicago. He is a professor
of finance and economic history at UCEMA (Buenos Aires), where he also
leads the Center for the Study of Economic History.

Wolf Heinrich Reuter has been secretary general of the German Council
of Economic Experts since May 2018. Between May 2016 and April 2018,
he already worked as economist for macroeconomics at the Council's staff.
Prior to this, he worked as a research economist at the Austrian National Bank
(OeNB) and as research assistant at the Vienna University of Economics and
Business (WU Vienna) and the International Institute for Applied Systems
Analysis (IIASA), as well as shorter periods for the European Central Bank
and the European Commission. From 2004 to 2010 he studied Economics at
the Vienna University of Economics and Business and received his doctorate
(topic: "Measurement, Determinants and Effects of Fiscal Frameworks") at
the same university in 2013.

Thomas R. Saving is the director emeritus of the Private Enterprise Research
Center and a university distinguished professor of economics emeritus at
Texas A&M University. Dr. Saving received his PhD from the University of

Chicago and served on the faculty at the University of Washington at Seattle and Michigan State University before moving to Texas A&M University in 1968. Dr. Saving's research has covered the areas of antitrust, monetary, and health economics. He has served as a referee or as a member of the editorial board of the major U.S. economics journals and as co-editor of *Economic Inquiry* from 1997 to 2006. He is the co-editor of *Medicare Reform: Issues and Answers* (1999), and the co-author of *The Economics of Medicare Reform* (2000) and *The Diagnosis and Treatment of Medicare* (2007). He is currently emphasizing monetary economics research. He is the co-author, with Boris Pesek, of *Money Wealth and Economic Theory* (1966) and *The Foundations of Money and Banking* (1967). He recently authored *A Century of Federal Reserve Monetary Policy* (2019). Dr. Saving has been elected to the post of president of the Western Economics Association, the Southern Economics Association, and the Association of Private Enterprise Education. In 2000, President Clinton appointed Dr. Saving as a public trustee of the Social Security and Medicare Trust Funds; he served as trustee until 2007. He also served on President Bush's bipartisan Commission to Strengthen Social Security.

Jan-Egbert Sturm has been full professor of applied macroeconomics at the Department of Management, Technology and Economics (D-MTEC) as well as director of the KOF Swiss Economic Institute at ETH Zurich since October 2005. Sturm is editor of the *European Journal of Political Economy* and a member of various committees and boards in Switzerland and abroad. He studied and obtained his doctorate at the University of Groningen. From 2001 to 2003, he was head of the Department of Economic Forecasting and Financial Markets at the Ifo Institute for Economic Research in Munich and held a professorship in economics, with a focus on macroeconomics and monetary policy, at the Center for Economic Studies (CES) of the Faculty of Economics at the University of Munich. In 2003, he was appointed professor of economics, chair of monetary economics of open economies at the University of Konstanz (D), and at the same time became head of the TWI— Thurgau Institute of Economics at the University of Konstanz in Kreuzlingen (CH).